DEFINING DOCUMENTS
IN AMERICAN HISTORY

Business Ethics

DEFINING DOCUMENTS
IN AMERICAN HISTORY

Business Ethics

Volume 1

Editor
Michael Shally-Jensen, PhD

SALEM PRESS
A Division of EBSCO Information Services, Inc.
Ipswich, Massachusetts

GREY HOUSE PUBLISHING

Cover: Skyscrapers. Image by Circle Creative Studio via iStock. Charging document in the case of Bernie Madoff (page 395).

Copyright © 2019 by EBSCO Information Services, Inc., and Grey House Publishing, Inc.

Defining Documents in American History: Business Ethics, published by Grey House Publishing, Inc., Amenia, NY, under exclusive license from EBSCO Information Services, Inc.

All rights reserved. No part of this work may be used or reproduced in any manner whatsoever or transmitted in any form or by any means, electronic or mechanical, including photocopy, recording, or any information storage and retrieval system, without written permission from the copyright owner. For permissions requests, contact proprietary-publishing@ebsco.com.

∞ The paper used in these volumes conforms to the American National Standard for Permanence of Paper for Printed Library Materials, Z39.48 1992 (R2009).

Publisher's Cataloging-In-Publication Data
(Prepared by The Donohue Group, Inc.)

Names: Shally-Jensen, Michael, editor.
Title: Business ethics / volume editor, Michael Shally-Jensen, PhD.
Other Titles: Defining documents in American history (Salem Press)
Description: [First edition]. | Ipswich, Massachusetts : Salem Press, a division of EBSCO Information Services ; Amenia, NY : Grey House Publishing, [2019] | Includes bibliographical references and index.
Identifiers: ISBN 9781642652833 (set) | ISBN 9781642654158 (v. 1) | ISBN 9781642654165 (v. 2)
Subjects: LCSH: Business ethics--United States--History--Sources. | Corporations--Moral and ethical aspects--United States--History--Sources. | Commercial law--United States--History--Sources. | United States--Economic conditions--History--Sources.
Classification: LCC HF5387.5.U6 B87 2019 | DDC 174.40973--dc23

FIRST PRINTING
PRINTED IN THE UNITED STATES OF AMERICA

Contents

Publisher's Note ix
Editor's Introduction xi
Contributor List xv

Volume 1

EARLY EFFORTS—AND FAILINGS

From *The Prince* 3
"Advice to a Young Tradesman" 9
Adam Smith, from *The Theory of Moral Sentiments* 13
Fletcher v. Peck 21
Lowell Mill Girls 27
From "Bartleby the Scrivener: A Story of Wall Street" 39
From *The Life of P.T. Barnum* 47
Presidential Proclamations on Blockade and Commercial Trade 53
From *Utilitarianism* 61
"The Money Power" 69
Documents Relating to Black Friday, 1869 73
Verse and Cartoon about Boss Tweed and Tammany Hall 79
Crédit Mobilier Scandal 85
Pendleton Civil Service Reform Act 95

MOVING TOWARD THE MODERN

Andrew Carnegie: "The Gospel of Wealth" 105
Eugene Debs: "What Can We Do for Working People?" 113
Sherman Antitrust Act 119
"Wall Street Owns the Country" 123
Frick's Fracas—Henry Frick Makes His Case 129
"The Absurd Effort to Make the World Over" 137
From *The Theory of the Leisure Class* 145
Coal Strike Hearings: The Miners Testify 153
An Immigrant Garment Worker's "Days and Dreams" 159
Theodore Roosevelt on Corporate Trusts 165

"Echoes from the Recent Pennsylvania Coal Strike"... 175
Jane Addams: "Child Labor and Other Dangers of Childhood"... 185
From *The Jungle*... 191
Fire Hazards in New York City Factories... 197
Clayton Act... 209
On the Teapot Dome Scandal... 221
From *My Life and Work*, by Henry Ford... 227

Volume 2

CRISIS AND RENOVATION

President Hoover Responds to the Stock Market Crash... 235
Stuart Chase: *Waste and the Machine Age*... 240
Memories of the Flint Sit-Down Strike... 243
From *What Makes Sammy Run?*... 251
From *The Fountainhead*... 255
From *The Road to Serfdom*... 263
From *The Hidden Persuaders*... 269
Eisenhower's Farewell Address... 275

ENTERPRISE AND ETHICS IN THE LATE TWENTIETH CENTURY

Rachel Carson: *Silent Spring*... 283
Equal Pay Act... 287
From *Unsafe at Any Speed*... 293
"The Social Responsibility of Business Is to Increase Its Profits"... 297
The "Powell Memo": Attack on the Free Enterprise System... 305
Bill Gates: Letter to Hobbyists... 319
Foreign Corrupt Practices Act—U.S. Justice Department Overview... 323
From *The Culture of Narcissism*... 327
"What Is Business Ethics?"... 333
United States v. Kelly—An "Abscam" Case... 343
"Greed Is Good"... 349
Exxon Valdez Oil Spill: A Report to the President... 353
From *Glengarry Glen Ross*... 359

Testimony from the 1994 Tobacco Hearings 365
Adarand Constructors, Inc. v. Peña 373

BIG BUSINESS AND BIG GOVERNMENT TODAY

Sarbanes-Oxley Act 383
Halliburton Overcharges Report 389
Charging Document in the Case of Bernie Madoff 395
Dodd-Frank Wall Street Reform and Consumer Protection Act—A Synopsis 403
Report on the *Deepwater Horizon* Oil Spill 409
Citizens United v. Federal Election Commission 415
"Countrywide Protected Fraudsters by Silencing Whistleblowers..." 427
EPA Notice of Violation of Clean Air Act to Volkswagen Group of America, Inc. 439
Wells Fargo Account Fraud Scandal 447
Summary of Letter Requesting Further Review of the Dakota Access Pipeline (DAPL) and Memorandum
  Opinion re. Vacatur 453
Equifax Data Breach Announcement 463
Statement to the U.S. Senate Judiciary Committee concerning Cambridge Analytica 469
From *Big Business: A Love Letter to an American Anti-Hero* 481

APPENDIXES

Chronological List 491
Web Resources 493
Bibliography 495
Index 505

Publisher's Note

Defining Documents in American History series, produced by Salem Press, offers a closer look at important historical documents by pairing primary source documents on a broad range of subjects with essays written especially for the series by expert writers, including historians, professors, researchers, and other authorities in the subject under examination. This established series includes thirty-four titles that present documents selected to illuminate specific eras in American history—including *Postwar 1940s, The Civil Rights*, and *World War II*—or to explore significant themes and developments in American society—*Slavery, Immigration & Immigrant Communities*, and *Native Americans*.

This set, *Defining Documents in American History: Business Ethics*, offers in-depth analysis of sixty-seven documents, including letters, newspaper accounts, book excerpts, speeches, political debates, testimony, firsthand accounts, memoirs, court rulings, legal texts, legislative acts, excerpts from both fiction and nonfiction books, and dialogues from dramatic works. These selections explore the intricacies of business ethics, from labor relations and corporate profits to consumer safety and political lobbying.

The material is organized into five sections, and each section begins with a brief introduction that defines questions and problems underlying the subjects addressed in the historical documents.

- **Early Efforts—And Failings** including a selection from Niccolò Macchievelli's *The Prince*, written in the early sixteenth century, but which is still considered a seminal work by many business (and military) leaders today; Benjamin Franklin's "Advice to a Young Tradesman," excerpts from Adam Smith's *Theory of Moral Sentiments* and John Stuart Mills's *Utilitarianism*, and documents and cartoons related to business debacles including Black Friday, Tammany Hall, and the Crédit Mobilier Scandal and civil service reform;

- **Moving toward the Modern** considers significant documents as the Sherman Antitrust Act meant to stem anticompetitive behavior, working conditions in Chicago's meatpacking industry described in *The Jungle*, reports about safety and worker treatment in the factories and tenements of large U.S. cities, Theodore Roosevelt's speech concerning the dangerous power of trusts, and the Teapot Dome scandal that led to the sentencing of the first U.S. cabinet official (Albert B. Fall, who was President Warren G. Harding's Secretary of the Interior);

- **Crisis and Renovation** includes such significant writers as Ayn Rand and the libertarian philosophy of *The Fountainhead*), Stuart Chase and his calls to protect the environment as well as the economy in *Waste and the Machine Age*, as well as such pivotal events as the stock market crash in 1929 that led to the Great Depression, and Eisenhower's farewell address in which he described the potential threat of government contracts and public policy to create a "scientific-technological elite";

- **Enterprise and Ethics in the Late Twentieth Century** begins with the publication of Rachel Carson's *Silent Spring* and its warnings about the dangers of DDT presented, Ralph Nader's exposé of the auto industry and its disregard of consumer safety in favor of design in *Unsafe at Any Speed*, the decision in *United States v. Kelly* (an Abscam case) and dialogue from the movie *Wall Street* ("Greed Is Good"); and

- **Big Business and Big Government Today** evaluates ethical implications of business practices including the Bernie Madoff "ponzi" scheme, Dodd-Frank Wall Street reforms following the Great Recession of 2008, the Deepwater Horizon oil spill and its aftermath, Equifax's data breach, and Facebook's sharing of user data with Cambridge-Analytica.

These documents provide an overview of business ethics and how it affects all of society, from the heads of corporations in industries like oil, energy, social media, food, and transportation to the workers that produce the goods and services to the consumers of those goods and services. They present a wide array of legal and moral opinions, descriptions of the effects that business ethics can play in the national and global economy, and they take a closer look at the way that business ethics relates to politics.

Essay Format

Each Historical Document is supported by a critical essay, written by historians and teachers, that includes a Summary Overview, Defining Moment, Author Biography, Document Analysis, and Essential Themes. An important feature of each essay is a close reading of the primary source that develops broader themes, such as the author's rhetorical purpose, social or class position, point of view, and other relevant issues. Each essay also includes a Bibliography and Additional Reading section for further research.

Appendixes
- **Chronology** arranges all documents by year.
- **Web Resources** is an annotated list of websites that offer valuable supplemental resources.
- **Bibliography** lists helpful articles and books for further study.

Contributors
Salem Press would like to extend its appreciation to all involved in the development and production of this work. The essays have been written and signed by scholars of history, humanities, and other disciplines related to the essays' topics. Without these expert contributions, a project of this nature would not be possible.

Editor's Introduction

All societies have standards of ethical conduct. Generally, there are restrictions against theft, violence, and other forms of harm. Often, there is some version of the golden rule, too. *Ethics* is that branch of philosophy concerned with both the content and nature of morality in society. And *business ethics* is a type of applied ethics that concerns itself with practical moral questions in the world of commerce. Oftentimes, such questions overlap into legal and political matters, particularly when one looks at concrete cases from the past, as we do in the present volume. Thinkers as diverse as Machiavelli, Adam Smith, John Stuart Mill, and F.A. Hayek have considered the place of business in society, and we look here at those authors along with numerous examples of corporate behavior that raise questions of morality—the "good" and the "bad," the "right," and the "wrong."

Business Ethics and Corporate History

Corporations have existed for centuries. In early modern Europe, they were set up to create and control such entities as universities, churches, trading firms, and associations. In England, the Netherlands, and elsewhere, the king granted corporate status to these entities, charging them with overseeing themselves in a manner appropriate to the royal realm. One of the first such corporations of note was the East India Company (EIC), established in 1602 to extend British commercial interests in South Asia. The EIC may have been the first "multinational" corporation to issue stocks held by investors. It indeed spread British influence, but after a long and rather checkered history (involving wars and ethnic division), it finally was "disestablished" in 1857 by the crown.

Colonial Americans disliked many of the British corporations that oversaw the American colonies. The American Revolution was launched in part to rid the colonies of British monopolistic rule. During the founding era of the United States, corporate charters (licenses to exist) were granted for limited time periods and could readily be revoked for violating laws. Corporations could engage in activities necessary to fulfill their chartered purpose—and little more. They could not make any political or unauthorized charitable contributions or spend money to influence legislation. They could not own stock in other corporations or own property that was not essential to fulfilling their purpose. They could be terminated if they exceeded their authority or caused public harm. Corporate owners and managers were generally responsible for criminal acts taking place in their name.

This long-ago version of the American corporation began to change during the Industrial Revolution. In the mid-nineteenth century a U.S. Supreme Court decision, *Santa Clara County v. Southern Pacific R.R. Co.* (1866), granted corporations "personhood," meaning that they could enjoy many of the rights and responsibilities of individual citizens. These rights and responsibilities included ownership of diverse properties, freedom of investment, signing of contracts, and the ability to sue and be sued. As the Court affirmed in subsequent cases, a corporation could be thought of as an "association of individuals" united for a particular purpose. By such means, the corporation achieved a break from the restrictions of its Colonial past and began to exercise a greater degree of control over its own business activities.

Corporations of the eighteenth and nineteenth centuries engaged in many questionable acts. Trading in and exploiting enslaved African Americans is one example; another is taking over land inhabited by Native Americans to use for commercial (and political) purposes. Both such goals were aided and abetted by different American governments, at both the state and national levels.

The Industrial Revolution served to expand enterprise in the late eighteenth century and throughout the nineteenth century, producing wealthy and influential companies and owners. These businesses often were able to avoid regulation and control even as they engaged in activities such as fraud, price gouging, labor exploitation, and stock manipulation—not to mention the use of unsafe work environments where workers were routinely injured or died.

At this time, the United States was rapidly expanding both economically and geographically. Production and manufacturing grew exponentially, as did international trade. In order to protect themselves from competition, larger-sized operations became corporations. Such corporations, in turn, began to dominate not only the business scene but also American politicians, the courts, the cities, and society generally.

Under the principle of limited liability, it was held that a corporation could not have criminal charges brought against it. Finding a corporation liable for breaches of law or ethics, especially from the beginning of the Gilded Age (c. 1870–1900) through the early twentieth century, was difficult on a number of grounds. Although legally counted as "persons," corporations were, and remain, collective enterprises. Thus, proving that a corporation had formulated the necessary "criminal intent" and proceeded to carry it through, was almost impossible. In addition, courts of this period had difficulty attributing breaches to companies when the specific acts for which they were accused were not identified in their own charters. Furthermore, the accused was required to be brought to court to face his or her accusers—an unlikely prospect in the case of large holding companies. These legal stipulations did not prevent the charging of many individual businessmen (and politicians) with crimes, but they did make the prosecution of corporations improbable.

By the 1910s, however, as the Progressive Era took hold, it began to be recognized that a corporation could be held liable for the deeds of "agents" acting in a professional capacity on the company's behalf. A key component of attributing liability to corporations was the notion that employees had the authority to carry out the behavior in question. The goal of prosecutors was to find a company liable for actions taken by an employee (as had once been the case in the Colonial Era). Partly because of these legal changes, and partly because of the growth of business generally, the early 1900s came to be known as the antitrust era in American history, where large corporate monopolies (like Standard Oil Co.) were challenged by "trust busters" such as Theodore Roosevelt. Other abuses, such as the use of child labor, also were challenged by Progressive reformers. Labor unions gained significant ground, too, by promoting the need to protect workers.

A tentative consensus on the nature of corporations and their legal and ethical responsibilities toward society was sustained for decades thereafter. This consensus survived two world wars, a decade of flourishing enterprise known as the "Roaring Twenties," and an equally great economic collapse named the Great Depression. Major ups and downs in the legal, ethical, and economic landscape occurred in these decades, and yet ultimately a working balance between business and government, enterprise and regulation, was left intact. The corporate "excesses" of the early twentieth century were tamed, and the government "excesses" of the New Deal during the Depression were challenged in turn. With the onset of World War II, massive economic programs benefited both sectors—and served the populace as well.

By the 1950s and 1960s, the economic consensus was deeply entrenched as part of American culture. These two decades were good ones for the American nation and the American people. Workers could look forward to good pay and strong benefits (health care, pensions, etc.), and businesses thrived by entering into long-term commitments with their employees, their customers, their suppliers, and their shareholders. Profits and investors' interests were important pieces of the picture, but they were by no means the only pieces. If a business wanted to grow, it had to invest in the community as much as it did in the corporate balance sheet. States and localities in which businesses operated received their fair share in the form of corporate taxes, and businesses benefited from state and local infrastructure built to aid the flow of commerce. It was a system that seemed to work well for everyone and that few questioned or criticized (though there were always dissenters). Through it all, the U.S. economy became the envy of the world.

This state of affairs began to erode in the 1970s. The change was caused in part by an economic downturn; it was propelled as well by a new brand of economic thinking—at the center of which stood the economist Milton Friedman and a band of libertarian-leaning colleagues. On the political scene, conservatives such as William F. Buckley Jr. and William F. Powell Jr. began to advance the new perspective. All of these thinkers argued for an economic and cultural rebellion, one that sought to raise the profile of the free market and serve the interests of business leaders. As a result, corporations began to set up lobbying organizations in Washington, D.C., and to join new, pro-free market associations such as the Business Roundtable. Political and economic think tanks such as the Cato Institute and the Heritage Foundation promoted an antilabor, probusiness policy agenda. The message among corporate elites became one of profit over social principle, commerce over community, employers over employees, and stockholders over ordinary citizens.

With the election of Ronald Reagan in 1980 and the opening of the "Reagan Revolution," this new business environment took center stage. There was a strong emphasis on lowering of tax rates and eliminating of some taxes; weakening of union organization and expanding nonunion businesses; reducing or eliminating the minimum wage; abandoning traditional pensions in favor of 401(k) plans (which shifted some financial risk from employers to employees); cutting costs for business measures, such as using cheaper overseas firms instead of local suppliers; and paying chief executive officers (CEOs) and other top executives large sums of money in recognition of their unique talents—even in years when profits were down. From the 1980s through the early

2000s, corporations, and an increasing number of their supporters in government, successfully shifted the paradigm away from the "social responsibility" of business—an oxymoron to the likes of Friedman—and toward the deregulation of industry, the privatization of government functions, the offshoring of production facilities, and the loosening of financial restrictions. Reagan's appointee to the chair of the U.S. Federal Reserve, Alan Greenspan, was himself a libertarian and worked hard to realize these goals.

The new vision lasted for years, even after Reagan left office. The American economy was roaring despite major ethical and environmental lapses including Wall Street scandals, banking crises, unscrupulous industry practices (as in the tobacco business), damaging oil spills, and the like. The prevailing premise was that corporate wealth would "trickle down" to workers and the economy as a whole, and one could argue that had happened; but by the late 1990s and early 2000s, the reality seemed to be indicating something different. Businesses and investors seemed to be profiting at the expense of ordinary Americans, as an increasing wealth gap between the haves and have-nots became evident. Massive corporate corruption cases (WorldCom, Enron, Tyco, and others) erupting in the early 2000s seemed only to prove the case, resulting in major government legislation (the Sarbanes-Oxley Act, 2002) designed to curb the tide. Corporations could no longer be viewed by the public as inherently ethical, good for the economy and society; rather, they seemed to be in it for themselves.

In 2008, another series of profound corporate mishaps came to light, in events leading to the Great Recession of that period. While the full story of the financial crisis of 2008 and its aftermath is still being written, one of its central chapters concerns a hyperinflated housing market, risky lending by mortgage banks, and Wall Street financial wizardry (in the form of "collateralized debt obligations"). The wave of home foreclosures that followed led to the loss of trillions in wealth from American households along with the failure—and federal bailout—of dozens of top banking and investment institutions. In Washington, D.C., legislators responded by enacting the Dodd-Frank Wall Street Reform and Consumer Protection Act (2010)—legislation that has since been chipped away at by conservative critics.

The same year that Dodd-Frank became law the U.S. Supreme Court, in *Citizens United v. FEC*, ruled that corporations not only are "legal persons" whose rights may not be abridged, but, *as* persons, they are entitled to unlimited spending in the area of political advertising. Essentially equating money with speech, the justices argued that to curtail spending on political ads would amount to limiting free speech. Technically, the type of ads in question are not permitted to endorse individual candidates (without restrictions being applied) but must instead focus on *ideas* or *messages*; yet in most cases, it is very clear which candidates an ad's sponsors favor and which ones they dislike. *Citizens United* gave political action committees (PACs)—a type of corporation—a bullhorn with which to steer the political conversation. Corporate influence in politics remains strong as a result.

More recently the major legal and ethical problems have centered on large digital technology firms and their misuse of private customer data. Numerous security breaches have occurred in which data collected by companies was found to have been inadequately protected, resulting in tens or even hundreds of millions of personal records (including social security numbers and credit card information) being stolen. In another famous case, the social media company Facebook improperly shared its customer data with the political research firm Cambridge Analytica, placing both companies in legal jeopardy and raising the ire of Facebook users. Companies such as Apple, Google, and Microsoft have also faced antitrust challenges, particularly in Europe. The tech sector is a fast-evolving one and often laws have yet to catch up with it. No doubt it will face more such challenges in the future.

Conclusion

The business corporation has been a subject of controversy and public scrutiny ever since its development. It can no longer be considered merely a passive though necessary component of the free-market economy. Rather, it is an institution that, however much it may have been shaped by ethics and economics, is also an instrument of social and political power. It is true that some corporations today seek to cultivate a socially responsible perspective, and many make valuable philanthropic contributions; but by and large the capture and control of revenues and profits remain the driving force. Whether one sees this as "good" or "bad" may depend on where one stands on the ethical, economic, and political spectrum. These and other such matters will continue to be examined by future researchers seeking to understand the nature, operation, and morality of the modern corporation.

Michael Shally-Jensen

Bibliography and Additional Reading

Baida, Peter. *Poor Richard's Legacy: American Business Values from Benjamin Franklin to Donald Trump.* New York: W. Morrow, 1990.

Balleisen, Edward J. *Fraud: An American History from Barnum to Madoff.* Princeton, NJ: Princeton University Press, 2017.

Carroll, Archie B., et al. *Corporate Responsibility: The American Experience.* New York: Cambridge University Press, 2012.

Christiansen, Christian. *Progressive Business: An Intellectual History of the Role of Business in American Society.* New York: Oxford University Press, 2015.

Smith, Hedrick. *Who Stole the American Dream?* New York: Random House, 2012.

Contributor List

Michael P. Auerbach, MA
Marblehead, Massachusetts

William E. Burns, PhD
George Washington University

Jennifer L. Henderson Crane, PGDip
Fife, Scotland

Steven L. Danver, PhD
Walden University

KP Dawes, MA
Chicago, IL

Amber Dickinson, PhD
Oklahoma State University

Tracey DiLascio, JD
Framingham, Massachusetts

Bethany Groff Dorau, MA
Historic New England

Ashleigh Fata, MA
University of California, Los Angeles

Kay Tilden Frost
Washington, D.C.

Aaron George, PhD
Tarleton State University

Aaron Gulyas, MA
Mott Community College

Melissa A. Hale, JD
Loyola University Chicago

Micah Issitt, MA
Philadelphia, Pennsylvania

Mark S. Joy, PhD
Jamestown University

Jonathan Rees, PhD
Colorado State University, Pueblo

Hannah Rich, MA
Philadelphia, PA

Michael Shally-Jensen, PhD
Amherst, MA

Michelle McBride Simonelli, JD
Poland, Ohio

Scott A. Merriman, PhD
Troy University

Scott C. Monje, PhD
Tarrytown, NY

Michael Seth, PhD
James Madison University

David Simonelli, PhD
Youngstown State University

Noëlle Sinclair, JD, MLS
University of Iowa Law Library

Robert Surbrug, PhD
Bay Path University

Anthony Vivian, MA
University of California, Los Angeles

Donald A. Watt, PhD
Middleton, ID

DEFINING DOCUMENTS
IN AMERICAN HISTORY

Business Ethics

Early Efforts—And Failings

In this first section, we present an array of documents concerning early literary and philosophical treatments of the subject of ethics (or "morals") in business and related areas. We also include several concrete examples of commercial activities in the nineteenth century that raise questions about ethics and legality in that era and describe how people approached such questions and found solutions.

Literary and Philosophical Works

We begin with an examination of a seminal work, *The Prince*, by a famous Renaissance writer, Niccolò Machiavelli. Although focusing primarily on the leadership qualities needed by a European prince in the 1500s, the work remains relevant today to those interested in the subject of executive leadership. Machiavelli himself worked in the military and politics for a time and was intimately familiar with the Medici family, who then ran the great commercial city of Florence.

Next, we jump to the 1700s and consider two thinkers from that period: Benjamin Franklin and Adam Smith. Franklin, of course, is well known as a Founding Father, diplomat, inventor, and printer. He was also deeply interested in commercial affairs and enjoyed writing about a number of different topics. Here, he combines his interests in a piece offering "Advice to a Young Tradesman." His Scottish contemporary, Adam Smith, was and is just as well known as a founder of the field of political economy and as a "moral philosopher" of note. He published *The Theory of Moral Sentiments* (1759) and *The Wealth of Nations* (1776). It is from the former work that we draw here to illustrate Smith's vision of "the prudent man" in business and in life.

Moving to the 1800s, we present works by two iconic American figures: the writer Herman Melville and the showman-entrepreneur P.T. Barnum. Although Melville is best known for his classic *Moby Dick*, he published other works as well. In his story "Bartleby, the Scrivener" (1853) Melville tells of a clerk in a law office who refuses to carry out the tasks assigned to him—and the effect that his refusal has. In the year after "Bartleby" was penned, the famed sideshow operator P.T. Barnum issued his autobiography, telling how he rarely refused anything if it looked like it could turn a profit. Barnum's life and story raise numerous questions about ethics in business and beyond.

We round out the selection of philosophical and literary reflections with a deep reflection by philosopher John Stuart Mill on the topic of "utilitarianism," or the doctrine that, that which serves the public interest best is that which satisfies most of the people most of the time—as opposed to that which satisfies fewer people to the same degree or greater. Mill's *Utilitarianism* (1863) is a landmark statement in the field, and we present an excerpt of it in the present section.

Concrete Examples/Questions

In this category we have the U.S. Supreme Court decision *Fletcher v. Peck* (1810), concerning a massive land fraud in Georgia—the Yazoo land scandal—and the fault the Court found in the deal. The Yazoo scheme benefitted politicians and business investors but negatively impacted Native American tribes.

In "Lowell Mill Girls" we look at work life in a New England textile mill in the 1830s, when business owners reigned supreme and workers had few if any rights.

In "Documents Relating to Black Friday 1869" we present a cartoon poking fun at one of two "robber barons"—Jay Gould—involved in market manipulation, along with a record of the crashing the price of gold, which gave this day (September 24) its name. Similarly, in "Verse and Cartoon about Boss Tweed and Tammany Hall, 1871," we show how the famed New York City political operator and his moneymaking "machine" were exposed in the press and came to be reviled by the public. Ethics, and legality, mattered, and Tweed was caught out as a result.

One of the most notable corruption cases of the nineteenth century is the Crédit Mobilier Scandal of 1872, a major railroad stock scheme involving elected officials who were in cahoots with businessmen to drive up the value of their investments and receive the dividends. Ten years later, the Pendleton Civil Service Reform Act sought to address one major aspect of this same problem, the reliance of politicians on hired "cronies" rather than on professional civil servants.

From *The Prince*

Date: 1513–1520
Author: Niccolò Machiavelli
Genre: Political treatise

Summary Overview

Niccolò Machiavelli was a writer and politician who lived and worked in Florence, Italy during the Renaissance period. He was an influential military and political leader during a chaotic political period for the city, and his most famous writings are treatises on the goals and methods of successful leaders. His most famous work, *The Prince*, is a treatise on the methods by which leaders can maintain control over their subjects. Machiavelli lived in a tumultuous political world, and the books he wrote after he left his political career are aimed at teaching leaders the best way to control a city. The apparent cynicism and immorality of this work led people to use the term "Machiavellian" to describe manipulative political practices.

Defining Moment

Renaissance Florence was a place of growth and change in political, artistic, and military spheres. The city was one of the largest and most economically significant cities in western Europe and, though the government was technically an elected council, a small group of powerful merchant families effectively controlled the political system. Florence was also home to many famous writers and artists of the late Medieval and early Renaissance periods, and it was known worldwide as a center of commerce and culture.

The city underwent huge political changes during Machiavelli's lifetime. In the early 1400s, a series of military leaders took control as the city waged wars against its neighbors. Eventually, the banker Cosimo de Medici established a political dynasty that allowed his family, the Medicis, to rule the city for decades. Three generations of Medicis managed the city's affairs from 1434 to 1492, though they maintained the illusion of a representative government. Lorenzo de Medici, Cosimo's grandson, was the patron of artists such as Botticelli, Leonardo da Vinci, and Michelangelo, and the family spent huge sums on construction and beautification projects.

After Lorenzo de Medici died, his son Piero was unable to maintain political control. The Medici family was exiled in 1494. In their absence, a charismatic preacher named Girolamo Savonarola briefly took power and encouraged the citizens of Florence to reform the government. His sermons encouraged the people to live spiritual and abstinent lives and he criticized what he saw as the excessive worldliness and greed of the Medicis and their followers. He was popular in the city until the government in Florence and the pope in Rome grew concerned that his preaching was destabilizing their institutions. Florence banned him from preaching and Pope Alexander VI excommunicated him. He lost his sway with the people and was arrested, tortured, and executed.

Savonarola's death left a temporary power vacuum in Florence. For the first time in decades, the government was a democratic republic led by a council of mostly elected officials. One politician who rose to prominence during the republican period was a young aristocrat named Niccolò Machiavelli.

Author Biography

Niccolò Machiavelli was born in Florence in 1469 to a prominent but poor family. During his youth, Florence expelled the Medici family, a powerful dynasty that had ruled Florence since the early 1400s. Shortly after this, Machiavelli took office as a high-ranking official in charge of the city's foreign affairs and diplomatic relationships.

Machiavelli went on numerous diplomatic missions to Rome and was a respected politician during his time in office. He also had success as a military leader—his army of Florentine citizens defeated the neighboring city of Pisa in a major victory—but his political career did not last. The Medici family came back to power in 1512 and overthrew the republican government, taking power back into the hands of the family. The new leaders imprisoned and tortured Machiavelli and then exiled him from the city.

His political career over, Machiavelli turned to writing. He spent the next several years working on his major works, *Discourses on Livy* and *The Prince*, though neither were published during his lifetime. In his works, he attempts to guide and advise political leaders in Florence by drawing on his own experience as a leader in the republic.

In the 1520s, he was given the position of official historian of Florence and was commissioned to write a history of the city by Pope Clement VII, who was a member of the Medici family and one of Machiavelli's old enemies. Meanwhile, Florence was again shifting between rule by the Medicis and a republican government. Machiavelli hoped for another political position, but his recent patronage by the Medici Pope meant that he was viewed with suspicion by the new generation of politicians. He died in 1527 in Florence.

HISTORICAL DOCUMENT

XVII. Of Cruelty and Clemency, and Whether It Is Better to Be Loved or Feared

PASSING to the other qualities above referred to, I say that every Prince should desire to be accounted merciful and not cruel. Nevertheless, he should be on his guard against the abuse of this quality of mercy. Cesare Borgia was reputed cruel, yet his cruelty restored Romagna, united it, and brought it to order and obedience; so that if we look at things in their true light, it will be seen that he was in reality far more merciful than the people of Florence, who, to avoid the imputation of cruelty, suffered Pistoja to be torn to pieces by factions.

A Prince should therefore disregard the reproach of being thought cruel where it enables him to keep his subjects united and obedient. For he who quells disorder by a very few signal examples will in the end be more merciful than he who from too great leniency permits things to take their course and so to result in rapine and bloodshed; for these hurt the whole State, whereas the severities of the Prince injure individuals only.

And for a new Prince, of all others, it is impossible to escape a name for cruelty, since new States are full of dangers. Wherefore Virgil, by the mouth of Dido, excuses the harshness of her reign on the plea that it was new, saying:—

'A fate unkind, and newness in my reign
Compel me thus to guard a wide domain.'

Nevertheless, the new Prince should not be too ready of belief, nor too easily set in motion; nor should he himself be the first to raise alarms; but should so temper prudence with kindliness that too great confidence in others shall not throw him off his guard, nor groundless distrust render him insupportable.

And here comes in the question whether it is better to be loved rather than feared, or feared rather than loved. It might perhaps be answered that we should wish to be both; but since love and fear can hardly exist together, if we must choose between them, it is far safer to be feared than loved. For of men it may generally be affirmed, that they are thankless, fickle, false, studious to avoid danger, greedy of gain, devoted to you while you are able to confer benefits upon them, and ready, as I said before, while danger is distant, to shed their blood, and sacrifice their property, their lives, and their children for you; but in the hour of need they turn against you. The Prince, therefore, who without otherwise securing himself builds wholly on their professions is undone. For the friendships which we buy with a price, and do not gain by greatness and nobility of character, though they be fairly earned are not made good, but fail us when we have occasion to use them.

Moreover, men are less careful how they offend him who makes himself loved than him who makes himself feared. For love is held by the tie of obligation, which, because men are a sorry breed, is broken on every whisper of private interest; but fear is bound by the apprehension of punishment which never relaxes its grasp.

Nevertheless a Prince should inspire fear in such a fashion that if he do not win love he may escape hate. For a man may very well be feared and yet not hated, and this will be the case so long as he does not meddle with the property or with the women of his citizens and subjects.

And if constrained to put any to death, he should do so only when there is manifest cause or reasonable justification. But, above all, he must abstain from the property of others. For men will sooner forget the death of their father than the loss of their patrimony. Moreover, pretexts for confiscation are never to seek, and he who has once begun to live by rapine always finds reasons for taking what is not his; whereas reasons for shedding blood are fewer, and sooner exhausted.

But when a Prince is with his army, and has many soldiers under his command, he must needs disregard the reproach of cruelty, for without such a reputation in its Captain, no army can be held together or kept under any kind of control. Among other things remarkable in Hannibal this has been noted, that having a very great army, made up of men of many different nations and brought to fight in a foreign country, no dissension ever arose among the soldiers themselves, nor any mutiny against their leader, either in his good or in his evil fortunes. This we can only ascribe to the transcendent cruelty, which, joined with numberless great qualities, rendered him at once venerable and terrible in the eyes of his soldiers; for without this reputation for cruelty these other virtues would not have produced the like results.

Unreflecting writers, indeed, while they praise his achievements, have condemned the chief cause of them; but that his other merits would not by themselves have been so efficacious we may see from the case of Scipio, one of the greatest Captains, not of his own time only but of all times of which we have record, whose armies rose against him in Spain from no other cause than his too great leniency in allowing them a freedom inconsistent with military strictness. With which weakness Fabius Maximus taxed him in the Senate House, calling him the corrupter of the Roman soldiery. Again, when the Locrians were shamefully outraged by one of his lieutenants, he neither avenged them, nor punished the insolence of his officer; and this from the natural easiness of his disposition. So that it was said in the Senate by one who sought to excuse him, that there were many who knew better how to refrain from doing wrong themselves than how to correct the wrong-doing of others. This temper, however, must in time have marred the name and fame even of Scipio, had he continued in it, and retained his command. But living as he did under the control of the Senate, this hurtful quality was not merely disguised, but came to be regarded as a glory.

Returning to the question of being loved or feared, I sum up by saying, that since his being loved depends upon his subjects, while his being feared depends upon himself, a wise Prince should build on what is his own, and not on what rests with others. Only, as I have said, he must do his utmost to escape hatred.

GLOSSARY

Cesare Borgia: a Roman leader and contemporary of Machiavelli; he is a frequent example of leadership in *The Prince*

Dido: a queen in Virgil's epic poem *Aeneid* who rules the new city of Carthage in northern Africa

Fabius Maximus: another Roman general who was less successful than Scipio against Hannibal

Hannibal: a Carthaginian general in the 200s BCE who fought and almost conquered the Locrians

Locrians: a Greek tribe eventually conquered by the Romans

patrimony: inheritance

Pistoja: a small town near Florence

rapine: destruction and looting

Scipio: the ancient Roman general who eventually defeated Hannibal

Cover page of 1550 edition of Machiavelli's Il Principe *and* La Vita di Castruccio Castracani da Lucca. *(By omslagsbild)*

Document Analysis

In *The Prince*, Machiavelli discusses the correct way for a ruler to behave if he wishes to keep power. The actions he suggests have often been considered immoral or tyrannical. Throughout the work, he treats the maintenance of power, rather than virtue or goodness, as the most important goal for a leader. According to this philosophy, tyrannical, cruel, and dishonest actions are acceptable if they allow one to keep control. The ruthless practicality of his work led to the use of the term "Machiavellian" to describe cunning and unethical political behavior.

In this passage, Machiavelli discusses the distinction between love and fear. He asserts that they "can hardly exist together"; therefore, since love is a more selfish and changeable motivation, fear is a better way for the prince to motivate his subjects to do what he wants. Machiavelli also cautions against trust: if the leader believes what his subjects say and "builds wholly on their professions" of loyalty, he will be overthrown. In addition, Machiavelli believes strongly that "men are a sorry breed" and that they are fundamentally guided by greed, not loyalty. His statement that "men will sooner forget the death of their father than the loss of their patrimony" shows his belief that self-interest is the governing principle of humanity and therefore the best way to keep subjects in line.

Essential Themes

The Prince is the work that gave rise to the word "Machiavellian" to describe immoral, self-centered political manipulation. In this passage, Machiavelli suggests several such actions: he says that a prince can "quell disorder by a very few signal examples" and that a general should "disregard the reproach of cruelty" and accept that cruel actions are necessary. Machiavelli's prince does not treat his subjects with kindness but takes actions that can injure and frighten citizens. He suggests that it is better to be feared than loved because love is more fragile than fear, and a successful prince will not derive his power from something that can be easily broken.

Another central theme is the appeal to historical precedent as a way to justify political action. Throughout the passage, Machiavelli calls on ancient and modern Roman examples to demonstrate times when his philosophy has been correct. He begins by discussing the Roman Cesare Borgia, who had recently died when *The Prince* was written, and contrasts his actions with Florence's. He also uses a fictional poetic character, Dido (a character of the Roman poet Virgil), to justify the idea that a new leader will definitely acquire "a name for cruelty."

For these and other reasons *The Prince* continues to be read today by students of leadership, politics, business, history, and the humanities.

—*Hannah Rich*

Bibliography and Additional Reading

Benner, Erica. *Be Like the Fox: Machiavelli In His World*. New York: Norton, 2017.

Strathern, Paul. *The Medici: Power, Money, and Ambition in the Italian Renaissance*. New York: Pegasus, 2017.

Viroli, Maurizio, and Antony Shugaar. *Niccolò's Smile: A Biography of Machiavelli*. New York: Farrar Straus & Giroux, 2000.

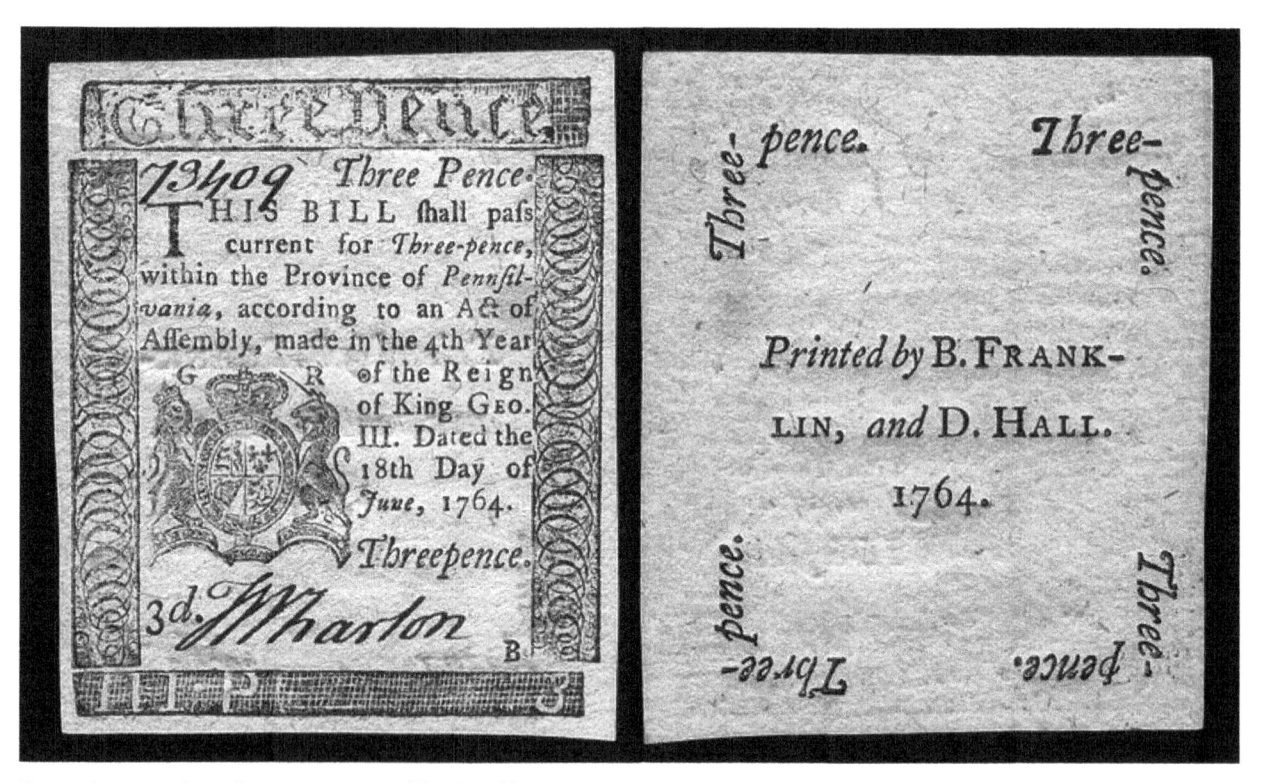

Pennsylvania colonial currency printed by Franklin in 1764.

■ "Advice to a Young Tradesman"

Date: 1748
Author: Benjamin Franklin
Genre: Essay

Summary Overview

Benjamin Franklin's 1748 essay giving "Advice to a Young Tradesman" offers us a glimpse into the financial and occupational world of Britain's American colonies in the mid-eighteenth century. Perhaps surprisingly, much of the financial wisdom Franklin conveys in this brief essay is broadly applicable to modern life (or is, at least, recognizable). In the twenty-first century, financial experts encourage business owners and consumers alike to live within their means, save for the future, and manage credit wisely. Franklin's examples of behaviors that can damage a tradesman's financial reputation are analogous to modern activities that might damage one's credit rating.

Despite these parallels, Franklin's essay shows us an America where communities are smaller—where personal reputations could be damaged and business growth shattered because the wrong person saw you in the tavern at the wrong time of day. At the same time, it helps establish a line of thought that would persist in Colonial America, and ultimately in the United States: namely, that a person's wealth and status are the direct result of individual decisions made and actions taken. Franklin's essay presents an early America where, for the independent tradesman, the possibilities are nearly limitless.

Defining Moment

This essay first appeared in 1748 as part of a book entitled *The American Instructor: or Young Man's Best Companion*. *The American Instructor* was one example of the several handbooks aimed at adolescent and young adult males that served as a guide not only to general business knowledge but also topics such as grammar, writing, mathematics, accounting, and penmanship—all useful subjects to a young man finishing his apprenticeship and beginning a career as a tradesman. This particular book was an Americanized version of *The Instructor*, compiled by George Fisher in Britain. For this American edition, publisher Benjamin Franklin replaced some chapters or essays with ones that spoke directly to issues that men would encounter in the American colonies. Franklin also added a brief discussion and historical account of the colonies as well as his own summary of advice for young men entering a trade.

"Tradesmen," in the context in which Franklin composed his advice, were artisans in a number of fields who had undergone a lengthy apprenticeship and were prepared to enter the workforce on their own. In the British American colonies, these trades ranged from carpenters to dressmakers and from printers (like Franklin had been) to tavern keepers. Thus, any advice directed at tradesmen had to be sufficiently broad as to be applicable to this wide variety of occupations.

Books such as these are one indication of the rapid growth the British colonies in America were experiencing in the mid-eighteenth century. In cities like Franklin's Philadelphia, new arrivals to the colonies and internal migrants moving from rural areas to the city for new opportunities provided plenty of customers and laborers. Franklin's reprinting of a British book demonstrates the close cultural connection between the mother country and the colonies while his Americanization demonstrates the persistent cultural differences between the two lands.

Author Biography

One of the most well-known, multifaceted figures in the history of the United States, Benjamin Franklin has long served as a model for entrepreneurial spirit and civic engagement. Born in Boston in 1706, Franklin never completed a formal education but would nonetheless enter the worlds of publishing, science, politics, and diplomacy. Franklin initially made an impact in the newspaper business; a career that began when he was fifteen years old when he worked as an apprentice for his brother James. James had founded the first independent newspaper in the colonies, the *New-England Courant*.

Benjamin eventually abandoned his apprenticeship and, as a fugitive from the law because of this, moved to Philadelphia at age 17. It was in Philadelphia that he and other young men who sought to learn and improve themselves, established a library for their benefit—this collection of books would evolve into a library that would allow members of the public to purchase membership and, after being incorporated as the Library Company of Philadelphia would be the first library in the American colonies and is an example of the way in which much of Franklin's work blended business management with public benefit.

In 1728, Franklin took charge of the *Pennsylvania Gazette* and began publishing other newspapers, religious books, and pamphlets. He attempted to build a network of newspapers that would stretch across the many British colonies but the project never achieved the success he desired. Despite not achieving these ambitious goals, Franklin published the first monthly news magazine in the Americas, the *General Magazine and Historical Chronicle for All the British Plantations in America*. Franklin also found success as an author, with his *Poor Richard's Almanack* being incredibly popular. He used his skills for promotion to generate publicity for evangelist George Whitefield during the Great Awakening. Franklin's broad experience made him an ideal advisor to young tradesmen.

HISTORICAL DOCUMENT

Remember that Time is Money. He that can earn Ten Shillings a Day by his Labour, and goes abroad, or sits idle one half of that Day, tho' he spends but Sixpence during his Diversion or Idleness, ought not to reckon That the only Expence; he has really spent or rather thrown away Five Shillings besides.

Remember that Credit is Money. If a Man lets his Money lie in my Hands after it is due, he gives me the Interest, or so much as I can make of it during that Time. This amounts to a considerable Sum where a Man has good and large Credit, and makes good Use of it.

Remember that Money is of a prolific generating Nature. Money can beget Money, and its Offspring can beget more, and so on. Five Shillings turn'd, is *Six*: Turn'd again, 'tis Seven and Three Pence; and so on 'til it becomes an Hundred Pound. The more there is of it, the more it produces every Turning, so that the Profits rise quicker and quicker. He that kills a breeding Sow, destroys all her Offspring to the thousandth Generation. He that murders a Crown, destroys all it might have produc'd, even Scores of Pounds.

Remember that Six Pounds a Year is but a Groat a Day. For this little Sum (which may be daily wasted either in Time or Expence unperceiv'd) a Man of Credit may on his own Security have the constant Possession and Use of an Hundred Pounds. So much in Stock briskly turn'd by an industrious Man, produces great Advantage.

Remember this Saying, *That the good Paymaster is Lord of another Man's Purse*. He that is known to pay punctually and exactly to the Time he promises, may at any Time, and on any Occasion, raise all the Money his Friends can spare. This is sometimes of great Use: Therefore never keep borrow'd Money an Hour beyond the Time you promis'd, lest a Disappointment shuts up your Friends Purse forever.

The most trifling Actions that affect a Man's Credit, are to be regarded. The Sound of your Hammer at Five in the Morning or Nine at Night, heard by a Creditor, makes him easy Six Months longer. But if he sees you at a Billiard Table, or hears your Voice in a Tavern, when you should be at Work, he sends for his Money the next Day. Finer Cloaths than he or his Wife wears, or greater Expence in any particular than he affords himself, shocks his Pride, and he duns you to humble you. Creditors are a kind of People, that have the sharpest Eyes and Ears, as well as the best Memories of any in the World.

Good-natur'd Creditors (and such one would always chuse to deal with if one could) feel Pain when they are oblig'd to ask for Money. Spare 'em that Pain, and they will love you. When you receive a Sum of Money, divide it among 'em in Proportion to your Debts. Don't be asham'd of paying a small Sum because you owe a greater. Money, more or less, is always welcome; and your Creditor had rather be at the Trouble of receiving Ten Pounds voluntarily brought him, tho' at ten different Times or Payments, than be oblig'd to go ten Times to demand it before he can receive it in a Lump. It shews, besides, that you are mindful of what you owe; it makes you appear a careful as well as an honest Man; and that still encreases your Credit.

Beware of thinking all your own that you possess, and of living accordingly. 'Tis a Mistake that many People who have Credit fall into. To prevent this, keep an exact Account for some Time of both your Expences and your Incomes. If you take the Pains at first to mention Particulars, it will have this good Effect; you will discover how wonderfully small trifling Expences mount up to large Sums, and will discern what might have been, and may for the future be saved, without occasioning any great Inconvenience.

In short, the Way to Wealth, if you desire it, is as plain as the Way to Market. It depends chiefly on two Words, Industry and Frugality; i.e. Waste neither Time nor Money, but make the best Use of both. He that gets all he can honestly, and saves all he gets (necessary Expences excepted) will certainly become Rich; If that Being who governs the World, to whom all should look for a Blessing on their honest Endeavours, doth not in his wise Providence otherwise determine.

GLOSSARY

groat: a small amount of money, usually four pence

stock: in this context, money retained in savings

trifling: seemingly small or insignificant

Document Analysis

Franklin begins his advice with the aphorism "time is money." He expands on this by specific amounts of time and money as an easily understandable object lesson—illustrating that time spent away from profitable work results in more lost money than one might expect. The second piece of advice, rhetorically, echoes the first. Time is money, but credit is money as well. Here, Franklin explains the dangers of credit and interest for the debtor and the benefits to the creditor—the nature and use of credit is a theme on which Franklin will spend a great deal of time in this essay, giving modern readers some indication of the financial arrangements into which young artisans in the American colonies would enter when they launched their careers.

Franklin moves away from the subject of credit for the next two pieces of advice. He discusses the "prolific generating Nature" of money. As he talks about the "turning" of small amounts of money into larger ones, we can understand this in terms both of interest that can be earned on money that is deposited in banks or loaned out but also the benefit that can be gained through the investments in equipment that might be made by artisans and tradesmen who were making an effort to grow their businesses. The illustration of the shortsightedness of killing a breeding sow would very likely resonate with the largely agricultural British American colonies. Next, Franklin breaks down the virtues of saving even a small amount of money on a regular basis. In his example, he points out that a groat a day will total six pounds a year. A groat was—even in 1748—an outdated amount of currency. While it originally was valued at around four pence, more generally it denotes a small amount of money. Regardless of the mathematics of Colonial currency, Franklin's larger point is that small amounts of money, managed carefully, would build to larger amounts over time; the discipline of saving would eventually pay off. With additional careful management of credit, a scrupulous saver could build a great deal of wealth over time.

From here, Franklin moves into an extensive discussion of credit, beginning with the admonition to repay borrowed money on time, if not earlier. Doing so, he explains, will make it more likely that one would be able to borrow money when necessary in the future. Paying late—or not at all—will close off avenues of borrowing. Paying borrowed money back in a timely manner is not the only behavior to follow. Franklin next discusses activities that will set a creditor's mind at ease, and behaviors that will cause concern. The wise borrower, Franklin explains, will be diligent in his work, earning money to repay his debts on time. Unwise borrowers will waste their time—engaging in leisure activities when they should be working. Franklin's examples emphasize that creditors will learn of

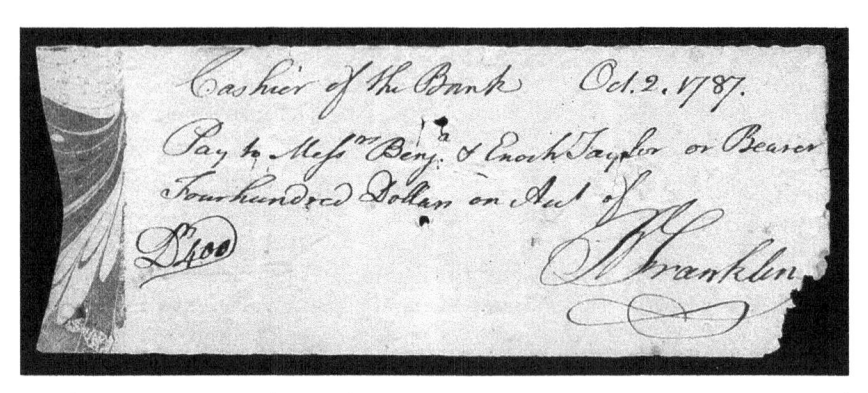

Franklin autograph check signed during his Presidency of Pennsylvania. (National Museum of History)

these activities, and either be satisfied that the borrower is a good bet and that his money is safe or be suspicious that the money lent may be in jeopardy and demand early repayment. In the same way, Franklin warns that those in debt should not spend money more extravagantly than they should—particularly, not more extravagantly than the people to whom they owe money.

Essential Themes

Franklin also recommends making payments on debts on a regular basis, even if one cannot repay the entire amount. Doing so demonstrates good management of income but also mindfulness of what today we might call "debt to income ratio." Following this, Franklin concludes with some more general advice. He emphasizes the importance of living within ones' means and not becoming overly reliant on credit. He closes with a brief discussion of the need for both industry and frugality: working hard at one's trade and managing one's money carefully. Echoing his advice earlier in the essay, he reiterates the importance of careful saving as the foundation of wealth. His final sentence, which he presents almost as a caveat, is that—basically—even the most careful planning can be upset by unexpected disasters, described spiritually here as the determination of God's providence. Throughout, we see the wit and wisdom of this founding figure at work, and can appreciate why he continues to be read as a "popular author" even today.

—*Aaron Gulyas*

Bibliography and Additional Reading

Isaacson, Walter. *Benjamin Franklin: An American Life.* New York: Simon & Schuster, 2003.

Taylor, Alan. *Colonial America: A Very Short Introduction.* London and New York: Oxford University Press, 2012.

Schultz, Ronald. "The Small-Producer Tradition and the Moral Origins of Artisan Radicalism in Philadelphia 1720–1810." *Past & Present*, no. 127 (1990): 84–116.

Stott, Richard. "Artisans and Capitalist Development." *Journal of the Early Republic* 16, no. 2 (1996): 257–71.

Adam Smith, from *The Theory of Moral Sentiments*

Date: 1759
Author: Adam Smith
Genre: Nonfiction book (excerpt)

Summary Overview

Adam Smith's first published book, *The Theory of Moral Sentiments*, elucidates a philosophical framework that would figure prominently in his later and more well-known work, *The Wealth of Nations*, a foundational text in classical economics. In this earlier work, Smith focuses on the origins of morality by analyzing how complex of psychological motives, including self-interest, fomented sociological connections. This was in contrast to previous writers like Bernard Mandeville and Thomas Hobbes, who had pessimistic views about benevolence and believed moral virtues derived primarily from self-interest. In sum, Smith argues that "sympathy," or the ability to identify and reflect others' emotions and consider the causes of them, produces feelings of moral approval or disapproval. A major feature in Smith's moral philosophy is the theory of the "impartial spectator," or an imagined self that humans use to consider the ramification of actions in a larger community. In this selection from the beginning of Part VI of *The Theory of Moral Sentiments*, Smith describes a particular virtue, prudence, and its relation to security (including financial). Smith travels from the individual level to the scope of the state, and ultimately asserts that the standards for assessing prudence should be analogous. That is, if a prudent man lives within his means and endeavors to live in harmony with conditions around him, so too should the leader of a state.

Defining Moment

The eighteenth century was a time of political, economic, and intellectual transformations in Scotland, the home of Adam Smith. The Acts of Union in 1707 officially made Scotland and England one political unit, but the two states had been dynastically linked since at least the seventeenth century when Queen Elizabeth made the reigning Stuarts in Scotland the heirs to her throne in England. Although the dynastic connection did not solve entirely the tumultuous relations between Scotland and England, the Glorious Revolution in 1688 threatened the tenuous political harmony. The Glorious Revolution was the bloodless overthrow of the Catholic James II, the Stuart king, and his infant son in favor of James II's Protestant son-in-law and daughter, William of Orange and Mary. For the Catholics in Scotland, the rejection of the Catholic Stuart line was intolerable.

The Jacobites were a political group that formed in reaction to the overthrow of James II and his son; adherents to the cause came from across the British Isles. In Scotland adherents primarily came from the Catholic minority in the Lowland and various Highland clans. Over time, however, the cause attracted individuals of various backgrounds who clashed with the religious and political status quo in Scotland and, after 1707, in Great Britain. Jacobite uprisings continued to flare until the disastrous Battle of Culloden in Scotland, the final Hanoverian success over the political rebels in 1745. This defeat resulted in a crackdown against all rebels and their supporters: officers were executed, Jacobite gentry had their lands stripped and sold, and punitive measures against traditional clothing were enacted in an attempt to integrate Scotland more closely with the rest of Britain.

Nonetheless, Scotland reaped the economic benefits of union with England, even if the political situation was often precarious throughout the eighteenth century. The political travails of the seventeenth century and a devastating famine in the 1690s kept the economy of Scotland small, especially in comparison to England. Laboring under these political and environmental complications, Scotland could not hope to compete on the global stage when the dominant European economic system at the time was mercantilism. As an economic theory, mercantilism held that a country should maximize exports, minimize imports (or at least place tariffs on them), and accumulate gold in the treasury. Colonialism aided mercantilist countries greatly. England, for example, implemented policies that restricted trade between English

Portrait of Smith by John Kay, 1790.

colonies and other nations to benefit the state coffers. Scotland, without any official colonies, could not build its commercial interests in the same way. In the late 1690s, nevertheless, Scotland attempted to enter into this market by establishing a colony called "Caledonia" on the Isthmus of Panama. This colonizing attempt, named the Darien scheme after the Gulf of Darién where the colony was located, suffered from poor planning, disease, and attacks from the Spanish military. A significant portion of circulating Scottish money had backed this venture, and so the collapse of the Darien scheme financially devastated the state. This botched colonizing experiment perhaps compelled Scotland to the Acts of Union in 1707 since closer political ties with England meant closer economic ties. A shared market with England and English colonies did prove fruitful for Scotland, which could now profit officially from trade with the Americas.

Scotland also benefited from a prominent intellectual climate at the same time as the Age of Enlightenment was transforming minds across the European continent. This philosophical movement stressed reason as the source of knowledge, whereas previous thinkers had stressed theological explanations. Although Scotland may have been relatively distant in terms of geography from the continent, the country was not remote from contemporary intellectual currents. In contrast to England's two universities, Oxford and Cambridge, Scotland had four long-standing and intellectually rigorous universities that produced important thinkers like Frances Hutcheson, David Hume, and Adam Smith (St. Andrews, Aberdeen, Glasgow, and Edinburgh). In addition to these universities, there were a number of clubs promoting discussion about reason and philosophy. David Hume and Adam Smith were both members of clubs like the Political Economy Club and The Select Society. These intellectual associations, publications, and universities mutually interacted with each other and fostered dialogue about the tumultuous contemporary developments, both in Scotland and globally.

Author Biography

Adam Smith (1723–1790) was a prominent member of the Scottish Enlightenment whose writings contributed to his reputation as one of the founding fathers of the modern economics. His pioneering philosophy also earned him the moniker "Father of Capitalism." Not much is known about Smith's childhood in Kirkcaldy, Scotland, but his education at the University of Glasgow and Balliol College, Oxford would prove to be formative for his later work. Francis Hutcheson, in particular, was an influential teacher of Smith's in Glasgow: Smith's philosophy reflects Hutcheson's interest in moral sense theory. Smith would not enjoy his time at Oxford as much, and he soon returned to Glasgow with an unfavorable opinion about the quality of English instruction.

Back in Glasgow, Smith began delivering public lectures in 1748 and became a professor in his own right in 1751. During this time Smith established a friendship with another heavyweight of the Scottish Enlightenment, David Hume; this friendship would prove intellectually fruitful for both men. It was in this academic position that Smith also formulated many of the ideas that would garner him respect in his lectures and find publication in *The Theory of Moral Sentiments* (1759).

When he received the opportunity to travel and tutor a Scottish nobleman in 1764, Smith resigned his professorship and took to the road. On this tour Smith met leading figures of the day, including Voltaire, Francois

Quesnay, and Benjamin Franklin. Smith's service as professional tutor only lasted two years before he returned to Great Britain. He spent the next decade working on the book *The Wealth of Nations* (1776), which became an instant success upon publication.

This work would be the last of Smith's writings to achieve acclaim or to survive his last bequests. In the remainder of his career, Smith served as commissioner of customs in Scotland starting in 1778 and became a founding member of the Royal Society of Edinburgh, an academic organization, in 1783. He died in 1790 from illness, and left instructions to destroy any writing unsuitable for publication. Although his published works undeniably influenced economic theory, Smith's dearth of writing, combined with a nebulous personal life, has contributed to continued debate about the nature and intent of his philosophical thought.

HISTORICAL DOCUMENT

We suffer more, it has already been observed, when we fall from a better to a worse situation, than we ever enjoy when we rise from a worse to a better. Security, therefore, is the first and the principal object of prudence. It is averse to expose our health, our fortune, our rank, or reputation, to any sort of hazard. It is rather cautious than enterprising, and more anxious to preserve the advantages which we already possess, than forward to prompt us to the acquisition of still greater advantages. The methods of improving our fortune, which it principally recommends to us, are those which expose to no loss or hazard; real knowledge and skill in our trade or profession, assiduity and industry in the exercise of it, frugality, and even some degree of parsimony, in all our expences.

The prudent man always studies seriously and earnestly to understand whatever he professes to understand, and not merely to persuade other people that he understands it; and though his talents may not always be very brilliant, they are always perfectly genuine. He neither endeavours to impose upon you by the cunning devices of an artful impostor, nor by the arrogant airs of an assuming pedant, nor by the confident assertions of a superficial and imprudent pretender. He is not ostentatious even of the abilities which he really possesses. His conversation is simple and modest, and he is averse to all the quackish arts by which other people so frequently thrust themselves into public notice and reputation. For reputation in his profession he is naturally disposed to rely a good deal upon the solidity of his knowledge and abilities; and he does not always think of cultivating the favour of those little clubs and cabals, who, in the superior arts and sciences, so often erect themselves into the supreme judges of merit; and who make it their business to celebrate the talents and virtues of one another, and to decry whatever can come into competition with them. If he ever connects himself with any society of this kind, it is merely in self-defence, not with a view to impose upon the public, but to hinder the public from being imposed upon, to his disadvantage, by the clamours, the whispers, or the intrigues, either of that particular society, or of some other of the same kind.

The prudent man is always sincere, and feels horror at the very thought of exposing himself to the disgrace which attends upon the detection of falsehood. But though always sincere, he is not always frank and open; and though he never tells any thing but the truth, he does not always think himself bound, when not properly called upon, to tell the whole truth. As he is cautious in his actions, so he is reserved in his speech; and never rashly or unnecessarily obtrudes his opinion concerning either things or persons.

The prudent man, though not always distinguished by the most exquisite sensibility, is always very capable of friendship. But his friendship is not that ardent and passionate, but too often transitory affection, which appears so delicious to the generosity of youth and inexperience. It is a sedate, but steady and faithful attachment to a few well-tried and well-chosen companions; in the choice of whom he is not guided by the giddy admiration of shining accomplishments, but by the sober esteem of modesty, discretion, and good conduct. But though capable of friendship, he is not always much disposed to general sociality. He rarely frequents, and more rarely figures in those convivial societies which are distinguished for the jollity and gaiety of their conversation. Their way of life might too often interfere with the regularity of his temperance, might interrupt the steadiness of his industry, or break in upon the strictness of his frugality.

But though his conversation may not always be very sprightly or diverting, it is always perfectly inoffensive. He hates the thought of being guilty of any petulance or rudeness. He never assumes impertinently over any body, and, upon all common occasions, is willing to place himself rather below than above his equals. Both in his conduct and conversation, he is an exact observer of decency, and respects with an almost religious scrupulosity, all the established decorums and ceremonials of society. And, in this respect, he sets a much better example than has frequently been done by men of much more splendid talents and virtues; who, in all ages, from that of Socrates and Aristippus, down to that of Dr. Swift and Voltaire, and from that of Philip and Alexander the Great, down to that of the great Czar Peter of Moscovy, have too often distinguished themselves by the most improper and even insolent contempt of all the ordinary decorums of life and conversation, and who have thereby set the most pernicious example to those who wish to resemble them, and who too often content themselves with imitating their follies, without even attempting to attain their perfections.

In the steadiness of his industry and frugality, in his steadily sacrificing the ease and enjoyment of the present moment for the probable expectation of the still greater ease and enjoyment of a more distant but more lasting period of time, the prudent man is always both supported and rewarded by the entire approbation of the impartial spectator, and of the representative of the impartial spectator, the man within the breast. The impartial spectator does not feel himself worn out by the present labour of those whose conduct he surveys; nor does he feel himself solicited by the importunate calls of their present appetites. To him their present, and what is likely to be their future situation, are very nearly the same: he sees them nearly at the same distance, and is affected by them very nearly in the same manner. He knows, however, that to the persons principally concerned, they are very far from being the same, and that they naturally affect them in a very different manner. He cannot therefore but approve, and even applaud, that proper exertion of self-command, which enables them to act as if their present and their future situation affected them nearly in the same manner in which they affect him.

The man who lives within his income, is naturally contented with his situation, which, by continual, though small accumulations, is growing better and better every day. He is enabled gradually to relax, both in the rigour of his parsimony and in the severity of his application; and he feels with double satisfaction this gradual increase of ease and enjoyment, from having felt before the hardship which attended the want of them. He has no anxiety to change so comfortable a situation, and does not go in quest of new enterprises and adventures, which might endanger, but could not well increase, the secure tranquillity which he actually enjoys. If he enters into any new projects or enterprises, they are likely to be well concerted and well prepared. He can never be hurried or drove into them by any necessity, but has always time and leisure to deliberate soberly and coolly concerning what are likely to be their consequences.

The prudent man is not willing to subject himself to any responsibility which his duty does not impose upon him. He is not a bustler in business where he has no concern; is not a meddler in other people's affairs; is not a professed counsellor or adviser, who obtrudes his advice where nobody is asking it. He confines himself, as much as his duty will permit, to his own affairs, and has no taste for that foolish importance which many people wish to derive from appearing to have some influence in the management of those of other people. He is averse to enter into any party disputes, hates faction, and is not always very forward to listen to the voice even of noble and great ambition. When distinctly called upon, he will not decline the service of his country, but he will not cabal in order to force himself into it; and would be much better pleased that the public business were well managed by some other person, than that he himself should have the trouble, and incur the responsibility, of managing it. In the bottom of his heart he would prefer the undisturbed enjoyment of secure tranquillity, not only to all the vain splendour of successful ambition, but to the real and solid glory of performing the greatest and most magnanimous actions.

Prudence, in short, when directed merely to the care of the health, of the fortune, and of the rank and reputation of the individual, though it is regarded as a most respectable and even, in some degree, as an amiable and agreeable quality, yet it never is considered as one, either of the most endearing, or of the most ennobling of the virtues. It commands a certain cold esteem, but seems not entitled to any very ardent love or admiration.

Wise and judicious conduct, when directed to greater and nobler purposes than the care of the health, the fortune, the rank and reputation of the individual, is frequently and very properly called prudence. We talk of the prudence of the great general, of the great statesman, of the great legislator. Prudence is, in all these cases, combined with many greater and more splendid virtues, with valour, with extensive and strong benevolence, with a sacred regard to the rules of justice, and all these supported by a proper degree of self-command. This superior prudence, when carried to the highest degree of perfection, necessarily supposes the art, the talent, and the habit or disposition of acting with the most perfect propriety in every possible circumstance and situation. It necessarily supposes the utmost perfection of all the intellectual and of all the moral virtues. It is the best head joined to the best heart. It is the most perfect wisdom combined with the most perfect virtue. It constitutes very nearly the character of the Academical or Peripatetic sage, as the inferior prudence does that of the Epicurean.

Mere imprudence, or the mere want of the capacity to take care of one's-self, is, with the generous and humane, the object of compassion; with those of less delicate sentiments, of neglect, or, at worst, of contempt, but never of hatred or indignation. When combined with other vices, however, it aggravates in the highest degree the infamy and disgrace which would otherwise attend them. The artful knave, whose dexterity and address exempt him, though not from strong suspicions, yet from punishment or distinct detection, is too often received in the world with an indulgence which he by no means deserves. The awkward and foolish one, who, for want of this dexterity and address, is convicted and brought to punishment, is the object of universal hatred, contempt, and derision. In countries where great crimes frequently pass unpunished, the most atrocious actions become almost familiar, and cease to impress the people with that horror which is universally felt in countries where an exact administration of justice takes place. The injustice is the same in both countries; but the imprudence is often very different. In the latter, great crimes are evidently great follies. In the former, they are not always considered as such. In Italy, during the greater part of the sixteenth century, assassinations, murders, and even murders under trust, seem to have been almost familiar among the superior ranks of people. Caesar Borgia invited four of the little princes in his neighbourhood, who all possessed little sovereignties, and commanded little armies of their own, to a friendly conference at Senigaglia, where, as soon as they arrived, he put them all to death. This infamous action, though certainly not approved of even in that age of crimes, seems to have contributed very little to the discredit, and not in the least to the ruin of the perpetrator. That ruin happened a few years after from causes altogether disconnected with this crime. Machiavel, not indeed a man of the nicest morality even for his own times, was resident, as minister from the republic of Florence, at the court of Caesar Borgia when this crime was committed. He gives a very particular account of it, and in that pure, elegant, and simple language which distinguishes all his writings. He talks of it very coolly; is pleased with the address with which Caesar Borgia conducted it; has much contempt for the dupery and weakness of the sufferers; but no compassion for their miserable and untimely death, and no sort of indignation at the cruelty and falsehood of their murderer. The violence and injustice of great conquerors are often regarded with foolish wonder and admiration; those of petty thieves, robbers, and murderers, with contempt, hatred, and even horror upon all occasions. The former, though they are a hundred times more mischievous and destructive, yet when successful, they often pass for deeds of the most heroic magnanimity. The latter are always viewed with hatred and aversion, as the follies, as well as the crimes, of the lowest and most worthless of mankind. The injustice of the former is certainly, at least, as great as that of the latter; but the folly and imprudence are not near so great. A wicked and worthless man of parts often goes through the world with much more credit than he deserves. A wicked and worthless fool appears always, of all mortals, the most hateful, as well as the most contemptible. As prudence combined with other virtues, constitutes the noblest; so imprudence combined with other vices, constitutes the vilest of all characters.

> **GLOSSARY**
>
> **bustler:** one who moves in an engergetic fashing
>
> **quackish:** presented falsely as having curative powers
>
> **Senigaglia (also spelled Sinigallia/Senigallia):** a location in Italy where Cesare Borgia lured would-be conspirators under false promises of security on December 31, 1502; after he had trapped the conspirators with his army, Borgia summarily executed them for disloyalty

Document Analysis

As a complete work, *The Theory of Moral Sentiments* is a wide-ranging examination of human psychology and society. Smith's character analysis of the prudent man, however, valorizes apolitical life at the same time as it shows the pernicious effects political engagement can have. While this is only a small section of a larger work, the attitude to political life in this section reflects Smith's involvement in Enlightenment thought, especially concerning issues of individual liberty, and political trends in Great Britain away from absolute monarchy.

At the beginning of this section on the prudent man, Smith leads the reader to believe that his character analysis will simply concern security and human livelihood. In his first detailed description of this character, however, it becomes clear that Smith has a greater point to make about political involvement. As Smith elaborates, the prudent man "is averse to all the quackish arts by which other people so frequently thrust themselves into public notice and reputation." Namely, the prudent man does not actively seek public recognition. Furthermore, "he does not always think of cultivating the favour of those little clubs and cabals." The link between "public notice" and specialized clubs does not automatically connote political aspirations, but Smith's description of these clubs as leading to competition and attention implies that they are connected to a struggle for power. As Smith continues to describe the conduct of the prudent man, he says that this character "never assumes impertinently over any body, and, upon all common occasions, is willing to place himself rather below than above his equals." By specifically placing this virtuous man as willing to humble himself for the sake of security, Smith associates virtue with lack of political ambition.

Aside from his general statements about the prudent man's behavior, Smith's specific references to historical individuals solidifies the author's antipathy toward politics based on a cult of personality. After Smith describes the prudent man's tendency to humble himself, he explains that this man is a better example than "men of much more splendid talents and virtues; who, in all ages, from that of Socrates and Aristippus, down to that of Dr. Swift and Voltaire, and from that of Philip and Alexander the Great, down to that of the great Czar Peter of Moscovy have too often distinguished themselves by the most improper and even insolent contempt of all the ordinary decorums." Half of the names Smith mentions were not actual political leaders, but they did concern themselves with political issues in their philosophical thoughts or writings. By linking personalities like Socrates with Peter the Great, Smith also generalizes the behavior of an absolute monarch with all individuals who interject on political matters. The last paragraph of this selection emphasizes the deleterious effect politics have on the individual in the explication of events at Senigaglia (or Senigallia). While Smith does not approve of Cesare Borgia's duplicitous behavior, he does acknowledge that great power tends to corrupt the ability of individuals to assess whether behavior is just or not. In this distortion between prosaic, quotidian behavior and great matters of state, Smith's sympathy clearly lies with the man who lives a simple, unambitious life.

In this small selection it is possible to see how Adam Smith's antipathy toward overbearing political rulership correlates with his disdain for mercantilism as an economic theory. Since mercantilism relied on strong rulers who could establish strong controls over trade and national spending, it interfered with individual freedom to buy and sell where one pleased. Smith's prioritization of individual liberty in this work would receive more attention in relation to economic theory in his magnum opus, *The Wealth of Nations*, but this earlier work establishes the psychological and political groundwork that made the later work such a success.

AN

INQUIRY

INTO THE

Nature and Causes

OF THE

WEALTH OF NATIONS.

By ADAM SMITH, LL.D. and F.R.S.
Formerly Professor of Moral Philosophy in the University of GLASGOW.

IN TWO VOLUMES.

VOL. I.

―――――

LONDON:
PRINTED FOR W. STRAHAN; AND T. CADELL, IN THE STRAND.
MDCCLXXVI.

The first page of The Wealth of Nations, *1776 London edition.*

Essential Themes

This selection from *The Theory of Moral Sentiments* illustrates Adam Smith's optimism about human behavior and economics. Smith was aware of a pessimistic current in philosophical thought which decried the effect of self-interest in society (such as in Jean-Jacques Rousseau's *Discourse on Inequality*). Equally Smith was aware of the uproar caused by a satirical poem written by Bernard Mandeville, *The Fable of the Bees*. This parable describes a fictitious bee colony that thrived while vice ruled, but the introduction of moral virtue caused the collapse of the bee colony's economy. Mandeville's satire upholds a view of society that financial profit and self-interest could not coexist with higher concerns about human rights. In response Smith conceived of an economic system where human self-interest and financial gain could be mutually beneficial for all involved.

As Smith describes in the character of the prudent man, the self-interested desire to provide oneself with security yields positive social gains. Smith ascribes part of this positive social effect to the assessment of the "impartial spectator," essentially a form of social consciousness. This separate conscience determines human virtues based on which behaviors are most aware and agreeable with community well-being. The "impartial spectator" as described here naturally values the prudent man's desire not to importune the present at the expense of future pleasure. Smith recognizes, however, that this assessment is not always impartial and often the scale of an action distorts the impartial spectator, as he explains in the case of Cesare Borgia and Machiavelli. Nevertheless, Smith remains convinced that the unintended positive consequences of evil actions, such as Borgia successfully preventing a coup against himself through duplicitous means, does not diminish the cruelty of these behaviors in a universal assessment.

Smith's equivocation on this dichotomy between positive consequences and unjust behavior to others underlies a larger issue with his overall optimistic outlook. Although the idea of the "invisible hand," that is, the unintended social benefits of self-interested behavior, does appear in *The Theory of Moral Sentiments*, it is most often associated with Smith's later work, *The Wealth of Nations*. This later work proposes in general that nations would experience more profit in a free market where human self-interest dictated the flow of goods and division of labor. Although Smith's economic system is of course more complicated, it does presuppose that an abundance of resources would be available; it also presupposes that in most people and in most contexts exists the natural inclination to operate according to this "mutual sympathy," which Smith argues negotiates human behavior toward one another. As the "father of capitalism," Smith also does not seem to account for the role that advanced technology would play in this type of economy. At what point should a more authoritative power like a political government step in to enact restrictions to prevent rising income inequality, or unfair commercial practices? Smith could not have predicted the consequences of his system, both good and bad, as increased profit interacted with more global connections and industrial advancements.

—Ashleigh Fata

Bibliography and Additional Reading

Milgate, Murray and Shannon C. Stimson. *After Adam Smith: A Century of Transformation in Politics and Political Economy*. Princeton, NJ: Princeton University Press, 2009.

Muller, Jerry Z. *Adam Smith in His Time and Ours: Designing the Decent Society*. Princeton, NJ: Princeton University Press, 1993.

Norman, Jesse. *Adam Smith: Father of Economics*. New York: Basic Books, 2018.

Rasmussen, Dennis C. *The Infidel and the Professor: David Hume, Adam Smith, and the Friendship That Shaped Modern Thought*. Princeton, NJ: Princeton University Press, 2017.

Smith, Adam. *The Wealth of Nations*. 1776. New York: Bantam Books, 2003.

■ Fletcher v. Peck

Date: 1810
Author: John Marshall
Genre: Court decision

Summary Overview

The 1810 Supreme Court case *Fletcher v. Peck* represented the first instance of the highest court in the land declaring a state law to be unconstitutional. Additionally, it strengthened notions of property rights and affirmed the inviolability of contracts. As the budding nation moved westward, these were to be vitally important concepts for securing economic growth.

The circumstances surrounding *Fletcher v. Peck* also highlight the practical, legal, and financial difficulties of the nation's initial burst of westward expansion in the late eighteenth and early nineteenth centuries. Multiple factors, such as inaccurate surveying and incomplete or missing paperwork, meant that there were often competing claims for the same property. Add to this the fact that people at every level, from state governments to individual farmers, had a financial stake in this expansion, and one often finds corruption and fraud entering the mix.

Defining Moment

The roots of *Fletcher v. Peck* go back to the 1790s and America's southwestern frontier. It involves one of the most widespread and astounding instances of land fraud in the history of the United States. This was the Yazoo land fraud. The Yazoo lands were comprised of territory that belonged to the state of Georgia in the 1790s. At that time, Georgia's land extended all the way west to the Mississippi River, which, in the eighteenth century, was the western border of the United States. Georgia's state government wanted to encourage settlement of these areas by white farmers for a number of reasons, including the continued claim on the areas by American Indian tribes, Spanish claims on some of the territories bordering Spanish Florida, and Georgia's own interest in obtaining revenue from these lands.

To accomplish this, four land speculation companies were created in 1794. Their purpose was to buy the Yazoo lands from the state of Georgia and then sell parcels of them to farmers for a profit. This type of land speculation was common on the American frontier. The state legislature of Georgia agreed to sell over 40 million acres to the companies for $500,000. This was made official when the Yazoo Land Act was signed into law in 1795.

Not long after the passage of the act, several issues came to light. One was that some of the land was claimed by American Indian tribes. Another was that many members of the Georgia state legislature had received bribes from land speculators as an enticement to pass the land act and generally support their efforts. Many of these lawmakers subsequently lost their reelection bids and, in 1796, a new legislature repealed the Yazoo Land Act, declaring, moreover, that any transactions taking place as a result of it were invalid.

But that was hardly the end of the situation. What about people who had bought land under the 1795 law? Georgia offered refunds of their money but some still wanted the land. Georgia did not recognize these people's ownership of the land. Disputes continued for years, the matter becoming the responsibility of the federal government when Georgia gave up its western land claims in 1802. The case of *Fletcher v. Peck* embodied the key questions that the government had to address in the wake of the Yazoo land fraud.

Author Biography

John Marshall was born in 1755 in Virginia. He served in the Continental Army during the American War of Independence. Leaving the army in 1780, he studied law at the College of William and Mary and entered politics, holding a seat in the Virginia House of delegates during the 1780s and 1790s while continuing his private law practice. He supported the ratification of the U.S. Constitution.

As the First Party System began to emerge in the 1790s, Marshall found himself part of the Federalist faction, which, in general, advocated a strong national government and support for commercial endeavors. During the presidency of John Adams, Marshall was part of the diplomatic contingent sent to France to negotiate an end to France's seizure of American merchant ships; this mission resulted in the infamous XYZ Affair, in which French officials attempted to extract a bribe from the Americans in order to even begin the negotiations.

Marshall briefly served as Secretary of State, from June 1800 to early 1801, when he was sworn in as Chief Justice of the Supreme Court, a post which he held until his death at age 79 in June 1835. During his time on the court, he presided over some of the most significant cases in American legal and Constitutional history. In addition to *Fletcher v. Peck*, his court decided *Marbury v. Madison*, which established the precedent for the principle of judicial review, or the right of the Supreme Court to rule on the constitutionality of federal laws.

HISTORICAL DOCUMENT

The question whether a law be void for its repugnancy to the Constitution is, at all times, a question of much delicacy, which ought seldom, if ever, to be decided in the affirmative in a doubtful case. The court, when impelled by duty to render such a judgment, would be unworthy of its station could it be unmindful of the solemn obligations which that station imposes. But it is not on slight implication and vague conjecture that the Legislature is to be pronounced to have transcended its powers, and its acts to be considered as void. The opposition between the Constitution and the law should be such that the judge feels a clear and strong conviction of their incompatibility with each other.

The importance and the difficulty of the questions, presented by these pleadings are deeply felt by the Court. The lands in controversy vested absolutely in James Gunn and others, the original grantees, by the conveyance of the Governor, made in pursuance of an act of assembly to which the Legislature was fully competent. Being thus in full possession of the legal estate, they, for a valuable consideration, conveyed portions of the land to those who were willing to purchase. If the original transaction was infected with fraud, these purchasers did not participate in it, and had no notice of it. They were innocent. Yet the Legislature of Georgia has involved them in the fate of the first parties to the transaction, and, if the act be valid, has annihilated their rights also.

The Legislature of Georgia was a party to this transaction, and for a party to pronounce its own deed invalid, whatever cause may be assigned for its invalidity, must be considered as a mere act of power which must find its vindication in a train of reasoning not often heard in courts of justice.

But the real party, it is said, are the people, and when their agents are unfaithful, the acts of those agents cases to be obligatory.

It is, however, to be recollected that the people can act only by these agents, and that, while within the powers conferred on them, their acts must be considered as the acts of the people. If the agents be corrupt, others may be chosen, and, if their contracts be examinable, the common sentiment, as well as common usage of mankind, points out a mode by which this examination may be made, and their validity determined.

If the Legislature of Georgia was not bound to submit its pretensions to those tribunals which are established for the security of property, and to decide on human rights, if it might claim to itself the power of judging in its own case, yet there are certain great principles of justice, whose authority is universally acknowledged, that ought not to be entirely disregarded.

If the Legislature be its own judge in its own case, it would seem equitable that its decision should be regulated by those rules which would have regulated the decision of a judicial tribunal. The question was, in its nature, a question of title, and the tribunal which decided it was either acting in the character of a court of justice, and performing a duty usually assigned to a court, or it was exerting a mere act of power in which it was controlled only by its own will.

If a suit be brought to set aside a conveyance obtained by fraud, and the fraud be clearly proved, the conveyance will be set aside as between the parties, but the rights of third persons who are purchasers without notice, for a valuable consideration, cannot be disregarded. Titles, which, according to every legal test, are perfect are acquired with that confidence which is inspired by the opinion that the purchaser is safe. If there be any concealed defect, arising from the conduct of those who had held the property long before he acquired it, of which he had no notice, that concealed defect cannot be set up against him. He has paid his money for a title good at law; he is innocent, whatever may be the guilt of others, and equity will not subject him to the penalties attached to that guilt. All titles would be insecure, and the intercourse between man and man would be very seriously obstructed if this principle be overturned.

A court of chancery, therefore, had a bill been brought to set aside the conveyance made to James Gunn and others as being obtained by improper practices with the Legislature, whatever might have been its decision as respected the original grantees, would have been bound, by its own rules and by the clearest principles of equity, to leave unmolested those who were purchasers without notice for a valuable consideration.

If the Legislature felt itself absolved from those rules of property which are common to all the citizens of the United States, and from those principles of equity which are acknowledged in all our courts, its act is to be supported by its power alone, and the same power may devest any other individual of his lands if it shall be the will of the Legislature so to exert it.

It is not intended to speak with disrespect of the Legislature of Georgia, or of its acts. Far from it. The question is a general question, and is treated as one. For although such powerful objections to a legislative grant as are alleged against this may not again exist, yet the principle on which alone this rescinding act is to be supported may be applied to every case to which it shall be the will of any legislature to apply it. The principle is this: that a legislature may, by its own act, devest the vested estate of any man whatever, for reasons which shall, by itself, be deemed sufficient.

In this case the Legislature may have had ample proof that the original grant was obtained by practices which can never be too much reprobated, and which would have justified its abrogation so far as respected those to whom crime was imputable. But the grant, when issued, conveyed an estate in fee simple to the grantee, clothed with all the solemnities which law can bestow. This estate was transferrable, and those who purchased parts of it were not stained by that guilt which infected the original transaction. Their case is not distinguishable from the ordinary case of purchasers of a legal estate without knowledge of any secret fraud which might have led to the emanation of the original grant. According to the well known course of equity, their rights could not be affected by such fraud. Their situation was the same, their title was the same, with that of every other member of the community who holds land by regular conveyances from the original patentee.

Is the power of the Legislature competent to the annihilation of such title, and to a resumption of the property thus held?

The principle asserted is that one Legislature is competent to repeal any act which a former legislature was competent to pass, and that one legislature cannot abridge the powers of a succeeding legislature.

The correctness of this principle, so far as respects general legislation, can never be controverted. But if an act be done under a law, a succeeding legislature cannot undo it. The past cannot be recalled by the most absolute power. Conveyances have been made, those conveyances have vested legal estate, and, if those estates may be seized by the sovereign authority, still that they originally vested is a fact, and cannot cease to be a fact.

When, then, a law is in its nature a contract, when absolute rights have vested under that contract, a repeal of the law cannot devest those rights; and the act of annulling them, if legitimate, is rendered so by a power applicable to the case of every individual in the community.

It may well be doubted whether the nature of society and of government does not prescribe some limits to the legislative power; and, if any be prescribed, where are they to be found if the property of an individual, fairly and honestly acquired, may be seized without compensation?

To the Legislature all legislative power is granted, but the question whether the act of transferring the property of an individual to the public be in the nature of the legislative power is well worthy of serious reflection.

It is the peculiar province of the legislature to prescribe general rules for the government of society; the application of those rules to individuals in society would seem to be the duty of other departments. How far the power of giving the law may involve every other power, in cases where the Constitution is silent, never has been, and perhaps never can be, definitely stated.

The validity of this rescinding act, then, might well be doubted, were Georgia a single sovereign power. But Georgia cannot be viewed as a single, unconnected, sovereign power, on whose legislature no other restrictions are imposed than may be found in its own Constitution. She is a part of a large empire; she is a member of the American Union; and that Union has a Constitution the supremacy of which all acknowledge, and which imposes limits to the legislatures of the several States which none claim a right to pass. The Constitution of the United States declares that no State shall pass any bill of attainder, ex post facto law, or law impairing the obligation of contracts.

Does the case now under consideration come within this prohibitory section of the Constitution?

In considering this very interesting question, we immediately ask ourselves what is a contract? Is a grant a contract?

A contract is a compact between two or more parties, and is either executory or executed. An executory contract is one in which a party binds himself to do, or not to do, a particular thing; such was the law under which the conveyance was made by the Governor. A contract executed is one in which the object of contract is performed, and this, says Blackstone, differs in nothing from a grant. The contract between Georgia and the purchasers was executed by the grant. A contract executed, as well as one which is executory, contains obligations binding on the parties. A grant, in its own nature, amounts to an extinguishment of the right of the grantor, and implies a contract not to reassert that right. A party is therefore always estopped by his own grant.

Since, then, in fact, a grant is a contract executed, the obligation of which still continues, and since the Constitution uses the general term "contract" without distinguishing between those which are executory and those which are executed, it must be construed to comprehend the latter as well as the former. A law annulling conveyances between individuals, and declaring that the grantors should stand seised of their former estates, notwithstanding those grants, would be as repugnant to the Constitution as a law discharging the vendors of property from the obligation of executing their contracts by conveyances. It would be strange if a contract to convey was secured by the Constitution, while an absolute conveyance remained unprotected.

It is, then, the unanimous opinion of the Court that, in this case, the estate having passed into the hands of a purchaser for a valuable consideration, without notice, the State of Georgia was restrained, either by general principles which are common to our free institutions or by the particular provisions of the Constitution of the United States, from passing a law whereby the estate of the plaintiff in the premises so purchased could be constitutionally and legally impaired and rendered null and void.

GLOSSARY

agents: representatives

devest: to legally take away property

James Gunn: one of the speculators who bought Yazoo lands under the original 1795 law

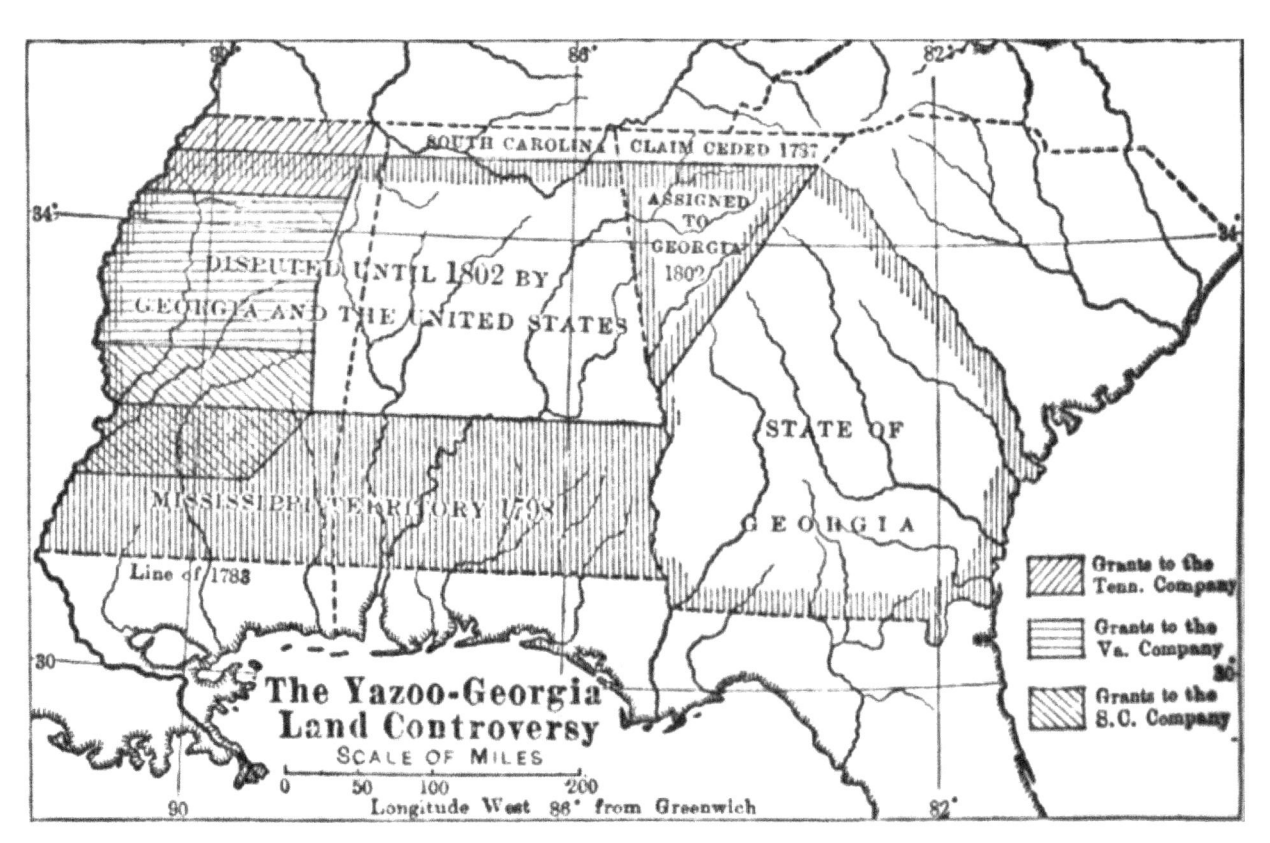

Map of the American Deep south, showing the three areas which constituted the 1789 Yazoo land scandal. (From Allen Johnson - Johnson, Allen (1915). Union and Democracy. *Cambridge, Massachusetts: Houghton Mifflin Company.)*

Document Themes and Analysis

This excerpt from John Marshall's opinion in *Fletcher v. Peck* encapsulates the significant constitutional and legal issues settled by the case. The Marshall court had already, in *Marbury v. Madison*, established the principle of judicial review, under which the Supreme Court could rule on the constitutionality of federal laws. In the first paragraph of this excerpt, Marshall discusses this power and reiterates his opinion that this should be done very rarely.

Marshall then goes over some of the facts of the case, observing that even if Georgia's sale of land to speculators was tainted with fraud, those people who bought their farms or other property from the speculators were innocent of wrongdoing and their purchases were legal and proper. However, the state's 1796 law that invalidated the purchases brought them into the mess and, in Marshall's words, "annihilated their rights." While a state legislature has the right to amend or abolish laws passed by a previous session of the legislature, does that legislature have the authority to meddle in or eliminate a contract which—at the time it was entered into—was completely valid and legal? Looking at this issue from the purchaser's perspective, Marshall observes, "He has paid his money for a title good at law; he is innocent, whatever may be the guilt of others, and equity will not subject him to the penalties attached to that guilt. All titles would be insecure, and the intercourse between man and man would be very seriously obstructed if this principle be overturned."

What is at risk is the very nature of legal contracts. It would be a dangerous precedent for a state legislature to have the power to, for whatever reason, void lawful contracts. This is an issue, Marshall discusses, that has a great importance and there is a question of whether or not a government has the power to do this. Basically, Marshall says, the original land act of 1795 sold property to individual businesses—this is a contract, even it was an act of a legislature. Does the legislature have the ability (as it did in 1796) to abolish a contract the same as it would abolish any other law?

For Marshall, the answer is no, because Georgia is part of the United States and subject to the strictures of the U.S. Constitution. The Constitution, he argues, prohibits this very thing, forbidding states from passing any act "impairing the obligation of contracts." Marshall, in unanimous agreement with the court, declared that the State of Georgia did not have the power, under the limits placed on it by the Constitution, to nullify contracts.

In years to come, *Fletcher v. Peck* would provide valuable precedent both for the authority of the Supreme Court to rule on the constitutionality of state acts as well as for the establishment of the inviolable nature of contracts that are legally entered into. On a darker note, in the full decision authored by Marshall, there is a suggestion that Native American tribes who possessed land in this region did not have the same full, legal title to their property. This would provide justification for seizure of Indian lands through various means by the federal government throughout the nineteenth century.

—*Aaron Gulyas*

Bibliography and Additional Reading

Atkins, Jonathan M. *From Confederation to Nation: The Early American Republic, 1789–1848*. New York: Routledge, 2016.

Banner, Stuart. *How the Indians Lost Their Land: Law and Power on the Frontier*. Cambridge, MA: Harvard University Press, 2005.

Hobson, Charles F. *The Great Yazoo Land Sale: The Case of* Fletcher v. Peck. Lawrence: University of Kansas Press, 2016.

Magrath, C. Peter. *Yazoo: Law and Politics in the New Republic*. New York: Norton, 1967.

Smith, Jean Edward. *John Marshall: Definer of a Nation*. Reprint Ed. New York: Henry Holt and Company, 2014.

■ Lowell Mill Girls

Date: 1883 (publication of report)
Author: Harriet H. Robinson
Genre: Memoir; report

Summary Overview

The middle of the first half of the nineteenth century saw the boom of the cotton industry in New England, spurring the creation of vast mill buildings in towns such as Manchester, New Hampshire; Biddeford, Maine; and Lawrence and Lowell, Massachusetts. The mills created hundreds of jobs, particularly for young women for whom employment options were severely limited. Harriet H. Robinson wrote a memoir entitled *Loom and Spindle; or, Life among the Early Mill Girls* (1898), an indispensable piece for research into the women and girls who worked within the mills; the second piece below is an excerpt of that book and was likely written in 1883. The first excerpt below comes from Robinson's essay "Early Factory Labor in New England," published in an 1883 Massachusetts Bureau of Statistics of Labor report. Robinson herself was a Lowell mill girl who began her career at a young age. As she grew, so too did the industry, but unfortunately, the changes that came were not for the better. Robinson and those like her found themselves working harder for fewer wages and, as a result, tried to push for reform. Her memoir provides a frank narrative of her plight and that of other mill girls and describes those who chose not to back down.

Defining Moment

This excerpt of Harriet H. Robinson's writing, while providing historical background initially, is an impassioned attempt to show how it came to pass that she and others within the mills decided to "turn out," or strike. Simply put, the mill owners were taking advantage of them, lowering wages and increasing work for higher profits. As Robinson states aptly, "Help was too valuable to be ill-treated"; the girls and women employed by the mills exerted themselves day in and day out, starting at dawn and ending fourteen hours later, with two breaks in between for meals. Initially, as she mentions, the cost of bed and board ($1.50) was partially subsidized by the employer; this certainly would have been an excellent incentive for those thinking of factory work. However, this fee eventually became payable by the employee alone, along with an overall reduction in wages, and of course, this change in compensation did not come with a reduction of expected output.

Many historians, as well as contemporaries, utilized a comparison of the mill workers with their cotton "counterparts" in the South: the slaves. Robinson, in fact, recounts a song sung during turn outs that included the repeated line, "I will not be a slave." Slave owners treated their human property however they saw fit, but the mill workers were not considered property; they were *help*. They were employees who therefore should have been treated properly. It is vital to remember that, at this stage of American history, in the 1830s and 1840s, the country had not yet been inundated with the influx of immigrants from eastern and southern Europe. Harriet H. Robinson was working, predominantly, in the years preceding the first wave of Irish immigration, which was spurred by the famine in Ireland during the late 1840s. For the most part, the employee pool in her time was made up of native-born Anglo-American women. In her memoir, Robinson writes, "Before 1840, the foreign element in the factory population was almost an unknown quantity" (*Loom* 12). The mill workers were proud of their work, proud to help earn their livelihood and that of their families, and were not prepared to be basely treated, especially considering the amount of labor they provided at the rate of pay offered and hours endured.

Author Biography

Harriet Jane Hanson Robinson was born on February 8, 1825, in Boston, Massachusetts, to William and Harriet Browne Hanson. Robinson, one of four children, lost her father in 1831. As recounted in her book, an affluent neighbor offered to adopt her, thereby easing, if only slightly, the family's financial obligations, a proposal her mother refused, preferring to keep all the children with

Detail from Plan of the city of Lowell, Massachusetts. *(Sidney & Neff Publisher: Moody, S. Date: 1850 Location: Lowell (Mass.)*

her. Her mother was soon helped by friends of her late husband who assisted her in the opening of a small shop, where she sold confectionary and other small goods, but it did not garner a healthy income for the family.

In *Loom and Spindle*, Robinson writes that the family's move to Lowell had been suggested and facilitated by her widowed maternal aunt, who worked there as a boardinghouse matron. It was there, at the age of ten, that Robinson started working in a Lowell mill, the Tremont Corporation, as a doffer, changing out empty bobbins for full ones in the spinning room. While she doffed, her mother kept a boardinghouse for young men, and it was during this time that young Robinson, a future suffragist, took to joining them in games such as checkers, which helped inspire her belief in the equality of the sexes.

While still in her mid-teens, Robinson added to her role as a mill girl by becoming a writer for the *Lowell Offering*, a magazine for the workers; topics included childhood stories, their work and experience in the mills, and poems. As historian William Moran relates in his book *Belles of New England: The Women of the Textile Mills and the Families whose Wealth They Wove*, the magazine's initial bright start began to wane within a few years, receiving criticism that writers were too sympathetic to the mill owners and that the publication voiced the workers' concerns too little. The *Lowell Offering* ended in 1845.

Robinson's rich life, as a mill girl and writer, eventually included that of wife, mother of four, abolitionist, and suffragist, fighting valiantly for equality for women. She died at the age of eighty-six, on December 22, 1911, in Malden, Massachusetts, a suburb close to the city of her birth.

HISTORICAL DOCUMENT

"Early Factory Labor in New England"
In 1832, Lowell was little more than a factory village. Five "corporations" were started, and the cotton mills belonging to them were building. Help was in great demand and stories were told all over the country of the new factory place, and the high wages that were offered to all classes of work-people; stories that reached the ears of mechanics' and farmers' sons and gave new life to lonely and dependent women in distant towns and farm-houses. . . . Troops of young girls came from different parts of New England, and from Canada, and men were employed to collect them at so much a head, and deliver them at the factories. . . .

At the time the Lowell cotton mills were started the caste of the factory girl was the lowest among the employments of women. In England and in France, particularly, great injustice had been done to her real character. She was represented as subjected to influences that must destroy her purity and self-respect. In the eyes of her overseer she was but a brute, a slave, to be beaten, pinched and pushed about. It was to overcome this prejudice that such high wages had been offered to women that they might be induced to become mill-girls, in spite of the opprobrium that still clung to this degrading occupation. . . .

The early mill-girls were of different ages. Some were not over ten years old; a few were in middle life, but the majority were between the ages of sixteen and twenty-five. The very young girls were called "doffers." They "doffed," or took off, the full bobbins from the spinning-frames, and replaced them with empty ones. These mites worked about fifteen minutes every hour and the rest of the time was their own. When the overseer was kind they were allowed to read, knit, or go outside the mill-yard to play. They were paid two dollars a week. The working hours of all the girls extended from five o'clock in the morning until seven in the evening, with one half-hour each, for breakfast and dinner. Even the doffers were forced to be on duty nearly fourteen hours a day. This was the greatest hardship in the lives of these children. Several years later a ten-hour law was passed, but not until long after some of these little doffers were old enough to appear before the legislative committee on the subject, and plead, by their presence, for a reduction of the hours of labor.

Those of the mill-girls who had homes generally worked from eight to ten months in the year; the rest of the time was spent with parents or friends. A few taught school during the summer months. Their life in the factory was made pleasant to them. In those days there was no need of advocating the doctrine of the proper relation between employer and employed. *Help was too valuable to be ill-treated.* . . .

The most prevailing incentive to labor was to secure the means of education for some *male* member of the family. To make a *gentleman* of a brother or a son, to give him a college education, was the dominant thought in the minds of a great many of the better class of mill-girls. I have known more than one to give every cent of her wages, month after month, to her brother, that he might get the education necessary to enter some profession. I have known a mother to work years in this way for her boy. I have known women to educate young men by their earnings, who were not sons or relatives. There are many men now living who were helped to an education by the wages of the early mill-girls. . . .

It is well to digress here a little, and speak of the influence the possession of money had on the characters of some of these women. We can hardly realize what a change the cotton factory made in the status of the working women. Hitherto woman had always been a money *saving* rather than a money earning, member of the community. Her labor could command but small return. If she worked out as servant, or "help," her wages were from 50 cents to $1.00 a week; or, if she went from house to house by the day to spin and weave, or do tailoress work, she could get but 75 cents a week and her meals. As teacher, her services were not in demand, and the arts, the professions, and even the trades and industries, were nearly all closed to her.

As late as 1840 there were only seven vocations outside the home into which the women of New England had entered. At this time woman had no property rights. A widow could be left without her share of her husband's (or the family) property, an "incumbrance" to his estate. A father could make his will without reference to his daughter's share of the inheritance. He usually left her a home on the farm as long as she remained single. A woman was not supposed to be capable of spending her own, or of using other people's money. In Massachusetts, before 1840, a woman could not, legally, be treasurer of her own sewing society, unless some man were responsible for her.

The law took no cognizance of woman as a moneyspender. She was a ward, an appendage, a relict. Thus it happened, that if a woman did not choose to marry, or, when left a widow, to remarry, she had no choice but to enter one of the few employments open to her, or to become a burden on the charity of some relative....

Loom and Spindle; or, Life among the Early Mill Girls

One of the first strikes of cotton-factory operatives that ever took place in this country was that in Lowell, in October, 1836. When it was announced that the wages were to be cut down, great indignation was felt, and it was decided to strike, *en masse*. This was done. The mills were shut down, and the girls went in procession from their several corporations to the "grove" on Chapel Hill, and listened to "incendiary" speeches from early labor reformers.

One of the girls stood on a pump, and gave vent to the feelings of her companions in a neat speech, declaring that it was their duty to resist all attempts at cutting down the wages. This was the first time a woman had spoken in public in Lowell, and the event caused surprise and consternation among her audience.

Cutting down the wages was not their only grievance, nor the only cause of this strike. Hitherto the corporations had paid twenty-five cents a week towards the board of each operative, and now it was their purpose to have the girls pay the sum; and this, in addition to the cut in the wages, would make a difference of at least one dollar a week. It was estimated that as many as twelve or fifteen hundred girls turned out, and walked in procession through the streets. They had neither flags nor music, but sang songs, a favorite (but rather inappropriate) one being a parody on "I won't be a nun."

"Oh! isn't it a pity, such a pretty girl as I—
Should be sent to the factory to pine away and die?
Oh! I cannot be a slave,
I will not be a slave,
For I'm so fond of liberty
That I cannot be a slave."

My own recollection of this first strike (or "turn out" as it was called) is very vivid. I worked in a lower room, where I had heard the proposed strike fully, if not vehemently, discussed; I had been an ardent listener to what was said against this attempt at "oppression" on the part of the corporation, and naturally I took sides with the strikers. When the day came on which the girls were to turn out, those in the upper rooms started first, and so many of them left that our mill was at once shut down. Then, when the girls in my room stood irresolute, uncertain what to do, asking each other, "Would you?" or "Shall we turn out?" and not one of them having the courage to lead off, I, who began to think they would not go out, after all their talk, became impatient, and started on ahead, saying, with childish bravado, "I don't care what you do, *I* am going to turn out, whether anyone else does or not;" and I marched out, and was followed by the others.

As I looked back at the long line that followed me, I was more proud than I have ever been since at any success I may have achieved, and more proud than I shall ever be again until my own beloved State gives to its women citizens the right of suffrage.

The agent of the corporation where I then worked took some small revenges on the supposed ringleaders; on the principle of sending the weaker to the wall, my mother was turned away from her boarding-house, that functionary saying, "Mrs. Hanson, you could not prevent the older girls from turning out, but your daughter is a child, and *her* you could control."

It is hardly necessary to say that so far as results were concerned this strike did no good. The dissatisfaction of the operatives subsided, or burned itself out, and though the authorities did not accede to their demands, the majority returned to their work, and the corporation went on cutting down the wages.

And after a time, as the wages became more and more reduced, the best portion of the girls left and went to their homes, or to the other employments that were fast opening to women, until there were very few of the old guard left; and thus the *status* of the factory population of New England gradually became what we know it to be to-day.

GLOSSARY

bravado: audacity, daring, boldness

en masse: as a group, all together

incendiary: aggressive, stirring, rousing

incumbrance (encumbrance): burden, impediment, strain

irresolute: indecisive, unsure

Lowell: a city in Massachusetts, approximately twenty-five miles north of Boston, named for industrialist Francis Cabot Lowell

old guard: workers native to the New England area

Cover of The Lowell Offering, *Series 1, Number 1 (1840, Merrimac Valley Textile Museum)*

Document Analysis

The wide, towering red brick buildings in Lowell, Massachusetts, are silent now. While some house historical societies, offices, museums, and apartments, the rest, like those in other former mill cities throughout New England, stand as hushed reminders to an era of bustle and noise, back when the buildings reverberated with the din of heavy machinery and the voices of hundreds of workers. Lowell began as an ideal planned city, combining the mill buildings and company boardinghouses with plenty of greenery; the location of the city was strategic, as the mill could operate by harnessing the waterpower of the nearby Merrimack River.

Mill Beginnings

This system of mills was inspired by those functioning within Great Britain, such as in Manchester, England, in the early nineteenth century. These were viewed by Francis Cabot Lowell and one of his associates, Nathan Appleton. While Lowell and Appleton admired the mills and their place within the English textile industry, they were shocked and astounded by the treatment of the workers therein. They were determined to bring the English mill idea to New England, but with a completely different ethos for dealing with their employees. *Their employees would be cared for and without the stigma attached to the factory girls of England.* Robinson devotes time to this phase in the history of the Lowell mills: "'The Lowell factory system' went into operation, a practice which included the then new idea, that corporations should have souls, and should exercise a paternal influence over the lives of their operatives" (*Loom* 7). Clearly, what Lowell and Appleton saw had an effect, and they were determined not to follow England's example. As Robinson notes in the first excerpt above,

> The factory girl was the lowest among the employments of women.... [In Europe] great injustice had been done to her real character. She was represented as subjected to influences that must destroy her purity and self-respect. In the eyes of her overseer she was but a brute, a slave, to be beaten, pinched and pushed about.

Lowell and his initial counterparts sought to make their operatives' position one of esteem, an employ of which

Tintype of two young women in Lowell, Massachusetts.

to be proud. The paternal influence remarked upon earlier in *Loom and Spindle* was to be incorporated into the mills and boardinghouses; the corporations would help their help. Sandra Adickes, in her work "Mind among the Spindles," relates that careful attention was paid to the boardinghouses; they were installed with "resident chaperones" who upheld the girls' "standards of moral conduct" and enforced "mandatory Sunday church attendance," Robinson's memoir verifies this part of boardinghouse living: "The mill-girls went regularly to meeting and 'Sabbath school;' and every Sunday the streets of Lowell were alive with neatly dressed young women, going or returning therefrom." The houses themselves, as remembered by Robinson, were homey and attractive and even admired by such illustrious persons as English author Charles Dickens; she quotes him as saying, "'There is a piano in a great many of the boarding-houses, and nearly all the young ladies subscribe to circulating libraries,'" Given his reputation for wanting better working and living conditions for the working man, woman, and child, the Lowell mills could not have wished for a better endorsement.

The Mill Girls
The first generation of this workforce was predominantly from New England and was relatively young. Robinson states that the average worker was in her mid-teens to mid-twenties, but it was not unusual for a younger girl to be found among the other workers. Historian Thomas Dublin, in his article "Women, Work, and Protest," reveals the following statistics for Lowell's Hamilton Company around the time of Robinson's introduction to mill work: "more than 85 per cent of those employed in July 1836 were women and that over 96 percent were native-born." Robinson was among the youngest workers, the doffers, when her mill career began. In "Early Factory Labor," Robinson writes of what a girl could expect in such a position: "The very young girls were called 'doffers.' They 'doffed,' or took off, the full bobbins from the spinning-frames, and replaced them with empty ones. These mites worked about fifteen minutes every hour and the rest of the time was their own. When the overseer was kind they were allowed to read, knit, or go outside the mill-yard to play." Despite working a quarter of every hour, the doffers were still required to be "on duty" for the full day; this was continued until a law was passed in Massachusetts in 1842 attempting to limit a child's working hours. Of course, it is really left to history as to how faithfully this law was regularly enforced by a company desperate for profits or by a family desperate for income. The workforce did contain men, but as documented in "The Family and Industrial Discipline in Ante-Bellum New England" by Barbara Tucker, this segment of employees consisted of higher-paying skilled or managerial positions such as overseer. Dublin notes that while the mill girls worked primarily in the weaving and spinning rooms, male employees typically served in other roles such as pickers, carders, or mechanics.

To many of the girls making their way through the factory gates every morning, their position held much promise and pride, both to them and their families in many ways. William Moran quotes Ann Swett Appleton, a mill worker from New Hampshire, as having written, "The thought that I am living on no one is a happy one, indeed." Despite the fourteen-hour days for six days out of the week, mill work could be seen as liberating as compared to domestic service. Historian Sandra Adickes writes that the work in a factory garnered higher pay when compared with other employment opportunities for women. Live-in work in domestic service, depending on the employer, included the requirement to be "on-call" at any or all hours.

The average age of the mill girls is intriguing; they were young and still under the typical marital age, allowing ample time to settle down. Young workers, in general, did not seek to make their positions within the mill lifelong endeavors; this is a topic a number of historians have touched upon, as does Robinson herself. The motives bringing in the workers were varied but not attached with indefinite participation. Some, as mentioned in the excerpt above, labored to finance a brother's education; Robinson terms this "the most prevailing incentive." Mortgages for the family home or farm were another motivation for their earnings. Sarah G. Bagley, another mill worker, writer, and suffragist like Robinson, used her wages to put a down payment on a piece of land for her family in 1840. Bagley's ability to do this, as outlined by Helena Wright in her article "Sarah G. Bagley: A Biographical Note," demonstrates that the earning power of female workers like Bagley was "not as insignificant as has been generally supposed of many mill women." Others sought to earn their dowry before marriage.

Even if they did not seek to labor for their brother's education or to secure payment for their family's home, some early mill girls saved to fund their own education or to save money before marrying. These early mill girls, like Ann Swett Appleton, Sarah G. Bagley, and Harriet Robinson, saw their position as operatives as temporary, not a lifelong occupation. Their time within the vast buildings, before they moved on to higher education, marriage, or perhaps another vocation, served to heightened their own self-importance, as well as providing for themselves. Were it not for these opportunities, many of these girls would have been left "to become a burden on the charity of some relative," as Robinson notes.

CONSTITUTION OF THE
Lowell Factory Girls Association.

PREAMBLE.

Whereas we, the undersigned, residents of Lowell, moved by a love of honest industry and the expectation of a fair and liberal recompence, have left our homes, our relatives and youthful associates, and come hither, and subjected ourselves to all the danger and inconvenience, which necessarily attend young and unprotected females, when among strangers, and in a strange land; and however humble the condition of Factory Girls, (as we are termed,) may seem, we firmly and fearlessly (though we trust with a modesty becoming our sex,) claim for ourselves, that love of moral and intellectual culture, that admiration of, and desire to attain and preserve pure, elevated and refined characters, a true reverence for the divine principle which bids us render to every one his due; a due appreciation of those great and cardinal principles of our government, of justice and humanity, which enjoins on us " to live and let live "—that chivalrous and honorable feeling, which with equal force, forbids us to invade others rights, or suffer others, upon any consideration, to invade ours; and at the same time, that utter abhorence and detestation of whatever is mean, sordid, dishonorable or unjust—all of which, can alone, in our estimation, entitle us to be called the daughters of freemen, or of Republican America.

And, whereas, we believe that those who have preceded us have been, we know that ourselves are, and that our successors are liable to be, assailed in various ways by the wicked and unprincipled, and cheated out of just, legal and constitutional dues, by ungenerous, illiberal and avaricious capitalists,—and convinced that "union is power," and that as the unprincipled consult and advise, that they may the more easily decoy and seduce—and the capitalists that they may the more effectually defraud—we (being the weaker,) claim it to be our undeniable right, to associate and concentrate our power, that we may the more successfully repel their equally base and iniquitous aggressions.

And, whereas, impressed with this belief, and conscious that our cause is a common one, and our conditions similar, we feel it our imperative duty to stand by each other through weal and woe; to administer to each others wants, to prevent each others back-sliding—to comfort each other in sickness, and advise each other in health, to incite each other to the love and attainment of those excellences, which can alone constitute the perfection of female character—unsullied virtue, refined tastes and cultivated intellects—and in a word, do all that in us lies, to make each other worthy ourselves, our country and Creator.

Therefore, for the better attainment of those objects, we associate ourselves together, and mutually pledge to each other, a females irrefragable vow, to stand by, abide by, and be governed by the following

PROVISIONS.

ARTICLE 1st. It shall be denominated the LOWELL FACTORY GIRLS' ASSOCIATION.

ART. 2d. Any female of good moral character, and who works in any one of the Mills in this city, may become a member of this Association, by subscribing to this Constitution.

ART. 3d. The officers of the Association shall be, a President, Vice President, a Recording Secretary, a Corresponding Secretary, a Treasurer, a Collector, and a Prudential Committee, two of whom shall be selected from each Corporation in this city.

ART. 4th. The officers shall be chosen by the vote of the Association; that is, by the vote of a majority of the members present.

ART. 5th. The duties of the President, Vice President, Secretaries, Treasurer, and Collector, shall be the same as usually appertain to such offices. The duties of the Prudential Committee shall be to watch over the interests of the Association generally; to recommend to the Association, for their consideration and adoption, such By-Laws and measures as in their opinion the well-being of the Association may require; and also to ascertain the necessities of any of its members, and report the same, as soon as may be, to the Association. And whenever, in the opinion of the Committee, there are necessities so urgent as to require immediate relief, they shall forthwith report the same to the President, who shall immediately draw upon the Treasurer for the sum recommended, and which sum the Committee shall forthwith apply to the relief of the necessitous.

ART. 6th. The Treasurer and Collector shall be subject to the supervision of the Prudential Committee, to whom they shall be accountable, and to whom they shall give such security for the faithful discharge of their duties, as the Committee shall require.

ART. 7th. All moneys shall be raised by vote of a majority of the Association, or of the members present, and shall be assessed equally on all the members.

ART. 8th. All the officers shall hold their office for the term of one year, with the privilege of resigning, and subject to be removed by vote of the Association, for good cause.

ART. 9th. The Association shall meet once in three months, and may be convened oftener, if occasion require, by the President, upon a petition of twenty of the members first petitioning her for that purpose.

ART. 10th. It shall forever be the policy of the members of this Association, to bestow their patronage, so far as is practicable, upon such persons as befriend, but never upon such as oppose our cause.

ART. 11th. The Association shall have power to make all necessary By-Laws, which shall be consistent with these Provisions, and such By-Laws, when made, shall be binding upon all the members.

ART. 12th. Any member may dissolve her connection with the Association, by giving two weeks notice to the Recording Secretary; and any member shall be expelled from the Association by a vote of a majority of the members present, for any immoral conduct or behavior unbecoming respectable and virtuous females.

ART. 13th. This Constitution may be altered or amended at any time, by a vote of two thirds of the members present.

1836 Constitution of the Lowell Factory Girls Association. (Factory Girls' Association - Center for Lowell History, University of Massachusetts Lowell Libraries)

Turn outs

The idyllic vision of the mills and their operatives did not last long, and soon changes were brought that faded the luster from Lowell and its sister cities. Years passed, and overproduction led to a fall in the price allotted to the finished product. This then led to wage cuts and an increase in expected output. Robinson points out that this instigated the first strike, as related above, in October 1836. Despite her young age of eleven, she, too, took part, later recalling, "As I looked back at the long line that followed me, I was more proud than I have ever been since at any success I may have achieved, and more proud than I shall ever be again until my own beloved State gives to its women citizens the right of suffrage" (*Loom* 85). Although this initial strike was not successful, it did not stop the mill workers from taking action again and again. Historian Thomas Dublin cites further attempts between the years 1834 and 1848, both to maintain pay and to demand more reasonable hours.

Although wishing to recapture a better income was, indeed, a fundamental part of turning out, Dublin stresses something more formed a part of the drive to strike, a feeling alluded to by Robinson in the excerpt. He writes that "the wage cuts undermined the sense of dignity and social equality which was an important element in their Yankee heritage" and that such cuts were considered "an attack on their economic independence" (Dublin 108). This again brings to mind the refrain of the song sung by strikers in which they declare they will not be slaves. The mill operatives were not going to labor fourteen hours a day for a pittance of a wage. Earning their own income freed their families from having to support them and freed charities from offering them assistance, not to mention the added incentive of helping a brother through school or purchasing the family home, as Sarah G. Bagley did. These women knew they deserved better than how the mills chose to treat them, having strayed from the original vision held by Francis Cabot Lowell, Nathan Appleton, and their associates.

Although she mentions it only briefly, Robinson does allude to the dire consequences the mill girls faced for striking. Robinson calls the actions of the company agent against the strike's organizers "some small revenges," yet goes on to say that her mother "was turned away from her boarding-house" for not having prevented her from participating in the strike. Recalling what Robinson relates earlier in her memoir, this suggests that her mother, who was struggling to support four children on her own, lost her best employment. As William Moran notes in *The Belles of New England*, terminating striking workers was not uncommon, and later on, the corporations "blacklisted" known agitators, preventing them from gaining employment at other mills in the city. It is obvious from her own account that Robinson was not one of those unfortunates who were blacklisted, as she says elsewhere in her memoir that she continued her factory work into her twenties, when she received an "honorable discharge" and married.

As the years brought more wage reductions and consequently more strikes, the young women of New England moved away from mill work, their places taken by different waves of immigrants: first the Irish and French Canadians, before the boats brought those from eastern and southern Europe. "Thus," as Robinson notes, "the status of the factory population of New England gradually became what we know it to be to-day."

Essential Themes

Throughout Robinson's essay "Early Factory Labor in New England," and even more so within the length of her book, *Loom and Spindle*, there reads inherent pride in the work performed in the mills. The early days of the mills helped to promote this feeling. Moran writes that Maine's Bates Mills boasted that "their bedspreads were 'Loomed to be Heirloomed.'" The New England mills produced materials that were made into the uniforms worn by Civil War soldiers, as well as those serving in the World Wars. It is no wonder these women held such pride in their participation within the industry.

This pride played into their distress at the changes wrought within the mills. Earning their own income and thereby able to contribute to their families or to gain their independence, allowed these women to recognize a new and dynamic level of self-worth. In legal terms, as recalled by Robinson, a woman "was a ward, an appendage, a relict." Mill employment had shown these young women a glimpse of more freedom within their restricted lives. The lowered wages and increased production degraded them, setting the stage for the later women's and labor movements and for the corporations' replacement of the increasingly dissatisfied mill girls with foreign immigrant laborers, whom they could exploit more readily.

—*Jennifer L. Henderson Crane*

Bibliography and Additional Reading

Adickes, Sandra. "Mind among the Spindles: An Examination of Some of the Journals, Newspapers, and Memoirs of the Lowell Female Operatives." *Women's Studies* 1.3 (1973): 279–87.

Dublin, Thomas. "Women, Work, and Protest in the Early Lowell Mills: 'The Oppressing Hand of Avarice Would Enslave US.'" *Labor History* 16.1 (1975): 99–116.

Farfield, Roy P. "Labor Conditions at the Old York: 1831–1900." *New England Quarterly* 30.2 (1957): 166–80.

Gersuny, Carl. "Industrial Causalities in Lowell, 1890–1905." *Labor History* 20.3 (1979): 435–42.

Moran, William. *The Belles of New England: The Women of the Textile Mills and the Families Whose Wealth They Wove*. New York: St. Martin's, 2004.

Robinson, Harriet J. Hanson. "Early Factory Labor in New England." In *Fourteenth Annual Report of the Bureau of Statistics of Labor*, 337–401. Boston: Wright, 1883.

———. *Loom and Spindle; or, Life among the Early Mill Girls*. New York: Crowell, 1898.

Schlereth, Thomas J. *Victorian American: Transformations in Everyday Life*. New York: Harper, 1991.

Tucker, Barbara M. "The Family and Industrial Discipline in Ante-Bellum New England." *Labor History* 21.1 (1979): 55–74.

Weiss, Jane. "'In the Mills, We Are Not So Far from God and Nature': Industrialization and Spirituality in Nineteenth-Century New England." *Journal for the Study of Religion, Nature & Culture* 5.1 (2011): 82–100.

Wolfe, Allis Rosenberg, and H.E. Back, eds. "Letters of a Lowell Girl and Friends, 1845–1846." *Labor History* 17.1 (1976): 96–102.

Wright, Helena. "Sarah G. Bagley: A Biographical Note." *Labor History* 20.3 (1979): 398–413.

1847 map showing the street layout and ferry routes for lower Manhattan.

From "Bartleby the Scrivener: A Story of Wall Street"

Date: 1853
Author: Herman Melville
Genre: Story; fiction

Summary Overview

The excerpt reprinted here is taken from a longer story called "Bartleby, the Scrivener: A Story of Wall Street," written by Herman Melville. The story was serialized in two parts, both published in *Putnam's Magazine*. The parts appeared in November and December of 1853; the whole was later reprinted in *The Piazza Tales*, an 1856 collection of Melville's short stories, with some minor alterations to the text.

Defining Moment

Scholars consider Melville to be the greatest American fiction writer of his time. He is most famous for his novel *Moby Dick* (1851), the story of Captain Ahab and his quest to find and kill the great white whale that bit off his leg. *Moby Dick* was considered a commercial failure at the time it was published, but Melville's other fiction, published in the 1840s and 1850s, was often considered very successful. "Bartleby, the Scrivener" is considered the best of Melville's short stories.

During the 1850s, while Melville was most prolific in his fiction writing, there were two major events occurring in the United States. First is the lead-up to the Civil War. During the 1850s, the U.S. government was focused on trying to prevent a war over slavery. Various compromises were enacted to try and maintain a balance of power between slaveholders and abolitionists. Of course, ultimately, war broke out in 1861, leading to the bloodiest conflict in American history.

Meanwhile, the time period known as the First Industrial Revolution ended somewhere between 1830 and 1840 (scholars disagree on the exact time). This revolution was, as the name implies, a dramatic change in how business was conducted, particularly in England and its former and current colonies. Industry moved from what is known as hard labor—people making things themselves—to machinery. This change was first noticed in the textile industry where spinning and weaving moved from the home into textile mills. While this industrial change arguably created the middle class and raised the standard of living for people across Europe and the Americas, it also dramatically changed the nature of work and products. The idea of going into a factory and repetitively working a machine was very different from the idea of spinning or weaving in a home.

"Bartleby, the Scrivener" was written between these time periods—the First Industrial Revolution and the Civil War—and understanding them is crucial to understanding the story's significance.

Author Biography

Herman Melville was born on August 1, 1819 in New York City. He was one of seven children. At the age of 11, his father, a merchant, moved his entire family to Albany where he believed he could find more successful work. Unfortunately, the family was quickly bankrupted, and Melville's father died suddenly. He and his siblings left school in order to support the family; many siblings chose to continue in the family trade of fur and imports, but Melville sought out teaching jobs, clerked at local banks, and even worked at his uncle's farm. He continued his studies independently, was a voracious reader, and began writing at an early age. He was always fascinated by the sea, particularly the story of the ship *Essex*, which was attacked and sunk by a whale in 1820. This story was an influence on *Moby Dick* later in his life.

When Melville was 20 (in 1839), he began to work on ships and sailing vessels, including the whaling ship *Charles and Henry*. By 1844, he decided to return to his mother's home and begin to write about his adventures. His first short stories and novels were successful both in England and the United States, but in 1851, he published what would become his first complete and total flop of a book: *Moby Dick*. After that, Melville was constantly struggling with financial ruin and total obscurity. He wrote short stories and poems to try and maintain his writing career, but by 1863 he had taken a job as a dock worker, where he continued for twenty years. While he continued to publish smaller pieces, they went largely unrecognized; Melville died of a heart attack on September 28, 1891. Few papers even bothered to print an obituary. His work was not rediscovered until the 1920s, when scholars uncovered *Moby Dick* and began to consider its allegorical significance. One novel, *Billy Budd*, was published posthumously. Melville had been working on it when he died.

HISTORICAL DOCUMENT

Now my original business—that of a conveyancer and title hunter, and drawer-up of recondite documents of all sorts—was considerably increased by receiving the master's office. There was now great work for scriveners. Not only must I push the clerks already with me, but I must have additional help. In answer to my advertisement, a motionless young man one morning, stood upon my office threshold, the door being open, for it was summer. I can see that figure now—pallidly neat, pitiably respectable, incurably forlorn! It was Bartleby.

After a few words touching his qualifications, I engaged him, glad to have among my corps of copyists a man of so singularly sedate an aspect, which I thought might operate beneficially upon the flighty temper of Turkey, and the fiery one of Nippers.

I should have stated before that ground glass folding-doors divided my premises into two parts, one of which was occupied by my scriveners, the other by myself. According to my humor I threw open these doors, or closed them. I resolved to assign Bartleby a corner by the folding-doors, but on my side of them, so as to have this quiet man within easy call, in case any trifling thing was to be done. I placed his desk close up to a small side-window in that part of the room, a window which originally had afforded a lateral view of certain grimy back-yards and bricks, but which, owing to subsequent erections, commanded at present no view at all, though it gave some light. Within three feet of the panes was a wall, and the light came down from far above, between two lofty buildings, as from a very small opening in a dome. Still further to a satisfactory arrangement, I procured a high green folding screen, which might entirely isolate Bartleby from my sight, though not remove him from my voice. And thus, in a manner, privacy and society were conjoined.

At first Bartleby did an extraordinary quantity of writing. As if long famishing for something to copy, he seemed to gorge himself on my documents. There was no pause for digestion. He ran a day and night line, copying by sun-light and by candle-light. I should have been quite delighted with his application, had he been cheerfully industrious. But he wrote on silently, palely, mechanically.

It is, of course, an indispensable part of a scrivener's business to verify the accuracy of his copy, word by word. Where there are two or more scriveners in an office, they assist each other in this examination, one reading from the copy, the other holding the original. It is a very dull, wearisome, and lethargic affair. I can readily imagine that to some sanguine temperaments it would be altogether intolerable. For example, I cannot credit that the mettlesome poet Byron would have contentedly sat down with Bartleby to examine a law document of, say five hundred pages, closely written in a crimpy hand.

Now and then, in the haste of business, it had been my habit to assist in comparing some brief document myself, calling Turkey or Nippers for this purpose. One object I had in placing Bartleby so handy to me behind the screen, was to avail myself of his services on such trivial occasions. It was on the third day, I think, of his being with me, and before any necessity had arisen for having his own writing examined, that, being much hurried to complete a small affair I had in hand, I abruptly called to Bartleby. In my haste and natural expectancy of instant compliance, I sat with my head bent over the original on my desk, and my right hand sideways, and somewhat nervously extended with the copy, so that immediately upon emerging from his retreat, Bartleby might snatch it and proceed to business without the least delay.

In this very attitude did I sit when I called to him, rapidly stating what it was I wanted him to do—namely, to examine a small paper with me. Imagine my surprise, nay, my consternation, when without moving from his privacy, Bartleby in a singularly mild, firm voice, replied,

"I would prefer not to."

I sat awhile in perfect silence, rallying my stunned faculties. Immediately it occurred to me that my ears had deceived me, or Bartleby had entirely misunderstood my meaning. I repeated my request in the clearest tone I could assume. But in quite as clear a one came the previous reply, "I would prefer not to."

"Prefer not to," echoed I, rising in high excitement, and crossing the room with a stride. "What do you mean? Are you moon-struck? I want you to help me compare this sheet here—take it," and I thrust it towards him.

"I would prefer not to," said he.

I looked at him steadfastly. His face was leanly composed; his gray eye dimly calm. Not a wrinkle of agitation rippled him. Had there been the least uneasiness, anger, impatience or impertinence in his manner; in other words, had there been any thing ordinarily human about him, doubtless I should have violently dismissed him from the premises. But as it was, I should have as soon thought of turning my pale plaster-of-paris bust of Cicero out of doors. I stood gazing at him awhile, as he went on with his own writing, and then reseated myself at my desk. This is very strange, thought I. What had one best do? But my business hurried me. I concluded to forget the matter for the present, reserving it for my future leisure. So calling Nippers from the other room, the paper was speedily examined.

A few days after this, Bartleby concluded four lengthy documents, being quadruplicates of a week's testimony taken before me in my High Court of Chancery. It became necessary to examine them. It was an important suit, and great accuracy was imperative. Having all things arranged I called Turkey, Nippers and Ginger Nut from the next room, meaning to place the four copies in the hands of my four clerks, while I should read from the original. Accordingly Turkey, Nippers and Ginger Nut had taken their seats in a row, each with his document in hand, when I called to Bartleby to join this interesting group.

"Bartleby! quick, I am waiting."

I heard a slow scrape of his chair legs on the uncarpeted floor, and soon he appeared standing at the entrance of his hermitage.

"What is wanted?" said he mildly.

"The copies, the copies," said I hurriedly. "We are going to examine them. There"—and I held towards him the fourth quadruplicate.

"I would prefer not to," he said, and gently disappeared behind the screen.

For a few moments I was turned into a pillar of salt, standing at the head of my seated column of clerks. Recovering myself, I advanced towards the screen, and demanded the reason for such extraordinary conduct.

"*Why* do you refuse?"

"I would prefer not to."

With any other man I should have flown outright into a dreadful passion, scorned all further words, and thrust him ignominiously from my presence. But there was something about Bartleby that not only strangely disarmed me, but in a wonderful manner touched and disconcerted me. I began to reason with him.

"These are your own copies we are about to examine. It is labor saving to you, because one examination will answer for your four papers. It is common usage. Every copyist is bound to help examine his copy. Is it not so? Will you not speak? Answer!"

"I prefer not to," he replied in a flute-like tone. It seemed to me that while I had been addressing him, he carefully revolved every statement that I made; fully comprehended the meaning; could not gainsay the irresistible conclusions; but, at the same time, some paramount consideration prevailed with him to reply as he did.

"You are decided, then, not to comply with my request—a request made according to common usage and common sense?"

He briefly gave me to understand that on that point my judgment was sound. Yes: his decision was irreversible.

It is not seldom the case that when a man is browbeaten in some unprecedented and violently unreasonable way, he begins to stagger in his own plainest faith. He begins, as it were, vaguely to surmise that, wonderful as it may be, all the justice and all the reason is on the other side. Accordingly, if any disinterested persons are present, he turns to them for some reinforcement for his own faltering mind.

"Turkey," said I, "what do you think of this? Am I not right?"

"With submission, sir," said Turkey, with his blandest

tone, "I think that you are."

"Nippers," said I, "what do *you* think of it?"

"I think I should kick him out of the office."

(The reader of nice perceptions will here perceive that, it being morning, Turkey's answer is couched in polite and tranquil terms, but Nippers replies in ill-tempered ones. Or, to repeat a previous sentence, Nippers' ugly mood was on duty and Turkey's off.)

"Ginger Nut," said I, willing to enlist the smallest suffrage in my behalf, "what do you think of it?"

"I think, sir, he's a little *luny*," replied Ginger Nut with a grin.

"You hear what they say," said I, turning towards the screen, "come forth and do your duty."

But he vouchsafed no reply. I pondered a moment in sore perplexity. But once more business hurried me. I determined again to postpone the consideration of this dilemma to my future leisure. With a little trouble we made out to examine the papers without Bartleby, though at every page or two, Turkey deferentially dropped his opinion that this proceeding was quite out of the common; while Nippers, twitching in his chair with a dyspeptic nervousness, ground out between his set teeth occasional hissing maledictions against the stubborn oaf behind the screen. And for his (Nippers') part, this was the first and the last time he would do another man's business without pay.

Meanwhile Bartleby sat in his hermitage, oblivious to every thing but his own peculiar business there.

Some days passed, the scrivener being employed upon another lengthy work. His late remarkable conduct led me to regard his ways narrowly. I observed that he never went to dinner; indeed that he never went any where. As yet I had never of my personal knowledge known him to be outside of my office. He was a perpetual sentry in the corner. At about eleven o'clock though, in the morning, I noticed that Ginger Nut would advance toward the opening in Bartleby's screen, as if silently beckoned thither by a gesture invisible to me where I sat. The boy would then leave the office jingling a few pence, and reappear with a handful of ginger-nuts which he delivered in the hermitage, receiving two of the cakes for his trouble.

He lives, then, on ginger-nuts, thought I; never eats a dinner, properly speaking; he must be a vegetarian then; but no; he never eats even vegetables, he eats nothing but ginger-nuts. My mind then ran on in reveries concerning the probable effects upon the human constitution of living entirely on ginger-nuts. Ginger-nuts are so called because they contain ginger as one of their peculiar constituents, and the final flavoring one. Now what was ginger? A hot, spicy thing. Was Bartleby hot and spicy? Not at all. Ginger, then, had no effect upon Bartleby. Probably he preferred it should have none.

Nothing so aggravates an earnest person as a passive resistance. If the individual so resisted be of a not inhumane temper, and the resisting one perfectly harmless in his passivity; then, in the better moods of the former, he will endeavor charitably to construe to his imagination what proves impossible to be solved by his judgment. Even so, for the most part, I regarded Bartleby and his ways. Poor fellow! thought I, he means no mischief; it is plain he intends no insolence; his aspect sufficiently evinces that his eccentricities are involuntary. He is useful to me. I can get along with him. If I turn him away, the chances are he will fall in with some less indulgent employer, and then he will be rudely treated, and perhaps driven forth miserably to starve. Yes. Here I can cheaply purchase a delicious self-approval. To befriend Bartleby; to humor him in his strange willfulness, will cost me little or nothing, while I lay up in my soul what will eventually prove a sweet morsel for my conscience. But this mood was not invariable with me. The passiveness of Bartleby sometimes irritated me. I felt strangely goaded on to encounter him in new opposition, to elicit some angry spark from him answerable to my own. But indeed I might as well have essayed to strike fire with my knuckles against a bit of Windsor soap. But one afternoon the evil impulse in me mastered me, and the following little scene ensued:

"Bartleby," said I, "when those papers are all copied, I will compare them with you."

"I would prefer not to."

"How? Surely you do not mean to persist in that mulish vagary?"

No answer.

I threw open the folding-doors near by, and turning upon Turkey and

Nippers, exclaimed in an excited manner—

"He says, a second time, he won't examine his papers. What do you think of it, Turkey?"

It was afternoon, be it remembered. Turkey sat glowing like a brass boiler, his bald head steaming, his hands reeling among his blotted papers.

"Think of it?" roared Turkey; "I think I'll just step behind his screen, and black his eyes for him!"

So saying, Turkey rose to his feet and threw his arms into a pugilistic position. He was hurrying away to make good his promise, when I detained him, alarmed at the effect of incautiously rousing Turkey's combativeness after dinner.

"Sit down, Turkey," said I, "and hear what Nippers has to say. What do you think of it, Nippers? Would I not be justified in immediately dismissing Bartleby?"

"Excuse me, that is for you to decide, sir. I think his conduct quite unusual, and indeed unjust, as regards Turkey and myself. But it may only be a passing whim."

"Ah," exclaimed I, "you have strangely changed your mind then—you speak very gently of him now."

"All beer," cried Turkey; "gentleness is effects of beer—Nippers and I dined together to-day. You see how gentle *I* am, sir. Shall I go and black his eyes?"

"You refer to Bartleby, I suppose. No, not to-day, Turkey," I replied; "pray, put up your fists."

I closed the doors, and again advanced towards Bartleby. I felt additional incentives tempting me to my fate. I burned to be rebelled against again. I remembered that Bartleby never left the office.

"Bartleby," said I, "Ginger Nut is away; just step round to the Post Office, won't you? (it was but a three minute walk,) and see if there is any thing for me."

"I would prefer not to."

"You *will* not?"

"I *prefer* not."

I staggered to my desk, and sat there in a deep study. My blind inveteracy returned. Was there any other thing in which I could procure myself to be ignominiously repulsed by this lean, penniless wight?—my hired clerk? What added thing is there, perfectly reasonable, that he will be sure to refuse to do?

"Bartleby!"

No answer.

"Bartleby," in a louder tone.

No answer.

"Bartleby," I roared.

Like a very ghost, agreeably to the laws of magical invocation, at the third summons, he appeared at the entrance of his hermitage.

"Go to the next room, and tell Nippers to come to me."

"I prefer not to," he respectfully and slowly said, and mildly disappeared.

"Very good, Bartleby," said I, in a quiet sort of serenely severe self-possessed tone, intimating the unalterable purpose of some terrible retribution very close at hand. At the moment I half intended something of the kind. But upon the whole, as it was drawing towards my dinner-hour, I thought it best to put on my hat and walk home for the day, suffering much from perplexity and distress of mind.

Shall I acknowledge it? The conclusion of this whole business was, that it soon became a fixed fact of my chambers, that a pale young scrivener, by the name of Bartleby, and a desk there; that he copied for me at the usual rate of four cents a folio (one hundred words); but he was permanently exempt from examining the work done by him, that duty being transferred to Turkey and Nippers, one of compliment doubtless to their superior acuteness; moreover, said Bartleby was never on any account to be dispatched on the most trivial errand of any sort; and that even if entreated to take upon him such a matter, it was generally understood that he would prefer not to—in other words, that he would refuse pointblank.

GLOSSARY

conveyancer: a specialist lawyer

dyspeptic: someone who suffers from indigestion or irritability (or who appears to do)

pallid: pale or insipid

recondite: a subject of which little is known

sanguine: optimistic or positive

scrivener: a desk clerk or notary

Document Analysis

This excerpt includes roughly the first half of Melville's short story. The narrator, whose name we never learn, hires a new scrivener (clerk) for his busy law office. The scrivener, Bartleby, is at first an industrious employee, and the narrator is glad to have hired him—although he notices that Bartleby takes no joy in his work. He works "silently, palely, mechanically." A few days into Bartleby's employment, he is called on to complete the secondary work of a copyist—to compare word by word a copy to the original to ensure no mistakes have been made in the rewriting. The narrator admits that it is tedious work, but also understands it as necessary. Here we first see Bartleby's singular answer: "I would prefer not to."

The narrator is furious; how dare Bartleby refuse to do the work for which he was hired. But even when the narrator expresses his anger and gets the other two clerks to agree that Bartleby must do this, and that he should be fired immediately if he won't, Bartleby continues to repeat, in his "mild, firm voice," that he would prefer not to. The narrator is at an impasse. If Bartleby were at all antagonistic, he thinks, he would throw him out immediately. But the evenly delivered refusal has him completely at a loss. Eventually, he sits down and goes back to work.

The narrator's frustration repeats itself; he is bewildered by Bartleby's calm, quiet rebuttal. He reflects frequently that if Bartleby reacted in some way or showed some elevated state of emotion, he could react to that, but Bartleby's steady evenness leaves the narrator feeling helpless. The narrator even calls on his other office employees for their opinions. They agree that Bartleby should be fired immediately, but the narrator still cannot bring himself to do it. Eventually, it is agreed that Bartleby will not do any menial task in the office.

In the second half of the story, not reprinted here, Bartleby does less and less work, until he simply stares out the window at a blank wall all day. It is revealed that he is living there; the narrator finds it simpler to move his offices to a new location rather than to remove Bartleby. When new tenants take the office, Bartleby is still there; when he is removed, he sleeps in the building's doorway. He is arrested; in jail he starves to death.

Throughout the story, we see Bartleby's quiet refusal to complete various tasks; he won't complete tedious work; he won't complete any work; he won't thrive; finally, he won't survive. Bartleby's preference "to not" ultimately ends his life.

Essential Themes

Many of Melville's works explore the majesty that human beings can experience. He often writes about the broad expanse of the ocean, as so much of life revolved around the sea. But what seems to particularly fascinate Melville is what happens when, even in the face of such potential, humans allow their lives to become small. Ahab's tragedy is his pinpoint focus on the whale on whom he blames his misfortune. Bartleby's tragedy is his unwillingness to engage with the life around him, allowing his life to become smaller and smaller until there is nothing left. In a modern context, Bartleby's condition might be interpreted as chronic and increasingly serious depression. At a minimum, his personal work ethic conflicts with that of the business firm that employs him. Although Wall Street itself, as a business center, was still comparatively small in the 1840s, business was business and employees were expected to carry out their work.

At one point in the story, the narrator uses the phrase "passive resistance" to describe Bartleby's behavior. The phrase is commonly associated with social movements, particularly those led by Mahatma Gandhi in India and Martin Luther King Jr. in the United States. The goal of passive resistance is to give an attacker no emotion or reaction to work with; the theory behind this passivity is to force attackers to see their own behavior in isolation. While it is unlikely that Bartleby was considering his behavior an act of resistance against social oppression, the boss's reaction certainly unfolds in the expected manner. His behavior escalates further, as he threatens Bartleby and shouts at him; yet, ultimately, he reaches a point where he cannot further escalate, given his character, so he simply gives in to Bartleby's peculiarities.

One can also connect this story to the concept of slavery and abolition. Melville never stated that he was an abolitionist, but his stories often considered similar topics. His later story "Benito Cereno," for example, seems to express a horror for the concept of slavery, and is often interpreted by scholars to be proof of Melville's views on the matter. Melville also chose to publish his stories in *Putnam's Magazine*. The magazine itself strongly supported abolitionists, frequently containing articles and statements supporting this cause. It is unlikely that Melville would have chosen this publisher if he (Melville) were proslavery; and is logical to consider him at least neutral to slavery, if not outright opposed.

Considering Bartleby's behavior as that of a worker is also important. A scrivener's work involved simply making copies of documents. In the narrator's office, it was often law documents, some of which might be hundreds of pages long, needing a scrivener's attention. Serving as a human photocopier would be tedious enough, but needing to verify the accuracy of the work by reviewing it as someone else reads it aloud is perhaps even more mind-numbing. The narrator even acknowledges the job as such, but states that it must be done. He and his other clerks have accepted that as true. Bartleby appears not to accept that truth. There is an interesting conundrum here, then: the reader may support Bartleby's refusal to do work that sounds boring and trying; but if all workers had the ability to pick and choose their own tasks, then how would the work get done? Melville seems to draw on the idea of the Industrial Revolution turning human beings into so many moving parts of a grand machinery.

What is especially curious about Bartleby's work ethic is that he seems to stand on his preference, his attitude, rather than on his abilities or even his willingness to perform a task. At one point, after a refusal, the narrator asks Bartleby, "You *will* not?" Bartleby responds: "I *prefer* not." One wonders what would have happened if Bartleby's boss had said "You must." He threatens Bartleby's employment regularly, but never simply informs Bartleby, in plain language, what *must* be done.

"Bartleby, the Scrivener: A Story of Wall Street" is considered Melville's best short story with good reason. In considering whether or not Bartleby's actions were correct and appropriate, the reader gets a chance to examine the nature of work and one worker's engagement with authority, his fellow workers, and the workplace in the mid-nineteenth century.

—*Kay Tilden Frost*

Bibliography and Additional Reading

"The Life of Herman Melville," PBS.org. https://www.pbs.org/wgbh/americanexperience/features/whaling-biography-herman-melville/.

Morrison, Toni. "Melville and the Language of Denial." *The Nation*, January 7, 2014. https://www.thenation.com/article/melville-and-language-denial/.

Mumford, Lewis. "From the Stacks: 'The Significance of Herman Melville.'" August 1, 2013. https://newrepublic.com/article/114098/significance-herman-melville-lewis-mumford-stacks.

Yothers, Brian. *Melville's Mirrors: Literary Criticism and America's Most Elusive Author*. Rochester, NY: Camden House, 2011.

Barnum with Commodore Nutt, photograph by Charles DeForest Fredricks.

From *The Life of P.T. Barnum*

Date: 1854
Author: P.T. Barnum
Genre: Autobiography; memoir

Summary Overview

Discussing Phineas Taylor Barnum—"Tale" to his friends and P.T. Barnum to history—is complicated. He was an extremely successful businessman who forever changed the concept of entertainment in the United States, but he made his fortune by exploiting slaves, disabled people, and animals. He told himself that he did not aim to deceive people in the usual sense, but rather to get them to participate in the act of deception—something he said that human beings enjoyed immensely.

Defining Moment

In the excerpt from Barnum's autobiography included here, the entertainment maestro relates how cheating was generally expected in the business world of his time, and how when he ran his store and trading business (before going into sideshows and circuses), everyone cheated in the normal course of affairs. This is a fundamental aspect of the way Barnum did business; he believed that no one was truly honest, or if they were they must be dupes and "suckers." This made it easier for Barnum to justify how he ran his small business, his newspaper, his famous American Museum, and arguably his political career later in life.

It is important to remember that Barnum was not unique in the Victorian era. In both the United States and England, "freak shows" were somewhat commonplace, part of the general interest in horror and astonishment that also fueled such works as *Dracula*, *Frankenstein*, and *The Picture of Dorian Gray*, to name just a few of the more literary books of the era. More widely marketed popular books and magazines, called "penny dreadfuls," contained stories designed to shock and horrify—to the delight of audiences. At the time when Barnum released his autobiography in 1854, his museum of oddities had been operating in New York City for about a dozen years but he had not yet cofounded the famed Barnum & Bailey Circus (launched in 1871).

Author Biography

Barnum was born in Bethel, Connecticut, on July 5, 1810. At the age of 15, his father died. He had five siblings and was primarily responsible for their support. After holding several different jobs, he began to manage a weekly newspaper in Danbury, Connecticut, called *Herald of Freedom*. Even then, Barnum's tendency towards sensationalism and showmanship showed its hand; he was arrested three times for libel during the years he managed the paper. On one occasion, he threw himself a party and a parade upon being released from jail.

Barnum married at 19, then moved to New York City in 1834. This is where the part of his career with which most people are familiar really began. He purchased a slave, Joice Heth, and labeled her the 161-year-old nurse to George Washington; he made his first big money by selling tickets to see her. Even when Heth died, Barnum managed to make money; he charged people to see a gruesome autopsy—which proved she was not as old as "she" had claimed.

With the money he made, Barnum purchased the American Museum in New York City, a five-story building then filled with conventional exhibits—stuffed animals and wax figures, mostly. Barnum quickly changed the tone of the museum; he filled it with "freak show" acts, dramatic theatrical performances, beauty contests, and more. He brought his distant cousin, Charles Stratton, to live with him. Stratton was just over two feet tall and 11 years old at the time. Barnum called him "Captain Tom Thumb" and billed him as older and more worldly than he was in order to sell more tickets. He also exhibited the "Siamese Twins" (conjoined twins) Cheng and Eng, along with a piece of fakery called the "Feejee Mermaid" consisting of the torso and head of a monkey sewed onto the tail of a large fish. He brought the soprano Jenny Lind from Sweden to perform at the museum; she was so well received that some music historians credit her with popularizing opera in the United States.

Later, Barnum took to politics and was elected as the mayor of Bridgeport, Connecticut. He continued to release revised versions of his autobiography, as critics argued with the details of his life as he presented it. Although Barnum is often associated with the circus, particularly Barnum & Bailey, he did not work in the circus until he was 60 years old. He took to the new role with the same verve he employed in his prior operations, seeking to make his circus "the Greatest Show on Earth."

Barnum died in 1891 at the age of 81. Knowing that he was gravely ill and likely to die, he had convinced a New York newspaper to publish his obituary early so that he could enjoy it before passing.

HISTORICAL DOCUMENT

There is something to be learned even in a country store. We are apt to believe that sharp trades, especially dishonest tricks and unprincipled deceptions, are confined entirely to the city, and that the unsophisticated men and women of the country do every thing "on the square." I believe this to be measurably true, but know that there are many exceptions to this rule. Many is the time I cut open bundles of rags, brought to the store by country women in exchange for goods, and declared to be all linen and cotton, that contained quantities of worthless woollen trash in the interior, and sometimes stones, gravel, ashes, etc. And sometimes, too, have I (contrary to our usual practice) measured the load of oats, corn or rye which our farmer-customer assured us contained a specified number of bushels, perhaps sixty, and found it four or five bushels short. Of course the astonished woman would impute the rag-swindle to a servant or neighbor who had made it up without her knowledge, and the man would charge carelessness upon his "help" who measured the grain, and by mistake "made a wrong count." These were exceptions to the general rule of honesty, but they occurred with sufficient frequency to make us watchful of our customers, and to teach me the truth of the adage, "There's cheating in all trades but ours."

* * * * *

Messrs. Keeler and Whitlock sold out their store of goods to Mr. Lewis Taylor in the summer of 1827. I remained a short time as clerk for Mr. Taylor. They have a proverb in Connecticut, that "the best school in which to have a boy learn human nature, is to permit him to be a tin peddler for a few years. "I think his chances for getting "his eye-teeth cut" would be equally great, in a country barter store like that in which I was clerk. As before stated, many of our customers were hatters, and we took hats in payment, for goods. The large manufacturers generally dealt pretty fairly by us, but some of the smaller fry occasionally shaved us prodigiously. There probably is no trade in which there can be more cheating than in hats. If a hat was damaged "in coloring" or otherwise, perhaps by a cut of half a foot in length, it was sure to be patched up, smoothed over, and slipped in with others to send to the store. Among the furs used for the nap of hats in those days, were beaver, Russia, nutria, otter, coney, muskrat, etc., etc. The best fur was otter, the poorest was coney.

The hatters mixed their inferior furs with a little of their best, and sold us the hats for "otter." We in return mixed our sugars, teas, and liquors, and gave them the most valuable names. It was "dog eat dog" "tit for tat." Our cottons were sold for wool, our wool and cotton for silk and linen; in fact nearly every thing was different from what it was represented. The customers cheated us in their fabrics: we cheated the customers with our goods. Each party expected to be cheated, if it was possible. Our eyes, and not our ears, had to be our masters. We must believe little that we saw, and less that we heard. Our calicoes were all "fast colors," according to our representations, and the colors would generally run "fast" enough and show them a tub of soap-suds. Our ground coffee was as good as burned peas, beans, and corn could make, and our ginger was tolerable, considering the price of corn meal. The "tricks of trade" were numerous. If a "peddler" wanted to trade with us for a box of beaver hats worth sixty dollars per dozen, he was sure to obtain a box of "coneys" which were dear at fifteen dollars per dozen. If we took our pay in clocks, warranted to keep good time, the chances were that they were no better than a chest of drawers for that purpose that they were like Pindar's razors, "made to sell," and if half the number of wheels necessary to form a clock could be found within the case, it was as lucky as extraordinary.

Such a school would "cut eye-teeth," but if it did not cut conscience, morals, and integrity all up by the roots, it would be because the scholars quit before their education was completed!

* * * * *

After a few hours, he good-naturedly said to me, "Mr. B., what are the requisite qualifications of a good showman?"

I smilingly replied, that "the first qualification necessary was a thorough knowledge of human nature, which of course included the faculty of judiciously applying soft soap."

"And what is that you call 'sof sup?'" eagerly inquired the anxious Professor Pinte.

I told him it was the faculty to please and flatter the public so judiciously as not to have them suspect your intention.

In passing the custom-house we had a large quantity of medals, books, and engravings (lithographs of the General.) I knew that these were subject to duty, but I was very prodigal in presenting them to the custom-house officers, and by that means got them through duty-free.

"Is that what you call 'sof sup?'" inquired Professor Pinte.

"Exactly," I replied.

GLOSSARY

"cut one's eye teeth on": to learn through experience

"fast colors": indicating that the color will not fade when the fabric is washed

judiciously: with good judgment or sense

"on the square": honestly or legitimately; above board

Document Analysis

This excerpt from Barnum's *Life* illustrates his notion that no one is entirely honest in his or her dealings with others, especially in the business world. He lays out the benefits of trusting with one's eyes (and sense) rather than with what one is told. He also suggests that virtually everyone expects to be cheated—the shopkeeper, the supplier, the customer—it is just a matter of anticipating this and trying to minimize your loses and maximizing your gains. According to this logic, there is basically no harm in cheating people, because they should be looking out for themselves, and they would cheat you if given the chance.

There is a saying in the world of commerce: "Let the buyer beware." The statement refers to the idea that, in any transaction, buyers are responsible for protecting their own interests; they, and they alone, must make sure that they are not overpaying for an item and that it meets their expectations in terms of quality and other characteristics they seek.

There is another saying that is often attributed to Barnum: "There's a sucker born every minute." Although no one knows for sure whether Barnum invented the saying, or even uttered it, it is easy to understand why it has been attributed to him. Barnum, as a shopkeeper, appears to see no harm in offering customers lesser quality goods in order to make a profit; after all, he argues, they typically offer him lesser quality goods in trade, which, as he sees it, means that any cheating he does is fair.

All who have looked at the life and writings of P.T. Barnum agree that he was a showman of the first order, someone who was always happy to draw attention to himself and his doings—particularly when he could parlay that attention into money from paying customers. One question that often comes up in discussing Barnum is whether he was cruel or deceptive in his efforts to "trick" people. He himself maintained that he never was. He claimed that people participated in transactions in ways that made them aware of the risks and benefits involved. Certainly in the passage reprinted here, there is no sense that he is out to harm his customers or ruin his relationship with them; or that he is doing anything beyond what they would do themselves. He is simply seeking to turn a transaction to his own ends, according to his own skewed

1866 newspaper advertisement for Barnum's American Museum located on Ann Street in Manhattan. (Barnum's American Museum - New York Times) perspective. He sees the nature of business as essentially unethical, and is simply trying to match it step by step by his own actions.

Essential Themes
Some aspects of Barnum's life and thought came into sharper relief when he began to operate his freak shows and circuses. He argued in his writing and during his life that no one ever actually believed that a monkey sewn onto a fish was a mermaid, but that people *wanted to believe* that it was and found enjoyment in discovering whether or not they could do so. He thought of himself as an entertainer who was giving people a chance to escape their real-life drudgery and be challenged by something different. Many of his "freaks" were people who had impressive talents—sword swallowing or fire breathing, for example. Some observers have even argued that Barnum gave a home and (possibly) fair wages to people like Cheng and Eng and Charles Sutton, who likely would not have found work otherwise and may even have been institutionalized.

After Barnum turned to politics in the 1860s and 1870s, before founding his circus, he claimed to have had something of a change of heart. He quickly took up the cause of the abolition of slavery, for example, even though he admits that he had once owned and whipped slaves. Is it possible that he saw the error of his ways? It is, of course; but then one must remember that Barnum's entire career was based on giving people what he thought they wanted or needed, regardless of its truthfulness. It is therefore difficult to trust much of anything he said or wrote during his lifetime.

It must also be remembered that Barnum had purchased, and profited off of, of Joice Heth—even exploiting her death. He helped to popularize the racially infused minstrel show in the United States. He showed off one William Henry Johnson as "Zip the Pinhead" and promoted him with ads and signs asking, "What is It?" He implied that Johnson was part ape and part man. He showed off children with skull deformities, presenting them as "Aztecs." He called a family with albinism "white Negros."

The same kind of questionable sensationalism continues into modern times. It could be argued that Barnum's influence extends into tabloid newspapers sold at grocery store checkout stands—publications that routinely swear they have evidence of, say, a human monkey baby being born in a remote town somewhere, or that they have definitive proof of an autopsy of an alien having taken place. On the internet, one is often bombarded with articles that have headlines like, "You won't believe how these 23 celebrities have aged"; or, "This worm will cure everything that's making you sick." Those who create such articles have found ways to make money following the Barnum tradition. If users click on them—well, they have made their choice, electing to be astonished rather than wary.

According to Barnum, "the American people like to be humbugged" (a reference to witnessing sideshows and fakeries). Perhaps such humbuggery has become a normal part of American life, in part thanks to Barnum; or maybe it always was and Barnum simply tapped into it.

—Kay Tilden Frost

Bibliography and Additional Reading
"History of Freak Shows." University of Sheffield. https://www.sheffield.ac.uk/nfca/researchandarticles/freakshows.

Kolbert, Elizabeth. "What P.T. Barnum Understood About America." *The New Yorker,* July 29, 2019. https://www.newyorker.com/magazine/2019/08/05/what-p-t-barnum-understood-about-america.

Mansky, Jackie. "P.T. Barnum Isn't the Hero 'The Greatest Showman' Wants You to Think." *Smithsonian Magazine,* December 22, 2017. https://www.smithsonianmag.com/history/true-story-pt-barnum-greatest-humbug-them-all-180967634/.

Parker, James. "The Spectacular P.T. Barnum." *The Atlantic,* August, 2019. https://www.theatlantic.com/magazine/archive/2019/08/pt-barnum-biography-robert-wilson/592780/.

Wilson, Robert. *Barnum: An American Life*. New York: Simon and Schuster, 2019.

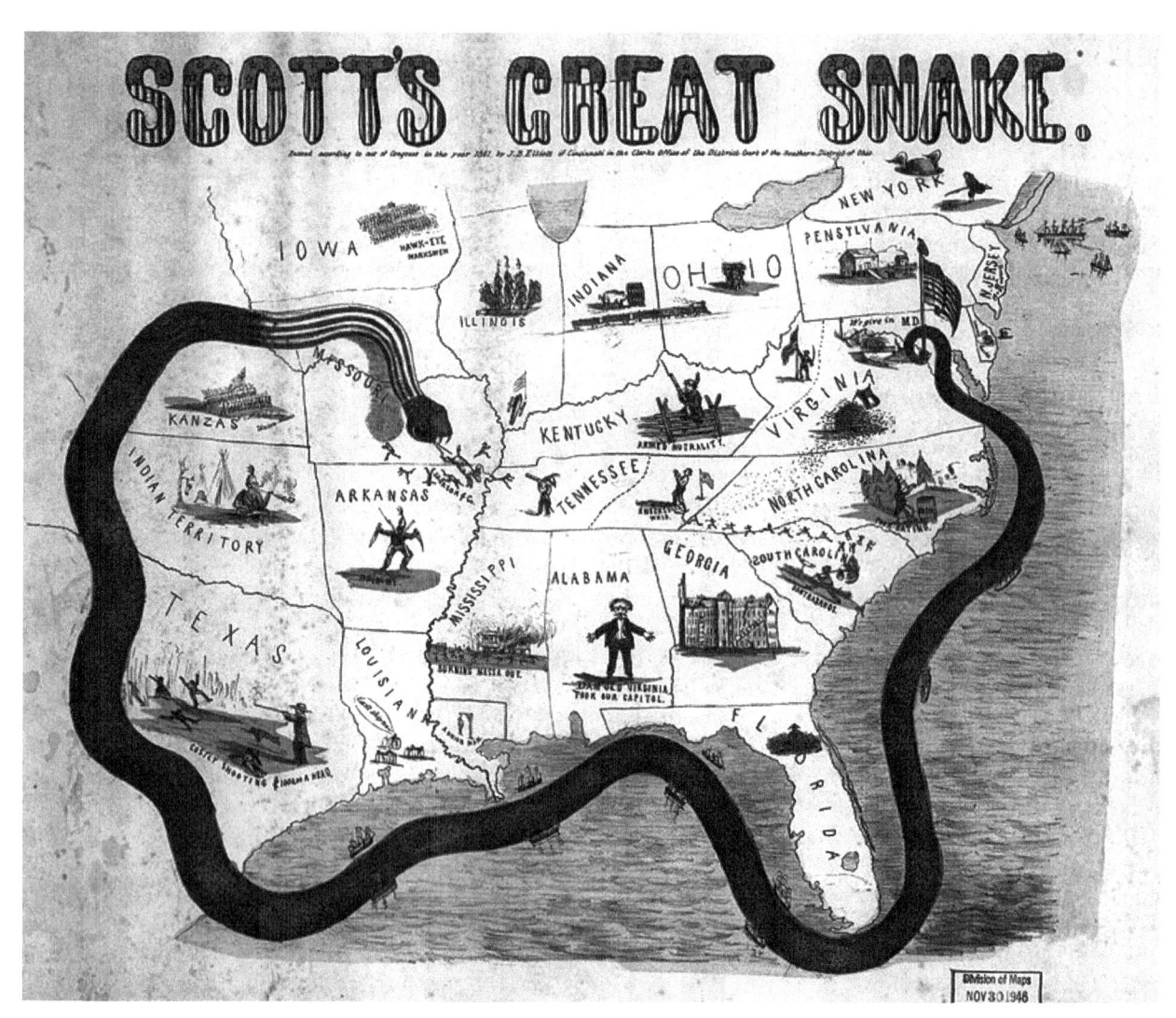

Scott's great snake. Cartoon map illustrating Gen. Winfield Scott's plan to crush the Confederacy. (J.B. Elliott - The Library of Congress/American Memory)

Presidential Proclamations on Blockade and Commercial Trade

Date: 1861
Author: Abraham Lincoln
Genre: Law

Summary Overview
At the start of the Civil War, President Abraham Lincoln, facing the secession of several Southern states, determined that the seceding states should be isolated and their collective economies stifled. The vehicle the Union would use to achieve this end was an extensive naval blockade of all ports participating in the rebellion. Not long after issuing his first proclamation of this blockade, the president issued two additional declarations, increasing the breadth of the blockade as well as the severity of punishment for those who attempted to smuggle goods past it. Lincoln's establishment of this blockade ultimately helped to shorten the Civil War's length and prevent foreign involvement in the conflict.

Defining Moment
Following the presidential election of 1860, South Carolina determined that Lincoln's presidency was a potential threat to the state's economy and way of life. The South Carolina state legislature called a special convention during which delegates opted to remove the state from membership in the United States. That state's secession prompted six other states—Mississippi, Florida, Alabama, Georgia, Louisiana, and Texas—to follow suit. In time, four more states joined what became known as the Confederate States of America.

Secession increased tensions between the U.S. military and those who lived in these states, and Southern leaders demanded the surrender of Union-held forts within Confederate territory. When the Union occupants of Fort Sumter in Charleston, South Carolina, refused to surrender the fort, Southern troops attacked. After thirty-four hours of constant cannon- and gunfire, the Union forces surrendered Fort Sumter and departed, ushering in the Civil War. In response, Lincoln called for the nation to raise 75,000 troops to engage the secessionists on the battlefield.

The key to the South's success would be trade. Through the many different ports in the Southeastern United States (such as those in Charleston; Mobile, Alabama; and Wilmington, North Carolina), the secessionists hoped to build a lucrative cotton exchange with major trading partners in Europe. Also aboard Southern and foreign ships were supplies and weapons to build the Confederacy's strength. With this economic lifeline in mind, Lincoln began exploring the idea of a blockade. Such a blockade would ideally halt foreign trade with these states and prevent smuggling as well.

Implementing the blockade would be extremely difficult in light of the geography of the states targeted. The Union would need to put security measures into place from the Carolinas to Florida, around the Florida panhandle, along the Gulf of Mexico, and up the Mississippi River. Secretary of the Navy Gideon Welles suggested that rather than send ships and troops to enforce such a broad stretch, the Union could implement the blockade in name only. Welles argued that a *de facto* blockade would send a clear message to foreign nations not to support the Southern states. Secretary of State William Henry Seward disagreed, arguing that only an actual blockade, no matter how difficult to form, would send this message to international governments and also prevent smuggling. Lincoln agreed with Seward and issued a proclamation on April 19, 1861, that applied the blockade to the original seceding states. A week later, he expanded the embargo to account for more seceding states, and extended it once more in August of that year.

Author Biography
Lincoln was born on February 12, 1809, near Hodgenville, Kentucky, to parents Thomas Lincoln (a farmer and frontiersman) and Nancy Hanks (who died when Abraham was only nine years old). Lincoln and his father moved through the frontier several times after Nancy's

death, first to Indiana and later to Illinois. Lincoln's childhood education was basic, a product of his upbringing in the rural areas of the Midwest. For example, his school in Indiana was a log cabin. His father assisted in Lincoln's education. Although his education was limited, young Lincoln developed a love for literature that continued throughout his life. As he grew older, he also gained a strong interest in law.

In 1832, the twenty-three-year-old Lincoln joined the army as a volunteer during the Black Hawk War. He was elected captain of his unit within months of joining and remained involved until the end of the conflict. After the war, Lincoln explored a number of business activities, including work on a riverboat and at his father's store, before he set up a law practice in New Salem, Illinois.

Lincoln soon pursued elected office. Though defeated in his first campaign for the Illinois state legislature, he remained involved in government until his next campaign opportunity, holding a number of local appointed positions such as surveyor and postmaster. He also continued to practice law from his own office. In 1834, he successfully campaigned for the state legislature and was reelected three times thereafter. After retiring from the state legislature, he returned to Springfield, Illinois, where he had established a new law practice after passing the Illinois bar. In 1842, he married Mary Todd, with whom he would have four children, although only one would survive into adulthood.

In 1847, Lincoln was elected as a member of the Whig Party to the U.S. House of Representatives, a post he held for one term. In 1855, he ran unsuccessfully for the Senate. He tried again in 1858, this time as a Republican. In 1860, undaunted by his previous electoral defeats, Lincoln ran successfully for president on the Republican ticket and was reelected in 1864.

President Lincoln's 1861–65 tenure was marked not only by his Civil War accomplishments. He also helped build the Republican Party, unify the Northern Democrats, and bring an end to slavery, and established the U.S. Department of Agriculture. During his second term, he led the effort to reconcile the nation's relationship with the secessionist South. However, he was unable to complete his work as president: On April 14, 1865, while attending a play at Ford's Theatre in Washington, D.C., he was assassinated by John Wilkes Booth. After three days of lying in state in the Capitol rotunda, he was interred at Oak Grove Cemetery in Springfield, Illinois.

Proclamation 81—Declaring a Blockade of Ports in Rebellious States
April 19, 1861
By the President of the United States of America

A Proclamation

WHEREAS an insurrection against the Government of the United States has broken out in the States of South Carolina, Georgia, Alabama, Florida, Mississippi, Louisiana, and Texas, and the laws of the United States for the collection of the revenue can not be effectually executed therein conformably to that provision of the Constitution which requires duties to be uniform throughout the United States; and

WHEREAS a combination of persons engaged in such insurrection have threatened to grant pretended letters of marque to authorize the bearers thereof to commit assaults on the lives, vessels, and property of good citizens of the country lawfully engaged in commerce on the high seas and in waters of the United States; and

WHEREAS an Executive proclamation has been already issued requiring the persons engaged in these disorderly proceedings to desist therefrom, calling out a militia force for the purpose of repressing the same, and convening Congress in extraordinary session to deliberate and determine thereon:

Now, THEREFORE, I, Abraham Lincoln, President of the United States, with a view to the same purposes before mentioned and to the protection of the public peace and the lives and property of quiet and orderly citizens pursuing their lawful occupations until Congress shall have assembled and deliberated on the said unlawful proceedings or until the same shall have ceased, have further deemed it advisable to set on foot a blockade of the ports within the States aforesaid, in pursuance of the laws of the United States and of the law of nations in such case provided. For this purpose a competent force will be posted so as to prevent entrance and exit of vessels from the ports aforesaid. If, therefore, with a view to violate such blockade, a vessel shall approach or shall attempt to leave either of the said ports, she will be duly warned by the commander of one of the blockading vessels, who will indorse on her register the fact and date of such warning, and if the same vessel shall again attempt to enter or leave the blockaded port she will be captured and sent to the nearest convenient port for such proceedings against her and her cargo as prize as may be deemed advisable.

And I hereby proclaim and declare that if any person, under the pretended authority of the said States or under any other pretense, shall molest a vessel of the United States or the persons or cargo on board of her, such person will be held amenable to the laws of the United States for the prevention and punishment of piracy.

In witness whereof I have hereunto set my hand and caused the seal of the United States to be affixed.

Done at the city of Washington, this 19th day of April, A.D. 1861, and of the Independence of the United States the eighty-fifth.

ABRAHAM LINCOLN.
By the President:
WILLIAM H. SEWARD, Secretary of State.

* * *

Proclamation 82—Extension of Blockade to Ports of Additional States
April 27, 1861
By the President of the United States of America

A Proclamation

WHEREAS, for the reasons assigned in my proclamation of the 19th instant, a blockade of the ports of the States of South Carolina, Georgia, Florida, Alabama, Louisiana, Mississippi, and Texas was ordered to be established; and

WHEREAS since that date public property of the United States has been seized, the collection of the revenue obstructed, and duly commissioned officers of the United States, while engaged in executing the orders of their superiors, have been arrested and held in custody as prisoners or have been impeded in the discharge of their official duties, without due legal process, by persons claiming to act under authorities of the States of Virginia and North Carolina, an efficient blockade of the ports of those States will also be established.

In witness whereof I have hereunto set my hand and caused the seal of the United States to be affixed.

Done at the city of Washington, this 27th day of April, A.D. 1861, and of the Independence of the United States the eighty-fifth.

ABRAHAM LINCOLN.
By the President:
WILLIAM H. SEWARD, Secretary of State.

* * *

Proclamation 86—Prohibiting Commercial Trade with States in Rebellion
August 16, 1861
By the President of the United States of America

A Proclamation

WHEREAS on the 15th day of April, 1861, the President of the United States, in view of an insurrection against the laws, Constitution, and Government of the United States which had broken out within the States of South Carolina, Georgia, Alabama, Florida, Mississippi, Louisiana, and Texas, and in pursuance of the provisions of the act entitled "An act to provide for calling forth the militia to execute the laws of the Union, suppress insurrections, and repel invasions, and to repeal the act now in force for that purpose," approved February 28, 1795, did call forth the militia to suppress said insurrection and to cause the laws of the Union to be duly executed, and the insurgents have failed to disperse by the time directed by the President; and

WHEREAS such insurrection has since broken out, and yet exists, within the States of Virginia, North Carolina, Tennessee, and Arkansas; and

WHEREAS the insurgents in all the said States claim to act under the authority thereof, and such claim is not disclaimed or repudiated by the persons exercising the functions of government in such State or States or in the part or parts thereof in which such combinations exist, nor has such insurrection been suppressed by said States:

Now, THEREFORE, I, Abraham Lincoln, President of the United States, in pursuance of an act of Congress approved July 13, 1861, do hereby declare that the inhabitants of the said States of Georgia, South Carolina, Virginia, North Carolina, Tennessee, Alabama, Louisiana, Texas, Arkansas, Mississippi, and Florida (except the inhabitants of that part of the State of Virginia lying west of the Alleghany Mountains and of such other parts of that State and the other States hereinbefore named as may maintain a loyal adhesion to the Union and the Constitution or may be from time to time occupied and controlled by forces of the United States engaged in the dispersion of said insurgents) are in a state of insurrection against the United States, and that all commercial intercourse between the same and the inhabitants thereof, with the exceptions aforesaid, and the citizens of other States and other parts of the United States is unlawful, and will remain unlawful until such insurrection shall cease or has been suppressed; that all goods and chattels, wares and merchandise, coming from any of said States, with the exceptions aforesaid, into other parts of the United States without the special license and permission of the President, through the Secretary of the Treasury, or proceeding to any of said States, with the exceptions aforesaid, by land or water, together with the vessel or vehicle conveying the same or conveying persons to or from said States, with said exceptions, will be forfeited to the United States; and that from and after fifteen days from the issuing of this proclamation all ships and vessels belonging in whole or in part to any citizen or inhabitant of any of said States, with said exceptions, found at sea or in any port of the United States will be forfeited to the United States; and I hereby enjoin upon all district attorneys, marshals, and officers of the revenue and of the military and naval forces of the United States to be vigilant in the execution of said act and in the enforcement of the penalties and forfeitures imposed or declared by it, leaving any party who may think himself aggrieved thereby to his application to the Secretary of the Treasury for the remission of any penalty or forfeiture, which the said Secretary is authorized by law to grant if in his judgment the special circumstances of any case shall require such remission.

In witness whereof I have hereunto set my hand and caused the seal of the United States to be affixed.

Done at the city of Washington, this 16th day of August, A.D. 1861, and of the Independence of the United States the eighty-sixth.

ABRAHAM LINCOLN.
By the President:
WILLIAM H. SEWARD, Secretary of State.

GLOSSARY

aggrieved: mistreated

blockade runner: light, fast ship used to smuggle supplies, weapons, and money to and from Confederate ports during the Civil War

chattels: property

insurrection: a violent, organized uprising against an established government

letter of marque: a government's written authorization for privateers to attack, capture, or loot an opposing government's ships on the high seas

repress: subdue

Document Analysis

Even before taking office in March 1861, Lincoln faced a harsh reality. South Carolina, which saw Lincoln's opposition to slavery as a threat to its economy, voted to cease its "membership" in the United States in December of 1860. Several other states, inspired by South Carolina's move, followed suit early in 1861. The push for Southern secession had sparked dangerous confrontations between Union troops stationed in these states and the rebel forces living there. Lincoln's predecessor, President James Buchanan, had told his troops to stand their ground, even when operating in siege conditions, as they were at Fort Sumter. Upon assuming office, Lincoln authorized the troops at that island fort to surrender their positions but by no means wanted to allow the secession to continue unanswered.

One month after his inauguration, Lincoln—after consulting with his cabinet—decided to take a major step to cut off the secessionists' economic lifelines. He did so through a series of proclamations, presidential statements that institute the necessary measures to deal with particular situations. In these documents, he declares that a civil war is at hand, a war that threatened to tear apart the Union. A blockade was necessary to contain and defeat the growing rebellion. Lincoln looked to Congress to support this policy and encouraged the legislature to implement any laws necessary to ensure that the blockade was imposed efficiently and effectively. He also looked to his own administration, including the military, federal attorneys, and other officials, urging them to do their respective parts to maintain the blockade's integrity and that of the Union.

Proclamation 81

On April 19, 1861, Lincoln issued the first of these documents. In the first line of Proclamation 81, he declares that the government of the United States faced an open insurrection in South Carolina, Georgia, Alabama, Florida, Mississippi, Louisiana, and Texas. Lincoln speaks initially to the fact that this insurrection directly affected the Union's ability to collect tax revenue from its citizens, a provision established in the Constitution. His list of grievances against these states, however, begins to grow from this statement.

For example, he accuses the seceding states of threatening to practice piracy against the Union's maritime commercial pursuits. He claims that the states were willing to use "pretended" letters of marque, written documents authorizing privateers to attack, capture, or loot Union ships. Letters of marque were commonly used throughout maritime history, particularly during times of open war, and the Constitution granted Congress the ability to issue such letters. The government of the Confederacy likewise claimed the ability to grant letters of marque, but as the United States did not consider the Confederate government to be legitimate, the seceded states were thus, in Lincoln's view, attempting to claim a power they did not have. To make matters worse, he writes, these seven states were threatening to use this power against the "good citizens" of the United States as they engaged in lawful commerce in their own waters.

Lincoln proclaims that the individuals committing these acts—the members of the seceding states—must cease their actions, and calls for the U.S. military to deploy and "repress" the rebels. In the interest of the public peace and safety, and with the integrity of the United States at stake, he writes, Congress must take into account the "unlawful proceedings" of the Southern states. He states that he believes it necessary to place a blockade around the ports of each of the states that has seceded. A navy force would be present to prevent any ships from entering or exiting these harbors. Any unauthorized ship caught in these waterways would be detained, examined, and catalogued. That ship would then be issued a formal warning not to repeat its actions and released. If the ship again tried to enter or leave a blockaded port, it would be captured and its crew prosecuted. Any cargo of value seized would be considered a prize (a ship and its cargo captured during war) and redistributed among Union circles.

Furthermore, he writes that any individual or group claiming to have the national authority (such as that of the United States or another legitimate country) to attack the interests of the federal government at sea would be captured and prosecuted to the fullest extent of the law. This statement serves as a warning to two audiences. First, it is a caution to any foreign party who may become involved in privateering against American ships using the aforementioned fraudulent letters of marque. Second and more importantly, it speaks to the secessionists themselves and advises them that the United States government will not tolerate any Rebel attacks on its ships.

Proclamation 82

Although Lincoln's first proclamation issues a stern warning to the secessionists not to attack American interests, they did not capitulate. In Proclamation 82, issued only a little more than a week after Lincoln declared the blockade, the president states that a number of Union officials who were simply collecting taxes and performing other duties as ordered by Washington had been arrested in North Carolina and Virginia and detained without due process of law. Their captors, Lincoln writes, claimed to be acting under the authority of the governments of their respective states. Virginia had only two months earlier opted to remain with the Union and seek a compromise with the new Lincoln administration. However, the state's government soon changed its position, and Virginia broke away from the United States on April 17, 1861. Its capital, Richmond, soon became the capital of the Confederacy.

North Carolina also remained on the sidelines early, seeking some sort of compromise with the federal government. However, after Lincoln issued his call for 75,000 troops on April 15, North Carolina refused to provide its share of volunteers. Although the state did not officially secede from the Union until the next month, North Carolina's leadership had already made the decision to defy the federal government, placing that state squarely on the side of the secessionists. Because of these actions on the part of the states, Proclamation 82 extends the blockade to Virginia's and North Carolina's ports as well.

The next few months saw a series of major changes that would shape the Civil War. In June, the western counties of Virginia took issue with the state government's decision to secede and in turn seceded from the Confederacy. This region was admitted into the Union on June 20, 1863, taking the name of West Virginia. Meanwhile, the Union continued a long-running series of political maneuvers to prevent many of the slave states from joining the Confederacy. These efforts proved fruitful, as Delaware, Missouri, Kentucky, and Maryland remained part of the Union. In July, Union and Confederate militias met on the battlefield for the first time at Manassas, Virginia, in the First Battle of Bull Run, wherein an untrained Union army was forced to retreat in the face of an overwhelming infusion of Confederate reinforcements. By then, Lincoln's blockade was finally in place, with improved naval vessels enforcing it against smaller, faster smuggling ships known as blockade runners. In addition to implementing the blockade, Congress on July 13, 1861, declared the Confederate States to be in an official state of insurrection against the United States.

Proclamation 86

On August 16, 1861, Lincoln issued Proclamation 86, which speaks to the effect of the above developments on the wartime situation. He states that he was within his rights as president when he called for the 75,000 troops to meet what was clearly an "insurrection against the laws, Constitution, and Government of the United States." He cites the Militia Act of 1795, passed by Congress to validate the actions of President George Washington, who had raised a militia to put down the Whiskey Rebellion the previous year. Despite Lincoln's use of the presidential power given him by Congress, however, the Confederate insurrection had continued and spread into Tennessee, Arkansas, and other states.

Lincoln notes that the rebels had been operating as if they were subject solely to the authority of the state governments. These governments, on the other hand, had done nothing to deny this perceived sovereignty. Furthermore, although the rebels had clearly been operating against the laws of the United States, the state governments claiming authority over them had done nothing to suppress the insurrection.

Since Congress had joined Lincoln in identifying the eleven insurgent states (excluding West Virginia, which Lincoln notes refused to join and in fact was taking steps to combat the insurgency), Lincoln felt empowered to elevate the effort against the Confederacy. His first move in this proclamation is to declare commerce with the secessionist states illegal until the end of the war. Any goods, merchandise, or other items brought into the Union by land or sea from these states or vice versa—unless granted an exemption by the president or his administration—would be "forfeited to the United States." Furthermore, any Confederate ships caught transporting people or goods into or out of the Union would also be confiscated. Once the blockade was in place, any unauthorized ship found attempting to travel between the United States and the Confederate ports in question would be captured and its cargo distributed in the Union.

Lincoln applied the full weight of his power to these proclamations and the blockade itself. At his disposal were not only the U.S. Navy and the War Department but also law enforcement, including marshals and district attorneys, and the U.S. Treasury. Lincoln mentions this last agency because of its responsibilities in collecting and processing revenues. Much of Lincoln's argument against the secessionist movement, as seen in these proclamations, was based on the fact that the states involved would cease to collect federal tax revenues and pay their federal obligations. The Treasury would thus recoup lost revenues by liquidating any confiscated ships and contraband. Implicit is the notion that once a blockade runner was captured by the Union, any item of value seized would not be returned to the perpetrator as long as the war persisted.

At the end of Proclamation 86, Lincoln attempts to show flexibility with regard to specific cases. For example, he suggests that parties detained for violating the blockade may, if they feel mistreated by the charges levied against them, appeal directly to the Treasury Department. The Treasury would, Lincoln writes, have the authority to review each case thoroughly and drop the charges in special cases. Lincoln also leaves open the possibility that the suspension of commerce between Union and secessionist states could be exempted if the latter "maintain[ed] a loyal adhesion" to the former. The newly created state of West Virginia, cited in Proclamation 86, provides an example of how a state may benefit economically from this declaration of loyalty. If a state wanted to avoid suffering from a lack of commerce with the Union, it could simply reverse course, rejoin the Union, and immediately return to economic vitality.

Nevertheless, it was Lincoln's intention to apply a strict, extensive, and far-reaching blockade that would weaken the maritime-reliant economies of the Southern states that declared themselves sovereign. In fact, the breakaway states had by this point not only seceded, an act that itself was illegal in Lincoln's view, but also taken up arms against the military and civilian agents of the federal government. Lincoln and his cabinet believed that the war could be ended if the Confederacy's maritime supply and revenue lines were cut. The only way to ensure the efficacy of such a policy was to apply the blockade in the strictest manner possible.

Essential Themes

Lincoln inherited from his predecessor a steadily deteriorating situation, as the divide between the free states of the North and the slave states of the South continued to widen. Opponents of Lincoln argued repeatedly during his first presidential campaign that he would not share Buchanan's apparent ambivalence on abolition and would outlaw slavery, on which the agrarian economy of the South relied. Although Lincoln asserted during this period that he had said nothing to support this rumor, his success on the campaign trail made the Southern states extremely wary. After he won the election, South Carolina decided it was time to break away from Lincoln's United States.

Lincoln's response to the secession of South Carolina was to take swift action, calling up 75,000 troops to confront the rebels. This action emboldened other states to follow South Carolina's example. As states continued to leave the Union, Lincoln issued three proclamations that were designed to cut off the port cities of the South. The blockade was within his presidential power to impose, he argues in the proclamations, as the country faced an insurrection that threatened the safety of its government and people. In Proclamation 86, the third proclamation concerning the blockade, Lincoln asserts his presidential authority again, outlining specific punishments for those who would violate the blockade. Still, he also sought to appear fair. Those who felt they were unjustly accused could appeal their cases, even during wartime. Furthermore, Lincoln makes it known that all involved states, even those that had already seceded, could avoid the blockade and the resulting economic disruption by re-dedicating themselves to the Union.

The proclamations include strong language identifying the secessionist states as criminals and belligerents against the United States. Such verbiage was likely included both to intimidate the Southern states and to make it clear to foreign governments that they were to stay away from the affected ports or else be seen as potential enemies of the Union. The U.S. government was largely successful in preventing foreign powers from allying with the Confederacy; although the Confederacy continued to trade with some foreign bodies, particularly British possessions in the Caribbean, the governments of such areas remained officially allied with the United States. However, the secessionists themselves were not intimidated by bellicose language, and the Confederate movement against the United States continued.

—*Michael Auerbach*

Bibliography and Additional Reading

"Abraham Lincoln." *Library of Congress*. The Library of Congress, 2013.

Beschloss, Michael, and Hugh Sidey. *The Presidents of the United States of America*. Washington, DC: White House Historical Association, 2009.

"The Blockade of Confederate Ports, 1861–1865." *Office of the Historian*. U.S. Department of State, n.d.

Canfield, Eugene B. "Birth of a Blockade." *Naval History* 21.5 (2007): 44–51.

Ekelund, Robert B. *Tariffs, Blockades, and Inflation: The Economics of the Civil War*. Lanham, MD: Rowman & Littlefield, 2004.

Faulkner, Ronnie W. "Secession." *North Carolina History Project*. John Locke Foundation, 2013.

"Fort Sumter." *Civil War Trust*. Civil War Trust, 2013.

Lankford, Nelson D. "Virginia Convention of 1861." In *Encyclopedia Virginia*. Virginia Foundation for the Humanities, April 5, 2011.

"Lincoln, Abraham." *Biographical Directory of the United States Congress*. U.S. Congress, 2005.

Lincoln, Abraham. "Call for 75,000 Volunteers." *Essential Documents of American History*. Compiled by Norman Desmarais and James H. McGovern, 2009.

Wise, Stephen R. *Lifeline of the Confederacy: Blockade Running during the Civil War*. Columbia: University of South Carolina Press, 1991.

■ From *Utilitarianism*

Date: 1863
Author: John Stuart Mill
Genre: Nonfiction book (excerpt)

Summary Overview

John Stuart Mill composed this selection from chapter two of his 1863 book *Utilitarianism* as a defense and explication of the principle of utility. In Mill's view, morality is defined by utility, that is, actions are proportionately more right or wrong in accordance with the amount of pleasure or lack thereof that they produce. Mill argues in this chapter against detractors who considered his definition of utility to be a "pig philosophy" because of its focus on pleasure. He assails this opposing position for not considering that humans may hold and be capable of higher values other than physical pleasure. Mill then offers a typology of pleasures: the higher (i.e., mental and moral) and the lower type (i.e., bodily appetites). Since Mill's theory of utilitarianism relies on a "felicific calculus" in order to evaluate how much happiness a specific action creates and thus determine its moral value, the author further explains how higher pleasures factor into this formula. Higher pleasures are more preferable innately to humans. Instead of balancing all types of pleasures by quantity, Mill argues that higher pleasures have a qualitative difference. Finally, Mill proposes that pleasure need not be self-centered but that a model exists where individuals consider the happiness of the whole to be in their self-interest.

Defining Moment

The Industrial Revolution dramatically affected almost every aspect of life in Great Britain in the early eighteenth century. The introduction of new mechanical tools increased production of goods that had previously been produced by hand; innovations like steam power allowed commercial agents to trade these goods to distant British colonies more quickly than ever before. As economic prosperity boomed for businesses employing these mechanical innovations, population shifted from dispersed rural settlements towards the sites of new factories. This rapid urbanization proved challenging for the working class, which struggled because of inadequate housing, poor sanitation, and poor compensation for long hours of factory work

Resistance to these difficult and dangerous conditions for the people fueling Britain's economic boom often struggled to find a sympathetic audience among the political elite. At the beginning of the eighteenth century, there was still no universal male suffrage, which meant that day laborers had no political franchise. Workers organized labor unions and strikes to try to change their unacceptable conditions. These actions, however, were met with resistance by political interests with money and land. Attempts were made to restrict the ability of workers to use collective action, such as in the Combination Act of 1799, but the grave conditions and the plight of the working man and child eventually reversed these restrictions by the 1830s.

Additionally, the Reform Act of 1832 extended political franchise in Britain, but it did not create universal suffrage for all men or women. This small extension of the vote, however, allowed more members of the Radical party to join Parliament. As an assemblage of various progressive opinions, the Radicals generally supported reform that would extend the right to vote, valorized personal liberties, and drove measures to ameliorate the life of the working class. Jeremy Bentham (1748–1832) was a prominent member of the Radical movement and public intellectual. As the underlying framework for his legal philosophy, Bentham developed an influential theory of utilitarianism eagerly promulgated by his students. Proposing that the happiness of the greatest number of people equated with the moral rectitude of an action, Bentham supported extended rights for typically disenfranchised members of society and gained devoted followers, such as James Mill, the father of John Stuart Mill. The son in time would inherit the political and philosophical leanings of his father and intellectual mentor. John Stuart Mill joined Parliament himself as a member of the Liberal Party, the successor to the Radicals, and developed the ideas of utilitarianism to argue forcefully for societal change.

Author Biography

John Stuart Mill (1806–1873) was one of the most influential British philosophers of the nineteenth century. His father, James Mill, was a philosopher and historian in his own right, and he fostered his son's precocious nature with an early and rigorous Classical education. As a young teen, Mill was reading Aristotle in the original Greek, the works of Adam Smith, and engaging with his father's notable intellectual friends. The elder Mill was a follower of Jeremy Bentham, the father of modern utilitarianism and a political Radical. As part of this association, the elder Mill positioned himself politically against the prevailing Whigs and Tories at the time, and considered the Radical position more fit to address issues of nonaristocratic segments of society. The younger Mill, because of this early education in a wide range of ancient texts and modern intellectual movements, was well-disposed for radical social and political thinking as well.

By 1826, however, the stress of this education and his father's hopes began to weigh upon him. As a result, Mill moved away from his father's emphasis on Enlightenment ideals of reason. Instead, Mill explored the poetry and philosophical thought associated with Romanticism, which predominantly rejected naturalistic and secular explanations for knowledge and human experience. Renewed by his intellectual explorations, Mill remained eclectic in his intellectual proclivities: he engaged in a pen-friendship with Auguste Comte, the (French) founder of positivism; he was a nonconformist with the Church of England; and he enjoyed the poetry of Samuel Coleridge.

At the same time as this intellectual crisis, Mill began working with his father for the East India Company. Afforded the financial means and time to write, Mill began publishing on a variety of topics, including his *System of Logic* (1843) and *Principles of Political Economy* (1848). After many years of friendship, in 1851 Mill married Harriet Taylor, who significantly impacted her husband's work and development of ideas. Unfortunately Taylor died in 1858, around the same time that Mill retired from the East India Company and the firm itself was dissolved. She may have influenced her husband to support the cause of women's suffrage, however, and he cites her as an influence in his final revision of another of his notable works, *On Liberty*.

In the final part of his career, Mill continued to write on and develop his theories of utilitarianism as well as engaging in political affairs. He served as a member of Parliament from 1865-68, in which position he strongly argued for radical labor reforms and extending suffrage. When he was not reelected, Mill spent his remaining years in France in quietude until his death in 1873.

HISTORICAL DOCUMENT

A PASSING remark is all that needs be given to the ignorant blunder of supposing that those who stand up for utility as the test of right and wrong, use the term in that restricted and merely colloquial sense in which utility is opposed to pleasure. An apology is due to the philosophical opponents of utilitarianism, for even the momentary appearance of confounding them with any one capable of so absurd a misconception; which is the more extraordinary, inasmuch as the contrary accusation, of referring everything to pleasure, and that too in its grossest form, is another of the common charges against utilitarianism: and, as has been pointedly remarked by an able writer, the same sort of persons, and often the very same persons, denounce the theory "as impracticably dry when the word utility precedes the word pleasure, and as too practicably voluptuous when the word pleasure precedes the word utility." Those who know anything about the matter are aware that every writer, from Epicurus to Bentham, who maintained the theory of utility, meant by it, not something to be contradistinguished from pleasure, but pleasure itself, together with exemption from pain; and instead of opposing the useful to the agreeable or the ornamental, have always declared that the useful means these, among other things. Yet the common herd, including the herd of writers, not only in newspapers and periodicals, but in books of weight and pretension, are perpetually falling into this shallow mistake. Having caught up the word utilitarian, while knowing nothing whatever about it but its sound, they habitually express by it the rejection, or the neglect, of pleasure in some of its forms; of beauty, of ornament, or of amusement. Nor is the term thus ignorantly misapplied solely in disparagement, but occasionally in compliment; as though it implied superiority to frivolity and the mere pleasures of the moment. And this perverted use is the only one in which the word is popularly known, and the one from which the new generation are acquiring their sole notion of its meaning. Those who introduced the word, but who had for many years discontinued it as a distinctive appellation, may well feel themselves called upon to resume it, if by doing so they can hope to contribute anything towards rescuing it from this utter degradation.

The creed which accepts as the foundation of morals, Utility, or the Greatest Happiness Principle, holds that actions are right in proportion as they tend to promote happiness, wrong as they tend to produce the reverse of happiness. By happiness is intended pleasure, and the absence of pain; by unhappiness, pain, and the privation of pleasure. To give a clear view of the moral standard set up by the theory, much more requires to be said; in particular, what things it includes in the ideas of pain and pleasure; and to what extent this is left an open question. But these supplementary explanations do not affect the theory of life on which this theory of morality is grounded- namely, that pleasure, and freedom from pain, are the only things desirable as ends; and that all desirable things (which are as numerous in the utilitarian as in any other scheme) are desirable either for the pleasure inherent in themselves, or as means to the promotion of pleasure and the prevention of pain.

Now, such a theory of life excites in many minds, and among them in some of the most estimable in feeling and purpose, inveterate dislike. To suppose that life has (as they express it) no higher end than pleasure—no better and nobler object of desire and pursuit—they designate as utterly mean and grovelling; as a doctrine worthy only of swine, to whom the followers of Epicurus were, at a very early period, contemptuously likened; and modern holders of the doctrine are occasionally made the subject of equally polite comparisons by its German, French, and English assailants.

When thus attacked, the Epicureans have always answered, that it is not they, but their accusers, who represent human nature in a degrading light; since the accusation supposes human beings to be capable of no pleasures except those of which swine are capable. If this supposition were true, the charge could not be gainsaid, but would then be no longer an imputation; for if the sources of pleasure were precisely the same to human beings and to swine, the rule of life which is good enough for the one would be good enough for the other. The comparison of the Epicurean life to that of beasts is felt as degrading, precisely because a beast's pleasures do not satisfy a human being's conceptions of happiness. Human beings have faculties more elevated than the animal appetites, and when once made conscious of them, do not regard anything as happiness which does not include their gratification. I do not, indeed, consider the Epicureans to have been by any means faultless in drawing out their scheme of consequences from the utilitarian principle. To do this in any sufficient manner, many Stoic, as well as Christian elements require to be included. But there is no known Epicurean theory of life which does not assign to the pleasures of the intellect, of the feelings and imagination, and of the moral sentiments, a much higher value as pleasures than to those of mere sensation. It must be admitted, however, that utilitarian writers in general have placed the superiority of mental over bodily pleasures chiefly in the greater permanency, safety, uncostliness, etc., of the former-that is, in their circumstantial advantages rather than in their intrinsic nature. And on all these points utilitarians have fully proved their case; but they might have taken the other, and, as it may be called, higher ground, with entire consistency. It is quite compatible with the principle of utility to recognise the fact, that some kinds of pleasure are more desirable and more valuable than others. It would be absurd that while, in estimating all other things, quality is considered as well as quantity, the estimation of pleasures should be supposed to depend on quantity alone.

If I am asked, what I mean by difference of quality in pleasures, or what makes one pleasure more valuable than another, merely as a pleasure, except its being greater in amount, there is but one possible answer. Of two pleasures, if there be one to which all or almost all who have experience of both give a decided preference, irrespective of any feeling of moral obligation to prefer it, that is the more desirable pleasure. If one of the two is, by those who are competently acquainted with both, placed so far above the other that they prefer it, even though knowing it to be attended with a greater amount of discontent, and would not resign it for any quantity of the other pleasure which their nature is capable of, we are justified in ascribing to the preferred enjoyment a superiority in quality, so far outweighing quantity as to render it, in comparison, of small account....

I must again repeat, what the assailants of utilitarianism seldom have the justice to acknowledge, that the happiness which forms the utilitarian standard of what is right in conduct, is not the agent's own happiness, but that of all concerned. As between his own happiness and that of others, utilitarianism requires him to be as strictly impartial as a disinterested and benevolent spectator. In the golden rule of Jesus of Nazareth, we read the complete spirit of the ethics of utility. To do as you would be done by, and to love your neighbour as yourself, constitute the ideal perfection of utilitarian morality. As the means of making the nearest approach to this ideal, utility would enjoin, first, that laws and social arrangements should place the happiness, or (as speaking practically it may be called) the interest, of every individual, as nearly as possible in harmony with the interest of the whole; and secondly, that education and opinion, which have so vast a power over human character, should so use that power as to establish in the mind of every individual an indissoluble association between his own happiness and the good of the whole; especially between his own happiness and the practice of such modes of conduct, negative and positive, as regard for the universal happiness prescribes; so that not only he may be unable to conceive the possibility of happiness to himself, consistently with conduct opposed to the general good, but also that a direct impulse to promote the general good may be in every individual one of the habitual motives of action, and the sentiments connected therewith may fill a large and prominent place in every human being's sentient existence. If the, impugners of the utilitarian morality represented it to their own minds in this its, true character, I know not what recommendation possessed by any other morality they could possibly affirm to be wanting to it; what more beautiful or more exalted developments of human nature any other ethical system can be supposed to foster, or what springs of action, not accessible to the utilitarian, such systems rely on for giving effect to their mandates....

Utility is often summarily stigmatised as an immoral doctrine by giving it the name of Expediency, and taking advantage of the popular use of that term to contrast it with Principle. But the Expedient, in the sense in which it is opposed to the Right, generally means that which is expedient for the particular interest of the agent himself; as when a minister sacrifices the interests of his country to keep himself in place. When it means anything better than this, it means that which is expedient for some immediate object, some temporary purpose, but which violates a rule whose observance is expedient in a much higher degree. The Expedient, in this sense, instead of being the same thing with the useful, is a branch of the hurtful. Thus, it would often be expedient, for the purpose of getting over some momentary embarrassment, or attaining some object immediately useful to ourselves or others, to tell a lie. But inasmuch as the cultivation in ourselves of a sensitive feeling on the subject of veracity, is one of the most useful, and the enfeeblement of that feeling one of the most hurtful, things to which our conduct can be instrumental; and inasmuch as any, even unintentional, deviation from truth, does that much towards weakening the trustworthiness of human assertion, which is not only the principal support of all present social well-being, but the insufficiency of which does more than any one thing that can be named to keep back civilisation, virtue, everything on which human happiness on the largest scale depends; we feel that the violation, for a present advantage, of a rule of such transcendant expediency, is not expedient, and that he who, for the sake of a convenience to himself or to some other individual, does what depends on him to deprive mankind of the good, and inflict upon them the evil, involved in the greater or less reliance which they can place in each other's word, acts the part of one of their worst enemies. Yet that even this rule, sacred as it is, admits of possible exceptions, is acknowledged by all moralists; the chief of which is when the withholding of some fact (as of information from a malefactor, or of bad news from a person dangerously ill) would save an individual (especially an individual other than oneself) from great and unmerited evil, and when the withholding can only be effected by denial. But in order that the exception may not extend itself beyond the need, and may have the least possible effect in weakening reliance on veracity, it ought to be recognised, and, if possible, its limits defined; and if the principle of utility is good for anything, it must be good for weighing these conflicting utilities against one another, and marking out the region within which one or the other preponderates....

John Stuart Mill. (London Stereoscopic Company - Hulton Archive)

Document Analysis

The nineteenth century in Britain was a paradoxical era. Great technological innovations expanded the realm of what was thought to be humanly possible; artistic and intellectual movements incorporated more voices into popular dialogue; and it was also a period of entrenched political and religious conservatism. Although John Stuart Mill was in many ways a nonconformist in his political and writing career, this selection from *Utilitarianism* shows that he still desired to appeal to this conservative element in his philosophy. Unlike his intellectual mentor, Jeremy Bentham, who made no qualitative difference between types of pleasures, Mill's concern for spiritual interests shows that he wished for traditionally minded readers to see the value in the utilitarianism.

Mill's desire to characterize utilitarianism as a philosophy compatible with spiritual interests reveals itself in his offense at detractors who consider utilitarianism "a doctrine worthy of a swine." As he says, "Human beings have faculties more elevated than the animal appetites": rather than see humans as a more articulate kind of animal, Mill believes that, by nature, humans have the capacity to think beyond self-interest. He decries his opponents' view of utilitarianism, and reverses their arguments to show that it is they who truly denigrate the human condition (e.g., "To suppose that life has (as they express it) no higher end than pleasure—no better and nobler object of desire and pursuit—they designate as utterly mean and grovelling.") This belief in natural human capacity is at variance with Mill's rather relativistic adherence to the socially constructed nature of moral principles (e.g., "education and opinion, which have so vast a power over human character"). Mill's explanation of utilitarian morality, however, implies a nearly spiritual faith in the capacity for humans to rise above their potential to increase the well-being of all. He says: "the happiness which forms the utilitarian standard of what is right in conduct, is not the agent's own happiness, but that of all concerned." The general well-being of all supplies the faith by which utilitarian adherents abide. Mill's appeal, next, to the model of Jesus and the creed of "love your neighbour as yourself" only confirms that the English intellectual desired to appeal to an audience with traditionally religious beliefs.

Ultimately, Mill's faith in the better nature of human beings compels him to this appeal to traditionally minded readers as well as to more sympathetic radicals. As a rhetorical move, it is not without merit. Without the support or favor of conservative skeptics, Mill could not hope to achieve any societal changes that he proposed in his other works. He was aware that he needed more people to see the value in the common welfare when it had not been common at the time to see the humanity in others who were different by virtue of gender or social class.

Essential Themes

Mill conceived of his utilitarianism as a way to inform political, economic, and social policy. His ethical calculus could, in his mind, provide a fair and just means to evaluate and change the status quo. What measures could mathematically increase the amount of happiness in a society? What existing conditions were inhibiting human progress by their lack of regard for the general welfare? As a man of progressive ideals for his time, Mill used his ethical calculus to argue for expanded rights for women and protections for the working class. As both an author and a member of Parliament, Mill used the tenets of utilitarianism to espouse radical changes to society.

For example, although Mill composed *Principles of Political Economy* (1848) before this passage from *Utilitarianism*, the principles of utility are still vital to his vision of an improved economy. Additionally, this earlier text remained incredibly influential in teaching economics. In this text, Mill considers the moral impact of rapid industrialization and the treatment of workers in such a system. He argues for "co-operatives" which would permit workers to compete economically with traditional firms. Through profit-sharing or ownership in capital, Mill believed that workers could invest themselves with a communal purpose and defeat divisive self-interest. Careful to stipulate that he did not advocate socialism, Mill nonetheless proposed that his system would increase the happiness of all individuals involved in economic growth.

On the other hand, In *The Subjugation of Women*, an essay published in 1869, Mill argued that the advancement of women, both in their education and political franchise, was a matter of utilitarian importance. Expanding rights for women would only contribute to the greater happiness of society as a whole. Not only did the lack of educational opportunities for women limit their happiness, Mill posited, but the lack of rights afforded to women stymied men's ability to interact with woman equally, and thus limited men's achievement.

Even though Mill was not successful in his day at passing measures in support of these goals, his intellectual legacy contributed to the rationale used by later activists. At the root of Mill's theory of utilitarianism is the idea that values are socially constructed rather than being naturally predetermined. This perspective, along with the forward-thinking proposals in his writings, empowered other progressive proponents to push for both expanded individual rights and protections from powerful and greedy institutions.

—*Ashleigh Fata*

Bibliography and Additional Reading

Larsen, Timothy. *John Stuart Mill: A Secular Life*. Oxford: Oxford University Press, 2018.

Mill, John S., and Collini Stefan. *On Liberty and Other Writings*. Cambridge: Cambridge University Press, 1989.

Miller, Dale E. *John Stuart Mill: Moral, Social, and Political Thought*. Malden, MA: Polity Press, 2010.

Rosen, F. *Classical Utilitarianism from Hume to Mill*. London: Routledge, 2003.

Lincoln in February 1865, two months before his death. (Alexander Gardner - Library of Congress)

■ "The Money Power"

Date: November 21, 1864
Author: Abraham Lincoln (attributed to)
Genre: Letter

Summary Overview

In this excerpt from a letter to Colonel William F. Elkins, attributed to President Abraham Lincoln, the author expresses fears about the growth of the "money power" in the United States. The notion of a shadowy "money power" exercising undue influence over government policies at the state and federal level had surfaced in American political rhetoric at various times over the previous decades, often in response to specific controversies. With the rapid growth of industry in the second half of the nineteenth century and the accompanying rise in the wealth and power of those who controlled these industries, the specter of the "money power" once again flourished.

The language in the letter is dramatic, verging on apocalyptic, framing the emerging dominance of the "money power" as the greatest challenge the nation could face—and as a calamity even more destructive to the United States than the Civil War, which in 1864 was nearing its conclusion.

Historians have long debated the authenticity of this letter; the question of Lincoln's authorship provides an additional layer of significance to the document. At the most basic level, this is a denunciation of corporate dominance. Subsequent debates over authorship illustrate the ways in which people seek to "claim" historical figures as representatives for their views.

Regardless of the ultimate authorship of these words, they provide insight into concerns about the changing American business landscape in the nineteenth century and beyond.

Defining Moment

The letter is dated November 21, 1864. At that time, the American Civil War would continue on for nearly six months until it finally ended. At this point, however, the eventual Union victory was all but assured. President Abraham Lincoln, and others, began to look to developing policies that would shape the postwar United States. While the status of former slaves and reincorporating the seceded Confederate states back into the Union were of primary concern, this excerpt illustrates emerging fears about the growing economic and political dominance of business, industrial, and financial entities in the United States.

While the explosive growth of the financial and industrial sectors in the United States is usually seen as a phenomenon of the later nineteenth and early twentieth centuries, this growth and development had been incubating for several decades. Lincoln's own history working with and for some of these entities is discussed in the Author Biography below; but, broadly, the political party with which Lincoln was affiliated for most of his career—the Whig party—was a powerful force for a growing, national economy. The policies supported by the Whigs recognized the importance of both the agricultural and developing industrial sectors and called for the federal government to support the development of business through protective tariffs, infrastructure improvements, and a central banking system to manage the money supply. Thus, the question of business and corporate influence on the political system was an established concern in the United States.

The Democratic party—particularly under President Andrew Jackson—opposed the use of the federal government's resources to support economic growth, largely because they perceived this support as primarily benefiting a narrow sector of the economy: the burgeoning industrial manufacturing sector. The Democratic opposition to the central banking system, controlled by the Second Bank of the United States, is one of the first historical episodes where the concept of the "money power" emerged (although the phrase "money power" was not prevalent until later in the century).

This letter, with its concern about the growth of the money power and the dominance of industry over the United States, began to be cited in the early twentieth century (one of the reasons for its disputed authorship) during the progressive era's push for increased regulation and public oversight of corporations. These concerns, however, had persisted in American politics for decades.

Author Biography
Abraham Lincoln was born in Kentucky on February 12, 1809. His father, Thomas, engaged in a number of jobs, including farming and land speculation. The confusing and easily contestable nature of land titles in Kentucky was a key factor in encouraging the family's move across the Ohio River to Indiana (where land was surveyed and property described using the more accurate "township and range" system) in 1816. Lincoln's time in formal schools was limited, as their family was far enough out on the western frontier that there were few teachers who were in the area consistently. As a result, he was self-taught in a number of areas, particularly enjoying reading a wide variety of literature. The family moved west to Illinois in 1831, but Abraham, now in his early 20s, moved out on his own, settling in New Salem, Illinois. There, he co-owned a store and attempted to begin a political career running, but losing, a race for the Illinois state legislature.

During the 1830s, he also served in the Illinois militia during the Black Hawk War. His eclectic career continued with stints as a land surveyor and postmaster. Eventually, he began teaching himself from legal textbooks, hoping to become a lawyer. His attempts to enter politics succeeded in 1834 when he was elected to the Illinois legislature, where he served four terms and he passed the bar exam in 1836 and moved to Springfield and began his legal career.

Lincoln married Mary Todd in 1840. His political career expanded in 1847, when he served a single term in the U.S. House of Representatives. Returning to Illinois fulltime in 1849, Lincoln continued his legal practice, often representing railroad companies.

He returned to politics in the 1850s, joining the new Republican Party that had emerged following the collapse of the Whigs in 1856. Losing a contest for the U.S. Senate, Lincoln emerged as the moderate Republican nominee for President in 1860. His election triggered the first wave of southern secession and the establishment of the Confederate States of America.

Aside from the Civil War, Lincoln's policies as president reflected the long-standing goals of the defunct Whig party that had been adopted by the Republicans. Lincoln signed into law the Pacific Railways Acts in 1862 and 1864, which provided support from the federal government for a transcontinental railroad. He supported tariffs to promote domestic industrial growth. Under Lincoln's leadership, the federal government issued paper currency for the first time—a move back toward the central banking of earlier decades. Lincoln's track record of business activity and corporate-friendly policies and positions is one reason why his authorship of these document has been challenged.

HISTORICAL DOCUMENT

We may congratulate ourselves that this cruel war is nearing its end. It has cost a vast amount of treasure and blood.... It has indeed been a trying hour for the Republic; but I see in the near future a crisis approaching that unnerves me and causes me to tremble for the safety of my country. As a result of the war, corporations have been enthroned and an era of corruption in high places will follow, and the money power of the country will endeavor to prolong its reign by working upon the prejudices of the people until all wealth is aggregated in a few hands and the Republic is destroyed.

I feel at this moment more anxiety for the safety of my country than ever before, even in the midst of war. God grant that my suspicions may prove groundless.

GLOSSARY

enthroned: placed in a position of power and authority

"the money power": a pejorative term that characterizes the financial elite as a corrupt and destructive influence in American politics

"the Republic": a reference to the United States

Document Analysis

In this brief passage in his letter to Colonel Elkins, the author begins by observing (or, perhaps, hopefully predicting) that the "cruel" Civil War is approaching its conclusion. Despite the massive manhunts of money spent and lives lost in the War, the author claims to be "unnerve[d]" by a future "crisis": the fact that "corporations have been enthroned" is the cause for his concern and he predicts that corruption in "high places" will follow. The "high places" referred to here is left undefined but can reasonably be assumed to refer to corruption in the federal government. The author also outlines his suspicions of a campaign in which the "money power" will exploit divisions and "prejudices" among the American people in an effort to concentrate wealth "in a few hands."

Like the reference to "high places," the discussion of the means and method by which the "money power" will "work" upon the peoples' prejudices is left vague; likewise, the concern that the American republic will be "destroyed" is left up to the imagination. Rhetorically, we see the "money power" referred to in monarchical terms, with terms such as "enthroned" and "reign." This is contrasted with the nation, which is explicitly referred to as "the Republic"—a way of contrasting the sides of the struggle between the wealthy elite and the American people in a manner that causes readers to recall the American War of Independence. The author explains that he is more concerned about these potential developments than about the ongoing Civil War and concludes with a prayer that his "suspicions may prove groundless."

Essential Themes

The vague and almost prophetic nature of this excerpt is akin to what we often see in writing from a viewpoint of conspiracy theory or political paranoia. At the same time, it is also possible to interpret the vagueness as being due to this being a brief personal letter rather than an organized, well thought-out treatise. From the standpoint of late 1864, we can see the roots of the author's concern being clear in the growth of northern industry during the Civil War, supported by the many hundreds of contracts with the federal government for weapons, ammunition, food, uniforms, and other supplies needed for the war effort, in addition to the increasing amount of consumer goods being produced. The war itself provided fuel for the growth of the corporations that the author predicts will be the next enemy of the American people.

—*Aaron Gulyas*

Bibliography and Additional Reading

Appleby, Joyce. *The Relentless Revolution: A History of Capitalism.* New York: W.W. Norton, 2011.

Boritt, Gabor S. *Lincoln and the Economics of the American Dream.* Champaign-Urbana: University of Illinois Press, 1994.

Licht, Walter. *Industrializing America: The Nineteenth Century.* Baltimore: The Johns Hopkins University Press, 1995.

McPherson, James M. *Abraham Lincoln.* London and New York: Oxford University Press, 2009.

■ Documents Relating to Black Friday, 1869

Date: 1869 and September 24, 1869
Authors: Currier & Ives; New York Gold Exchange
Genre: Editorial, report

Summary Overview

The Currier & Ives editorial cartoon reproduced here, along with the picture of the chalkboard tracking gold prices at the New York Gold Exchange, were two images representing one of several scandals occurring during the administration of President Ulysses S. Grant—although this particular one, the financial crash known as Black Friday (1869), was not of Grant's making. Attempts to rig markets that traded in various commodities have happened for centuries. In 1869, two wealthy financiers, Jay Gould and James Fisk, decided to rig the gold market; they also sought at least tacit consent from the president. The scheme seemed to be working well for the two investors until September 24, when Grant determined that the dramatic increase in gold prices was not welcome. The results of the president's actions came to be reflected in the price board, which showed the price of gold peaking at $162.50 at 11:36 a.m., holding most of its value for the next few hours, and then plummeting to $133.375 at 2:52 p.m., when trading closed for a short time. The illustrators Currier & Ives captured the situation by depicting Fisk prodding bulls and bears—symbols of Wall Street growth and decline, respectively—just as Grant comes charging out from the Treasury. Both of these graphic portrayals of events proved effective in conveying the dramatic developments of that day to the public.

Defining Moment

The economic pressures wrought by the Civil War forced great changes on the operation of the government of the United States. In 1861, Congress authorized the printing of paper money, "Demand Notes," to help finance the war. Prior to that, June 1776 had been the last time that paper money (a $2 Continental note) had been authorized by the central government (such as it was at the time). In the interim, currency meant coins, which contained precious metals such as gold or silver; this gave them an intrinsic value in addition to the face value ascribed to them by the federal government. The "Demand Notes" of 1861 were followed in 1862 by "Legal Tender Notes," which were not received enthusiastically by the public. At times during the Civil War, one hundred paper dollars were valued at only thirty-seven gold or silver dollars. In the years after the war, when both forms of currency were still widely circulated, the "exchange" rate settled at about one hundred thirty-seven paper to one hundred gold/silver.

Early in 1869, the price of gold rose to $131, and Jay Gould was able to buy it and make a handsome profit by selling it at $145 before the price settled back to its normal range. This started him thinking about the profits that could be made if gold rose to $200. With James Fisk Jr. as his major partner, Gould began strategically buying gold to force up the price. On September 24, Grant realized that he had been led by Gould into indirectly supporting this scheme, by agreeing to not sell government gold during September. Now Grant, however, authorized the immediate sale of $5-million worth of gold (some sources say $4 million) by the Treasury, an amount that was actually more than the government had on hand (or at least readily available). The authorization served its purpose. The price of gold, which had been at $132 in August, was at $150 on September 10, according to the data on the chalkboard. After fluctuations, the price closed at $145 on September 23. Thus, on the 24 of September gold had a swing from up twelve points to down nine points, before trading was temporarily halted. The price board documented this change, while the cartoon ridiculed Fisk and Gould for the attempt. Yet, Gould had discovered on the 23rd that Grant was considering making a change, which caused him to begin selling more than he was buying. In the end the financier netted about $12 million from his scheme.

Author Biography

Nathan Currier (1813–1888) and James Merritt Ives (1824–1895) were artists and lithographers, running the most successful lithography studio in nineteenth century America. While today, the partnership is best known for its sentimental Victorian-style illustrations of life in the United States, Currier's initial success was in depicting through lithography current and historically significant events. His depictions of disasters, such as the fire at the New York Merchant's Exchange, gained him a contract with the *New York Sun* for weekly prints. This was the venue for the publication of items such as "The Boy of the Period Stirring up the Animals." Ives had joined the firm by the mid-1850s, and became a partner in 1857. His understanding of trends and demands for lithographs was his contribution to the firm. While the two published their own work (which ranged over the breadth of life in the United States), they also brought the work of other artists to the general population, making and coloring lithographs of artists' works. It was estimated that during the pair's partnership, their company produced over 7,000 distinct lithographs, printing hundreds of thousands of copies overall.

The chalkboard was the ongoing record of the prices of transactions and the time of those transactions, kept by the New York Gold Exchange. This was established in 1862, when the government began printing paper money. The New York Gold Exchange became part of the New York Stock Exchange in 1865, and closed its operations in 1897. This board was used as evidence before the Committee of Banking and Currency in 1870, which may explain why the caption, which was written then, mistakenly gives the year of Black Friday as 1870 rather than 1869.

HISTORICAL DOCUMENT

Panic in Gold Room on Black Friday.

SCENE IN THE GOLD ROOM ON "BLACK FRIDAY."

A cartoon showing Jim Fisk stirring up the gold market in New York. Grant is shown running holding a bag of gold. By Currier & Ives, 1869—Library of Congress.

* * *

76 • EARLY EFFORTS—AND FAILINGS

Photograph of the blackboard in the New York Gold Room, September 24, 1869, showing the collapse of the price of gold. Handwritten caption by James A. Garfield indicates it was used as evidence before the Committee of Banking & Currency during hearings in 1870.

GLOSSARY

Black Friday: refers to a day when financial markets collapse, such as Black Friday, September 24, 1869, and Black Monday, October 19, 1987

Document Themes and Analysis

The chalkboard (called a bulletin board in the photo's caption) showing the price of gold during the day of September 24, 1869, was captured in a photograph that was used as evidence in a Congressional hearing occurring in 1870. When Rep. James A. Garfield, as chairperson of the House Committee on Banking and Currency, was given the task of coordinating a full investigation of what had occurred, he made certain that the task was completed in such a manner that Grant, a fellow Republican, might once again have the public's confidence. While there have been times when a dramatic price increase for a stock or commodity has been justified, the significant increase during that month, and even the past twenty-four hours, indicate that the market was not operating efficiently. Prior to September 1869, the U.S. government held weekly gold auctions to keep the supply relatively equal to the demand. However, Gould, making use of Grant's brother-in-law (Abel Corbin) and a political ally (Daniel Butterfield) who was subtreasurer in New York, convinced Grant that it would be beneficial to farmers if the government did not hold gold sales in September. (Many farmers' profits depended on the crop prices, which were pegged to the international price of their crops, with international sales being conducted in gold currency, not paper money; thus with high gold prices, they would be better off when they converted their revenue into paper currency.) When Grant finally realized that he had been tricked and issued an order to release gold from the Treasury, the collapse in prices was reflected on the board. Among other things, the price collapse caused many farmers to lose money on that year's crops. While the judgment of history has been that Grant did not knowingly participate in the plan to corner the gold market, it was one of a number of scandals that seemed to indicate he was an incompetent chief executive.

When Currier and Ives produced their editorial cartoon about the events surrounding Black Friday, they depicted the "zoo" that the New York Gold Exchange (often referred to as the Gold Room) had become. Jim Fisk, a key driver of the turmoil, is shown using a prod to stir up the bears and bulls in the cage. Although it was unclear when, or why, these animals first became associated with an upward market (bull) or a downward market (bear), by the time of this cartoon these images were coming to be widely understood in America. Fisk (the "boy of the period") was attempting to stir up a bull market to get the price of gold to climb another $40. He partially succeeded, by having his agents announce on the morning of September 24 that they would pay $160 for the commodity, up to $1-million worth, hence the inscription on the prod. Fisk is clearly identified by the toy Erie Railroad engine in his hip pocket, a rail line he owned with Gould, and by other possessions of his. Attempting to calm the disturbance, President Grant runs out from the U.S. Treasury building toward the Gold Room, carrying a bag marked "5 million gold." Even without a sale of that much gold, a statement that such a sale could take place is enough to cause a collapse in gold prices.

In this case, when the bursting of the bubble occurred and brought gold prices back to their normal range, it spilled over into the stock market, which similarly lost about 25 percent of its value. The millions that were lost led to great financial hardship, widespread bankruptcies, and some suicides. Because Gould and Fisk were allies of William Marcy Tweed, who controlled New York politics, when they were brought to trial a combination of good lawyers and Tweed-appointed judges meant that they were found innocent on all charges. An 1870 Congressional hearing, in which the picture of the blackboard was used, found President Grant innocent of any involvement in the scheme and identified the true culprits as Gould and Fisk.

—Donald A. Watt

Bibliography and Additional Reading

American Experience. "Black Friday, September 24, 1869." *PBS: American Experience.* Boston: WGBH Educational Foundation, 2018.

Armstrong Economics. "Panic of 1869" *Armstrong Economics.* Princeton: Armstrong Economics, 2018.

Garfield, James A. and the House Committee on Banking and Currency. Investigation into the Causes of the Gold Panic. Report of the majority of the Committee on banking and currency. March 1, 1870. Washington, DC: United States Printing Office, 1870 at Internet Archive. San Francisco: Internet Archive, 2009.

Renehan, Edward J., Jr. *Dark Genius of Wall Street: The Misunderstood Life of Jay Gould, King of the Robber Barons.* New York: Basic Books, 2005.

A Group of Vultures Waiting for the Storm to "Blow Over" – *"Let Us Prey."* Cartoon denouncing the corruption of New York's Boss Tweed and other Tammany Hall figures, drawn in 1871 by Thomas Nast and published in Harper's Weekly.

Verse and Cartoon about Boss Tweed and Tammany Hall

Date: November, 1871; August 19, 1871
Authors: William J. Linton; Thomas Nast
Genre: Political tract; poem; cartoon

Summary Overview

The satirical poem and cartoon reproduced here were only two of numerous attacks (written or drawn) directed against William Marcy "Boss" Tweed, as his grip on political power in New York City faltered during 1871. A leader in New York City politics for almost two decades, and chairman of the Tammany Hall association for eight years, Tweed and his corrupt hold over city politics were held in contempt by many. Cartoonist Thomas Nast was the first major spokesperson (via political cartoons) among those seeking to end the corruption. Linton's poem was written regarding the most visible symbol of Tweed's corruption, the construction of the New York County Courthouse. This external criticism of Tweed and his associates laid the foundation for others critics, some with direct knowledge of Tammany corruption and who became willing to testify against the participants.

Defining Moment

During the 1780s, the Federalist party (or faction) was the prime political movement in American politics. In New York City, a political association was created in opposition to some of the Federalist's views. This was known as Tammany Hall. (Several years later, it became identified with the Democratic Party, continuing in various forms until the 1960s.) Tammany Hall became totally dominant in New York City politics during the 1820s, after it had obtained the right to vote for all white males, rather than just property owners. When William Marcy Tweed moved into leadership positions in the 1850s and '60s, he used the city government as a source of revenue for himself and his friends. Ranging from creating imaginary jobs for friends, who gave Tweed part of their salaries, to kickbacks for city contracts and the hiring of his own companies to do the work at inflated rates, Tweed's schemes served to build his wealth and consolidate his power. At the same time, Tweed used the income provided by such projects to pay off politicians and political operatives in order to keep himself in business.

The misuse of the public trust came to a head when people finally understood what was happening with the construction of the New York County (Manhattan) Courthouse. In 1858, Tweed was the deciding vote to have the Board of Supervisors for New York County, i.e., the city of New York, rather than the state, oversee the building's construction. By 1871, the courthouse was nearing completion, its cost having spiraled to $13 million dollars, including furnishings. During the few years prior to July 1871 (when things began to fall apart for Tweed), Nast and others had been hammering away at the waste and overexpenditures in the courthouse project. In July, the *New York Times* began an exposé on the courthouse construction project in which the actual costs of various phases were documented. Just as the *Times* was printing the "facts," others such as Linton increased their anti-Tweed efforts by poking fun at the man, in this case by adapting a children's rhyme. Taken as a whole, the efforts of Linton, Nast, and others successfully focused public attention on the corruption of Boss Tweed. The result was demonstrated in the 1871 election, when most candidates that had been supported by Tweed and Tammany Hall were soundly defeated. This allowed an indictment of Tweed to move forward, in December 1871, thus bringing to an end his political dominance in New York City. (Tweed and James Ingersoll were the only individuals convicted of crimes related to this project, as the other leaders fled New York until the fervor to prosecute them had died down. Ingersoll was pardoned for his testimony against Tweed.)

Author Biographies

The author of the poem, William James Linton (1812–1897; signing himself "W.M.T." in this case), was born in London, moving to the United States in 1866. He apprenticed as a wood engraver, a profession he practiced throughout his life. He also was a prolific author. In Britain, he was a leader among those who were politically active on the Left, supporting Socialist and Chartist/labor goals, as well as strongly supporting the republican form of government. While obviously not totally abandoning his political writing, once in America he focused on engraving and more commercially viable genres of writing.

Thomas Nast (1840–1902) was born in Landau, Germany, moving to the United States in the late 1840s. His aptitude for drawing was expressed at a young age, and his first published work appeared when he was eighteen.

For fifteen years, beginning in 1862, Nast was a regular contributor to *Harper's Weekly*, with sporadic contributions after that. His cartoons against Tweed began appearing in 1867. His continuing influence includes having created the popular depictions of the figures of Columbia, Uncle Sam, and Santa Claus. He also originated using elephants for Republicans and popularized using donkeys for Democrats.

HISTORICAL DOCUMENT

The House that TWEED Built
Dedicated to Every True Reformer
(Republican or Democrat)
by W. M. T.

This is THE PLASTERER,
Garvey by name,
The Garvey who made it his little game
To lay on the plaster, and plaster it thick
On the roof
And the walls
And the wood
And the brick
Of the wonderful House
That TWEED built.
This is DICK CONNOLLY,
("Slippery Dick,")
Who controll'd the plastering laid on so thick
By the comptroller's plasterer, Garvey by name,
The Garvey who made it his little game
To lay on the plaster, and lay it on thick,
On the roof and the walls
And the wood and the brick
Of the wonderful House
That TWEED built.
This, Sir! is SWEENY, Peter B.,
In the plastering deepest of all the three,
Sweeny,
Garvey,
And Connolly, —
Otherwise known as "Slippery Dick,"
Who controll'd the plastering laid on so thick

From roof to cellar, on wood and brick,
In the wonderful House
That TWEED built.
These are THE CARPETS,
At so much a roll,
Supplied by the firm of Ingersoll,
The very best carpets of Ingersoll's make,
Which some one or other did often take
To the doors of the House that TWEED built.
This is THE METROPOLITAN,
Boss'd, they tell us, by Tweed's young man,
With carpets and furniture, spick and span,
Of the very best patterns of Ingersoll's make,
Like the carpets that somebody else did take
To the doors
Of the House
That TWEED built.
These are THERMOMETERS,
Only a few,
Good to tell you the atmosphere too,
And sold to the City by—never mind who!
You'll find the name on the City Roll,
With Sweeny and Garvey and Ingersoll,
And Connolly (known as "Slippery Dick"),
Who controll'd the plastering laid on so thick
On each blessed inch of wood or brick
Of the wonderful House that TWEED built.
This is BOSS TWEED,
Nast's man with the brains,
The Tammany Atlas who all sustains,
(A Tammany Samson perhaps for his pains,)
Who rules the City where Oakey reigns,

The father of that very nice young man
Who furnish'd the new Metropolitan,
The master of Woodward and Ingersoll
And all of the gang on the City Roll,
And formerly lord of "Slippery Dick,"
Who controll'd the plastering laid on so thick
By the comptroller's plasterer, Garvey by name,
The Garvey whose fame is the little game
Of laying on plaster and knowing the trick
Of charging as if he himself were a brick
Of the well-plaster'd House
That TWEED built ....
THE LAWS OF NEW YORK!
Well, indeed!
They are capital stuffing for cushions for Tweed.
What matter so long as the City is freed,—
Say free of the guild and the guilt and the greed
Of the Halls and the Garveys, the Sweenies and TWEED,
Boss Tweed, Nast's man with the wonderful brains,
The Tammany Atlas that all sustains,
(Tammany's Samson for all his gains,)
Who rules the City where Oakey reigns,
The father of that very nice young man
Who runs the new Metropolitan,
Master of Woodward and Ingersoll,
And all of the gang on the City Roll,
And formerly lord of "Slippery Dick"—
Controller of plastering laid on so thick,
By the controller's plasterer, known to fame
As thickest of plasterers, Garvey by name,
Who plaster'd the House that TWEED built ...

* * *

Only the New Court House

"During the years 1869, 1870, and part of 1871, in which, according to the 'Ring's' own acknowledgment, the sum of about $8,223,979.89 was expended on the new Court House, the legislative appropriation amounts to only $ 1,400,000. From 1858 to 1868 the Legislature appropriated the sum of $4,500,000. .... The building is still incomplete.

"In the neighboring County of Kings there was built, between the fall of 1861 and 1865, when work and materials were at their highest, a court-house which covers within one sixth of the area occupied by that of New York. The structure is of marble, brick, and iron, and the internal furnishing is in most respects equal to and in many superior to that of the New York Court House. The original cost of the building in Brooklyn was $551,758.28, and its cost up to the present time $745,601.54. The cost up to the present time of the unfinished New York Court House would, therefore, be sufficient to build and maintain, during six years, sixteen such court-houses as that of Brooklyn.

"COURT HOUSE.

Furniture ... $1,575,782.96
Carpets, Shades, and Curtains ... 675,534.44
Plastering-work ... 531,594.22
Thermometers ... 7,500.00
Other Items ... 2,780,411.62
$6,052,045.96
Repairs on Wood-work ... $750,071.92
Repairs on Plaster-work ... 1,294,684.13
Repairs on Plumbing-work ... 51,461.75
Repairs, not defined ... 75,716.13
$2,171,933.93"

Printed and Published by the Author at Cambridge, Mass., November, 1871.

GLOSSARY

County of Kings: Borough of Brooklyn

House that Tweed Built: New York County Courthouse (Manhattan)

Nast's man with the brains: a reference to a cartoon by Nast that depicted Tweed with a bag of money in place of his head

82 • EARLY EFFORTS—AND FAILINGS

Nast depicts the Tweed Ring: "Who stole the people's money?" / "'Twas him." From left to right: William Tweed, Peter B. Sweeny, Richard B. Connolly, and Oakey Hall. To the left of Tweed in the background are James H. Ingersoll and Andrew Garvey, city contractors involved with much of the city construction.

Document Themes and Analysis

The Linton poem, based loosely upon the children's verse "This Is the House that Jack Built," was a clever attempt to give its readers information about the New York County Courthouse project in an entertaining format. Knowing that newspaper columns of statistics, such as were printed at the end of the poem, were boring, Linton hoped to hook readers with the comical images created with his words. He alleged that this was written by William Marcy Tweed (Tweed's middle name was actually Magear, but he liked the name Marcy), however it was clear to all that this was *about* him, not by him. Because describing how Tweed took a 65-percent commission on all contracts would have bored readers, Linton began with the most visible excessive charge for a building with marble walls, a charge for plaster. Obviously, Andrew Garvey (a former fireman, whose name was on the plastering contract) did not really "lay on the plaster" to the roof, walls, wood, and brick. This was just an image of what might have been needed to justify the close to $2.9-million charge for plaster, or plaster repairs ($1.3 million even before the building was completed). Having Comptroller (i.e., auditor of expenditures and overseer of contracts) Richard Connolly and Chamberlain (collector and treasurer of public funds) Peter Sweeny, as part of the Tweed Ring of conspirators, made it easier to overcharge or misuse funds, as illustrated by the reference to them in the plastering section.

The reference to James Ingersoll, the individual given the contract for much of the furnishings, in the poem dealt with carpets, which cost more than $600,000. His reason for the high charge was that carpets in public buildings needed to be replaced quite often, although only a small section of the building was actually open by 1871. On another bill, Ingersoll charged the city just under $180,000 for three tables and forty chairs. Tweed placed eleven thermometers in the courthouse, with the scale being crudely drawn on paper, charging $7,500 for materials estimated to cost just over $12.

Linton referred to Boss Tweed as "Nast's man with the brains" and "The Tammany Atlas who all sustains," or the one who is at the head of the organization. The bag of money, which replaced Tweed's head in one of Nast's political cartoons, demonstrates what was on the minds of most of the men in the corruption ring. According to Linton's description, Tweed was the one inspiring the others with his greed. As for legal considerations, Linton states that laws served merely as "stuffing for cushions" as far as Tweed was concerned. He and his ring of associates ignored legal as well as moral limits when it came to their actions. As shown by the numbers listed after the poem, there was a large amount of money to be made via courthouse construction corruption. The Tammany Hall Ring was able to make millions from this one project, with some people having estimated the total amount skimmed from all Tweed-related projects to be, conservatively judged, in excess of $75 million, and possibly as high as $200 million (both astronomical sums for that era).

Thomas Nast's famous "Who Stole the People's Money—Twas Him" was printed within a month after the *New York Times* had published its exposé of Tweed. In a period when not everyone was literate, Tweed feared the cartoons that Nast produced about him because, of course, everyone could understand pictures. Tweed was so furious with Nast that, in 1871, he attempted to bribe the cartoonist with an offer of a fully paid European vacation in exchange for ceasing publication.

In this particular cartoon the figures in front, where the main focus is, represent Tweed, Peter Sweeny, Richard Connolly, and Abraham Oakey Hall. To the left of Tweed are James Ingersoll and Andrew Garvey. Because the term the *Tweed Ring* was used for the group dominating New York City politics and making millions of dollars on the courthouse project, it was logical for Nast to place Tweed and his associates in a circle. This helped to reinforce their identity for those who were unable to read the captions.

The message of the cartoon is clear; no one wanted to take responsibility for the cost overruns and inflated prices. The image shows that the Tweed Ring believed these things were part of the normal cost of doing business in the city/county. Most of the other individuals in the circle carry the names of companies that were involved in the courthouse project. However, one individual standing third on the right-hand side is labeled "Tom, Dick & Harry"—to demonstrate just how widespread the corruption was.

This cartoon has been seen as one of the most powerful in sending a political message and played a major role in undercutting Tweed. As clearly understood by Tweed, Nast was the preeminent political cartoonist of the 1860s and 1870s, and his work had a major impact on how average people understood this scheme and other current events. When Nast began focusing his work on Tweed in 1870, he became part of a growing number of forces that ultimately pushed Tweed out of power.

—*Donald A. Watt*

Bibliography and Additional Reading

Ashby, Ruth. *Boss Tweed and Tammany Hall.* San Diego, CA: Blackbirch Press, 2002.

Callow, Alexander B. "The House That Tweed Built." *American Heritage.* Rockville, MD: American Heritage Publishing Company, 1965.

Golway, Terry. *Machine Made: Tammany Hall and the Creation of Modern American Politics.* New York: Liveright Publishing Corporation, 2014.

Halloran, Fiona Deans. *Thomas Nast: The Father of Modern Political Cartoons.* Chapel Hill: The University of North Carolina Press, 2013.

Hendrick, Burton J. "William James Linton." *The New England Magazine.* Boston: Bay State Monthly Company, April, 1898.

Linton, William J. *The House That Tweed Built.* Ann Arbor, MI: Hathi Trust Digital Library, 1871.

■ Crédit Mobilier Scandal

Date: 1873
Author: Representative Luke Potter Poland
Genre: Government document

Summary Overview

Crédit Mobilier was the name of a construction company established by the Union Pacific Railroad in the wake of the passage of the Pacific Railway Act in 1862. That construction company was secretly controlled by the same men who ran the Union Pacific. As a result, it won many contracts to build the Transcontinental Railroad through noncompetitive bidding. The scandal broke in 1872 when the *New York Sun* revealed that railroad executives had bribed Republican congressman and then vice president of the United States, Schuyler Colfax. Another prominent Republican, Oakes Ames of Massachusetts, had sold significantly underpriced stock to congressmen in return for the passage of legislation favorable to the company. While many congressmen were implicated in the scandal, little punishment resulted from it.

Defining Moment

Crédit Mobilier was originally an investment company named the Pennsylvania Fiscal Agency. It was purchased by Thomas Durant, vice president of the Union Pacific Railroad, in 1864 and renamed the same as a French firm to make its actions harder to follow. It performed contract work for the Union Pacific Railroad even though it was largely controlled by many of the same investors as the railroad was. This relationship remained secret until the scandal broke in September 1872.

The *New York Sun* broke the story of the Crédit Mobilier scandal in a story about a Philadelphia lawsuit by Congressman Henry S. McComb against the men who controlled the Crédit Mobilier Company. He accused Congressman Oakes Ames of distributing stock to his fellow legislators. All this came at the height of President Ulysses Grant's reelection campaign and included Grant's outgoing vice president, Schuyler Colfax, and his incoming vice president, Henry Wilson—both of whom had been named as recipients of the stock. While the scandal did not stop Grant from winning reelection, it was the subject of an immediate congressional investigation.

Two congressional committees investigated the scandal: one in the House of Representatives, the other in the Senate. These committees investigated a total of thirteen members. They reached their conclusions very quickly—by late February 1873. Despite obvious evidence for congressmen having taken bribes, only two legislators, Ames (a Republican) and James Brooks of New York (a Democrat), were censured. Another representative named in the report was the future president James A. Garfield, who at the time was a (Republican) representative from Ohio.

None of the money that any of the congressmen earned from Crédit Mobilier stock was ever recovered. When the government threatened to sue the Union Pacific Railroad to make recovery possible, a federal court ruled that it had no standing. It did alter the railroad's charter to make further stock issuance more difficult, leaving the company at a competitive disadvantage.

Crédit Mobilier was the largest scandal of the Ulysses S. Grant administration and a defining moment in the history of the Republican Party. It demonstrated that many of the party's members cared as much about self-enrichment as they did about building a transcontinental railroad or ensuring the civil rights of black southerners. The affair was scandalous for at least three reasons. First, there was the flat-out bribery. Second, there was the sale of discounted stock to congressmen in exchange for favors. Third, they got caught red-handed.

Moreover, the scandal exposed the shady connection between the Union Pacific Railroad and Crédit Mobilier. Many people had expected more of a major railroad, viewing it as a responsible steward of the public's interest and the federal government's money. Instead, the Union Pacific men schemed to have Crédit Mobilier build the railroad at far above cost. In doing so, they both exploited government funding (which provided a variety of supports) and raked in excess profits on the basis of

86 • EARLY EFFORTS—AND FAILINGS

Dale Creek Bridge Union Pacific Railroad Company. (Andrew J. Russell, completed in 1868)

the shares they owned in Crédit Mobilier, whose stock value soared as a result of the growth in business. Both the owners and their friends in Congress benefited from the arrangement. Besides promoting favorable legislation, the owners' distribution of stock to legislators was supposed to curtail the possibility that Congress would investigate the relationship between these two firms.

The disputes between Ames and Vice President Colfax was particularly interesting. Colfax claimed he never earned any dividends on the stock he received. Ames claimed to have given it to him. One of them was lying, and a parallel deposit in his bank account strongly suggested that it was Colfax. Nevertheless, President Grant would send Colfax a letter attesting to his integrity. When that letter was published, Grant looked as if he had been taken advantage of by his associate, which was something that happened to Grant fairly often in his career. Grant's name would be tarnished by the scandal because it occurred during his administration even though he had nothing to do with its operation and obtained no benefit from the corruption himself.

While accepting bribes was illegal, Crédit Mobilier itself had broken no laws despite its cozy relationship with Union Pacific; its bids always remained just under the legal maximums, and there was no rule or regulation stating that the railroad had to build the transcontinental line at the lowest cost possible. However, the lavish salaries paid to executives, whose relationship with the company had to be kept secret, suggested knowledge of unethical behavior, if not outright violations of law.

Crédit Mobilier was the inspiration for one of two scandals featured in the famous novel *The Gilded Age: A Tale of Today*, published in 1873 by Mark Twain and Charles Dudley Warner. The scandal, then, is not just a notable historical event but one of the defining sociopolitical events of the era.

Author Biography

Representative Luke Potter Poland was a Republican congressman from Vermont who served from 1867 to 1875. He had briefly served in the U.S. Senate, replacing a Senator who had died in office, before being denied reappointment. He also chaired a committee investigating the outrages of the Ku Klux Klan and another concerning Reconstruction measures in Arkansas.

The official poster announcing the Pacific Railroad's grand opening.

HISTORICAL DOCUMENT

In order to [gain] a clear understanding of the facts hereinafter stated as to contracts and dealings in reference to stock of the Crédit Mobilier of America, between Mr. Oakes Ames and others, and members of Congress, it is necessary to make a preliminary statement of the connection of that company with the Union Pacific Railroad Company, and their relations to each other.

The Company called the "Crédit Mobilier of America" was incorporated by the legislature of Pennsylvania, and in 1864 control of its charter and franchises had been obtained by certain persons interested in the Union Pacific Railroad Company, for the purpose of using it as a construction company to build the Union Pacific road. In September, 1864, a contract was entered into between the Union Pacific Company and H. M. Hoxie, for the building by said Hoxie of one hundred miles of said road from Omaha west.

This contract was at once assigned by Hoxie to the Crédit Mobilier Company, as it was expected to be when made. Under this contract and extensions of it some two or three hundred miles of road were built by the Crédit Mobilier Company, but no considerable profits appear to have been realized therefrom. The enterprise of building a railroad to the Pacific was of such vast magnitude, and was beset by so many hazards and risks, that the capitalists of the country were generally averse to investing in it, and, notwithstanding the liberal aid granted by the Government, it seemed likely to fail of completion.

In 1865 or 1866, Mr. Oakes Ames, then and now a member of the House from the State of Massachusetts, and his brother Oliver Ames, became interested in the Union Pacific Company and also in the Crédit Mobilier Company as the agents for the construction of the road. The Messrs. Ames were men of very large capital, and of known character and integrity in business. By their example and credit, and the personal efforts of Mr. Oakes Ames, many men of capital were induced to embark in the enterprise, and to take stock in the Union Pacific Company and also in the Crédit Mobilier Company. Among them were the firm of S. Hooper & Co., of Boston, the leading member of which, Mr. Samuel Hooper, was then and is now a member of the House; Mr. John B. Alley, then a member of the House from Massachusetts, and Mr. Grimes, then a Senator from the State of Iowa. Notwithstanding the vigorous efforts of Mr. Ames and others interested with him, great difficulty was experienced in securing the required capital.

In the spring of 1867 the Crédit Mobilier Company voted to add 50 per cent. to their capital stock, which was then two and a half millions of dollars; and to cause it to be readily taken, each subscriber to it was entitled to receive as a bonus an equal amount of first-mortgage bonds of the Union Pacific Company. The old stockholders were entitled to take this increase, but even the favorable terms offered did not induce all the old stockholders to take it, and the stock of the Crédit Mobilier Company was never considered worth its par value until after the execution of the Oakes Ames contract hereinafter mentioned.

On the 16th day of August, 1867, a contract was executed between the Union Pacific Railroad Company and Oakes Ames, by which Mr. Ames contracted to build six hundred and sixty-seven miles of the Union Pacific road at prices ranging from $42,000 to $96,000 per mile, amounting in the aggregate to $47,000,000. Before the contract was entered into it was understood that Mr. Ames was to transfer it to seven trustees, who were to execute it, and the profits of the contract were to be divided among the stockholders in the Crédit Mobilier Company, who should comply with certain conditions set out in the instrument transferring the contract to the trustees. The Ames contract and the transfer to trustees are incorporated in the evidence submitted, and therefore further recital of their terms is not deemed necessary.

Substantially, all the stockholders of the Crédit Mobilier complied with the conditions named in the transfer, and thus became entitled to share in any profits said trustees might make in executing the contract.

All the large stockholders in the Union Pacific were also stockholders in the Crédit Mobilier, and the Ames contract and its transfer to trustees were ratified by the Union Pacific, and received the assent of the great body of stockholders, but not of all.

After the Ames contract had been executed, it was expected by those interested that by reason of the enormous prices agreed to be paid for the work very large profits would be derived from building the road, and very soon the stock of the Crédit Mobilier was understood by those holding it to be worth much more than its par value. The stock was not in the market and had no fixed market-value, but the holders of it, in December, 1867, considered it worth at least double the par value, and in January and February, 1868, three or four times the par value, but it does not appear that these facts were generally or publicly known, or that the holders of the stock desired they should be.

The foregoing statement the committee think gives enough of the historic details, and condition and value of the stock, to make the following detailed facts intelligible:

Mr. Oakes Ames was then a member of the House of Representatives, and came to Washington at the commencement of the session, about the beginning of December, 1867. During that month Mr. Ames entered into contracts with a considerable number of members of Congress, both Senators and Representatives, to let them have shares of stock in the Crédit Mobilier Company at par, with interest thereon from the first day of the previous July. It does not appear that in any instance he asked any of these persons to pay a higher price than the par value and interest, nor that Mr. Ames used any special effort or urgency to get these persons to take it. In all these negotiations Mr. Ames did not enter into any details as to the value of the stock or the amount of dividend that might be expected upon it, but stated generally that it would be good stock, and in several instances said he would guarantee that they should get at least 10 per cent. on their money.

Some of these gentlemen, in their conversations with Mr. Ames, raised the question whether becoming holders of this stock would bring them into any embarrassment as members of Congress in their legislative action. Mr. Ames quieted such suggestions by saying it could not for the Union Pacific had received from Congress all the grants and legislation it wanted, and they should ask for nothing more. In some instances those members who contracted for stock paid to Mr. Ames the money for the price of the stock, par and interest; in others, where they had not the money, Mr. Ames agreed to carry the stock for them until they could get the money or it should be met by the dividends.

Mr. Ames was at this time a large stockholder in the Crédit Mobilier, but he did not intend any of these transactions to be sales of his own stock, but intended to fulfill all these contracts from stock belonging to the company.

At this time there were about six hundred and fifty shares of the stock of the company, which had for some reason been placed in the name of Mr. T. C. Durant, one of the leading and active men of the concern.

Mr. Ames claimed that a portion of this stock should be assigned to him to enable him to fulfill engagements he had made for stock. Mr. Durant claimed that he had made similar engagements that he should be allowed stock to fulfill. Mr. McComb, who was present at the time, claimed that he had also made engagements for stock which he should have stock given him to carry out. This claim of McComb was refused, but after the stock was assigned to Mr. Ames, McComb insisted that Ames should distribute some of the stock to his (McComb's) friends, and named Senators Bayard and Fowler, and Representatives Allison and Wilson, of Iowa.

It was finally arranged that three hundred and forty-three shares of the stock of the company should be transferred to Mr. Ames to enable him to perform his engagements, and that number of shares were set over on the books of the company to Oakes Ames, trustee, to distinguish it from the stock held by him before. Mr. Ames at the time paid to the company the par of the stock and interest from the July previous, and this stock still stands on the books in the name of Oakes Ames, trustee, except thirteen shares which have been transferred to parties in no way connected with Congress. The committee do not find that Mr. Ames had any negotiation whatever with any of these members of Congress on the subject of this stock prior to the session of December, 1867, except Mr. Scott and it was not claimed that any obligation him as the result of it …

The members of Congress with whom he dealt were generally those who had been friendly and favorable to a Pacific Railroad, and Mr. Ames did not fear or expect to find them favorable to movements hostile to it; but he desired to stimulate their activity and watchfulness in opposition to any unfavorable action by giving them a personal interest in the success of the enterprise, especially so far as it affected the interest of the Crédit Mobilier Company. On the 9th day of December, 1867, Mr. C. C. Washburn, of Wisconsin, introduced in the House a bill to regulate by law the rates of transportation over the Pacific Railroad.

Mr. Ames, as well as others interested in the Union Pacific road, was opposed to this, and desired to defeat it. Other measures apparently hostile to that company were subsequently introduced into the House by Mr. Washburn of Wisconsin, and Mr. Washburne of Illinois. The committee believe that Mr. Ames, in his distributions of stock, had specially in mind the hostile efforts of the Messrs. Washburn, and desired to gain strength to secure their defeat. The reference in one of his letters to "Washburn's move" makes this quite apparent.

The foregoing is deemed by the committee a sufficient statement of facts as to Mr. Ames, taken in connection with what will be subsequently stated of his transactions with particular persons.

[Source: United States House of Representatives, "Report of the Select Committee to Investigate the Alleged Crédit Mobilier Bribery ... ." Washington, D.C.: Government Printing Office, 1873.]

GLOSSARY

dividend: a share of profits paid to a stockholder

par value: the stated minimum price of a firm and/or holdings; face value

Pacific Railroad Bond, City and County of San Francisco, 1865.

92 • EARLY EFFORTS—AND FAILINGS

Editorial cartoon: Uncle Sam directs U.S. Congressmen implicated in the Crédit Mobilier scheme to commit hara-kiri. (Joseph Ferdinand Keppler - Frank Leslie's Illustrated Newspaper, *March 8, 1873, p. 420)*

Document Themes and Analysis

The story of the Crédit Mobilier scandal has confused people ever since it happened. The railroad executive Charles Francis Adams' assessment is a good one: "They receive money into one hand as a corporation, and pay it out into the other as a contractor." Like that Adams quotation, the section of the House Special Select Committee Report on the scandal is notable because of how simply the committee tells the story of the governmental portion of the scandal. For example, the reason for the corruption was the difficulty in completing the task at hand—namely, building the railroad. Few investors thought that the Central Pacific and Union Pacific Railroads—two firms stocked with amateurs—would complete the project successfully. The corruption that emerged served to make investing in the railroad more lucrative, so that the operation attracted crucial capital. The congressmen involved in the project acted to protect the capital and subsidize the investment, since they benefitted from growing stock values.

Giving stock to congressmen was a good way of keeping that money flowing. That explains why this House report on the scandal focuses on Oakes Ames. Crédit Mobilier stock was not available on the open market. Purchasing it from Ames was the only way that it could be obtained. Ames kept a large portion of stock for himself while distributing it to others and holding it for those who couldn't quite afford it.

Oakes Ames was a very wealthy man before he entered Congress and began looking into profiting from the building of the Union Pacific Railroad. Ames actually contracted to take over the building of a large section of the road himself—a move that would have been scandalous had a sitting politician attempted it; but he ended up subcontracting that responsibility. Ames personally enticed many investors to participate in the project.

This section of Representative Poland's House report also explains why relatively few members of Congress were prosecuted. It is possible to appreciate the leniency shown a class of naïve legislator who got involved in the affair but did not necessarily know how business worked or that anything was amiss. Ames method of distributing the stock made it seem as though everything was above board, for the Union Pacific "had received from Congress all the grants and legislation it wanted." Crédit Mobilier, on the other hand, had not. Yet, because the personnel in the two companies were identical, the companies' interests were identical as well. Sophisticated investors understood that fact. Less experienced legislators did not.

On the other hand, many of the major investors whom Ames attracted were not just politicians looking to make extra money. They were wealthy men who just happened to be politicians willing to use their power to benefit their investment. Representative Samuel Hooper, for example, ran S. Hooper & Company in Boston. He almost certainly knew exactly what was going on. While there was outrage about the extent of this scandal, the relatively calm reaction even of a House select committee demonstrates that the American public was not so unwound by financial misdoings as to demand complete and systematic government ethics reform. The scandal did, however, inspire a number of lesser reform efforts—by the Grangers and civil service reformers—which did bear fruit in the ensuing years.

—*Jonathan Rees*

Bibliography and Additional Reading

Chernow, Ron. *Grant*. New York: Penguin, 2017.

"Poland, Luke Potter." In Virtual American Biographies.

Richardson, Heather Cox. *West from Appomattox: The Reconstruction of America After the Civil War*. New Haven, CT: Yale University Press, 2007.

White, Richard. *Railroaded: The Transcontinentals and the Making of Modern America*. New York: Norton, 2011.

Hayes kicking Chester A. Arthur out of the New York Custom House. (Frederick Burr Opper - United States Library of Congress's Prints and Photographs division)

Pendleton Civil Service Reform Act

Date: 1883
Author: George Hunt Pendleton
Genre: Legislation

Summary Overview

The Pendleton Civil Service Reform Act was reform legislation designed in reaction to the "spoils system," the corrupt way that people commonly got chosen for federal jobs. The act classified certain government jobs and put them under the oversight of a Civil Service Commission. That commission administered competitive examinations in order to guarantee that those selected were qualified to perform those duties instead of getting their jobs through personal connections or bribes. The law also structured a nonpartisan system for federal job holders to advance to better jobs within the government. Under the act, presidents could add jobs to the list of positions covered by the legislation—which they tended to do immediately before leaving the presidency to preserve positions against change by an incoming administration of the opposite party.

Defining Moment

The framers of the Constitution did not anticipate the party system. Therefore, there was no system in place at the beginning of the republic to deal with the massive influx of new office holders who came in when control of the presidency switched between parties. Staring with Andrew Jackson, scores of new office holders came in as part of a spoils system. Many of these new political appointments were poorly qualified and the effectiveness of the federal government—everything from the Department of State to the Post Office—suffered as a result.

The Spoils System meant that people who had no qualifications received appointments for government jobs and did those jobs badly. The collection of taxes, particularly of tariffs at ports, was so corrupt that the U.S. government lost an untold fortune in revenue every year. Pre–Pendleton Act civil servants were dependent upon patrons with political positions in order to keep their jobs, which bred corruption in otherwise ethical government employees. They were often forced to contribute money to the campaigns of their patrons and other politicians who belonged to the same party. Because of so much malfeasance, morale among civil servants was often very low.

Two of the most important reasons for the passage of the Pendleton Act were the numerous scandals that had surrounded the administration of Ulysses S. Grant (in office 1869–77) and the huge loss for Republicans in the midterm elections of 1882. However, the greatest impetus for the passage of the act was the assassination, in 1881, of President James A. Garfield of Ohio by Charles Guiteau, a disgruntled office seeker. Civil service reformers like George Hunt Pendleton, also of Ohio, used the assassination to stoke public opinion in support of reform, bringing on the defeat of Republicans in the midterms of 1882. The lame duck Congress passed Pendleton's bill early the next year.

The new president, Chester Arthur, had benefitted greatly from the spoils system as Collector of the Port of New York, one of the most potentially lucrative positions in the entire federal government at a time when that government depended primarily upon tariffs for its revenues. Nevertheless, Arthur championed the Pendleton Act through Congress even as Congress rejected most of his other ideas for reform. The law not only protected future executives from disgruntled office seekers, but by giving them less discretion in making appointments they could devote more of their energy to more important matters of state.

The passage of the Pendleton Act allowed Republicans to pose as reformers during the 1884 election and to lock in as many officeholders as possible when the tide turned towards Democrats. To the surprise of many observers, President Chester Arthur quickly accepted nearly all the rules implemented by the Civil Service Commission before leaving office, making the system much more effective than it might have been had he held on to partisan interests on his way into retirement.

The first real test of the Pendleton Act came when Democrat Grover Cleveland became president in 1885. Despite partisans clamoring for new jobs, Cleveland agreed to abide by the act's provisions. He also promised not to fire people from positions outside of the civil service system except for cause. Cleveland's scrupulousness in filling civil service jobs won him many new enemies within his own party. William McKinley actually took jobs out of the civil service system, but this did not change the overall trend towards increased coverage. The Pendleton Act became the basis for civil service reform at the state and local levels.

The Pendleton Act covered relatively few federal workers upon its immediate passage, but presidents greatly expanded its scope over time. By 1900, over half the jobs in the federal government were covered by the Pendleton Act. The reason for this was that with each change of party in the presidency, the chief executive from the outgoing party would use his power under the Pendleton Act to insulate his appointees from being fired by the incoming president. The Pendleton Act still serves as the basis for the civil service today. Out of approximately 2.7 million federal workers, over 90 percent are covered by the civil service protections the act put in place. As the number of civil service positions grew, the social class of the people who served in the civil service rose as its reputation improved.

After the passage of the Pendleton Act, actions that seemed scandalous but were not really illegal became so.

The Pendleton Act was one of the first good government measures embraced by Republican reformers derisively dismissed at the time as "Goo-Goos" ("good government guys"). Its effective implementation and gradual expansion quickly put an end to the movement for civil service reform. Theodore Roosevelt served on the U.S. Civil Service Commission from 1889–95.

Author Biography

Born in 1825, George Hunt Pendleton was a Democratic Ohio congressman beginning in 1856. His opposition to the Union effort during the Civil War made him one of the nation's most prominent "Copperheads." He was prominent enough, in fact, that George McClellan selected him to run for vice president during McClellan's unsuccessful bid to unseat President Abraham Lincoln in 1864. After running unsuccessfully for other offices, Pendleton became a U.S. Senator from Ohio in 1878. While in office, he championed civil service reform.

Pendleton's campaign for civil service reform made him unpopular with members of his own party who favored the spoils system. As a result, he lost reelection to the Senate in 1884 at a time when U.S. senators were still elected by politicians serving in state legislatures rather than by the people at large. President Grover Cleveland appointed Pendleton as ambassador to Germany in 1885. Pendleton died while returning home from that appointment in 1889.

HISTORICAL DOCUMENT

An act to regulate and improve the civil service of the United States.

Be it enacted by the Senate and House of Representatives of the United States of America in Congress assembled, That the President is authorized to appoint, by and with the advice and consent of the Senate, three persons, not more than two of whom shall be adherents of the same party, as Civil Service Commissioners, and said three commissioners shall constitute the United States Civil Service Commission. Said commissioners shall hold no other official place under the United States.

The President may remove any commissioner; and any vacancy in the position of commissioner shall be so filled by the President, by and with the advice and consent of the Senate, as to conform to said conditions for the first selection of commissioners.

The commissioners shall each receive a salary of three thousand five hundred dollars a year. And each of said commissioners shall be paid his necessary traveling expenses incurred in the discharge of his duty as a commissioner.

SEC. 2. That it shall be the duty of said commissioners:

FIRST. To aid the President, as he may request, in preparing suitable rules for carrying this act into effect, and when said rules shall have been promulgated it shall be the duty of all officers of the United States in the departments and offices to which any such rules may relate to aid, in all proper ways, in carrying said rules, and any modifications thereof; into effect.

SECOND. And, among other things, said rules shall provide and declare, as nearly as the conditions of good administration will warrant, as follows:

First, for open, competitive examinations for testing the fitness of applicants for the public service now classified or to be classified here-under. Such examinations shall be practical in their character, and so far as may be shall relate to those matters which will fairly test the relative capacity and fitness of the persons examined to discharge the duties of the service into which they seek to be appointed.

Second, that all the offices, places, and employments so arranged or to be arranged in classes shall be filled by selections according to grade from among those graded highest as the results of such competitive examinations.

Third, appointments to the public service aforesaid in the departments at Washington shall be apportioned among the several States and Territories and the District of Columbia upon the basis of population as ascertained at the last preceding census. Every application for an examination shall contain, among other things, a statement, under oath, setting forth his or her actual bona fide residence at the time of making the application, as well as how long he or she has been a resident of such place.

Fourth, that there shall be a period of probation before any absolute appointment or employment aforesaid.

Fifth, that no person in the public service is for that reason under any obligations to contribute to any political fund, or to render any political service, and that he will not be removed or otherwise prejudiced for refusing to do so.

Sixth, that no person in said service has any right to use his official authority or influence to coerce the political action of any person or body.

Seventh, there shall be non-competitive examinations in all proper cases before the commission, when competent persons do not compete, after notice has been given of the existence of the vacancy, under such rules as may be prescribed by the commissioners as to the manner of giving notice.

Eighth, that notice shall be given in writing by the appointing power to said commission of the persons selected for appointment or employment from among those who have been examined, of the place of residence of such persons, of the rejection of any such persons after probation, of transfers, resignations, and removals and of the date thereof, and a record of the same shall be kept by said commission. And any necessary exceptions from said eight fundamental provisions of the rules shall be set forth in connection with such rules, and the reasons there-for shall be stated in the annual reports of the commission.

THIRD. Said commission shall, subject to the rules that may be made by the President, make regulations for, and have control of, such examinations, and, through its members or the examiners, it shall supervise and preserve the records of the same; and said commission shall keep minutes of its own proceedings.

FOURTH. Said commission may make investigations concerning the facts, and may report upon all matters touching the enforcement and effects of said rules and regulations, and concerning the action of any examiner or board of examiners hereinafter provided for, and its own subordinates, and those in the public service, in respect to the execution of this act.

FIFTH. Said commission shall make an annual report to the President for transmission to Congress, showing its own action, the rules and regulations and the exceptions thereto in force, the practical effects thereof, and any suggestions it may approve for the more effectual accomplishment of the purposes of this act.

SEC. 3. That said commission is authorized to employ a chief examiner, a part of whose duty it shall be, under its direction, to act with the examining boards, so far as practicable, whether at Washington or elsewhere, and to secure accuracy, uniformity, and justice in all their proceedings, which shall be at all times open to him. The chief examiner shall be entitled to receive a salary at the rate of three thousand dollars a year, and he shall be paid his necessary traveling expenses incurred in the discharge of his duty The commission shall have a secretary, to be appointed by the President, who shall receive a salary of one thousand six hundred dollars per annum. It may, when necessary, employ a stenographer, and a messenger, who shall be paid, when employed, the former at the rate of one thousand six hundred dollars a year, and the latter at the rate of six hundred dollars a year. The commission shall, at Washington, and in one or more places in each State and Territory where examinations are to take place, designate and select a suitable number of persons, not less than three, in the official service of the United States, residing in said State or Territory, after consulting the head of the department or office in which such persons serve, to be members of boards of examiners, and may at any time substitute any other person in said service living in such State or Territory in the place of anyone so selected. Such boards of examiners shall be so located as to make it reasonably convenient and inexpensive for applicants to attend before them; and where there are persons to be examined in any State or Territory, examinations shall be held therein at least twice in each year. It shall be the duty of the collector, postmaster, and other officers of the United States at any place outside of the District of Columbia where examinations are directed by the President or by said board to be held, to allow the reasonable use of the public buildings for holding such examinations, and in all proper ways to facilitate the same.

SEC. 4. That it shall be the duty of the Secretary of the Interior to cause suitable and convenient rooms and accommodations to be assigned or provided, and to be furnished, heated, and lighted, at the city of Washington, for carrying on the work of said commission and said examinations, and to cause the necessary stationery and other articles to be supplied, and the necessary printing to be done for said commission.

SEC. 5. That any said commissioner, examiner, copyist, or messenger, or any person in the public service who shall willfully and corruptly, by himself or in co-operation with one or more other persons, defeat, deceive, or obstruct any person in respect of his or her right of examination according to any such rules or regulations, or who shall willfully, corruptly, and falsely mark, grade, estimate, or report upon the examination or proper standing of any person examined hereunder, or aid in so doing, or who shall willfully and corruptly make any false representations concerning the same or concerning the person examined, or who shall willfully and corruptly furnish to any person any special or secret information for the purpose of either improving or injuring the prospects or chances of any person so examined, or to be examined, being appointed, employed, or promoted, shall for each such offense be deemed guilty of a misdemeanor, and upon conviction thereof, shall be punished by a fine of not less than one hundred dollars, nor more than one thousand dollars, or by imprisonment not less than ten days, nor more than one year, or by both such fine and imprisonment.

SEC. 6. That within sixty days after the passage of this act it shall be the duty of the Secretary of the Treasury, in as near conformity as may be to the classification of certain clerks now existing under the one hundred and sixty-third section of the Revised Statutes to arrange in classes the several clerks and persons employed by the collector, naval officer, surveyor, and appraisers, or either of them, or being in the public service, at their respective offices in each customs district where the whole number of said clerks and persons shall be all together as many as fifty. And thereafter, from time to time, on the direction of the President, said Secretary shall make the like classification or arrangement of clerks and persons so employed, in connection with any said office or offices, in any other customs district. And, upon like request, and for the purposes of this act, said Secretary shall arrange in one or more of said classes, or of existing classes, any other clerks, agents, or persons employed under his department in any said district not now classified; and every such arrangement and classification upon being made shall be reported to the President.

Second. Within said sixty days it shall be the duty of the Postmaster-General, in general conformity to said one hundred and sixty-third section, to separately arrange in classes the several clerks and persons employed, or in the public service at each post-office, or under any postmaster of the United States, where the whole number of said clerks and persons shall together amount to as many as fifty. And thereafter, from time to time, on the direction of the President, it shall be the duty of the Postmaster-General to arrange in like classes the clerks and persons so employed in the postal service in connection with any other post-office; and every such arrangement and classification upon being made shall be reported to the President.

Third. That from time to time said Secretary, the Postmaster-General, and each of the heads of departments mentioned in the one hundred and fifty-eighth section of the Revised Statutes, and each head of an office, shall, on the direction of the President, and for facilitating the execution of this act, respectively revise any then existing classification or arrangement of those in their respective departments and offices, and shall, for the purposes of the examination herein provided for, include in one or more of such classes, so far as practicable, subordinate places, clerks, and officers in the public service pertaining to their respective departments not before classified for examination.

SEC. 7. That after the expiration of six months from the passage of this act no officer or clerk shall be appointed, and no person shall be employed to enter or be promoted in either of the said classes now existing, or that may be arranged hereunder pursuant to said rules, until he has passed an examination, or is shown to be specially exempted from such examination in conformity herewith. But nothing herein contained shall be construed to take from those honorably discharged from the military or naval service any preference conferred by the seventeen hundred and fifty-fourth section of the Revised Statutes, nor to take from the President any authority not inconsistent with this act conferred by the seventeen hundred and fifty-third section of said statutes; nor shall any officer not in the executive branch of the government, or any person merely employed as a laborer or workman, be required to be classified hereunder; nor, unless by direction of the Senate, shall any person who has been nominated for confirmation by the Senate be required to be classified or to pass an examination.

SEC. 8. That no person habitually using intoxicating beverages to excess shall be appointed to, or retained in, any office, appointment, or employment to which the provisions of this act are applicable.

SEC. 9. That whenever there are already two or more members of a family in the public service in the grades covered by this act, no other member of such family shall be eligible to appointment to any of said grades.

SEC. 10. That no recommendation of any person who shall apply for office or place under the provisions of this act which may be given by any Senator or member of the House of Representatives, except as to the character or residence of the applicant, shall be received or considered by any person concerned in making any examination or appointment under this act.

SEC. 11. That no Senator, or Representative, or Territorial Delegate of the Congress, or Senator, Representative, or Delegate elect, or any officer or employee of either of said houses, and no executive, judicial, military, or naval officer of the United States, and no clerk or employee of any department, branch or bureau of the executive, judicial, or military or naval service of the United States, shall, directly or indirectly, solicit or receive, or be in any manner concerned ill soliciting or receiving, any assessment, subscription, or contribution for any political purpose whatever, from any officer, clerk, or employee of the United States, or any department, branch, or bureau thereof, or from any person receiving any salary or compensation from moneys derived from the Treasury of the United States.

SEC. 12. That no person shall, in any room or building occupied in the discharge of official duties by any officer or employee of the United States mentioned in this act, or in any navy-yard, fort, or arsenal, solicit in any manner whatever, or receive any contribution of money or any other thing of value for any political purpose whatever.

SEC. 13. No officer or employee of the United States mentioned m this act shall discharge, or promote, or degrade, or in manner change the official rank or compensation of any other officer or employee, or promise or threaten so to do, for giving or withholding or neglecting to make any contribution of money or other valuable thing for any political purpose.

SEC. 14. That no officer, clerk, or other person in the service of the United States shall, directly or indirectly, give or hand over to any other officer, clerk, or person in the service of the United States, or to any Senator or Member of the House of Representatives, or Territorial Delegate, any money or other valuable thing on account of or to be applied to the promotion of any political object whatever.

SEC. 15. That any person who shall be guilty of violating any provision of the four foregoing sections shall be deemed guilty of a misdemeanor, and shall, on conviction thereof, be punished by a fine not exceeding five thousand dollars, or by imprisonment for a term not exceeding three years, or by such fine and imprisonment both, in the discretion of the court.

Approved, January sixteenth, 1883.

GLOSSARY

bona fide: done in good faith; authentic

customs (as in "customs district"): areas where tariffs are collected

In memoriam--our civil service as it was, a political cartoon by Thomas Nast showing statue of Andrew Jackson on a pig, which is over "fraud," "bribery," and "spoils," eating "plunder." Included in Harper's Weekly *on 28 April 1877, p. 325.*

Document Themes and Analysis
The text of the Pendleton Civil Service Reform Act serves as an excellent window into the activities of the federal government in the late nineteenth century. Indeed, its textual emphasis on selecting jobs like postal clerks and tax collectors rather than anything having to do with government policy, suggests just how limited the functions of the federal government were before the New Deal of the 1930s. Much of the law describes the Civil Service Commission, which the act creates, rather than the jobs that it regulates. The few jobs mentioned include clerks, collectors, surveyors, and appraisers. While all of these positions served crucial functions, few of their actions were likely to affect the day-to-day existence of most Americans.

It is no coincidence that the offices mentioned in the text of the act were situated in places where the government collected money. In the absence of an income tax (which was not instituted until 1913), much of the federal government's revenue came through tariffs. Thus, clerks in customs offices were very important positions. They could also be very lucrative for people of questionable ethics. Appraisers worked in these same customs offices in order to determine the value of imported goods, which then defined the exact tariffs that had to be paid. Corruption in these areas was difficult to detect, so the kind of competence that could be measured on a civil service examination mattered.

These potentially lucrative jobs mentioned in the law were the kinds of positions that the Republicans who passed the law were most interested in keeping. This kind of power grab seemed scandalous in a way, but in the long run even the most political of appointees would become less partisan once they had to meet civil service requirements.

The act did its best to assure that appointees would be as non-political as possible in order to increase the government's effectiveness. The ban on contributions to political candidates and office holders in the Pendleton Act served as the precedent for future reforms in the same direction, such as the Hatch Act of 1939 (which also banned political activity by federal civil servants).

Many historians have taken the position that the Pendleton Act was weak reform legislation. Nevertheless, it passed overwhelmingly at a time when Congress passed little significant legislation thanks to a general belief in laissez-faire, or the free operation of enterprise without regulation. In fact, the Pendleton Act and the Sherman Antitrust Act of 1890 may be the only two really important federal laws passed between the end of Reconstruction and the beginning of the Progressive Era.

—*Jonathan Rees*

Bibliography and Additional Reading
Garraty, John A. *The New Commonwealth 1877–1890*. New York: Harper, 1968.
"George Pendleton." In Ohio History Central.
Hoogenboom, Ari. *Outlawing the Spoils: A History of the Civil Service Reform Movement 1865–1883*. Urbana: University of Illinois Press, 1968.
———. "The Pendleton Act and the Civil Service." *American Historical Review* 64 (January, 1959): 301–18.
Theriault, Sean M. "Patronage, the Pendleton Act, and the Power of the People." *The Journal of Politics* 65 (February, 2003): 50–68.

Moving Toward the Modern

The later decades of the nineteenth century comprised what is known as the Gilded Age because of the great wealth that accrued to the owners of the nation's major industries, together with their financiers. For millions of working-class Americans, however, the era was anything but golden. Unions were in their infancy, and factory owners and managers held considerable freedom in exercising their authority in order to extract the most from their workers. The Gilded Age, in other words, was also a battleground between capital and labor.

First, we hear from one of the top industrialists at the turn of the century, Andrew Carnegie. Carnegie, in an essay called "The Gospel of Wealth" (1889), lays out the virtues of being blessed with wealth, particularly when it has come through hard work and individual effort. Philanthropy, for which Carnegie is remembered, was also part of the picture.

One of the most prominent labor leaders in these decades was Eugene V. Debs, an advocate of labor socialism and an eventual five-time candidate for president of the United States. In an 1890 essay by Debs included here, "What Can We Do for Working People?" we read in somewhat mocking tones of Debs' disdain for industry leaders and social reformers who seek to "help" workers raise themselves up in society. Debs felt that, given the proper respect, they could do it on their own.

Another movement emerging at this time was the Populist movement. Here, we hear from one Populist sympathizer complaining that "Wall Street Owns the Country." Her complaint was printed the same year (1890) that Congress passed the Sherman Antitrust Act, aimed precisely at curbing business "combinations in restraint of trade," otherwise known as monopolies. Even after the law was enacted, however, it took a while to take hold in the real world. A key mover and shaker in that regard was President Theodore Roosevelt, from whom we also hear a word regarding monopolistic corporate trusts and their ill effects. A later piece of legislation, the Clayton Act of 1914 (also included), served to fill in some of the gaps not addressed by the Sherman Act.

By way of contrast, Henry Clay Frick, a captain of industry, discusses the fact that workers do not know what is in their own best interest. In an interview reprinted here, Frick propounds the need to break labor strikes by any means possible (including the use of private security agents) and reduce wages as necessary to deal with downturns in business. Frick was arguing his case in the midst of a noted labor strike, the 1892 Homestead Strike at a Carnegie Steel plant.

Another workers' strike explored in this section is a 1902 coal miners' strike organized by the United Mine Workers (UMW). Two documents, from opposing points of view, lay out the issues involved and the different perspectives brought to bear. We learn from the workers themselves about the appalling conditions they faced in the mines ("Coal Strike Hearings: The Miners Testify"). And we learn from an industry leader about the economic difficulties caused by the strike ("Echoes from the Recent Pennsylvania Coal Strike").

In this section, too, we look at the social reformers and the "muckraking" journalists of the era who shined a light on unethical and illegal corporate practices. The social worker Jane Addams writes about "Child Labor and Other Dangers of Childhood" (1906), followed by an excerpt by the noted writer and activist Upton Sinclair from his famous novel *The Jungle* (1906). The latter supplies insight into the grim meatpacking industry in Chicago at the time. Another document examined here deals with fire hazards in New York City factories. Prepared in response to the devastating 1911 Triangle Shirtwaist Factory fire that killed 146 workers, the report noted that the same problems identified in the Triangle factory could be found in any number of other New York work sites at the time.

Not everyone believed that social reform was a worthwhile enterprise, of course. One such critic, William Graham Sumner, was an advocate of the philosophy of Social Darwinism, which held that society advanced according to principles of evolution, and individuals were foolish to think that they could somehow alter the trajectory. It was all a matter of the right sort of "breeding" and the "survival of the fittest." Although regarded as a failed school of thought in subsequent decades, one of its sympathizers was Henry Ford, from whom we also hear in this section (albeit more about his industrial policy than his social views).

In 1922, a noted instance of corruption involving government officials and industry executives, known as the Teapot Dome scandal, erupted on the scene. While President Warren G. Harding had little to do with it, the scandal caught up members of his cabinet and came to color public opinion about the 34th president. In this case, Harding's own ethics could not save him.

Andrew Carnegie: "The Gospel of Wealth"

Date: June 1889
Author: Andrew Carnegie
Genre: Article; editorial; essay

Summary Overview

For the extremely wealthy, the Gilded Age of the late nineteenth century was a time of excess. Many of the so-called robber barons amassed huge fortunes while spending extravagantly on themselves and giving little thought to the morality of what they did with their wealth. However, one of the wealthiest men in the world, who also happened to grow up in poverty, would speak to and define the responsibility of the wealthy toward society at large and the poor in particular. Andrew Carnegie, owner of the largest steel company in the world, was certainly a product of his time, and the way he treated his employees was not much different than the way many of his contemporaries treated theirs. But after selling his company, Carnegie put his words into action by using his vast fortune to improve society and offer the poor an opportunity to change their futures themselves.

Defining Moment

The term "Gilded Age" may imply a sense of glamour. However, when Mark Twain and Charles Dudley Warner wrote the 1873 novel *The Gilded Age: A Tale of Today*, they had something else in mind, satirizing the wealthy and powerful, who gave the illusion of glitter and shine but instead were hollow and corrupt. "Robber barons" is a derogatory term popularized in the nineteenth century. It was used to refer to wealthy businessmen who amassed even more wealth through dishonest or unscrupulous means, particularly when dealing with one another, smaller business owners, or with the workers they employed.

In some ways, Carnegie agreed with Twain and Warner's assessment of Gilded Age business practices and social relations, and in some ways he embodied them; more significantly, however, he viewed the accumulation of wealth by the robber barons as beneficial. Indeed, these businessmen were instrumental in transforming the United States from a predominantly agricultural, rural nation to an urbanized, industrialized world power.

Carnegie believed that the actions of the robber barons were the engine of the American economy, which, in turn, led to an increase in industrial jobs, the start of the American Industrial Revolution, and ultimately the creation of the middle class.

Carnegie was as ruthless as other businessmen of the era in stifling dissent and minimizing the strength of unions among his workers. Though his partner, Henry Clay Frick, did the dirty work, Carnegie gave Frick a free hand, making him chairman of Carnegie Steel. In 1892, Frick shut down Carnegie's massive Homestead mill rather than accede to union demands that he not cut wages. He hired Pinkerton detectives to act as the company's army, waging a gun battle with strikers that resulted in ten deaths. After the National Guard arrived to establish order, Homestead reopened as a nonunion mill.

Carnegie saw no benefit in giving workers' wages higher than the market would force him to pay, and he viewed giving money to the poor as morally bankrupting the recipients. His goal was to give common people the chance to succeed in the same way he had: by pulling themselves up from poverty through determination, hard work, and force of will. His "Gospel of Wealth" embodied this ethos. Carnegie was willing to use the bulk of his massive fortune to provide the tools for those people who had the kind of determination to achieve through their own efforts.

Author Biography

Andrew Carnegie was born the son of a linen weaver in the town of Dunfermline, Scotland, in 1835. When the burgeoning Industrial Revolution in Britain put his father out of work, the Carnegies moved to the United States when Andrew was thirteen. He then began work as a bobbin boy in a cotton factory, but his drive for knowledge and self-improvement enabled him to move up. After making a good living at the Pennsylvania Railroad, he left to take over the Keystone Bridge Company, and there, he saw that the future of the nation's prosperity lay in steel. Investing in the new Bessemer steelmaking process, he quickly outstripped his competitors' profits by producing steel at a lower cost. Wanting to use his fortune to pursue his vision of social uplift, he sold Carnegie Steel to financier John Pierpont (J.P.) Morgan in 1903, becoming the wealthiest man in the world. He devoted the rest of his life to philanthropy, building libraries and supporting cultural and higher educational institutions.

HISTORICAL DOCUMENT

The problem of our age is the proper administration of wealth, so that the ties of brotherhood may still bind together the rich and poor in harmonious relationship. The conditions of human life have not only been changed, but revolutionized, within the past few hundred years. In former days there was little difference between the dwelling, dress, food, and environment of the chief and those of his retainers. The Indians are to-day where civilized man then was. When visiting the Sioux, I was led to the wigwam of the chief. It was just like the others in external appearance, and even within the difference was trifling between it and those of the poorest of his braves. The contrast between the palace of the millionaire and the cottage of the laborer with us to-day measures the change which has come with civilization.

This change, however, is not to be deplored, but welcomed as highly beneficial. It is well, nay, essential for the progress of the race, that the houses of some should be homes for all that is highest and best in literature and the arts, and for all the refinements of civilization, rather than that none should be so. Much better this great irregularity than universal squalor. Without wealth there can be no Maecenas. The "good old times" were not good old times. Neither master nor servant was as well situated then as to-day. A relapse to old conditions would be disastrous to both—not the least so to him who serves—and would sweep away civilization with it. But whether the change be for good or ill, it is upon us, beyond our power to alter, and therefore to be accepted and made the best of. It is a waste of time to criticise the inevitable.

Objections to the foundations upon which society is based are not in order, because the condition of the race is better with these than it has been with any others which have been tried. Of the effect of any new substitutes proposed we cannot be sure. The Socialist or Anarchist who seeks to overturn present conditions is to be regarded as attacking the foundation upon which civilization itself rests, for civilization took its start from the day that the capable, industrious workman said to his incompetent and lazy fellow, "If thou dost net sow, thou shalt net reap," and thus ended primitive Communism by separating the drones from the bees. One who studies this subject will soon be brought face to face with the conclusion that upon the sacredness of property civilization itself depends—the right of the laborer to his hundred dollars in the savings bank, and equally the legal right of the millionaire to his millions. To these who propose to substitute Communism for this intense Individualism the answer, therefore, is: The race has tried that. All progress from that barbarous day to the present time has resulted from its displacement. Not evil, but good, has come to the race from the accumulation of wealth by those who have the ability and energy that produce it. But even if we admit for a moment that it might be better for the race to discard its present foundation, Individualism—that it is a nobler ideal that man should labor, not for himself alone, but in and for a brotherhood of his fellows, and share with them all in common, realizing Swedenborg's idea of Heaven, where, as he says, the angels derive their happiness, not from laboring for self, but for each other—even admit all this, and a sufficient answer is, This is not evolution, but revolution. It necessitates the changing of human nature itself a work of eons, even if it were good to change it, which we cannot know. It is not practicable in our day or in our age. Even if desirable theoretically, it belongs to another and long-succeeding sociological stratum. Our duty is with what is practicable now; with the next step possible in our day and generation. It is criminal to waste our energies in endeavoring to uproot, when all we can profitably or possibly accomplish is to bend the universal tree of humanity a little in the direction most favorable to the production of good fruit under existing circumstances. We might as well urge the destruction of the highest existing type of man because he failed to reach our ideal as favor the destruction of Individualism, Private Property, the Law of Accumulation of Wealth, and the Law of Competition; for these are the highest results of human experience, the soil in which society so far has produced the best fruit. Unequally or unjustly, perhaps, as these laws sometimes operate, and imperfect as they appear to the Idealist, they are, nevertheless, like the highest type of man, the best and most valuable of all that humanity has yet accomplished.

We start, then, with a condition of affairs under which the best interests of the race are promoted, but which inevitably gives wealth to the few. Thus far, accepting conditions as they exist, the situation can be surveyed and pronounced good. The question then arises—and, if the foregoing be correct, it is the only question with which we have to deal—What is the proper mode of administering wealth after the laws upon which civilization is founded have thrown it into the hands of the few? And it is of this great question that I believe I offer the true solution. It will be understood that *fortunes* are here spoken of, not moderate sums saved by many years of effort, the returns on which are required for the comfortable maintenance and education of families. This is not *wealth*, but only *competence* which it should be the aim of all to acquire.

There are but three modes in which surplus wealth can be disposed of. It can be left to the families of the descendants; or it can be bequeathed for public purposes; or, finally, it can be administered during their lives by its possessors. Under the first and second modes most of the wealth of the world that has reached the few has hitherto been applied. Let us in turn consider each of these modes. The first is the most injudicious. In monarchical countries, the estates and the greatest portion of the wealth are left to the first son, that the vanity of the parent may be gratified by the thought that his name and title are to descend to succeeding generations unimpaired. The condition of this class in Europe to-day teaches the futility of such hopes or ambitions. The successors have become impoverished through their follies or from the fall in the value of land. Even in Great Britain the strict law of entail has been found inadequate to maintain the status of an hereditary class. Its soil is rapidly passing into the hands of the stranger. Under republican institutions the division of property among the children is much fairer, but the question which forces itself upon thoughtful men in all lands is: Why should men leave great fortunes to their children? If this is done from affection, is it not misguided affection? Observation teaches that, generally speaking, it is not well for the children that they should be so burdened. Neither is it well for the state. Beyond providing for the wife and daughters moderate sources of income, and very moderate allowances indeed, if any, for the sons, men may well hesitate, for it is no longer questionable that great sums bequeathed oftener work more for the injury than for the good of the recipients. Wise men will soon conclude that, for the best interests of the members of their families and of the state, such bequests are an improper use of their means.

Poor and restricted are our opportunities in this life; narrow our horizon; our best work most imperfect; but rich men should be thankful for one inestimable boon. They have it in their power during their lives to busy themselves in organizing benefactions from which the masses of their fellows will derive lasting advantage, and thus dignify their own lives. The highest life is probably to be reached, not by such imitation of the life of Christ as Count Tolstoi gives us, but, while animated by Christ's spirit, by recognizing the changed conditions of this age, and adopting modes of expressing this spirit suitable to the changed conditions under which we live; still laboring for the good of our fellows, which was the essence of his life and teaching, but laboring in a different manner.

This, then, is held to be the duty of the man of Wealth: First, to set an example of modest, unostentatious living, shunning display or extravagance; to provide moderately for the legitimate wants of those dependent upon him; and after doing so to consider all surplus revenues which come to him simply as trust funds, which he is called upon to administer, and strictly bound as a matter of duty to administer in the manner which, in his judgment, is best calculated to produce the most beneficial results for the community—the man of wealth thus becoming the mere agent and trustee for his poorer brethren, bringing to their service his superior wisdom, experience and ability to administer, doing for them better than they would or could do for themselves.

We are met here with the difficulty of determining what are moderate sums to leave to members of the family; what is modest, unostentatious living; what is the test of extravagance. There must be different standards for different conditions. The answer is that it is as impossible to name exact amounts or actions as it is to define good manners, good taste, or the rules of propriety; but, nevertheless, these are verities, well known although indefinable. Public sentiment is quick to know and to feel what offends these. So in the case of wealth. The rule in regard to good taste in the dress of men or women applies here. Whatever makes one conspicuous offends the canon. If any family be chiefly known for display, for extravagance in home, table, equipage, for enormous sums ostentatiously spent in any form upon itself, if these be its chief distinctions, we have no difficulty in estimating its nature or culture. So likewise in regard to the use or abuse of its surplus wealth, or to generous, freehanded cooperation in good public uses, or to unabated efforts to accumulate and hoard to the last, whether they administer or bequeath. The verdict rests with the best and most enlightened public sentiment. The community will surely judge and its judgments will not often be wrong.

The best uses to which surplus wealth can be put have already been indicated. These who, would administer wisely must, indeed, be wise, for one of the serious obstacles to the improvement of our race is indiscriminate charity. It were better for mankind that the millions of the rich were thrown in to the sea than so spent as to encourage the slothful, the drunken, the unworthy. Of every thousand dollars spent in so called charity to-day, it is probable that $950 is unwisely spent; so spent, indeed as to produce the very evils which it proposes to mitigate or cure. A well-known writer of philosophic books admitted the other day that he had given a quarter of a dollar to a man who approached him as he was coming to visit the house of his friend. He knew nothing of the habits of this beggar; knew not the use that would be made of this money, although he had every reason to suspect that it would be spent improperly. This man professed to be a disciple of Herbert Spencer; yet the quarter-dollar given that night will probably work more injury than all the money which its thoughtless donor will ever be able to give in true charity will do good. He only gratified his own feelings, saved himself from annoyance—and this was probably one of the most selfish and very worst actions of his life, for in all respects he is most worthy.

In bestowing charity, the main consideration should be to help those who will help themselves; to provide part of the means by which those who desire to improve may do so; to give those who desire to use the aids by which they may rise; to assist, but rarely or never to do all. Neither the individual nor the race is improved by alms-giving. Those worthy of assistance, except in rare cases, seldom require assistance. The really valuable men of the race never do, except in cases of accident or sudden change. Every one has, of course, cases of individuals brought to his own knowledge where temporary assistance can do genuine good, and these he will not overlook. But the amount which can be wisely given by the individual for individuals is necessarily limited by his lack of knowledge of the circumstances connected with each. He is the only true reformer who is as careful and as anxious not to aid the unworthy as he is to aid the worthy, and, perhaps, even more so, for in alms-giving more injury is probably done by rewarding vice than by relieving virtue.

The rich man is thus almost restricted to following the examples of Peter Cooper, Enoch Pratt of Baltimore, Mr. Pratt of Brooklyn, Senator Stanford, and others, who know that the best means of benefiting the community is to place within its reach the ladders upon which the aspiring can rise—parks, and means of recreation, by which men are helped in body and mind; works of art, certain to give pleasure and improve the public taste, and public institutions of various kinds, which will improve the general condition of the people;—in this manner returning their surplus wealth to the mass of their fellows in the forms best calculated to do them lasting good.

Thus is the problem of Rich and Poor to be solved. The laws of accumulation will be left free; the laws of distribution free. Individualism will continue, but the millionaire will be but a trustee for the poor; entrusted for a season with a great part of the increased wealth of the community, but administering it for the community far better than it could or would have done for itself. The best minds will thus have reached a stage in the development of the race in which it is clearly seen that there is no mode of disposing of surplus wealth creditable to thoughtful and earnest men into whose hands it flows save by using it year by year for the general good. This day already dawns. But a little while, and although, without incurring the pity of their fellows, men may die sharers in great business enterprises from which their capital cannot be or has not been withdrawn, and is left chiefly at death for public uses, yet the man who dies leaving behind many millions of available wealth, which was his to administer during life, will pass away "unwept, unhonored, and unsung," no matter to what uses he leaves the dross which he cannot take with him. Of such as these the public verdict will then be: "The man who dies thus rich dies disgraced."

Such, in my opinion, is the true Gospel concerning Wealth, obedience to which is destined some day to solve the problem of the Rich and the Poor, and to bring "Peace on earth, among men Good-Will."

GLOSSARY

Maecenas: Gaius Maecenas, the first Emperor of Rome (as Caesar Augustus)

Herbert Spencer (1820–1903): British philosopher and sociologist who was a proponent of Social Darwinism (survival of the fittest)

Swedenborg: Emanuel Swedenborg (1688–1772), Swedish philosopher, theologian, and mystic

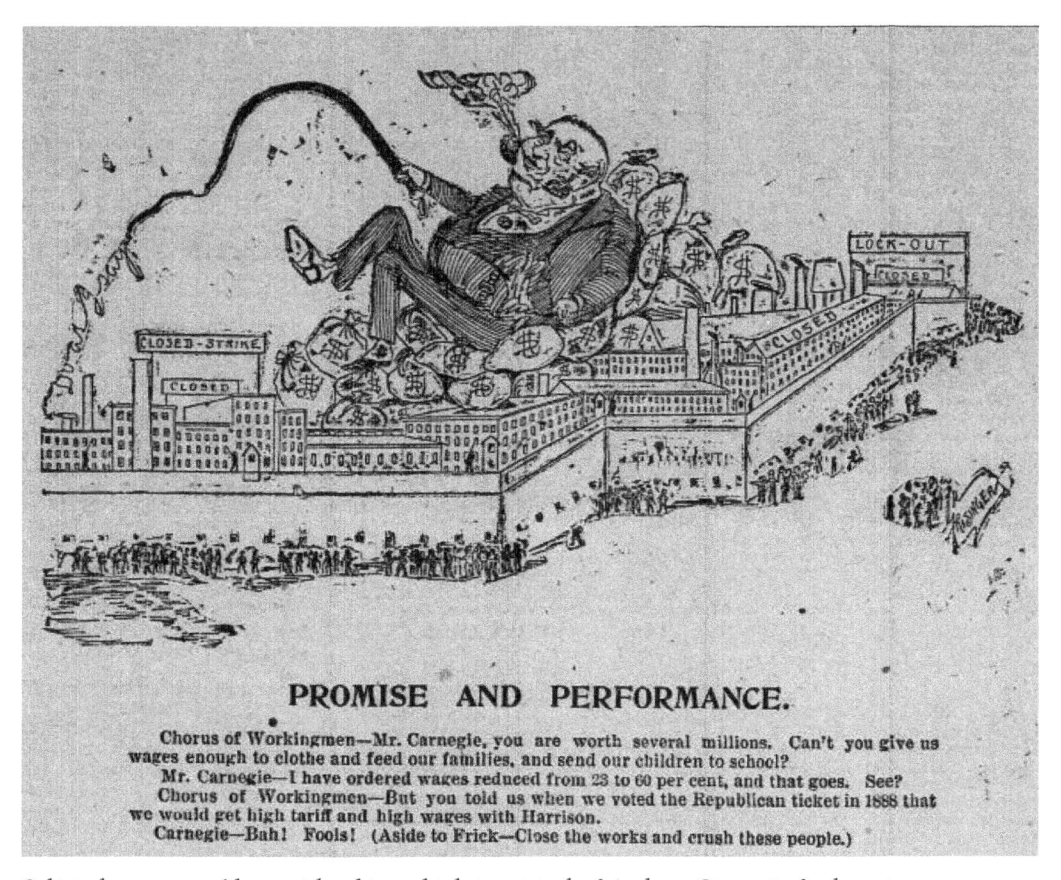

Political cartoon, of boss with whip, which is critical of Andrew Carnegie for lowering wages even though protective tariffs were implemented for industry. (St. Paul Daily Globe. Saint Paul, Minn., 03 July 1892)

Andrew Carnegie's philanthropy. (Puck *magazine cartoon by Louis Dalrymple, 1903*)

Document Analysis

When Andrew Carnegie wrote "The Gospel of Wealth" in 1889, he transferred the notion of *noblesse oblige* (the social responsibility of the European nobility) to the context of industrialized America. He believed that the business leaders of the time had a responsibility to use their wealth not just for self-aggrandizement but also for the common good of humanity. The idea of the common good was shaped by one of the most popular ideologies among the wealthy of the time, Social Darwinism.

It is ironic that a man who would become the wealthiest man in the world would state, "the man who dies thus rich dies disgraced," but the saying, which Carnegie often repeated, encapsulated his viewpoint. Carnegie also believed that an increased gap between the wealthy and the poor defined civilization in a positive way. Earlier, less "civilized" societies, Carnegie argues, had equality, but only an equality of poverty, meaning civilization could not progress because there were no wealthy individuals to fund it.

Following the ideas of Herbert Spencer, who coined the term "survival of the fittest" as it relates to societal organization, Carnegie believes that individualism and the drive to become wealthy were "the soil in which society so far has produced the best fruit." He states that collectivism and forced equality were to be abhorred, and the wealthy were obligated by their position in society to lead and to provide opportunities for others who had the ability to achieve more, thus uplifting civilization as a whole. Charity, as it was commonly practiced—giving money or other necessities to the poor—is an unwise use of money according to Carnegie because it only serves to perpetuate the social ills they were trying to cure.

Though a product of the ideas of his time, Carnegie's application of those ideas was far ahead of his contemporaries. He criticizes those who bequeathed their wealth to their children as both depriving society and doing a disservice to their children by not forcing them to earn their success. Instead, the wealthy are obligated by their position to use their wealth "in the manner which, in his judgment, is best calculated to produce the most beneficial results for the community." The wealthy are trustees for the poor, "doing for them better than they would or could do for themselves."

Essential Themes

Carnegie proposed a new and different solution to the crisis of poverty in the United States in his "Gospel of Wealth" essay. Indeed, the fact that he was so willing to tell his fellow millionaires what to do with their money was controversial, as were his ideas about Social Darwinism and the futility of the most common type of charity. Regardless of the debate his ideas generated, he would not back down and continued to write on the topic of philanthropy. He devoted his life and fortune to realizing his vision after he sold Carnegie Steel. At the time of his death in 1919, he had given away more than ninety-five percent of his personal fortune.

Though very few of the wealthy have followed Carnegie's advice to the extent that he did, many have followed the Carnegie pattern of donating and dispersing their money. Today, the Carnegie Corporation, the Carnegie Foundation for the Advancement of Teaching, and the Carnegie Endowment for the Humanities still carry on the philanthropic work started by Carnegie's fortune.

Even if the terminology has changed, the Social Darwinistic bent of Carnegie's philanthropy has lived far beyond his years. Many among the wealthy see themselves as possessing a unique responsibility to society. Additionally, some political philosophies common to the wealthy hold to this view of the proper use of wealth: not giving direct charity to the poor, but instead enabling them to rise out of poverty if they possess the drive to do so.

—Steven L. Danver

Bibliography and Additional Reading

Burgoyne, Arthur G. *The Homestead Strike of 1892*. Pittsburgh: University of Pittsburgh Press, 1979.

Josephson, Matthew. *The Robber Barons: The Great American Capitalists, 1861–1901*. New Brunswick, NJ: Transactions Publishers, 2011.

Kahan, Paul. *The Homestead Strike: Labor, Violence, and American Industry*. New York: Routledge, 2014.

Lagemann, Ellen Condliff. *The Politics of Knowledge: The Carnegie Corporation, Philanthropy, and Public Policy*. Chicago: University of Chicago Press, 1989.

Nasaw, David. *Andrew Carnegie*. New York: Penguin, 2007.

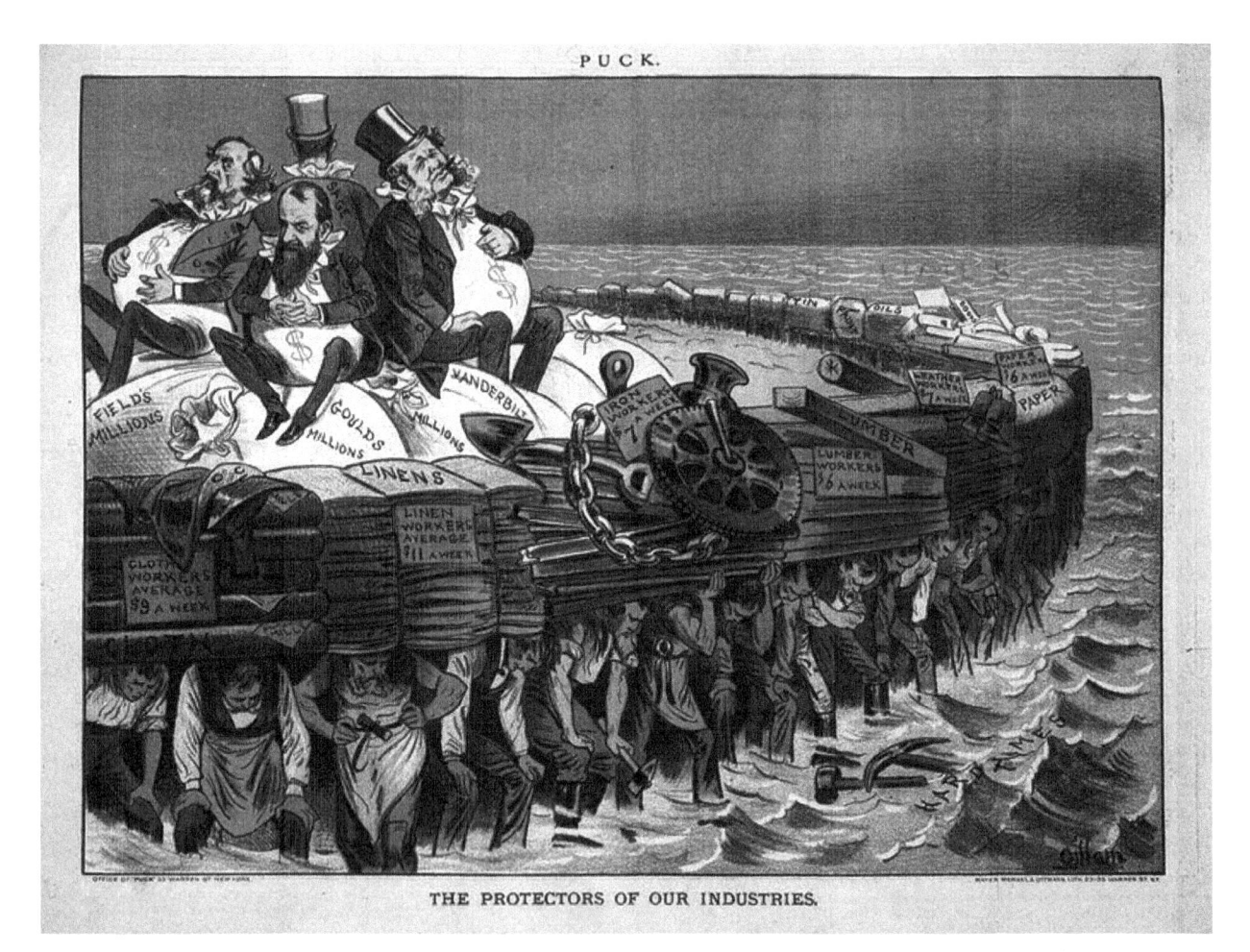

Cartoon showing Cyrus Field, Jay Gould, Cornelius Vanderbilt, and Russell Sage, seated on bags of "millions", on large heavy raft being carried by workers. (Puck (magazine); Mayer Merkel & Ottmann lith., N.Y.; Published by Keppler & Schwarzmann - Library of Congress)

Eugene Debs: "What Can We Do for Working People?"

Date: April 1890
Author: Eugene V. Debs
Genre: Article; editorial; essay

Summary Overview

During the so-called Gilded Age of the late nineteenth century, two competing visions of America were propagated. One, put forth by people such as industrialist Andrew Carnegie, emphasized the beneficial role of the wealthy in society. The other, which was held by union and Socialist Party leader Eugene Victor Debs, was more focused on working-class Americans whose well-being was often at the mercy of factory owners' desire for more wealth. In his essay "What Can We Do for Working People?," Debs presents the case that organizing into unions will allow working people to control their destiny and throw off the ideals of the wealthy, whose goal is to ensure that workers are employed for as little money as possible. By utilizing the power of the ballot box during elections and incorporating collective action in the workplace, working people will be better able to determine the course of their lives.

Defining Moment

Debs wrote his essay at a very difficult time for America's nascent labor movement. The prosperity of Gilded Age America was concentrated in the hands of those who owned the means of production. Men such as John D. Rockefeller, Andrew Carnegie, and John Pierpont Morgan controlled entire industries and spent as little as possible on their workers' wages and safety. The working class saw little, if any, benefit from the booming economy of the Industrial Revolution, and they exercised little power over the terms of their employment.

Though trade unions had worked to organize skilled workers for over a century, common laborers had no such protection until the rise of the Knights of Labor, which sought to bring together common workers and collectively negotiate to improve their lot. However, because of the violence that occurred during a labor rally at Chicago's Haymarket Square in 1886, many U.S. citizens associated unions with foreign radicalism and the ideologies of anarchism and socialism.

Debs would not be deterred, however, and he continued to argue in favor of unions as the only way for working people to achieve higher wages, safe working conditions, and an eight-hour day. But the labor movement did not come together to create a united front: as trade unions such as the American Federation of Labor (AFL) organized to improve the conditions of specially skilled workers, the Knights of Labor, which represented the interests of common workers, declined in influence as they became associated with radicalism. The AFL sought to distance itself from partisan politics, whereas Debs encouraged workers to take action both in the workplace and at the polling place in order to elect prolabor candidates who would institute the long-term goals of the labor movement. Whereas AFL leader Samuel Gompers preferred an issues-based alliance with politicians from the major parties, Debs encouraged workers to become active participants in the political organizations dedicated to the working peoples' agenda, such as the Socialist Labor Party (SLP) and the People's Party (also known as the Populist Party).

Debs's perspective was much more in line with the view espoused two years earlier by utopian novelist Edward Bellamy in *Looking Backward* (1888). A thorough critique of Gilded Age capitalism, Bellamy's view appealed to working people, with whom his ideal society, free of social divisions and conflict, resonated. But the only way to achieve a utopia such as Bellamy espoused was through voting and through organizing industrial workers to take control of their own fate.

Author Biography

Eugene V. Debs was born in Terre Haute, Indiana, on November 5, 1855. Like many young men at that time, he left school and entered the workplace at the age of fourteen. Around 1870, he became active in the railways employees union, the Brotherhood of Locomotive Firemen and Enginemen, and started a career as an advocate for working people. During the 1880s, Debs, still a member of the Democratic Party, won a seat in the Indiana state legislature. However, his true calling was with the railroad workers, and he became national secretary of the Brotherhood in 1880. It was during this period that his essay, "What Can We Do for Working People?" appeared in the union's periodical, the *Locomotive Firemen's Magazine*.

During the 1890s, Debs would expand his role nationally and found and lead the American Railway Union (ARU) in 1893. The ARU, which would soon become the largest organized union in the nation, accepted any white railway worker below the position of foreman, and Debs became instrumental in some of the union's most important labor actions before becoming a national political figure and running for president of the United States as a Socialist in 1900, 1904, 1908, and 1912.

HISTORICAL DOCUMENT

In one form or another certain persons are continually asking, "What can we do, or, What can be done for working people?" Why should such a question be asked at all in the United States? What gives rise to it? Are there circumstances and conditions warranting such an interrogatory? Who propounds it?....

Philanthropists of a certain type ask, "What can be done for working people?" and recommend soup houses, free baths, and more stringent laws against idleness and tramping, together with improved machinery in penitentiaries.

Another class devote time and investigation to diet, to show if wages decline that a man can live on ten cents a day and keep his revolting soul within his wretched body.

Another class, in answering the question, "What can we do for the working people?" reply by saying, "We will organize an Insurance Bureau which shall insure workingmen against accident, sickness, and death. We will supply them with medicine, doctors, and hospitals, taking so much from their wages to maintain the Bureau, and then, by compelling them to sign a contract which virtually reduces them to chattels, and makes them a part of our machinery, we will permit them to work for such pay as we choose to determine."

Another class answer the question, "What can we do for working people?" by telling them that unless they consent to abandon their labor organizations, absolve themselves from all obligations to such organizations, so far as they are concerned they shall have no work at all.

There are others, still, who discuss schemes for doing great and good things for working people, excepting, so far as it has come under the notice of the writer, to pay fair, honest wages.

This whole business of doing something for working people is disgusting and degrading to the last degree. It is not desirable to deny that in some quarters the question is asked honestly, but in such cases it is always in order to manifest pity for the questioner.

He is not inconvenienced by a surplus of brains. The question, "What can we do for working people?" as a general proposition, finds its resemblance in a question that might be asked by the owner of a sheep ranch, "What can I do for the sheep?" The reply would be, doubtless, "shear them." The ranch man takes care of the sheep that he may shear them, and it will be found that the men who ask with so much pharisaical solicitude, "What can we do for working men?" are the very ones who shear them the closest when the opportunity offers—strip them of everything of value that they may the more easily subjugate them by necessities of cold and hunger and nakedness, degrade and brutalize them to a degree that they become as fixed in their servitude as the wheels, cogs, cranks, and pins in the machinery they purchase and operate.

The real question to be propounded is, "What can workingmen do for themselves?" The answer is ready. They can do all things required, if they are independent, self-respecting, self-reliant men.

Workingmen can organize. Workingmen can combine, federate, unify, cooperate, harmonize, act in concert. This done, workingmen could control governmental affairs. They could elect honest men to office. They could make wise constitutions, enact just laws, and repeal vicious laws. By acting together they could overthrow monopolies and trusts. They could squeeze the water out of stocks, and decree that dividends shall be declared only upon cash investments. They could make the cornering of food products of the country a crime, and send the scoundrels guilty of the crime to the penitentiary. Such things are not vagaries. They are not Utopian dreams. They are practical. They are honest, they are things of good report.

Workingmen are in the majority. They have the most votes. In this God-favored land, where the ballot is all powerful, peaceful revolutions can be achieved. Wrongs can be crushed—sent to their native hell, and the right can be enthroned by workingmen acting together, pulling together.

What can workingmen do for themselves? They can teach capitalists that they do not want and will not accept their guardianship; that they are capable of self-management, and that they simply want fair pay for an honest day's work, and this done, "honors are easy." Fidelity to obligation is not a one-sided affair. Mutual respect is not the offspring of arrogance. There may have been a time when it was proper for the Southern slave owner to ask himself, "What can I do to better the condition of my slaves?" He owned them, they were his property; he controlled their destiny. He made them work as he did his cattle, mules, and horses, and appropriated all their earnings. Their children were his property as were the calves and colts of his cows and mares. But there never was a time beyond the dark boundary line of slavery when an employer of American workingmen could ask himself such a question without offering a degrading insult to every self-respecting workingman, and when a workingman hears it or anything like it and his cheek does not burn with righteous indignation he may know that he is on the road to subjugation, and if there exists a more humiliating spectacle within the boundaries of all the zones that belt the earth, what is it?

At every turn the question recurs, "What can workingmen do for themselves?" The question demands an answer, and unbidden a thousand are ready. We have not space for them. Let each workingman answer for himself. For one, we say the workingman can educate himself. He can read, study, and vote. He can improve his time and perfect his skill. He can see as clearly as others coming events, and prepare for their advent.

GLOSSARY

chattel: property; a slave

pharisaical: hypocritically self-righteous; condemnatory

tramping: wandering, vagabondage

Octopus representing Standard Oil with tentacles wrapped around U.S. Congress and steel, copper, and shipping industries, and reaching for the White House.

Document Analysis

Having been involved in the trade union movement for over a decade, Debs was adjusting his beliefs as the labor movement began to transform. Rather than concern himself with the betterment of working conditions of a particular industry, Debs's essay reflects a growing awareness of the commonality of all industrial workers, skilled and unskilled. Debs was one of a growing number of reformers, often from the upper classes of American society, who were considering ways to appease American workers who were voicing and demonstrating their dissatisfaction with their pay, working conditions, or terms of employment.

Debs begins the essay by noting that reformers in his time sought to ensure that industrial workers were pacified enough to continue to provide the cheapest possible labor for the benefit of America's factory owners and industrialists (much as slaveholders had before them). Each group of reformers is addressed by Debs, who analyzes their proposals and notes that each refuses to consider paying "fair, honest wages," which, Debs claims, is "disgusting and degrading to the last degree." Debs asks, "What can workingmen do for themselves?," and then answers that they can organize into unions to collectively bargain for what is in their best interests and can utilize their voting power to choose candidates who will best represent them in state and federal government.

Essential Themes

After "What Can We Do for Working People?" was published, Debs became increasingly outspoken. His speeches became dominated by the ideals of socialism and argued that the model of industrial capitalism was fundamentally flawed. Many in the middle and upper classes condemned the labor movement for promoting what they considered to be radical ideologies, but Debs and the ideas he expressed persisted.

Debs led the American Railway Union through tumultuous times, including the April 1894 strike against robber baron Jay Gould's Great Northern Railroad and the massive Pullman Strike the following month. Debs was imprisoned for six months for his role in the Pullman

Strike, and when he was released he announced he was a socialist and helped to form the Social Democratic Party, which then became the Socialist Party. Debs ran as the Socialist Party candidate for U.S. president for four consecutive elections between 1900 and 1912.

In 1905, Debs helped to found the Industrial Workers of the World (IWW), which best represented his ideas about American industrial workers and socialism. The IWW's goal was to create "one big union" of industrial workers across the nation. Debs's ideas, however, were again considered too radical, and the IWW lacked the support of the American middle and upper classes.

Though Debs and AFL leader Samuel Gompers disagreed on some aspects of unionism, they saw each other as allies, and the AFL eventually became more inclusive of workers from across the broad spectrum of American industry, though it still organized on a per-industry basis. After losing the 1912 presidential election, Debs won an Indiana congressional seat in the 1916 election, running on a pacifist platform and in opposition to America's involvement in World War I. He continued to voice his opposition when the United States entered the war in 1918, which resulted in his arrest and incarceration for sedition and violation of the Espionage Act. Nominated for the presidency by the Socialist Party in 1920, Debs ran his campaign from prison and received six percent of the popular vote. He was released upon the order of President Warren Harding on Christmas Day, 1921. Debs died in 1926.

—Steven L. Danver

Bibliography and Additional Reading

Ginger, Ray. *The Bending Cross: A Biography of Eugene Victor Debs*. Chicago: Haymarket, 2007.

Kloppenberg, James T. *Uncertain Victory: Social Democracy and Progressivism in European and American Thought, 1870–1920*. New York: Oxford University Press, 1988.

Lipset, Seymour Martin, and Gary Marks. *It Didn't Happen Here: Why Socialism Failed in the United States*. New York: Norton, 2000.

Salvatore, Nick. *Eugene V. Debs: Citizen and Socialist*. 2nd ed. Urbana: University of Illinois Press, 2007.

Standard Oil (Refinery No. 1 in Cleveland, Ohio, pictured) was a major company broken up under United States anti-trust laws.

Sherman Antitrust Act

Date: 1890
Author: Senator John Sherman of Ohio
Genre: Legislation

Summary Overview

A trust is a way of organizing a company that allows a firm to operate on a very large scale. The Sherman Antitrust Act was one of the two most important pieces of legislation passed by Congress in the late nineteenth century. It enshrined in American law and to a certain degree American culture that a company that controls too much of the market for a particular good or service is not good for the nation as a whole and should be broken up into separate pieces. It is the basis of all subsequent antitrust legislation in American history.

Defining Moment

Industrialization during the late nineteenth century favored companies that were first movers and companies that could achieve economies of scale. Businessmen like James "Buck" Duke and Andrew Carnegie employed technology to manufacture products cheaper than their competitors. These firms could then use their efficiencies to harm competition. By underselling those competitors or buying them out, it became possible for one (or sometimes a few) large companies to dominate whole industries. Once this situation came about, these dominant firms could raise prices on consumers and make their stockholders even richer.

The Sherman Antitrust Act was a response to this tendency in industries of all kinds. By giving the federal government the power to sue to break up trusts, it held the potential to restore competition and benefit consumers. Unfortunately, the federal government seldom used the law during its first decade of existence. More importantly, the U.S. Supreme Court, which invariably reviewed major antitrust cases, was loathe to let the Justice Department's interpretation of the act stand, even though they agreed that the law itself was constitutional because of Congress' power under the Commerce Clause. In the law's first major test, the Supreme Court let the E.C. Knight Company (better known as the Sugar Trust) remain intact even though it controlled 98 percent of the market for that product.

Despite the existence of this act, the United States went through a great merger movement that began in the 1860s, but greatly accelerated during the 1890s. By the end of that movement, one or two giant companies controlled over half the market in seventy-eight different industries. What gradually changed was the public attitude towards this situation as the nineteenth century transitioned into the Progressive era.

The real difference in the antitrust situation came with the ascension of Theodore Roosevelt to the Presidency in 1901. Roosevelt was willing to distinguish between what he considered "good" and "bad" trusts, employing the Sherman Antitrust Act against the ones he thought hurt consumers and not employing it against the others. The Supreme Court showed more willingness to allow those decisions to stand, most notably in cases against the Northern Securities Company (a railroad holding company) and the infamous Standard Oil trust. While the existence of this act did not change the general trajectory of capitalism in the United States towards large corporations, it did set an outer limit on the anticompetitive behavior in which those large companies could engage.

Author Biography

John Sherman (1823–1900), Republican of Ohio, was a congressman, U.S. senator, secretary of the treasury, and secretary of state. He played a pivotal role in Congress on the slavery issue before the Civil War and on many pressing issues during the late nineteenth century such as Chinese immigration and Civil Service reform. His greatest impact, however, was on American economic policy through legislation such as the Sherman Silver Purchase Act and the Sherman Antitrust Act.

Sherman's brother was William Tecumseh Sherman, the Civil War general who marched through Georgia. Unlike his brother, John Sherman twice unsuccessfully sought the presidential nomination of his party, in 1880 and 1884. Unfortunately for him, his campaigns never caught on because he was an uninspiring leader and poor public speaker. Sherman's primary historical importance derives from the wide range of legislation he championed through Congress.

HISTORICAL DOCUMENT

An act to protect trade and commerce against unlawful restraints and monopolies.

Be it enacted by the Senate and House of Representatives of the United States of America in Congress assembled,

Sec. 1. Every contract, combination in the form of trust or other- wise, or conspiracy, in restraint of trade or commerce among the several States, or with foreign nations, is hereby declared to be illegal. Every person who shall make any such contract or engage in any such combination or conspiracy, shall be deemed guilty of a misdemeanor, and, on conviction thereof, shall be punished by fine not exceeding five thousand dollars, or by imprisonment not exceeding one year, or by both said punishments, at the discretion of the court.

Sec. 2. Every person who shall monopolize, or attempt to monopolize, or combine or conspire with any other person or persons, to monopolize any part of the trade or commerce among the several States, or with foreign nations, shall be deemed guilty of a misdemeanor, and, on conviction thereof; shall be punished by fine not exceeding five thousand dollars, or by imprisonment not exceeding one year, or by both said punishments, in the discretion of the court.

Sec. 3. Every contract, combination in form of trust or otherwise, or conspiracy, in restraint of trade or commerce in any Territory of the United States or of the District of Columbia, or in restraint of trade or commerce between any such Territory and another, or between any such Territory or Territories and any State or States or the District of Columbia, or with foreign nations, or between the District of Columbia and any State or States or foreign nations, is hereby declared illegal. Every person who shall make any such contract or engage in any such combination or conspiracy, shall be deemed guilty of a misdemeanor, and, on conviction thereof, shall be punished by fine not exceeding five thousand dollars, or by imprisonment not exceeding one year, or by both said punishments, in the discretion of the court.

Sec. 4. The several circuit courts of the United States are hereby invested with jurisdiction to prevent and restrain violations of this act; and it shall be the duty of the several district attorneys of the United States, in their respective districts, under the direction of the Attorney-General, to institute proceedings in equity to prevent and restrain such violations. Such proceedings may be by way of petition setting forth the case and praying that such violation shall be enjoined or otherwise prohibited. When the parties complained of shall have been duly notified of such petition the court shall proceed, as soon as may be, to the hearing and determination of the case; and pending such petition and before final decree, the court may at any time make such temporary restraining order or prohibition as shall be deemed just in the premises.

Sec. 5. Whenever it shall appear to the court before which any proceeding under section four of this act may be pending, that the ends of justice require that other parties should be brought before the court, the court may cause them to be summoned, whether they reside in the district in which the court is held or not; and subpoenas to that end may be served in any district by the marshal thereof.

Sec. 6. Any property owned under any contract or by any combination, or pursuant to any conspiracy (and being the subject thereof) mentioned in section one of this act, and being in the course of transportation from one State to another, or to a foreign country, shall be forfeited to the United States, and may be seized and condemned by like proceedings as those provided by law for the forfeiture, seizure, and condemnation of property imported into the United States contrary to law.

Sec. 7. Any person who shall be injured in his business or property by any other person or corporation by reason of anything forbidden or declared to be unlawful by this act, may sue therefor in any circuit court of the United States in the district in which the defendant resides or is found, without respect to the amount in controversy, and shall recover three fold the damages by him sustained, and the costs of suit, including a reasonable attorney's fee.

Sec. 8. That the word "person," or " persons," wherever used in this act shall be deemed to include corporations and associations existing under or authorized by the laws of either the United States, the laws of any of the Territories, the laws of any State, or the laws of any foreign country.

GLOSSARY

antitrust: opposed to a trust, which was a form of legal organization that first appeared during the late nineteenth century and which helped large companies become very large companies; antitrust legislation was designed to allow the federal government to break those companies into pieces or dissolve them entirely

monopoly: any company that has total or near-total domination of a market in a particular good; while all monopolies in this era were trusts, not all trusts were monopolies

Document Analysis

The Sherman Antitrust Act passed unanimously in the House of Representatives and with only one dissenting vote in the Senate. On the surface, this seems odd for such a seemingly significant piece of legislation. However, the reason it passed so easily was that it actually did very little to change fundamental business law. Companies that were in restraint of trade were already technically illegal under common law before its passage and remained so afterwards.

The most important section of the law is the part that reads: "Every contract, combination in the form of trust or otherwise, or conspiracy, in restraint of trade or commerce…is hereby declared illegal." The wording comes from common law, but is extraordinarily vague. The essential question became how exactly would the Executive Branch and the courts that reviewed antitrust cases define "in restraint of trade?" Moreover, who exactly would the government enforce the act against because, after all, more than just companies signed contracts. Many Americans believed that very large companies were the inevitable result of free-market capitalism, and did not think it would be right to enforce the law against those combinations.

The hole that courts most often used to gut the intention of the framers of the act was its failure to distinguish between manufacturing and commerce. Sherman had spoken of passing a bill that outlawed "trusts and combinations in restraint of trade and production." The final text of the law only covered "restraint of trade or commerce," not production or manufacturing. That explains how the Supreme Court, in its tortured decision in the E.C. Knight case (1895), could let such an obvious monopolist to remain intact. Sugar refining was manufacturing, not commerce. This monopoly obviously affected commerce, but the Court was unwilling to extend Congress' powers from the Commerce Clause to enact legislation that had indirect effects upon commerce until the New Deal cases of the late 1930s.

Essential Themes

Despite its problems, the Sherman Antitrust Act is still important because it essentially federalized the enforcement of limitations on capitalism that already existed. While states retained the power to give and withdraw charters, this was one of the first laws that allowed the federal government to regulate their conduct for the sake of the public good. It is nonetheless conservative in the sense that it reaffirmed the traditional notion that competition was the best way to check economic power, not the action of a central government, even if it required action by the federal government to keep competition alive.

The primary weakness of the law was its failure to define basic terms like "trust," "restraint of trade," and "monopoly." John Sherman defended that decision since the common law defined them for anyone who looked there for guidance, but this nonetheless allowed judges enormous discretion in how it was enforced. Indeed, the law would prove a greater bane to trade unions than to large corporations in the years immediately following its passage. Nonetheless, all future antitrust laws would build upon the assumptions behind this legislation, filling in more than a few of the gaps that this law left open.

—*Jonathan Rees*

Bibliography and Additional Reading

Garraty, John A. *The New Commonwealth: 1877–1890.* New York: Harper & Row, 1968.

Merry, Robert W. *President McKinley: Architect of the American Century.* New York: Simon & Schuster, 2017.

Painter, Nell Irvin. *Standing at Armageddon: A Grassroots History of the Progressive Era.* New York: W.W. Norton, 2008.

Rees, Jonathan. *Industrialization and the Transformation of American Life: A Brief Introduction.* Armonk, NY: M.E. Sharpe, 2013.

"Wall Street Owns the Country"

Date: ca. 1890
Author: Mary Elizabeth Lease
Genre: Speech

Summary Overview

The late nineteenth century marked a significant point in U.S. history. Following the Civil War, the United States expanded its reach, reincorporating the Southern states into the Union, as well as adding many new ones, especially in the West. The economies of these regions depended heavily on agriculture, but food prices and various policies that significantly affected farmers were not set by the farmers themselves. Instead, they were set by corporate and political interests that largely resided in the East. As farmers felt the burden of these policies, they banded together to form organizations such as the Farmers' Alliance and the Populist Party—officially known as the People's Party—in hopes of bringing their interests to the national stage and motivating significant change. Mary Elizabeth Lease was heavily involved in this movement in the early 1890s, and her speech "Wall Street Owns the Country" succinctly captures many of the issues and frustrations faced by farmers during this time.

Defining Moment

In the wake of the Civil War, many regions of the United States faced serious economic depression, especially in the West and South, where the economy relied heavily on agriculture. As droughts damaged crops and cotton prices plummeted, many farmers—especially tenant farmers, who rented the land on which they grew their crops—were severely in debt. Even once crop yield improved, farmers found their livelihoods dependent upon prices, taxes, availability of transportation and storage, and myriad other regulations established by corporate and political powers mainly located in the East.

These hardships paved the way for the rise of a new political party, focused primarily in the Western and Southern states. The People's Party focused on strengthening farmers' rights, as well as asserting economic and political independence from the manufacturing- and industry-dominated East Coast. Populists fought for fair crop pricing, improved and expanded options for transportation and storage, and freedom from regulations on implements, such as grain elevators, that had a serious negative impact on the economic viability of farming.

In 1890, the Populists won control of the Kansas state legislature and successfully elected their first U.S. senator. With these successes, the party set its sights on increasing its presence on the national stage, a role that speakers such as Lease undertook. They traveled the country sharing their ideals and ideas with voters in areas similar to their own, in hopes of gaining enough support to win national elections.

Unfortunately, there was disagreement within the party over how to best accomplish this goal. Some believed teaming up with a mainstream political party such as the Democrats, who already had a strong following in the South, would help build national credibility and provide the channels necessary to reach a larger audience. Others believed this would dilute the Populist message by trying to appeal to moderates and that it was not worth the risk. By the time the Populist Convention took place in St. Louis, Missouri, in July of 1896, tension within the party ran high. Loyalties split between "fusion" Populists who favored a merger with the Democratic Party, and "mid-roaders" who believed such a merger would only help the Democrats suppress the third-party influence they had already gained. The rift proved to be too great, and the People's Party soon fell out of favor in both national and state politics.

Author Biography

Mary Elizabeth Lease was born Mary Clyens in Ridgway, Pennsylvania, in either 1850 or 1853. Her parents immigrated to the United States from Ireland during the Irish Famine; her father and brother died fighting for the Union army in the Civil War. In the early 1870s, she moved to Kansas to teach at a Catholic missionary school, and shortly thereafter married pharmacist Charles L. Lease.

Portrait of Mary Elizabeth Lease (1850–1933), American lecturer, writer, and political activist.

The couple lost everything in the financial panic of 1873 and relocated to Texas, where Lease became active in several causes, including prohibition and women's suffrage. She and her husband had several children during this time.

When the family moved back to Kansas, Lease became involved with the labor movement, joining the Farmers' Alliance and People's Party. Between 1890 and 1896, she toured the United States, speaking at campaign rallies and political conventions. Lease eventually divorced her husband and moved to New York City with her children, where she continued her career as a lecturer and activist until her death in 1933.

HISTORICAL DOCUMENT

This is a nation of inconsistencies. The Puritans fleeing from oppression became oppressors. We fought England for our liberty and put chains on four million of blacks. We wiped out slavery and our tariff laws, and national banks began a system of white wage slavery worse than the first. Wall Street owns the country. It is no longer a government of the people, by the people, and for the people, but a government of Wall Street, by Wall Street, and for Wall Street. The great common people of this country are slaves, and monopoly is the master. The West and South are bound and prostrate before the manufacturing East. Money rules, and our Vice-President is a London banker. Our laws are the output of a system which clothes rascals in robes and honesty in rags. The [political] parties lie to us and the political speakers mislead us. We were told two years ago to go to work and raise a big crop, that was all we needed. We went to work and plowed and planted; the rains fell, the sun shone, nature smiled, and we raised the big crop that they told us to; and what came of it? Eight-cent corn, ten-cent oats, two-cent beef and no price at all for butter and eggs—that's what came of it. The politicians said we suffered from overproduction. Overproduction, when 10,000 little children, so statistics tell us, starve to death every year in the United States, and over 100,000 shopgirls in New York are forced to sell their virtue for the bread their niggardly wages deny them... We want money, land and transportation. We want the abolition of the National Banks, and we want the power to make loans direct from the government. We want the foreclosure system wiped out... We will stand by our homes and stay by our fireside by force if necessary, and we will not pay our debts to the loan-shark companies until the government pays its debts to us. The people are at bay; let the bloodhounds of money who dogged us thus far beware.

GLOSSARY

niggardly: scanty or meager

sell their virtue: a euphemism for engaging in sex work, or prostitution

shopgirl: a woman employed in a retail store or shop

Document Analysis

Lease begins her speech by noting that the United States is a "nation of inconsistencies." She observes that the United States was founded by individuals who sought freedom from the control of England during the seventeenth and eighteenth centuries, but then used that freedom to enslave Africans and black Americans. Once slavery was technically abolished, she says, Congress passed tax laws and established national banks that enabled rich people to remain wealthy, while trapping the "common people" into a life that Lease describes as "wage slavery."

Lease then calls attention to the sharp regional divide in economic prosperity within the United States: She notes that the West and South—regions heavily dependent on agriculture—are subject to the financial whims of eastern business and political interests. She clearly expresses her personal feelings about the individuals in charge, saying that "the [political] parties lie to us and the political speakers mislead us."

To illustrate her point, Lease describes a scenario where, two years prior to her speech, politicians and corporate leaders encouraged farmers in the South and West to raise a large yield to ensure their future prosperity. With some help from good weather, the farmers' work proved quite effective, and food was plentiful that year. However, when the time came to sell the crops, the farmers found that the purchase price offered for the crops had dropped dramatically—to the point, she claims, where no one would even pay at all for butter or eggs. The same politicians claimed that prices had fallen because the farmers had "overproduced," but Lease observes that in that same year, an estimated ten thousand

1892 People's Party campaign poster promoting James Weaver for President of the United States.

children starved to death in the United States, and a hundred thousand young girls in cities engaged in prostitution just to afford food.

Finally, Lease lays out the demands she and her supporters have for future policy reform. Specifically, they want money, land, and transportation, as well as the power to obtain loans directly from the government rather than through private loan sharks. She also wants to end the foreclosure system. She concludes her speech with a warning to the "bloodhounds of money": The people who have been harmed by these corporations are ready to take action, and reform is on its way.

Essential Themes
At the time of her speech, Lease and her family were living in Kansas, surrounded by farmers and others whose livelihoods relied upon agriculture. As the United States admitted new western states following the Civil War, many felt disconnected from the money-controlling corporate powers in the East and struggled to make ends meet despite the importance of their role in producing food for the country.

Lease's speech expressed the frustration felt by many farmers in the West and South at the control these economic powers had over their livelihood, particularly with respect to setting crop prices. Many felt duped by politicians who had assured farmers that they would be able to provide for themselves and their families by producing a large amount of high-quality crops. Yet when the time came for harvest, those same powers used their influence to suppress prices to satisfy their own self-interest; the set prices were often too low for the farmers to recoup their expenses and keep up with payments on their land. Many were forced to borrow money at exorbitant rates to keep their land, repay debts incurred during the farming and harvest seasons, or move their product to market.

Some farmers who could not keep up with mortgage or debt payments lost their land to foreclosure. They wound up as tenant farmers, renting land from wealthier owners to continue making a living. Lease and others argued to end the foreclosure system hoping to protect farmers and other working poor from being forced from their homes.

Lease's anecdote about plummeting crop prices illustrates yet another "inconsistency" in the U.S. approach. Politicians claimed that overproduction caused the low prices, since the amount of supply exceeded the demand. But Lease points out that many people in the United States literally starved to death that year, so she cannot accept the argument that there is simply too much food available in the country to demand a fair price. Overall, her speech captures the frustrations and hardships faced by farmers in the United States during a time when manufacturing, corporate interests, and other hallmarks of industrialization dominated policy and political concerns. Lease's speech is sometimes quoted today to draw parallels between the Gilded Age and now.

—*Tracey M. DiLascio*

Bibliography and Additional Reading
Edwards, Rebecca. "Mary E. Lease." In *1896: The Presidential Campaign*. Poughkeepsie, NY: Vassar College, 2000.

———. "The Populist Party." In *1896: The Presidential Campaign*. Poughkeepsie, NY: Vassar College, 2000.

Goodwyn, Lawrence. *The Populist Moment: A Short History of the Agrarian Revolt in America*. New York: Oxford University Press, 1978.

Nugent, Walter. *The Tolerant Populists: Kansas Populism and Nativism*. 2nd ed. Chicago: The University of Chicago Press, 2013.

Woestman, Kelly A. "Mary Elizabeth Lease: Populist Reformer." In *Gilder Lehrman Institute of American History: History by Era*. New York: Gilder Lehrman Institute of American History, 2014.

Zinn, Howard. *A People's History of the United States: 1492 to Present*. New York: Harper, 2005.

Homestead Strike.

Air—Lay Me on the Hillside.

Say, comrades, did you hear about the tow-boat "Little Bill,"
That caused so much excitement at Carnegie's Homestead Mill?
With model barges well equipped, Bill Rogers, sly and slick,
Took "Pinkerton Assassins" there, employed by H. C. FRICK.

On the sixth of July, ninety-two, just at the dawn of day,
The "Pinkerton Marauders" tried to land at Fort Frick Bay,
'Twas then they met their Waterloo from Vulcan's brawny sons,
Who repulsed their every movement, and silenced all their guns.

Some weeks before this tragic act Carnegie went away,
To see the Banks O'Bonny Doon, that FRICK might have his say;
'Twas then he wired to Pinkerton, I want eight hundred strong,
One "V" per day shall be the pay, so bring your thugs along.

A committee sat at Homestead to investigate the cause,
Of H. C. FRICK'S tenacity on sumtuary laws;
When asked to state the cost (per ton) of billets four by four,
Had he been in a swearing room, I fancy he'd have swore.

HUGH O'DONNELL as a leader was placed upon the stand;
Describe what you were doing when the Vultures tried to land,
I risked my life entreating men, for God's sake not to shoot,
And for my pains (by LOVEJOY) I was stigmatized a loot.

McLUCKIE as a witness proved that he'd been through the mill,
And gave some sturdy pointers on the famed McKINLEY Bill;
He boldly intimated that where benefits accrue,
They are not for the masses, but the highly favored few.

JUDGE EWING was appointed to see justice hold the sway,
And filled the bill (admirably) in an autocratic way;
To construe the law to meet his views he'll very seldom fail,
While officials strut around at large, the Workmen go to jail.

FRICK'S mode of action seems to say, I feel inclined to brag;
I'll bust the "AMALGAMATION" now; bring out the pirates' flag;
The skull and crossbones now display, to let the public know,
The UNION MEN have had their day, I'll give the "SCABS" a show.

The "SCABS" they are a filthy set; I can't discriminate,
And though I aint allowed to bet, I'll confidently state,
That with your shoulders to the wheel, they can't soil Homestead mats,
Thy'll seek more congenial quarters, where they're not so "Rough on Rats."

Price 5 Cents.

Pro-Union pamphlet with lyrics to a song in support of workers.

Frick's Fracas—Henry Frick Makes His Case

Date: July 8, 1892
Author: Henry Clay Frick
Genre: Interview; article

Summary Overview

During the 1892 strike at the Homestead Steel Works, a facility of Carnegie Steel, company chair Henry Clay Frick offered his thoughts on the tense standoff between the company and the plant's striking employees in an interview with the *Pittsburgh Post*. Frick argued for reduced wages for employees and defended Carnegie's employee policies. He also railed against the strikers' tactics, defending his use of private security agents from the Pinkerton National Detective Agency and calling upon the state of Pennsylvania to intervene in the strike.

Defining Moment

The late nineteenth century was marked by strong growth in the U.S. economy, spurred in large part by the expansion of the American railways. Major enterprises such as the Carnegie Steel Company thrived, generating massive profits even during occasional economic downturns. This growth and prosperity was made possible by the country's working class, and a vast majority of American laborers worked long hours in often hazardous environments at low wages. In light of these inadequate working conditions, labor unions also experienced significant growth and activity during this period of economic growth, as members sought better wages and working conditions.

In late June and early July of 1892, a major confrontation between labor and corporate leadership took place at the Carnegie Steel Company's Homestead Steel Works facility in Homestead, Pennsylvania. Tensions had begun earlier in February, when the Amalgamated Association of Iron and Steel Workers, which represented a large number of Carnegie's most skilled employees, negotiated to renew the union's contract, which was set to expire on June 30, 1892. Andrew Carnegie, the owner of Carnegie Steel, had the company's chair, Frick, make a bombshell offer to the union: he proposed a wage reduction of more than eighteen percent and the removal of a number of positions from the union's collective bargaining unit. For the Homestead workers, wages were tied to the selling price of steel (a practice known as "sliding scale" wages). While there was no cap for increasing prices and wages, there was a limit at which the decline of wages relative to prices stopped, and Frick and Carnegie had proposed lowering the minimum limit of compensation even further. Based on the recent increase in the Homestead facility's output, the union had entered the negotiations under the expectation that Carnegie would offer a wage increase. The move, which many historians believe was deliberately orchestrated by Carnegie himself in an attempt to provoke a strike in order to undermine organized labor, was both bold and unexpected.

In late June, several days prior to the expiration of the union's collective bargaining agreement, Frick closed portions of the mill and barred entry to union employees. Although less than eight hundred employees were members of Amalgamated, more than three thousand employees agreed to strike in protest. Left alone to manage the strike by Carnegie (who was touring Scotland), Frick quickly completed the construction of a tall fence around the plant in order to keep out striking workers; the workers organized picket lines to surround the facility and prevent its operations from resuming.

In an effort to regain control of the Homestead plant, Frick dispatched by boat three hundred armed Pinkerton agents on the night of July 5 to enter the facility by river. Upon their arrival at the mill, the Pinkerton agents were met by the striking employees. A violent confrontation ensued as the Pinkertons and workers exchanged heavy gunfire. Nine workers and several Pinkerton agents were killed, and several hundred people suffered injuries. In light of the violence, Frick contacted the governor of Pennsylvania, Robert E. Pattison, in Harrisburg. Pattison deployed the state militia to Homestead. The presence of the militia enabled Frick to resume operations at the plant by employing strikebreakers. An assassination attempt on Frick on July 23 dissolved public support for the strike, and the strikers voted to return to work on

Carnegie's terms. With the collapse of the union, Homestead workers saw their wages slashed, work hours increased, and the elimination of several hundred jobs at the facility.

Two days after the violent confrontation between Pinkerton agents and striking workers on July 6, a Pennsylvania newspaper published an interview with Frick, in which he justified his actions and unequivocally expressed his disdain for organized labor.

Author Biography

Henry Clay Frick was born in West Overton, Pennsylvania, on December 19, 1849. He briefly attended Otterbein College in Westerville, Ohio, but he did not finish his studies. Instead, he moved to Pittsburgh, where he entered the coal and coke (a fuel used in steelmaking) business with his cousins in 1871. By 1880, he bought his cousins out of their partnership and founded the H.C. Frick Coke Company. Within a decade of its founding, Frick's company was producing more than eighty percent of the Pittsburgh steel industry's coke, rapidly turning Frick into a millionaire. In 1882, Frick and industrialist Carnegie entered a major partnership, bringing together Carnegie's steel empire and Frick's growing coke industry. Later in life, Frick moved to New York, where he constructed a massive mansion to house his growing art collection. Frick died on December 2, 1919, and he bequeathed his extensive art collection to create The Frick Collection, a museum inside his New York City residence.

HISTORICAL DOCUMENT

In an interview yesterday afternoon with Mr. George N. McCain, correspondent of the Philadelphia Press, Mr. H. C. Frick, chairman of the Carnegie Steel Company, Limited, said:

The question at issue is a very grave one. It is whether the Carnegie Company or the Amalgamated Association shall have absolute control of our plant and business at Homestead. We have decided, after numerous fruitless conferences with the Amalgamated officials in the attempt to amicably adjust the existing difficulties, to operate the plant ourselves. I can say with the greatest emphasis that under no circumstances will we have any further dealings with the Amalgamated Association as an organization. This is final. The Edgar Thomson Works and our establishment at Duquesne are both operated by workmen who are not members of the Amalgamated Association with the greatest satisfaction to ourselves and to the unquestioned advantage of our employees. At both of these plants the work in every department; goes on uninterrupted; the men are not harassed by the interference of trade union officials, and the best evidence that their wages are satisfactory is shown in the fact that we have never had a strike there since they began working under our system of management.

What was the basis of the differences existing at present between the Carnegie company and their men, Mr. Frick?

FIRST POINT AT ISSUE.

There, were three points upon which we differed. The skilled workmen in the Amalgamated Association work under what is known as a sliding scale. As the price of steel advances the earnings of the men advance; as the prices fall their earnings decrease in proportion. While there is no limit to an advance of earnings on the scale, there is a limit at which the decline stops. It is known as the minimum, and the figure heretofore has been $25 per ton for 4 by 4 Bessemer billets. We believe that if earnings based on the selling price of steel can advance without limit the workmen should be willing to follow the selling price down to a reasonable minimum, and so this figure was finally fixed by the Carnegie Company at the rate of $23 instead of $25. The reason for asking this upon our part was that the Carnegie Company has spent large sums of money in the introduction of new machinery in its Homestead plant, by means of which the workmen were enabled to increase their daily output, thereby increasing the amount of their own earnings. We had originally asked a reduction to $22, but subsequently agreed to compromise the rate at $23. The Amalgamated Association was unwilling to consider a reduction below $24 on steel billets, notwithstanding the fact that the improved machinery would enable their members, even at $23, to earn more than is paid in other Amalgamated mills. This was the first point at issue.

OTHER STUMBLING BLOCKS.
Under the present Amalgamated system the date of the expiration of the sliding scale is June 30, annually. We asked that this date be changed to December 31 (same as at Edgar Thomson), for the reason that the change would permit us to take our estimate upon the wages that we must pay during the year, beginning on January 1, so that we would be enabled to make contracts for the year accordingly. This point the Amalgamated Association refused to accede, and demanded the old date. The third proposition was the reduction in tonnage rates in those departments in the mills where the improvements I have spoken of have been made and which enable the workingmen to increase the output and consequently their earnings. Where no such improvements had been made there was no request on our part for a reduction in tonnage rate. In other words, we asked no reduction in any department of which the output had not been greatly increased by reason of our expensive improvements since the scale of 1889 went into effect.

As a rule, the men who were making the largest wages in the mill were the ones who most bitterly denounced the proposed revision of the scale, for out of the 3,800 men employed in every department only 325 were directly affected by this reduction.

WORKMEN HELD SWAY.
Finding that it was impossible to arrive at any agreement with the Amalgamated Association we decided to close our works at Homestead. Immediately the town was taken possession of by the workmen. An advisory committee of 50 took upon itself the direction of the affairs of the place; the streets were patrolled by men appointed by this committee, and every stranger entering the town became an object of surveillance, was closely questioned, and if there was the slightest reason to suspect him he was ordered to leave the place instantly under the threat of bodily harm. Guards were stationed at every approach to Homestead by the self-organized local government. Our employees were prohibited from going to the mills, and we, as the owners of the property, were compelled to stand by powerless to conduct the affairs of our business or direct its management. This condition of affairs lasted until Tuesday, when I appealed to the sheriff of Allegheny County, stating the facts as I have outlined them. The sheriff visited Homestead and talked with the advisory committee. Its members asked that they be permitted to appoint men from their own number to act as deputy sheriffs; in other words, the men who were interfering with the exercise of our corporate rights, preventing us from conducting our business affairs, requested that they be clothed with the authority of deputy sheriffs to take charge of our plant. The sheriff declined their proposition, and the advisory committee disbanded. The rest of the story is a familiar one; the handful of deputies sent up by the Sheriff McCleary were surrounded by the mob and forced to leave the town, and then the watchmen were sent up to be landed on our own property for the protection of our plant.

Why did the Carnegie Company call upon the Pinkertons for watchmen to protect their property?

We did not see how else we would have protection. We only wanted them for watchmen to protect our property and see that workmen we would take to Homestead—and we have had applications from many men to go there to—were not interfered with.

DOUBTED THE SHERIFF'S POWER.

Did you doubt the ability of the sheriff to enforce order at Homestead and protect your property?

Yes sir; with local deputies.

Why?

For the reason that three years ago our concern had an experience similar to this. We felt the necessity of a change at the works; that a scale should be adopted based on the sliding price of billets, and we asked the county authorities for protection. The workmen began tactics similar to those employed in the present troubles. The sheriff assured the members of the firm that there would be no difficulty, that he would give them ample protection and see that men who were willing to work were not interfered with. What was the result? The posse taken up by the sheriff—something over 100 men—were not permitted to land on our property; were driven off with threats of bodily harm, and it looked as if there was going to be great destruction of life and property. That frightened our people. Mr. Abbott was then in charge of the Carnegie, Phipps & Co. business, and was asked by the Amalgamated officials for a conference, which he agreed to, fearful if he did not do so there might be loss of life and destruction of property. Under that stress, in fear of the Amalgamated Association, an agreement was made and work was resumed. We did not propose this time to be placed in that position.

The Pinkerton men, as generally understood, had been summoned and all arrangements made with them to be on hand in case of failure by the sheriff to afford protection. Is that a fact or not?

The facts concerning the engagement of the Pinkerton men are these: From past experience, not only with the present sheriff but with all others, we have found that he has been unable to furnish us with a sufficient number of deputies to guard our property and protect the men who were anxious to work on our terms. As the Amalgamated men from the 1st of July had surrounded our works placed guards at all the entrances, and at all avenues or roads leading to our establishment and for miles distant therefrom, we felt that for the safety of our property, and in order to protect our workmen, it was necessary for us to secure our own watchmen to assist the sheriff, and we knew of no other source from which to obtain them than from Pinkerton agencies, and to them we applied.

TRIED TO AVOID TROUBLE.

We brought the watchmen here as quietly as possible; had them taken to Homestead at an hour of the night when we hoped to have them enter our works without any interference whatever and without meeting anybody. We proposed to land them on our own property, and all our efforts were to prevent the possibilities of a collision between our former workmen and our watchmen. We are to-day barred out of our property at Homestead, and have been since the 1st of July. There is nobody in the mills up there now; they are standing a silent mass of machinery with nobody to look after them. They are in the hands of our former workmen.

Have the men made overtures for a settlement of the difficulties since this trouble commenced?

Yes, sir. A leading ex-official in the Amalgamated Association yesterday, when this rioting was going on, called on the sheriff and I am informed asked him to come down to see me, stating that if he could get a promise that we would confer with the representatives of the Amalgamated Association looking toward an adjustment of this trouble, that he would go to Homestead and try to stop the rioting.

Did you consider his proposal?

No, sir. I told the gentleman who called that we could not confer with Amalgamated Association officials. That it was their followers who were rioting and destroying our property, and we would not accept his proposition. At the same time this representative of our former workmen said that they were willing to accept the terms offered, and concede everything we asked except the date of the scale, which they insisted should be June 30 in place of December 31.

FUTURE OF IT ALL.

What of the future of this difficulty?

It is in the hands of the authorities of Allegheny County. If they are unable to cope with it, it is certainly the duty of the governor of the State to see that we are permitted to operate our establishment unmolested. The men engaged by us through the Pinkerton agencies were sent up to Homestead with the full knowledge sheriff and by him placed in charge of his chief deputy, Col. Gray, and, as we know, with instructions to deputize them in case it became necessary. We have made an impartial investigation and are satisfied beyond doubt that the watchmen employed by us were fired upon by our former workmen and their friends for twenty-five minutes before they reached our property, and were fired upon after they had reached our property. That they did not return the fire until after the boats had touched the shore, and after three of the watchmen had been wounded, one fatally. After a number of the watchmen were wounded, and Capt. Rodgers, in charge of the tow-boat, at their request, had taken the injured away, leaving the barges at our works unprotected, our former workmen refused to allow Capt. Rodgers to return to the barges that he might remove them from our property, but fired at him and fatally wounded one of the crew.

You doubtless are aware, Mr. Frick, that the troubles at the Homestead mill invited widespread attention, and as a result Congress proposes to investigate the trouble, as well as the employment of Pinkerton detectives?

I am aware of the fact, sir. While nobody could regret the occurrences of the last few days more than myself, yet it is my duty, as the executive head of the Carnegie Company, to protect the interests of the association. We desire to, and will protect our property at all hazards. So far as Congressional investigation is concerned, I can say with the utmost candor that we welcome the investigation proposed. We are prepared to submit facts and figures which will convince unprejudiced men of the equity of our position. More than this, I believe that when all of the facts are known revelations will be made which will emphasize the justice of all our claims.

AS TO POLITICS.

How do you regard the present troubles at Homestead from a political standpoint. What effect will it have as a tariff issue in the political campaign of the coming fall?

We have never given a thought as to what effect our affairs might have on either of the political parties. We cannot afford to run our business and run politics at the same time. It would prove very unprofitable if we were to trim our sails to meet political issues. At the same time I may say that it is not a matter in which the protective tariff is involved, and every intelligent man, whether he be a manufacturer or employee, is aware of the fact. It is, however, a question as to whether or not the proprietors or its workmen will manage the works.

We did not propose to reduce the earnings of our employees below those of Amalgamated men in other mills. As I have said, we have put in improved machinery which other mills do not possess; increased our output and increased the earnings of our men. We asked that a reduction be made in these departments so that the earnings of our employee's would be on a par with other workmen in other Amalgamated mills. It is not a question of starvation wages, for you will please bear in mind the fact that the proposed equalization of earnings affects only about 325 men out of 3,800, and they are the ones who earn the most money in our establishment. It has no effect upon the wages of more the 15,000 other employees engaged in our establishment at Duquesne, Braddock, Pittsburg, Beaver Falls, and in the coke region.

GLOSSARY

billet: a small bar of metal used in metals manufacturing

concern: a firm or company

sliding scale: a wage scale that varies with the selling price of goods produced, the cost of living, or profits

Berkman's attempt to assassinate Frick, as illustrated by W. P. Snyder for Harper's Weekly *in 1892*

> Tomorrow night, about 11 oclock, 300 Watchmen obtained from Pinkerton, will leave the cars at Bellvue Station on the Fort Wayne Road, and take passage on two barges, and two boats that will be there ready to receive them. They will go at once to Homestead, reaching there, we hope, about three or four oclock on the morning of the 6th. The barges are well fitted up, and well provisioned, as are also the Boats. The Boats contain the uniforms, the arms, the ammunition, etc.

Frick's letter to Carnegie describing the plans and munitions that will be on the barges when the Pinkertons arrive to confront the strikers in Homestead.

Document Analysis

Despite his stated willingness to negotiate in good faith with the union members, Frick was an outspoken opponent of organized labor. His comments to the *Pittsburgh Post* reflected this attitude: in his interview, Frick accuses the Amalgamated Association of Iron and Steel Workers of attempting to take over Carnegie Steel and of inciting the violence and destruction that occurred during the standoff with Pinkerton agents. He also places responsibility for keeping the peace in the hands of the local, regional, and state law enforcement authorities.

When asked about the events leading up to the strike, Frick declares that the Amalgamated Association is an unwelcome organization. Other Carnegie Steel Company plants, he argues, operate without the presence of Amalgamated personnel "with the greatest satisfaction to ourselves and to the unquestioned advantage of our employees." He adds that Amalgamated members have simply refused to hear Carnegie's side of the issue and were being intransigent in their demands. On the issue of sliding scale wages, for example, Frick argues that linking wages to the selling price of steel (and putting in place a minimum to prevent bottoming out) balances the interests of the corporation and its employees. Frick further argues that Carnegie initially requested a reduction in wages in order to purchase far more efficient machines and equipment that had boosted the daily output of Homestead workers, thereby increasing their earnings. Even the number of employees affected by wage reductions was relatively small (about 325 of 3,800 workers), he claims.

Frick claims that because Amalgamated and the striking workers refused to negotiate in good faith with Carnegie, it was necessary to cut ties with the union and close the plant to the striking workers. He accuses the union of essentially laying siege to the town and states that he appealed directly to the sheriff of Allegheny County, where Homestead was located. However, when the sheriff's deputies arrived, they too were intimidated by the large numbers of hostile striking workers. No local force could counter the union mob, Frick suggests, necessitating the arrival of the Pinkerton agents and the state militia. When asked whether he believed the strike had political implications, Frick responds that his job is to operate a business, regardless of how either political party views his company.

Essential Themes

Frick's comments to the media following the end of the Homestead Strike were defiant and accusatory, assigning responsibility for the strike and the violence that ensued entirely to the Amalgamated members. He remained adamant in his belief that Amalgamated had grossly misinterpreted the company's wage policies and was unnecessarily stubborn in their demands. He argued that the principal issue of the strike was the "question as to whether or not the proprietors or its workmen will manage the works." He further pointed at the union as the instigator of a violent situation so difficult to contain that Frick had to call in private contractors to ensure security. Frick's company, he stated, was well within its legal rights to make operational changes, while Amalgamated was engaged in blatantly illegal activities.

The aftermath of the Homestead Strike saw a significant diminishment in the power and influence of unions, not only in the Pittsburgh steel industry but also nationwide. Throughout the United States, many employers became reluctant to enter into contracts with unions. The violent confrontation at Homestead is illustrative of the tensions between organized labor and management that were playing out across the country at the end of the nineteenth century and the beginning of the twentieth.

—Michael P. Auerbach

Bibliography and Additional Reading

MacKay, James. *Andrew Carnegie: Little Boss*. New York: Random, 2012.

Skrabec, Quentin R., Jr. *Henry Clay Frick: The Life of the Perfect Capitalist*. Jefferson, NC: McFarland, 2010.

Standiford, Les. *Meet You in Hell: Andrew Carnegie, Henry Clay Frick, and the Bitter Partnership that Changed America*. New York: Broadway, 2006.

■ "The Absurd Effort to Make the World Over"

Date: March 1894
Author: William Graham Sumner
Genre: Editorial

Summary Overview
Writing in the *Forum*, a leading American general-interest intellectual magazine, Yale sociologist William Graham Sumner published an essay critiquing the push for "social reform" in the late nineteenth century. Sumner attacks Progressive-Era efforts to bring about social and economic reform, claiming that these efforts were both wrong-headed and doomed to failure because of the Progressive inability to come to grips with the intractable nature of social reality. According to Sumner, Progressives are also frequently in error in their assertions about change for the conditions of the working class, which had actually improved since the Colonial Era despite the Progressive claims that industrialization harmed workers. Sumner sketches a picture of economic progress celebrating the rise of the industrial organization that dominates society and provides a level of prosperity unequaled in history.

Defining Moment
The late nineteenth century in the United States was a time of capitalist economic transformation. The wealth and power of business magnates or "robber barons" was being challenged by Progressive reformers hoping to regulate it and by nascent labor unions organizing workers seeking better working conditions and higher wages. The extremely wealthy, whose wealth was not based as in the Colonial Era on land but rather on money, were an increasingly prominent presence in American life. Businesses, particularly large businesses, were more frequently organized into corporations. In reaction, socialism, an import from Europe, was also attracting much interest among Americans. The so-called Gilded Age saw a dramatic increase in the influence of business on government.

The growing power of capitalists was connected to an even more fundamental economic transformation: the rise of industry with the growth of the railroad system and the expansion of manufacturing. America, which had since Colonial times had been a predominantly agricultural economy, was becoming a more industrialized one. The Northeast, where Sumner spent his life, was a leading region in this transformation. Along with this transformation, the relatively high wages paid by American industry attracted increasing immigration from Europe and elsewhere. By fostering immigration, industrialization made the United States a more diverse and multicultural country, and by concentrating populations in industrial and commercial cities, it made the nation more urbanized. As enterprises grew larger, managers and business owners grew more removed from workers than they had been in small workshop enterprises.

Sumner was also writing at a time when the study of society was becoming professionalized and secularized, as exemplified by his own decision to leave the ministry and enter the world of the university. Influences from Europe were leading to the creation of the discipline of sociology, the study of society, of which Sumner was a leading early practitioner. Along with secularism went a growing tendency toward materialism, analyzing society not in terms of abstract principles but material benefits. Classical economics, with its exaltation of free trade and suspicion of government intervention in the economy, had arrived in the United States from Britain in the mid-nineteenth century, but its influence was continuing to grow in Sumner's time. This was frequently combined with the influence of Darwinian ideas about advances through struggle and the positivist prioritizing of facts over theory. The new ideas were arriving at a time when the academic curriculum was in turmoil, as the old curriculum based on religion and the Greek and Roman classics was increasingly seen as irrelevant to modern life, and academics like Sumner contended over what students should be required and expected to learn.

Author Biography

William Graham Sumner (1840–1910) was born to an English immigrant couple in Paterson, New Jersey. He briefly served as an Episcopal clergyman, but in 1872, he left the ministry to become professor of political economy at Yale University. Although his interests later shifted to the study of society, Sumner remained deeply influenced by the orthodox free-trade economics of the nineteenth century. Like other American economic conservatives, he supported a gold-backed currency, opposing the free silver movement and protectionism. He was also highly suspicious of labor unions, although he believed that they served morale-building and information-disseminating purposes. Later deemed a Social Darwinist (a term not widely used at the time), he became embroiled in a controversy with the Yale administration for employing the English Social Darwinist Herbert Spencer's *The Study of Sociology* (1873) as a textbook. Sumner pioneered the establishment of sociology as an academic discipline in America, teaching the first sociology course at an American university in 1875 and being elected the second president of the American Sociological Society in 1908.

HISTORICAL DOCUMENT

The burden of proof is on those who affirm that our social condition is utterly diseased and in need of radical regeneration! My task at present, therefore, is entirely negative and critical: to examine the allegations of fact and the doctrines which are put forward to prove the correctness of the diagnosis and to warrant the use of the remedies proposed.

The propositions put forward by social reformers nowadays are chiefly of two kinds. There are assertions in historical form, chiefly in regard to the comparison of existing with earlier social states, which are plainly based on defective historical knowledge, or at most on current stock historical dicta which are uncritical and incorrect....

The other class of propositions consists of dogmatic statements which, whether true or not, are unverifiable. This class of propositions is the pest and bane of current economic and social discussion. [Upon a more or less superficial view of some phenomenon a suggestion arises which is embodied in a philosophical proposition and promulgated as a truth. From the form and nature of such propositions they can always be brought under the head of "ethics." This word at least gives them an air of elevated sentiment and purpose, which is the only warrant they possess....

When anyone asserts that the class of skilled and unskilled manual laborers of the United States is worse off now in respect to diet, clothing, lodgings, furniture, fuel, and lights; in respect to the age at which they can marry; the number of children they can provide for; the start in life which they can give to their children, and their chances accumulating capital, than they ever have been at any former time, he makes a reckless assertion for which no facts have been offered in proof. Upon an appeal to facts, the contrary of this assertion would be clearly established. It suffices, therefore, to challenge those who are responsible for the assertion to make it good.

If it is said that the employed class are under much more stringent discipline than they were thirty years ago or earlier, it is true. It is not true that there has been any qualitative change in this respect within thirty years, but it is true that a movement which began at the first settlement of the country has been advancing with constant acceleration and has become a noticeable feature within our time.

This movement is the advance in the industrial organization. The first settlement was made by agriculturists, and for a long time there was scarcely any organization. There were scattered farmers, each working for himself, and some small towns with only rudimentary commerce and handicrafts. As the country has filled up, the arts and professions have been differentiated and the industrial organization has been advancing.

This fact and its significance has hardly been noticed at all; but the stage of the industrial organization existing at any time, and the rate of advance in its development, are the absolutely controlling social facts. Nine-tenths of the socialistic and semi-socialistic, and sentimental or ethical, suggestions by which we are overwhelmed come from failure to understand the phenomena of the industrial organization and its expansion. It controls us all because we are all in it. It creates the conditions of our existence, sets the limits of our social activity, regulates the bonds of our social relations, determines our conceptions of good and evil, suggests our life-philosophy, molds our inherited political institutions, and reforms the oldest and toughest customs, like marriage and property.

I repeat that the turmoil of heterogeneous and antagonistic social whims and speculations in which we live is due to the failure to understand what the industrial organization is and its all-pervading control over human life, while the traditions of our school of philosophy lead us always to approach the industrial organization, not from the side of objective study, but from that of philosophical doctrine. Hence it is that we find that the method of measuring what we see happening by what are called ethical standards, and of proposing to attack the phenomena by methods thence deduced, is so popular.

* * * * *

All organization implies restriction of liberty. The gain of power is won by narrowing individual range. The methods of business in colonial days were loose and slack to an inconceivable degree. The movement of industry has been all the time toward promptitude, punctuality, and reliability. It has been attended all the way by lamentations about the good old times; about the decline of small industries; about the lost spirit of comradeship between employer and employee; about the narrowing of the interests of the workman; about his conversion into a machine or into a "ware," and about industrial war.

These lamentations have all had reference to unquestionable phenomena attendant on advancing organization. In all occupations the same movement is discernible—in the learned professions, in schools, in trade, commerce, and transportation. It is to go on faster than ever, now that the continent is filled up by the first superficial layer of population over its whole extent and the intensification of industry has begun. The great inventions both make the intention of the organization possible and make it inevitable, with all its consequences, whatever they may be....

Now the intensification of the social organization is what gives us greater social power. It is to it that we owe our increased comfort and abundance. We are none of us ready to sacrifice this. On the contrary, we want more of it. We would not return to the colonial simplicity and the colonial exiguity if we could. If not, then we must pay the price. Our life is bounded on every side by conditions. We can have this if we will agree to submit to that. In the case of industrial power and product the great condition is combination of force under discipline and strict coordination. Hence the wild language about wage-slavery and capitalistic tyranny.

In any state of society no great achievements can be produced without great force. Formerly great force was attainable only by slavery aggregating the power of great numbers of men. Roman civilization was built on this. Ours has been built on steam. It is to be built on electricity. Then we are all forced into an organization around these natural forces and adapted to the methods or their application; and although we indulge in rhetoric about political liberty, nevertheless we find ourselves bound tight in a new set of conditions, which control the modes of our existence and determine the directions in which alone economic and social liberty can go.

If it is said that there are some persons in our time who have become rapidly and in a great degree rich, it is true; it if is said that large aggregations of wealth in the control of individuals is a social danger, it is not true. ...

If this poor old world is as bad as they say, one more reflection may check the zeal of the headlong reformer. It is at any rate a tough old world. It has taken its trend and curvature and all its twists and tangles from a long course of formation. All its wry and crooked gnarls and knobs are therefore stiff and stubborn. If we puny men by our arts can do anything at all to straighten them, it will only be by modifying the tendencies of some of the forces at work, so that, after a sufficient time, their action may be changed a little and slowly the lines of movement may be modified. This effort, however, can at most be only slight, and it will take a long time. In the meantime spontaneous forces will be at work, compared with which our efforts are like those of a man trying to deflect a river, and these forces will have changed the whole problem before our interferences have time to make themselves felt.

The great stream of time and earthly things will sweep on just the same in spite of us. It bears with it now all the errors and follies of the past, the wreckage of all the philosophies, the fragments of all the civilizations, the wisdom of all the abandoned ethical systems, the debris of all the institutions, and the penalties of all the mistakes. It is only in imagination that we stand by and look at and criticize it and plan to change it. Everyone of us is a child of his age and cannot get out of it. He is in the stream and is swept along with it. All his sciences and philosophy come to him out of it.

Therefore the tide will not be changed by us. It will swallow up both us and our experiments. It will absorb the efforts at change and take them into itself as new but trivial components, and the great movement of tradition and work will go on unchanged by our fads and schemes. The things which will change it are the great discoveries and inventions, the new reactions inside the social organism, and then changes in the earth itself on account of changes in the cosmic forces.

These causes will make of it just what, in fidelity to them, it ought to be. The men will be carried along with it and be made by it. The utmost they can do by their cleverness will be to note and record their course as they are carried along, which is what we do now, and is that which leads us to the vain fancy that we can make or guide the movement. That is why it is the greatest folly of which a man can be capable, to sit down with a slate and pencil to plan out a new social world.

GLOSSARY

dicta (pl. of dictum): authoritative pronouncements; maxims

exiguity: meagerness or scantiness

warrant: justification

Republican campaign poster of 1896 attacking free silver.

Document Analysis

Sumner's focus in this essay is less on the ends of Progressive reform than on the "absurd" reforming instinct itself, which he finds incompatible with the enormous difficulty of changing social habits and customs. Sumner believes that the reformers are intellectually sloppy, using words without a rigorous understanding of their meaning and making assertions, particularly about past societies, without awareness of their truth or falsity. This leads them to paint contemporary society as declining when it is in many ways improving.

All claims about the deteriorating condition of American workers are, in Sumner's belief, false and based on an inadequate knowledge of the past. Sentimentality and a tendency for making broad, abstract statements without a basis in social reality are also problems for Progressive activists and thinkers. Calling for more rigorous fact-checking of claims about society would also benefit his position as an academic by promoting professionalization of social thought. All social analysis that is not based on rigorous factual analysis Sumner attacks as "sentimental" or "ethical"; his use of the word "ethical" in a derogatory sense broke with its use in mainstream American culture.

Sumner's picture of history is one where the great forces underlying social and historical change are largely immune to conscious action. (In his emphasis on changes in economic relations driving history, his awareness of the significance of the rise of industry, and his materialism, Sumner resembles his older contemporary, Karl Marx, whose politics he held in low regard.) The great economic change of Sumner's own period as he saw it was the rise of large, disciplined organizations associated with the growth of industry. Sumner does not use the term "Industrial Revolution," generally accepted as having been popularized by the British economic historian Arnold Toynbee, but it is clear he sees the rise of industry as connected to major social transformation. These organizations regulate the life of the worker to a degree unprecedented in the less organized enterprises of the Colonial and early national periods, giving rise to (in his view) baseless charges of "wage slavery," but they have also, and far more importantly, delivered an unparalleled prosperity. Trying to pass laws to moderate the impact of these changing social forces is a waste of time, in Sumner's view.

Economic prosperity is close to a supreme good for Sumner, although he seems to prefer that all classes benefit. He argues that the material condition of American workers has improved greatly since the Colonial Era and that the increasing regimentation of work is a small price to pay.

Essential Themes

Sumner became one of America's leading and most respected intellectuals. His brand of laissez-faire conservatism, built on the defense of capitalism and economic inequality, has had a great influence on the politics of American business and has always had its champions among university professors (more economists than practitioners of Sumner's own discipline of sociology) and other scholars. There has also been a revival of interest in Sumner's economic thought among libertarians. However, if he thought his essay would stop the Progressive movement in its tracks, he was destined for disappointment. The antitrust campaign under the administrations of Republicans Theodore Roosevelt and William Howard Taft attempted to rein in the power of the wealthy with some success, and the New Deal of the 1930s saw the further expansion of the regulatory state as a response to the Great Depression. Labor unions, which attempted to ameliorate the conditions of work and increase wages through collective action, also survived and grew in the subsequent decades. Although Sumner believed that government should interfere with business as little as possible, he also feared the influence of business on government, and there is some evidence that by the early twentieth century, he was more skeptical of the extremely wealthy.

Debates about the effectiveness of social reform and the value of economic controls versus economic freedom have continued to the present day. Although Sumner and his intellectual allies are often referred to as "classical liberals," the skeptical position against reform movements and the belief that large enterprises and wealthy people should be allowed to go their own ways with minimal interference he put forth is now identified with conservative forces in American political and intellectual life. Furthermore, great concentrations of wealth and their effect on American society are now usually discussed under the heading of inequality.

—*William E. Burns*

Bibliography and Additional Readings

Curtis, Bruce. *William Graham Sumner*. Boston: Twayne, 1981.

Hofstadter, Richard. *Social Darwinism in American Thought*. Boston: Beacon, 1992.

McCloskey, Robert Green. *American Conservatism in the Age of Enterprise 1865–1910: A Study of William Graham Sumner, Stephen J. Field, and Andrew Carnegie*. New York: Harper, 1964.

Sumner, William Graham. *On Liberty, Society and Politics: The Essential Essays of William Graham Sumner*. Ed. Robert C. Bannister. Indianapolis: Liberty Fund, 1992.

THE THEORY OF THE LEISURE CLASS

CHAPTER I

INTRODUCTORY

THE institution of a leisure class is found in its best development at the higher stages of the barbarian culture; as, for instance, in feudal Europe or feudal Japan. In such communities the distinction between classes is very rigorously observed; and the feature of most striking economic significance in these class differences is the distinction maintained between the employments proper to the several classes. The upper classes are by custom exempt or excluded from industrial occupations, and are reserved for certain employments to which a degree of honour attaches. Chief among the honourable employments in any feudal community is warfare; and priestly service is commonly second to warfare. If the barbarian community is not notably warlike, the priestly office may take the precedence, with that of the warrior second. But the rule holds with but slight exceptions that, whether warriors or priests, the upper classes are exempt from industrial employments, and this exemption is the economic expression of their superior rank. Brahmin India affords

The Theory of the Leisure Class, *1924*

From *The Theory of the Leisure Class*

Date: 1899
Author: Thorstein Veblen
Genre: Nonfiction book (excerpt)

Summary Overview

In 1899, Thorstein Veblen's *The Theory of the Leisure Class* was one of the first extensive critiques of modern American conspicuous consumption, or acquiring things not for their usefulness but, rather, as a means of expressing wealth and power. The book was also an attempt to integrate into the study of economics a knowledge of how people actually behave—rather than relying on the traditional economic view that people will act reasonably and in their own self-interest.

Veblen argued that modern industrial societies were socially stratified—that is, organized based on inherited or perceived status rather than on measurable usefulness. In modern societies, he argued, the higher levels of the stratified society are a "leisure class" with time and resources to engage in activities and purchase goods that people of lower status positions are unable to. In this excerpt, from chapter 10, "Modern Survivals of Prowess," Veblen explains that since the leisure class does not engage in labor but, rather, only consumes what is produced by those who do the labor in an industrial society, any success that people in the leisure class enjoy is the result of the type of personality traits that have developed in a consumption-oriented society.

Defining Moment

American writer Mark Twain called it the Gilded Age. Although this phrase was from the title of an 1873 novel about corrupt politicians, since the early twentieth century the term "Gilded Age" has been broadly applied to the United States in the late nineteenth century. It was a time of rapid industrial expansion, the birth of new technologies, and the development of new ways of doing business. These expanding industries provided work for the millions of people who came to the United States from around the world. These growing businesses also led to an increase in wages across the board in the United States. Yet despite the general rise in pay, there was also an increasingly unequal distribution of wealth in the nation. During the second half of the nineteenth century, financial resources were increasingly concentrated in the hands a smaller and smaller portion of Americans.

However, it was not just the ultrawealthy railroad barons and industrial magnates who saw an increase in their wealth. There was an expanding middle class in the United States too, made up of the executives and experts that managed the growing operations of business and industry. These middle-class Americans were the target of an advertising industry that marketed products that not only had utility, but would broadcast status. Whether it was furniture, clothing, household goods, or sports equipment, the brand and style of products that someone bought and used sent messages about the wealth and status of the user. New department stores and mail-order houses provided a greater variety of goods than ever before, with different levels of style, quality, and price that reflected the increasingly stratified society that Veblen described in *The Theory of the Leisure Class*.

Author Biography

Thorstein Veblen was born in 1857 in Cato, Wisconsin, ten years after his parents, Thomas and Kari Veblen, had emigrated from Norway. The family later moved to Minnesota and farmed. Veblen attended local schools and enrolled at Carleton College in Northfield, Minnesota. At college, Veblen studied economics and philosophy at a time when social science as a field of study was beginning to take shape in American higher education. Veblen undertook graduate study at Johns Hopkins University in Baltimore, Maryland, but, unable to receive financial support from the university, moved on to Yale, from which in 1884 he received a PhD in philosophy. Among his instructors at Yale was Charles Graham Sumner, the first American to hold a professorship in sociology. This grounding in the emerging social sciences would inform Veblen's work throughout his career.

Veblen's scholarly career faltered after Yale and, unable to find an academic position, he returned for a time to the family farm in Minnesota. Later, in the 1890s, Veblen shifted his studies to economics, studying first at Cornell University, then obtaining a position at the University of Chicago. There, he published articles in economics and sociology journals and, in 1899, his first and most influential monograph, *The Theory of the Leisure Class*, which is excerpted here.

Veblen's career took him to Stanford University, where he left under a cloud following his involvement in a widely discussed extramarital affair. He briefly taught at the University of Missouri, writing another book. With the outbreak of the First World War in 1914, Veblen began to investigate the connections between war, peace, and economics. He also worked for the federal government during the war and, following, settled in New York City, where he edited *The Dial* magazine for a year. In 1926, Veblen and a group of like-minded academics—who emerged during the Progressive era—established the New School for Social Research in Manhattan.

HISTORICAL DOCUMENT

The physical vigor acquired in the training for athletic games—so far as the training may be said to have this effect—is of advantage both to the individual and to the collectivity, in that, other things being equal, it conduces to economic serviceability. The spiritual traits which go with athletic sports are likewise economically advantageous to the individual, as contradistinguished from the interests of the collectivity. This holds true in any community where these traits are present in some degree in the population. Modern competition is in large part a process of self-assertion on the basis of these traits of predatory human nature. In the sophisticated form in which they enter into the modern, peaceable emulation, the possession of these traits in some measure is almost a necessary of life to the civilized man. But while they are indispensable to the competitive individual, they are not directly serviceable to the community. So far as regards the serviceability of the individual for the purposes of the collective life, emulative efficiency is of use only indirectly if at all. Ferocity and cunning are of no use to the community except in its hostile dealings with other communities; and they are useful to the individual only because there is so large a proportion of the same traits actively present in the human environment to which he is exposed. Any individual who enters the competitive struggle without the due endowment of these traits is at a disadvantage, somewhat as a hornless steer would find himself at a disadvantage in a drove of horned cattle.

The possession and the cultivation of the predatory traits of character may, of course, be desirable on other than economic grounds. There is a prevalent aesthetic or ethical predilection for the barbarian aptitudes, and the traits in question minister so effectively to this predilection that their serviceability in the aesthetic or ethical respect probably offsets any economic unserviceability which they may give. But for the present purpose that is beside the point. Therefore nothing is said here as to the desirability or advisability of sports on the whole, or as to their value on other than economic grounds.

In popular apprehension there is much that is admirable in the type of manhood which the life of sport fosters. There is self-reliance and good-fellowship, so termed in the somewhat loose colloquial use of the words. From a different point of view the qualities currently so characterized might be described as truculence and clannishness. The reason for the current approval and admiration of these manly qualities, as well as for their being called manly, is the same as the reason for their usefulness to the individual. The members of the community, and especially that class of the community which sets the pace in canons of taste, are endowed with this range of propensities in sufficient measure to make their absence in others felt as a shortcoming, and to make their possession in an exceptional degree appreciated as an attribute of superior merit. The traits of predatory man are by no means obsolete in the common run of modern populations. They are present and can be called out in bold relief at any time by any appeal to the sentiments in which they express themselves—unless this appeal should clash with the specific activities that make up our habitual occupations and comprise the general range of our everyday interests. The common run of the population of any industrial community is emancipated from these, economically considered, untoward propensities only in the sense that, through partial and temporary disuse, they have lapsed into the background of subconscious motives. With varying degrees of potency in different individuals, they remain available for the aggressive shaping of men's actions and sentiments whenever a stimulus of more than everyday intensity comes in to call them forth. And they assert themselves forcibly in any case where no occupation alien to the predatory culture has usurped the individual's everyday range of interest and sentiment. This is the case among the leisure class and among certain portions of the population which are ancillary to that class. Hence the facility with which any new accessions to the leisure class take to sports; and hence the rapid growth of sports and of the sporting sentient in any industrial community where wealth has accumulated sufficiently to exempt a considerable part of the population from work.

A homely and familiar fact may serve to show that the predaceous impulse does not prevail in the same degree in all classes. Taken simply as a feature of modern life, the habit of carrying a walking-stick may seem at best a trivial detail; but the usage has a significance for the point in question. The classes among whom the habit most prevails—the classes with whom the walking-stick is associated in popular apprehension—are the men of the leisure class proper, sporting men, and the lower-class delinquents. To these might perhaps be added the men engaged in the pecuniary employments. The same is not true of the common run of men engaged in industry and it may be noted by the way that women do not carry a stick except in case of infirmity, where it has a use of a different kind. The practice is of course in great measure a matter of polite usage; but the basis of polite usage is, in turn, the proclivities of the class which sets the pace in polite usage. The walking-stick serves the purpose of an advertisement that the bearer's hands are employed otherwise than in useful effort, and it therefore has utility as an evidence of leisure. But it is also a weapon, and it meets a felt need of barbarian man on that ground. The handling of so tangible and primitive a means of offense is very comforting to anyone who is gifted with even a moderate share of ferocity. The exigencies of the language make it impossible to avoid an apparent implication of disapproval of the aptitudes, propensities, and expressions of life here under discussion. It is, however, not intended to imply anything in the way of deprecation or commendation of any one of these phases of human character or of the life process. The various elements of the prevalent human nature are taken up from the point of view of economic theory, and the traits discussed are gauged and graded with regard to their immediate economic bearing on the facility of the collective life process. That is to say, these phenomena are here apprehended from the economic point of view and are valued with respect to their direct action in furtherance or hindrance of a more perfect adjustment of the human collectivity to the environment and to the institutional structure required by the economic situation of the collectivity for the present and for the immediate future. For these purposes the traits handed down from the predatory culture are less serviceable than might be. Although even in this connection it is not to be overlooked that the energetic aggressiveness and pertinacity of predatory man is a heritage of no mean value. The economic value—with some regard also to the social value in the narrower sense—of these aptitudes and propensities is attempted to be passed upon without reflecting on their value as seen from another point of view. When contrasted with the prosy mediocrity of the latter-day industrial scheme of life, and judged by the accredited standards of morality, and more especially by the standards of aesthetics and of poetry, these survivals from a more primitive type of manhood may have a very different value from that here assigned them. But all this being foreign to the purpose in hand, no expression of opinion on this latter head would be in place here. All that is admissible is to enter the caution that these standards of excellence, which are alien to the present purpose, must not be allowed to influence our economic appreciation of these traits of human character or of the activities which foster their growth. This applies both as regards those persons who actively participate in sports and those whose sporting experience consists in contemplation only. What is here said of the sporting propensity is likewise pertinent to sundry reflections presently to be made in this connection on what would colloquially be known as the religious life.

The last paragraph incidentally touches upon the fact that everyday speech can scarcely be employed in discussing this class of aptitudes and activities without implying deprecation or apology. The fact is significant as showing the habitual attitude of the dispassionate common man toward the propensities which express themselves in sports and in exploit generally. And this is perhaps as convenient a place as any to discuss that undertone of deprecation which runs through all the voluminous discourse in defense or in laudation of athletic sports, as well as of other activities of a predominantly predatory character. The same apologetic frame of mind is at least beginning to be observable in the spokesmen of most other institutions handed down from the barbarian phase of life. Among these archaic institutions which are felt to need apology are comprised, with others, the entire existing system of the distribution of wealth, together with the resulting class distinction of status; all or nearly all forms of consumption that come under the head of conspicuous waste; the status of women under the patriarchal system; and many features of the traditional creeds and devout observances, especially the exoteric expressions of the creed and the naive apprehension of received observances. What is to be said in this connection of the apologetic attitude taken in commending sports and the sporting character will therefore apply, with a suitable change in phraseology, to the apologies offered in behalf of these other, related elements of our social heritage.

There is a feeling—usually vague and not commonly avowed in so many words by the apologist himself, but ordinarily perceptible in the manner of his discourse—that these sports, as well as the general range of predaceous impulses and habits of thought which underlie the sporting character, do not altogether commend themselves to common sense. "As to the majority of murderers, they are very incorrect characters." This aphorism offers a valuation of the predaceous temperament, and of the disciplinary effects of its overt expression and exercise, as seen from the moralist's point of view. As such it affords an indication of what is the deliverance of the sober sense of mature men as to the degree of availability of the predatory habit of mind for the purposes of the collective life. It is felt that the presumption is against any activity which involves habituation to the predatory attitude, and that the burden of proof lies with those who speak for the rehabilitation of the predaceous temper and for the practices which strengthen it. There is a strong body of popular sentiment in favor of diversions and enterprises of the kind in question; but there is at the same time present in the community a pervading sense that this ground of sentiment wants legitimation. The required legitimation is ordinarily sought by showing that although sports are substantially of a predatory, socially disintegrating effect; although their proximate effect runs in the direction of reversion to propensities that are industrially disserviceable; yet indirectly and remotely—by some not readily comprehensible process of polar induction, or counter-irritation perhaps—sports are conceived to foster a habit of mind that is serviceable for the social or industrial purpose. That is to say, although sports are essentially of the nature of invidious exploit, it is presumed that by some remote and obscure effect they result in the growth of a temperament conducive to non-invidious work. It is commonly attempted to show all this empirically or it is rather assumed that this is the empirical generalization which must be obvious to any one who cares to see it. In conducting the proof of this thesis the treacherous ground of inference from cause to effect is somewhat shrewdly avoided, except so far as to show that the "manly virtues" spoken of above are fostered by sports. But since it is these manly virtues that are (economically) in need of legitimation, the chain of proof breaks off where it should begin. In the most general economic terms, these apologies are an effort to show that, in spite of the logic of the thing, sports do in fact further what may broadly be called workmanship. So long as he has not succeeded in persuading himself or others that this is their effect the thoughtful apologist for sports will not rest content, and commonly, it is to be admitted, he does not rest content. His discontent with his own vindication of the practice in question is ordinarily shown by his truculent tone and by the eagerness with which he heaps up asseverations in support of his position. But why are apologies needed? If there prevails a body of popular sentient in favor of sports, why is not that fact a sufficient legitimation? The protracted discipline of prowess to which the race has been subjected under the predatory and quasi-peaceable culture has transmitted to the men of today a temperament that finds gratification in these expressions of ferocity and cunning. So, why not accept these sports as legitimate expressions of a normal and wholesome human nature? What other norm is there that is to be lived up to than that given in the aggregate range of propensities that express themselves in the sentiments of this generation, including the hereditary strain of prowess? The ulterior norm to which appeal is taken is the instinct of workmanship, which is an instinct more fundamental, of more ancient prescription, than the propensity to predatory emulation. The latter is but a special development of the instinct of workmanship, a variant, relatively late and ephemeral in spite of its great absolute antiquity. The emulative predatory impulse—or the instinct of sportsmanship, as it might well be called—is essentially unstable in comparison with the primordial instinct of workmanship out of which it has been developed and differentiated. Tested by this ulterior norm of life, predatory emulation, and therefore the life of sports, falls short.

The manner and the measure in which the institution of a leisure class conduces to the conservation of sports and invidious exploit can of course not be succinctly stated. From the evidence already recited it appears that, in sentient and inclinations, the leisure class is more favorable to a warlike attitude and animus than the industrial classes. Something similar seems to be true as regards sports. But it is chiefly in its indirect effects, though the canons of decorous living, that the institution has its influence on the prevalent sentiment with respect to the sporting life. This indirect effect goes almost unequivocally in the direction of furthering a survival of the predatory temperament and habits; and this is true even with respect to those variants of the sporting life which the higher leisure-class code of proprieties proscribes; as, e.g., prize-fighting, cock-fighting, and other like vulgar expressions of the sporting temper. Whatever the latest authenticated schedule of detail proprieties may say, the accredited canons of decency sanctioned by the institution say without equivocation that emulation and waste are good and their opposites are disreputable. In the crepuscular light of the social nether spaces the details of the code are not apprehended with all the facility that might be desired, and these broad underlying canons of decency are therefore applied somewhat unreflectingly, with little question as to the scope of their competence or the exceptions that have been sanctioned in detail.

Addiction to athletic sports, not only in the way of direct participation, but also in the way of sentiment and moral support, is, in a more or less pronounced degree, a characteristic of the leisure class; and it is a trait which that class shares with the lower-class delinquents, and with such atavistic elements throughout the body of the community as are endowed with a dominant predaceous trend. Few individuals among the populations of Western civilized countries are so far devoid of the predaceous instinct as to find no diversion in contemplating athletic sports and games, but with the common run of individuals among the industrial classes the inclination to sports does not assert itself to the extent of constituting what may fairly be called a sporting habit. With these classes sports are an occasional diversion rather than a serious feature of life. This common body of the people can therefore not be said to cultivate the sporting propensity. Although it is not obsolete in the average of them, or even in any appreciable number of individuals, yet the predilection for sports in the commonplace industrial classes is of the nature of a reminiscence, more or less diverting as an occasional interest, rather than a vital and permanent interest that counts as a dominant factor in shaping the organic complex of habits of thought into which it enters. As it manifests itself in the sporting life of today, this propensity may not appear to be an economic factor of grave consequence. Taken simply by itself it does not count for a great deal in its direct effects on the industrial efficiency or the consumption of any given individual; but the prevalence and the growth of the type of human nature of which this propensity is a characteristic feature is a matter of some consequence. It affects the economic life of the collectivity both as regards the rate of economic development and as regards the character of the results attained by the development. For better or worse, the fact that the popular habits of thought are in any degree dominated by this type of character can not but greatly affect the scope, direction, standards, and ideals of the collective economic life, as well as the degree of adjustment of the collective life to the environment.

Something to a like effect is to be said of other traits that go to make up the barbarian character. For the purposes of economic theory, these further barbarian traits may be taken as concomitant variations of that predaceous temper of which prowess is an expression. In great measure they are not primarily of an economic character, nor do they have much direct economic bearing. They serve to indicate the stage of economic evolution to which the individual possessed of them is adapted. They are of importance, therefore, as extraneous tests of the degree of adaptation of the character in which they are comprised to the economic exigencies of today, but they are also to some extent important as being aptitudes which themselves go to increase or diminish the economic serviceability of the individual.

As it finds expression in the life of the barbarian, prowess manifests itself in two main directions—force and fraud. In varying degrees these two forms of expression are similarly present in modern warfare, in the pecuniary occupations, and in sports and games. Both lines of aptitudes are cultivated and strengthened by the life of sport as well as by the more serious forms of emulative life. Strategy or cunning is an element invariably present in games, as also in warlike pursuits and in the chase. In all of these employments strategy tends to develop into finesse and chicanery. Chicanery, falsehood, browbeating, hold a well-secured place in the method of procedure of any athletic contest and in games generally. The habitual employment of an umpire, and the minute technical regulations governing the limits and details of permissible fraud and strategic advantage, sufficiently attest the fact that fraudulent practices and attempts to overreach one's opponents are not adventitious features of the game. In the nature of the case habituation to sports should conduce to a fuller development of the aptitude for fraud; and the prevalence in the community of that predatory temperament which inclines men to sports connotes a prevalence of sharp practice and callous disregard of the interests of others, individually and collectively. Resort to fraud, in any guise and under any legitimation of law or custom, is an expression of a narrowly self-regarding habit of mind. It is needless to dwell at any length on the economic value of this feature of the sporting character.

In this connection it is to be noted that the most obvious characteristic of the physiognomy affected by athletic and other sporting men is that of an extreme astuteness. The gifts and exploits of Ulysses are scarcely second to those of Achilles, either in their substantial furtherance of the game or in the éclat which they give the astute sporting man among his associates. The pantomime of astuteness is commonly the first step in that assimilation to the professional sporting man which a youth undergoes after matriculation in any reputable school, of the secondary or the higher education, as the case may be. And the physiognomy of astuteness, as a decorative feature, never ceases to receive the thoughtful attention of men whose serious interest lies in athletic games, races, or other contests of a similar emulative nature. As a further indication of their spiritual kinship, it may be pointed out that the members of the lower delinquent class usually show this physiognomy of astuteness in a marked degree, and that they very commonly show the same histrionic exaggeration of it that is often seen in the young candidate for athletic honors. This, by the way, is the most legible mark of what is vulgarly called "toughness" in youthful aspirants for a bad name.

The astute man, it may be remarked, is of no economic value to the community—unless it be for the purpose of sharp practice in dealings with other communities. His functioning is not a furtherance of the generic life process. At its best, in its direct economic bearing, it is a conversion of the economic substance of the collectivity to a growth alien to the collective life process—very much after the analogy of what in medicine would be called a benign tumor, with some tendency to transgress the uncertain line that divides the benign from the malign growths. The two barbarian traits, ferocity and astuteness, go to make up the predaceous temper or spiritual attitude. They are the expressions of a narrowly self-regarding habit of mind. Both are highly serviceable for individual expediency in a life looking to invidious success. Both also have a high aesthetic value. Both are fostered by the pecuniary culture. But both alike are of no use for the purposes of the collective life.

> **GLOSSARY**
>
> **contradistinguish:** to draw distinctions between two things by comparing them
>
> **deprecation:** to demean or dismiss
>
> **matriculation:** formal entry into a school or course of study
>
> **pecuniary occupations; pecuniary employment:** Veblen's term for work that is primarily managerial or financial as opposed to physical or industrial
>
> **propensity:** a habit or common practice

Document Analysis

Veblen begins this chapter of *The Theory of the Leisure Class* by establishing the frame of reference he will use throughout—that of sports, or athletic competition. In the opening paragraph, he argues that the physical skills and "spiritual traits" that are associated with sports and athletics are "economically advantageous to the individual." Veblen then asserts that "modern competition" consists of a process of people asserting themselves on the basis of what he calls "traits of predatory human nature." In the modern world, he explains, these traits are "peaceable" but—as is the case with the predation practiced by animals in the wild—they are chiefly of benefit to the individual rather than the community as a whole. Veblen closes out the paragraph by describing some of these predatory traits, such as efficiency, ferocity, and cunning—anyone not possessing these traits, he argues, is at a "disadvantage" in the "competitive struggle." Sports, he argues, help cultivate these traits.

The next paragraph is almost an aside, as Veblen muses on the noneconomic value of the predatory traits encouraged by sports, claiming that "there is a prevalent aesthetic or ethical predilection for the barbarian aptitudes. Here, he is basically observing that athletes and athletic competitions are popular. All of this, he admits, is "beside the point" and he is not going to argue about whether or not sports are valuable on anything other than an economic basis.

In the third paragraph, Veblen's language becomes more complex and—to casual readers—confusing as he expands on his argument about the utility of sports for nurturing the predatory traits necessary for thriving in a competitive economy. He observes that sport features "self-reliance and good-fellowship" (or, expressed in a less charitable manner "truculence and clannishness"). He also discusses the prevalence of the word "manly" to describe the qualities necessary for competition and explains that these aggressive traits continued to be valued by modern society. Veblen points to the popularity of sports and athletics to members of the leisure class, arguing that the popularity will grow "in any industrial community where wealth has accumulated sufficiently to exempt a considerable part of the population from work." Sports require time and practice to master—the upper classes, not having to work 12 hours a day in a factory or other job—have the luxury of the spare time in which to indulge these activities. Thus, they are able to hone their predatory traits in a more efficient way than members of the working classes.

For his next example, Veblen uses the illustration of a walking stick. He explains that the walking stick is—in the popular imagination—associated with the leisure class, sporting men, "lower-class delinquents," and those "engaged in the pecuniary employments"—work which involves, Veblen explained in an earlier chapter, "ownership or acquisition." Similarly, there are groups that are generally not seen to carry walking sticks: women and men "engaged in industry" that is, men who are working. The walking stick, Veblen explains, is a signal or "advertisement" that the person carrying it doesn't have to engage in physical work, either because they are sufficiently wealthy, are engaged in "pecuniary" work, or because they are a criminal. He then connects the walking stick to his theme of predatory traits by reminding the reader that the walking stick is a weapon as well as an accessory and is also associated with sport. Here, Veblen brings together several of his themes such as the importance of sport, and sporting symbolism to modern industrial societies and the ways in which status objects (like walking sticks) may carry multiple layers of meaning.

Veblen, in a very long paragraph, also addresses the seeming contradiction that although the predatory traits nurtured by athletic competition are, in general, perceived as negative "sports are conceived to foster a habit of mind that is serviceable for the social or industrial purpose." In the subsequent paragraph, Veblen reiterates a point from a previous chapter (that the leisure class tends to be "more favorable to a warlike attitude and animus than the industrial classes") and draws a parallel between combat and athletics. The upper classes, however, have developed a refined taste and have rejected sporting events ("prize-fighting, cock-fighting, and other like vulgar expressions of the sporting temper"). Thus, while there are lower-class expressions of sport (the "vulgar" ones), there are also upper-class expressions. The type of sport one enjoys are another signifier of social status.

Essential Themes

Veblen concludes the chapter by continuing the discussion of the leisure class's attraction to sports—both as participants and spectators—and comparing it to the manifestations of sporting life enjoyed by the working classes. He also discusses the concept of "prowess," which (for the "barbarian") is made up of two factors: force and fraud. Force and fraud, he argues, are important not only to sport but modern warfare as well as the pecuniary occupations, or business and finance. Veblen further breaks these ideas down into traits such as strategy, finesse, and chicanery. In all, he sees evidence of the workings of class-informed attitudes and behaviors that are not entirely "rational" in the economic sense and that also bolster his ideas about leisure and consumption in the modern world.

—*Aaron Gulyas*

Bibliography and Additional Reading

Diggins, John Patrick. *Thorstein Veblen: Theorist of the Leisure Class*. Princeton, NJ: Princeton University Press, 1999.

Hudson, Michael, and Ahmet Öncü, eds. *Absentee Ownership and its Discontents: Critical Essays on the Legacy of Thorstein Veblen*. Dresden: ISLET, 2016.

Jorgensen, Elizabeth, and Henry Jorgensen. *Thorstein Veblen: Victorian Firebrand*. London: Routledge, 1998.

Plotkin, Sidney, ed. *The Anthem Companion to Thorstein Veblen*. London: Anthem, 2017.

■ Coal Strike Hearings: The Miners Testify

Date: December 18, 1902
Author: Unknown
Genre: Article

Summary Overview

The anthracite coal strike of 1902 came on the heels of significant labor agitation in the preceding years. In 1897, the United Mine Workers of America (UMWA)—working in bituminous, or soft coal, mines— won both wage increases and improved conditions, and miners' union membership grew significantly. Workers in anthracite, or hard coal, mines in eastern Pennsylvania went on strike in May 1902, demanding a reduction in hours, an increase in pay, and an end to unsafe working conditions. The strike continued through the summer, but by October, when it seemed that the strike would interfere with the winter's heating supply, President Theodore Roosevelt intervened, calling a meeting of the UMWA, the mine owners, and government arbitrators. Though the union initially refused to end the strike, following the establishment of an arbitration commission, the strike was called off on October 23, 1902, after 163 days. An article on the testimony taken by the commission was published in the newspaper *Public Opinion* in December 1902.

Defining Moment

When anthracite coal miners in eastern Pennsylvania went on strike in 1902, it was with the knowledge that their fellow coal miners in the Midwest had made significant gains in their strike of 1897 and that in the following five years, both anthracite and bituminous coal miners had been able to gain small concessions through union activity. In 1900, a general strike had been called, and under pressure from a looming election, Republican Senator Mark Hanna persuaded the mine owners to make wage and arbitration concessions. The strike was called off, without the UMWA or any other union being recognized by the mine owners.

By 1902, many of the same issues that arose in 1900 were pressing again. Wages were low, conditions in the mines were dangerous, and hours were long. On May 12, 1902, union miners went on strike, and in June, maintenance employees, such as firemen and engineers, joined them. In total, nearly 150,000 workers participated in the strike.

Resentful of governmental interference in the 1900 strike, the mine owners were not interested initially in any federal involvement. During the summer, strikers clashed with strikebreakers, police, private security personnel hired by the mine owners, and even the Pennsylvania National Guard. As the situation escalated and became the focus of national attention, President Roosevelt sought to protect the nation's winter heating supply and return the miners to work. Though Attorney General Philander Knox counseled against Roosevelt's involvement, as the strike continued and neither side seemed willing to negotiate, the president decided to call a meeting of labor, management, and government representatives on October 3. Roosevelt found the mine owners stubborn and rigid, while John Mitchell, the president of the UMWA, saw the meeting as a *de facto* recognition of the union and so was eager for it to be a success. However, the workers voted to continue the strike three days after the meeting, as they were unwilling to trust the word of the mine owners.

Despite the overall failure of the meeting, the federal government did not end its attempt to resolve the strike peacefully. At the behest of the White House, Secretary of War Elihu Root and businessman John Pierpont (J.P.) Morgan used Morgan's influence with mine owners to propose the creation of a five-member commission composed of two engineers, a judge, a coal expert, and a sociologist, which would hear testimony from the mine workers and seek to address their grievances. The workers and mine owners agreed, and a Catholic bishop and the commissioner of labor, Carroll D. Wright, were soon added to the commission. After 163 days, the coal strike ended on October 23.

The commission toured the area immediately after the strike ended and heard testimony from more than five hundred witnesses over the next several months. The commission determined that there were grounds to demand improvements in working conditions and wages, but it also confirmed that striking miners had harmed and in some cases killed nonstriking workers and destroyed property. In the end, the strikers won a 10 percent wage increase and a reduction of work hours from ten to nine hours, and though the UMWA was not officially recognized, an arbitration board was set up to address labor disputes. Miller and the UMWA considered the strike an important victory not only for Pennsylvania mine workers but also for labor unions nationwide.

WPA poster.

HISTORICAL DOCUMENT

Since the anthracite coal strike commission resumed its sessions, on December 3, some very interesting testimony has been given by mine-workers relative to the conditions of their employment. The operators have already announced that they will rebut many of the statements made, and, if this is done, their side of the case will be given a hearing at a later date.

James Gallagher, who has worked for Markle & Co. for twenty-one years, stated that in all the time he worked for the company he only once had received any money, and that was $50. "We traded at the company store and got credit," he explained. "We had to buy provisions there, though the prices are from 10 to 12 per cent higher than at other stores; but clothing, which is 20 per cent higher, we could buy elsewhere. I made an average of $1.25 a day every day of the years I've been working, I guess, but I was never out of debt. Sometimes I've owed the company a big amount—as high as $211 once. Every time I worked hard and reduced the debt until I was nearly clear, the company would take me out of the place where I was making $60 or $70 a month and put me in a place where I could not make $25, and then back into debt I'd be again."

Andrew Chippa, a breaker boy, employed by the same company, started to work last spring to wipe out a debt of $54 owed the company by his father when he was killed in the company's mines. The lad has not received any money for his work, but his earnings have been credited against the company's bill. As he has a mother and three brothers and sisters, his earnings have not been enough to reduce the bill. Instead it has grown to $88.17.

The first description of the work of a fireman was given when Jacob Ansbach, a Coxe employee, took the stand. He said that he worked one week from 6 A.M. to 4:30 P.M., and the next reversed these hours. His pay was $1.57 a day. Every other Sunday he worked twenty-four hours at a stretch. In the six years he had had his place, he paid between $700 and $800 on a house which he had bought for $900.

The most pathetic story yet told to the commission was that of Henry Call, a Markle employee. The old miner, decrepit from many injuries, told under the examination how the evictions were carried on. The wife was sick and her 100-year-old mother was blind and unable to walk. The day on which they were "thrown out" was rainy. He took them the best way he could to Hazelton, seven miles away, and placed them in a cold, damp, empty house. This was last month, when the atmosphere on the Hazelton mountain was quite cold. His wife became worse. Medical aid was kindly furnished free by a Hazelton doctor, but it did not help her much. "We were greatly worried because of our having been turned out of our house, and, one night," the witness said, between sobs, "she died."

W. H. Dettry, president of a local union, employed as a miner by Coxe Bros., said that company men are paid an average of $7.20 a week, and all contractors are required to stay in the mines from 7 A.M. until 3 P.M., regardless of whether they have enough cars to fill with coal they had mined. He said a black-list exists at the Coxe mines, and that he was on it for nine months, because he refused to work a breast which netted him only three dollars a week. He also complained of the docking system.

James McMonigle, a miner formerly employed by Markle & Co., said the breast he was working in was so dangerous that he complained to the company officials that he might be killed. He was told if he worked any other breast he would not be given any cars. He went out on strike, and after the suspension he was refused work and evicted from his house.

John Early, a check weighman, employed at the Gypsy Grove colliery of the Erie company, who was president of the Gypsy Grove "local," told, on stand, of an alleged attempt made by a former mine foreman named Grimes to bribe two presidents of local unions of the miners to have ten men in each local use their influence to have a resolution passed sending the men to work, thus making a serious break in solid ranks of the strikers. Each of the president was to receive $2,500 and a good position as mine foreman, and each of the ten men was to get from $100 to $200 each. Early refused the money and told Grimes he would see him later. Early reported the matter to District President Nichols, of the union, who gave out a public statement, in which he intimated bribery was being resorted to in order break the strike, and the whole thing fell through.

The Delaware and Hudson company presented figures to the commission December 10, they being the first certified statistics to be handed in. They show the average earnings of the miner in 1901 to have been $622.63, and his laborer $449.47. Mr. Mitchell, on the stand, said that $600 should be the minimum wage.

Father J. V. Hussie, pastor of St. Gabriel's church of Hazelton who has been a close friend of the miners, said, of the living conditions: "There has been much change in the last six years. The condition in and about Hazelton is deplorable. I say it without any coloring. The people are barely able to exist. The deplorable condition is most strikingly evident in cases of sickness, the sick being unable to secure bare necessities. Markle & Co. have a burial fund, because their people cannot save enough money to insure them burial. The foreigners have burial societies. It is impossible to keep families together. The children have to leave their homes and get work. The average age when the miners' children leave school is little over eleven years."

GLOSSARY

breaker boy: a child worker in a coal-breaking plant who removes impurities (e.g., slate) from broken clumps of coal

breast: the face being worked at the end of a tunnel

check weighman: a worker who weighs and records other workers' loads

Document Analysis

Published on December 18, 1902, in the Pennsylvania newspaper *Public Opinion*, the article on the coal strike hearings documents some of the miners' testimony taken by the strike commission and a Catholic priest who was familiar with the workers' living conditions. The article states that the mine operators intended to call this testimony regarding working and living conditions into question and that the paper would report their side of the case as well. Throughout the strike of 1902, *Public Opinion* sought not only to present a balanced view of the strike and the activities of the commission, but also to record the varying opinions set forth in other newspapers. In this case, however, the newspaper records the testimony of miners who described a system that kept them in a state of virtual slavery and forced them to work in dangerous conditions.

Several of the workers testify that the mine stores, where workers were forced to purchase food at inflated prices, consumed their wages and left them in debt to the company. One miner, James Gallagher, testifies that each time he had repaid nearly all of his debt, he was transferred to a lower-paying position, ensuring that he would never be debt-free. A worker's debt to the company did not disappear when he died; rather, it was passed on to his family, as a young man working to pay off his deceased father's debt explains to the commission. Workers who were unable to pay their debt were forced from company-owned houses or houses on which the company held the note. One elderly miner testifies that his family was evicted during a particularly rainy and cold period, resulting in the death of his already-ill wife, while another miner tells the commission that he was evicted after refusing to work in a particularly dangerous area of the mine.

In addition to testimony concerning the financial peril of working in the mines, testimony is given about the mine owners' attempts to intimidate workers and infiltrate the union. One worker testifies that he was placed on a blacklist when he refused to work in a low-paying position. Another reports that the mine owners attempted to bribe the miners into voting against the strike. They refused and reported the attempted bribery to union officials.

The article concludes by documenting the testimony of a local priest, Father J.V. Hussie, who testifies that living conditions for miners and their families were "deplorable," particularly for those whose family members fell ill or died. In some cases, families could not afford to bury their dead and were forced to rely on charity. Hussie also reports that children were often forced to leave their homes around age eleven to look for work.

Coal Strike Hearings: The Miners Testify • 157

Shenandoah, Pennsylvania. John Mitchell, President of the UMWA (United Mine Workers of America), arriving in the coal town during the Anthracite coal strike of 1902. His open four-horse carriage is surrounded by a crowd of boys. The driver of the high front seat is wearing a derby hat.

Essential Themes

"The Coal Strike Hearings" illustrates the hardships faced by workers in the anthracite mines, shedding light on the union's justification for the strike. UMWA hoped that the union was seen by the commission and the American people not as the instigator of the coal shortage that would result from the strike but as a champion of working people who had been driven to extreme measures by unjust and inhumane treatment. Since the commission would determine any concessions to be made, testimony was given that supported that argument—firsthand accounts of men who were evicted from their homes when they fell ill, young men falling deeper into debt with no chance to get ahead, and companies that resorted to bribery and intimidation to keep their workers impoverished, indebted, and unable to advocate for themselves without penalty. The mine owners' testimony illustrated the darker side of the strike, including the violence dealt to workers who refused to strike and acts of arson and sabotage against company property. Still, the testimony of the workers made a powerful impression on the commission, whose findings were generally in favor of the strikers.

—*Bethany Groff Dorau*

Bibliography and Additional Reading

Cornell, Robert J. *The Anthracite Coal Strike of 1902*. Washington, DC: Catholic University of America, 1957.

Dublin, Thomas, and Walter Light. *The Face of Decline: The Pennsylvania Anthracite Region in the Twentieth Century*. Ithaca, NY: Cornell University Press, 2005.

Grossman, Jonathan. "The Coal Strike of 1902—Turning Point in U.S. Policy." *U.S. Department of Labor*. U.S. Department of Labor, n.d.

"Public Opinion: Part of Life in the Cumberland Valley." *Public Opinion*. Chambersburg Public Opinion, 2014.

■ An Immigrant Garment Worker's "Days and Dreams"

Date: September 25, 1902
Author: Sadie Frowne
Genre: Autobiography; article

Summary Overview

In 1898, a young Polish girl named Sadie Frowne and her mother immigrated to the United States in search of greater economic opportunities. Their journey was arduous: they traveled in steerage, crowded into dark and damp conditions along with many other immigrants. Less than a year after arriving in New York City, her mother died, leaving Frowne to fend for herself. Frowne found employment at one of New York's many sweatshops, working long hours in dangerous conditions. In 1902, she gave an interview to the New York *Independent*, a reform-minded newspaper, in which she describes her experiences immigrating to and living in America.

Defining Moment

Beginning in the late nineteenth century, immigrants began arriving in the United States at an unprecedented rate. Between 1881 and 1920, more than twenty-three million immigrants settled in the United States, and the country's population more than doubled in that time, increasing from fifty million in 1880 to more than one hundred million by 1920. On the East Coast, large numbers of eastern and southern European immigrants came to major city centers such as New York in search of better financial opportunities or to escape political or religious persecution in their homelands. According to data from the 1860 U.S. Census, New York City's population just prior to the outbreak of the Civil War was about 814,000; by 1890, the population of New York City exceeded 1.5 million. Immigrants often settled in ethnic neighborhoods, where they were crowded into dark and poorly made tenement houses. Most immigrants, particularly those who did not speak English well, earned meager wages at factories, dockyards, and sweatshops throughout the city.

Young Sadie Frowne was among a wave of eastern European Jewish immigrants arriving in New York just prior to the turn of the twentieth century. Frowne's parents had owned a small grocery business in their small village in eastern Poland. However, Frowne's father died when she was ten years old, and her mother struggled to maintain their business following his death. Like many immigrants, Frowne's mother reached out for assistance to a relative who had already immigrated to the United States. Frowne's Aunt Fanny, who was living in New York City, encouraged the Frownes to come join her in New York and even gave them the financial assistance needed to make the trip. After a long and dangerous transatlantic voyage in the ship's overcrowded steerage section, Frowne (who was now thirteen) and her mother arrived in New York.

Not long after their arrival, Frowne's mother died of tuberculosis, an infectious disease that spread quickly in the crowded tenement buildings of New York City's immigrant neighborhoods. Following the death of her mother, Frowne found work in one of the city's garment factories (also known as sweatshops). The substandard working conditions at these sweatshops are infamous—long hours, poor lighting and ventilation, a lack of emergency exits and other safety procedures, frequent injuries, and low pay were the norm for Frowne and her coworkers. She also experienced the sexual harassment of her male coworkers and other forms of workplace abuse.

Frowne was eager to assimilate into American society. She moved from the Lower East Side to Brownsville, a predominantly Jewish community in Brooklyn, and began attending night classes at a nearby public school. She also became involved with the local unions, paying a monthly union membership fee and taking part in several strikes to demand better pay and shorter workdays. At the age of seventeen, she agreed to be interviewed by a New York–based newspaper called the *Independent*, which was compiling a story about sweatshops and the experiences of the immigrants who worked therein.

Author Biography
Not much is known about Sadie Frowne beyond the information that she provided to the *Independent*. She was born in 1885 in a small village in eastern Poland. Her mother was a well-educated, multilingual owner of a grocery business, and her father was a farmer. After her father died, expenses became too great for Frowne and her mother to support themselves, and they moved to New York City in 1898. Her mother died of tuberculosis shortly after their arrival, leaving Frowne to fend for herself. She worked long hours in a sweatshop during the day and pursued her education at night. In 1902, she was interviewed by the *Independent*, which included her brief autobiography in an article that depicted the life of sweatshop workers.

HISTORICAL DOCUMENT

We came by steerage on a steamship in a very dark place that smelt dreadfully. There were hundreds of other people packed in with us, men, women and children, and almost all of them were sick. It took us twelve days to cross the sea, and we thought we should die, but at last the voyage was over, and we came up and saw the beautiful bay and the big woman with the spikes on her head and the lamp that is lighted at night in her hand.

Aunt Fanny and her husband met us at the gate of this country and were very good to us, and soon I had a place to live out while my mother got work in a factory making white goods.

I was only a little over thirteen years of age and a greenhorn, so I received $9 a month and board and lodging, which I thought was doing well. Mother, who, as I have said, was very clever, made $9 a week on white goods, which means all sorts of underclothing, and is high class work.

But mother had a very gay disposition. She liked to go around and see everything, and friends took her about New York at night and she caught a bad cold and coughed and coughed. She really had hasty consumption, but she didn't know it, and I didn't know it, and she tried to keep on working, but it was no use. She had not the strength. Two doctors attended her, but they could do nothing, and at last she died and I was left alone. I had saved money while out at service, but mother's sickness and funeral swept it all away and now I had to begin all over again.

I got a room in the house of some friends who lived near the factory. I pay $1 a week for the room and am allowed to do light housekeeping—that is, cook my meals in it. I get my own breakfast in the morning, just a cup of coffee and a roll, and at noon time I come home to dinner and take a plate of soup and a slice of bread with the lady of the house. My food for a week costs a dollar, just as it did in Allen Street, and I have the rest of my money to do as I like with. I am earning $5.50 a week now, and will probably get another increase soon.

It isn't piecework in our factory, but one is paid by the amount of work done just the same. So it is like piecework. All the hands get different amounts, some as low as $3.50 and some of the men as high as $16 a week. The factory is in the third story of a brick building. It is in a room twenty feet long and fourteen broad. There are fourteen machines in it. I and the daughter of the people with whom I live work two of these machines. The other operators are all men, some young and some old.

Henry has seen me home every night for a long time and makes love to me. He wants me to marry him, but I am not seventeen yet, and I think that is too young. He is only nineteen, so we can wait.

I have been to the fortune teller's three or four times, and she always tells me that though I have had such a lot of trouble I am to be very rich and happy. I believe her because she has told me so many things that have come true.

So I will keep on working in the factory for a time. Of course it is hard, but I would have to work hard even if I was married.

I get up at half-past five o'clock every morning and make myself a cup of coffee on the oil stove. I eat a bit of bread and perhaps some fruit and then go to work. Often I get there soon after six o'clock so as to be in good time, though the factory does not open till seven. I have heard that there is a sort of clock that calls you at the very time you want to get up, but I can't believe that because I don't see how the clock would know.

At seven o'clock we all sit down to our machines and the boss brings to each one the pile of work that he or she is to finish during the day, what they call in English their 'stint.' This pile is put down beside the machine and as soon as a skirt is done it is laid on the other side of the machine. Sometimes the work is not all finished by six o'clock and then the one who is behind must work overtime. Sometimes one is finished ahead of time and gets away at four or five o'clock, but generally we are not done till six o'clock.

The machines go like mad all day, because the faster you work the more money you get. Sometimes in my haste I get my finger caught and the needle goes right through it. It goes so quick, though, that it does not hurt much. I bind the finger up with a piece of cotton and go on working. We all have accidents like that. Where the needle goes through the nail it makes a sore finger, or where it splinters a bone it does much harm. Sometimes a finger has to come off. Generally, though, one can be cured by a salve.

All the time we are working the boss walks about examining the finished garments and making us do them over again if they are not just right. So we have to be careful as well as swift. But I am getting so good at the work that within a year I will be making $7 a week, and then I can save at least $3.50 a week. I have over $200 saved now.

The machines are all run by foot-power, and at the end of the day one feels so weak that there is a great temptation to lie right down and sleep. But you must go out and get air, and have some pleasure. So instead of lying down I go out, generally with Henry. Sometimes we go to Coney Island, where there are good dancing places, and sometimes we go to Ulmer Park to picnics...

For the last two winters I have been going to night school. I have learned reading, writing and arithmetic. I can read quite well in English now and I look at the newspapers every day. I read English books, too, sometimes.

GLOSSARY

hasty consumption: incurable tuberculosis

piecework: payment based on the number of pieces completed

steerage: the section of a passenger ship, originally amid or near the steering equipment, having the cheapest seats

A sweatshop in a New York tenement building, c. 1889. (Jacob Riis - Library of Congress's Prints and Photographs division)

Document Analysis

Prior to her arrival in the United States, Sadie Frowne lived with her parents in a small apartment behind their store in eastern Poland, while her father's farming income supported their grocery business. When he died, however, Frowne and her mother entered a period of great tumult—they fell behind on their rent and ultimately closed the store. On the advice of Frowne's Aunt Fanny, they traveled across the Atlantic to settle in New York City, where they had heard it was easier to earn a living.

The trip aboard the steamer was, as Frowne recalls, extremely trying. Steerage—the cheapest section—was packed with fellow immigrants, many of whom were ill with various ailments. The accommodations thus smelled "dreadfully," as she describes, and both Frowne and her mother worried that they too would fall ill and never make it to the "beautiful bay and the big woman with the spikes on her head" (the Statue of Liberty). They did arrive safely, however, and were greeted by Aunt Fanny and her husband, with whom they lived until they obtained lodging for themselves.

Frowne first found work as a household servant, while her mother worked at a garment factory. However, her mother quickly succumbed to tuberculosis, and the cost of her care and funeral wiped away all of their meager savings. Frowne, then sixteen years old, began working at a sweatshop on Allen Street in Manhattan. She had sewing skills but needed to quickly learn how to sew dresses and other complex clothes at a fast pace. Frowne accounts how she wakes up each day at 5:30 in the morning, eats a light breakfast, and gets to work an hour before the sweatshop opens. When the facility opens its doors at 7:00, Frowne and her coworkers immediately sit down at their respective machines, while the foreman brings around a large pile of materials—called a "stint"—that had to be completed by the end of the day, some eleven hours later. Frowne faced a daunting task daily: she needed to perform consistently high-quality work yet complete it within a strict time limit. She already worked long hours during a typical day—any mistakes she made resulted in a much longer day toiling at her machine.

Frowne's story illustrates the physically draining work performed at sweatshops. The machines "go like mad all day," she explains, with each worker's feet operating it. Sometimes, her finger would get caught under the needle, an injury that would occur so frequently she eventually would think nothing of it, even when it resulted in bone fractures. Meanwhile, the foreman would walk up and down the cramped aisles to review the workers' stints—if the project was not done to standards, the worker was verbally harangued and forced to remain at work after hours until the stint was completed in a satisfactory manner.

Frowne refused to allow the physical and psychological challenges of the sweatshop to overcome her. She was savvy with her money, carefully budgeting her limited pay in such a way that she could afford groceries and other living expenses and still pay for new clothes and outings with her boyfriend, Henry. While many of her coworkers spent their time off resting up from their long and arduous shifts, Frowne insists that one "must go out and get air, and have some pleasure." Frowne frequently used a portion of her earnings to go to the theater or go out dancing. She even used some of her savings to attend night school, learning English and obtaining a basic education so that she could better assimilate into American society.

Essential Themes

Frowne's story provides an illustration of the nineteenth-century immigrant experience in New York City. Frowne's account describes the frightening conditions aboard the transatlantic steamships that brought millions of European immigrants to New York Harbor. It also illustrates the daily challenges facing American laborers at the turn of the century, before the introduction of stringent labor laws, and Frowne's working experience illustrates the lack of safety regulations, the long hours, and inadequate pay that characterized the work lives of many American laborers at the time. Her enthusiasm for her local union and willingness to strike for better working conditions and pay reflects the nascent labor movement of the time.

Frowne's account is also illustrative of the increasing independence experienced by young working women of the time. These working women of the early twentieth century were often the first women in their families to experience some measure of independence—living outside of the family, often unmarried, and financially supporting themselves. Frowne's remarks regarding her boyfriend Henry's desire to get married and her decision to wait reflect the increasing financial and social independence of working women of the time.

—*Michael P. Auerbach*

Bibliography and Additional Reading

Anbinder, Tyler. *Five Points: The 19th-Century New York City Neighborhood That Invented Tap Dance, Stole Elections, and Became the World's Most Notorious Slum.* New York: Simon, 2001.

Katzman, David M., and William M. Tuttle, Jr. *Plain Folk: The Life Stories of Undistinguished Americans.* Champaign: University of Illinois Press, 1982.

Lubove, Roy. *The Progressives and the Slums: Tenement House Reform in New York City, 1890–1917.* Pittsburgh: University of Pittsburgh Press, 1963.

Markel, Howard. *Quarantine! East European Jewish Immigrants and the New York City Epidemics of 1892.* Baltimore: Johns Hopkins University Press, 1999.

Wenger, Beth S. *The Jewish Americans: Three Centuries of Jewish Voices in America.* New York: Random, 2007.

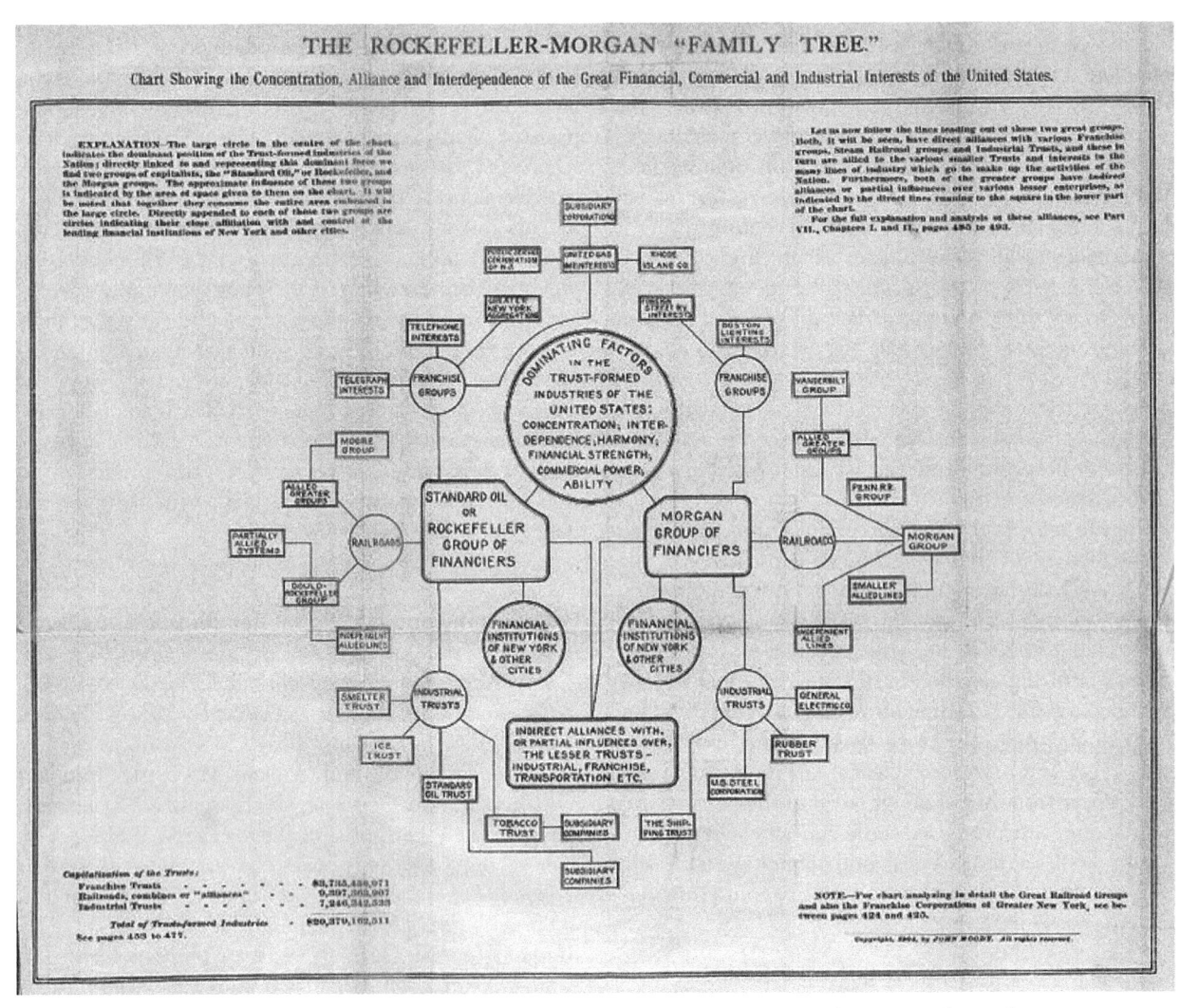

The Rockefeller-Morgan Family Tree (1904), which depicts how the largest trusts at the turn of the 20th century were in turn connected to each other. (John Moody - The Truth about The Trusts: A Description and Analysis of the American Trust Movement. *New York: Moody Publishing Company, 1904.)*

Theodore Roosevelt on Corporate Trusts

Date: September 20, 1902
Author: President Theodore Roosevelt
Genre: Political speech

Summary Overview

In the late summer of 1902, President Theodore Roosevelt set out on a speaking tour aimed at generating support for Republican congressional candidates in the off-year elections coming in November that year. Roosevelt gave this speech in the Music Hall in Cincinnati, Ohio, on September 20, 1902. This speech focused on the problem of the business trusts, and the need to regulate them. Roosevelt argued that while some action was needed to address the problems associated with the growth of the trusts, it must be done carefully and advisedly. He believed some solutions that had been proposed would hurt all corporations, not just those using trusts as a means of achieving monopoly. Roosevelt argued that a reckless approach to controlling the power of the trusts could destroy the general prosperity that the nation was experiencing at the time.

Defining Moment

The growth of big business in the late nineteenth and early twentieth centuries dramatically altered the American economy. Many of the founders and major stockholders in these new industrial firms grew very wealthy, and many Americans shared in some portion of the newly created prosperity. The growth of big business at this time was somewhat natural. The national railroad system provided relatively fast and reliable transportation, and the telegraph and later the telephone made instant communication possible. The corporate structure of business allowed companies to sell shares of stock to raise huge amounts of capital. In many ways, big business was growing simply because, for the first time, it was possible to do business on a truly large scale.

However, many believed that some of this growth was due to illegitimate business practices. Some consumers, journalists, and political reformers believed that some business firms tried to limit competition and to monopolize their particular industry. The trust was a common means of attempting this. As Roosevelt points out in this speech, many people used the word "trust" in a loose and often incorrect way, referring to any corporate business activity. The first trust that became known to the American public was the Standard Oil Trust, formed in 1882 but unknown to those outside the company for several years. In a business trust, the assets of several companies were put under the control of a group of trustees. Many of the early trusts were informal, with no legal structure, and were secret. But the managers of the trust could run the several businesses whose assets they controlled in such a way that competition was limited and the trust could move toward monopolistic control of the product or services they provided. Standard Oil soon became one of the favorite targets of muckraking journalists and crusading reformers. While Standard Oil apparently pioneered the trust, and became the most infamous example, there were trusts that attempted to control various businesses, such as the tobacco industry, meatpacking, and railroading. Congress had tried to address this issue with the Sherman Antitrust Act of 1890 but the legislation had little effect, in part because it was loosely worded and the types of illegal business combinations were not distinctly defined.

Theodore Roosevelt believed that the public's interest in rcining in the power of the trusts needed to be addressed. As the off-year elections of November 1902 drew near, he undertook a speaking tour to stimulate support for Republican candidates in Congress. He believed the Democratic Party would make the trusts a campaign issue, and if the Republicans did not address it they could lose seats in Congress. This was a speech made during that tour.

Author Biography

Theodore Roosevelt, the 26th president of the United States, was born in New York City on October 27, 1857. Roosevelt graduated from Harvard College in 1880, and studied law at Columbia University. He served one term in the New York State Assembly, and then served six years on the United States Civil Service Commission. He was assistant secretary of the Navy in President William McKinley's first administration, but resigned to serve in the army in the Spanish-American War. The notoriety he gained in that war led to his election as governor of New York in 1898. New York City political bosses who were unhappy with Roosevelt as governor and maneuvered to have him nominated for U.S. vice president when McKinley ran for a second term in 1900. McKinley was reelected with Roosevelt on the ticket, but the president was shot by an assassin on September 6, 1901; when he died (on September 14), Roosevelt became president and was easily elected in his own right in 1904.

HISTORICAL DOCUMENT

AT MUSIC HALL, CINCINNATI, OHIO, ON THE EVENING OF SEPTEMBER 20, 1902

Mr. Mayor, and you, my fellow-Americans:

I shall ask your attention to what I say to-night, because I intend to make a perfectly serious argument to you, and I shall be obliged if you will remain as still as possible; and I ask that those at the very back will remember that if they talk or make a noise it interferes with the hearing of the rest. I intend to speak to you on a serious subject and to make an argument as the Chief Executive of a nation, who is the President of all the people, without regard to party, without regard to section. I intend to make to you an argument from the standpoint simply of one American talking to his fellow-Americans upon one of the great subjects of interest to all alike; and that subject is what are commonly known as the trusts. The word is used very loosely and almost always with technical inaccuracy. The average man, however, when he speaks of the trusts means rather vaguely all of the very big corporations, the growth of which has been so signal a feature of our modern civilization, and especially those big corporations which, though organized in one State, do business in several States, and often have a tendency to monopoly.

The whole subject of the trusts is of vital concern to us, because it presents one, and perhaps the most conspicuous, of the many problems forced upon our attention by the tremendous industrial development which has taken place during the last century, a development which is occurring in all civilized countries, notably in our own. There have been many factors responsible for bringing about these changed conditions. Of these, steam and electricity are the chief. The extraordinary changes in the methods of transportation of merchandise and of transmission of news have rendered not only possible, but inevitable, the immense increase in the rate of growth of our great industrial centres that is, of our great cities. I want you to bring home to yourselves that fact. When Cincinnati was founded, news could be transmitted and merchandise carried exactly as had been the case in the days of the Roman Empire. You had here on your river the flatboat, you had on the ocean the sailing-ship, you had the pack-train, you had the wagon, and every one of the four was known when Babylon fell. The change in the last hundred years has been greater by far than the changes in all the preceding three thousand. Those are the facts. Because of them have resulted the specialization of industries, and the unexampled opportunities offered for the employment of huge amounts of capital, and therefore for the rise in the business world of those master minds through whom alone it is possible for such vast amounts of capital to be employed with profit. It matters very little whether we like these new conditions or whether we dislike them; whether we like the creation of these new opportunities or not. Many admirable qualities which were developed in the older, simpler, less progressive life, have tended to atrophy under our rather feverish, high-pressure, complex life of to-day. But our likes and dislikes have nothing to do with the matter. The new conditions are here. You can't bring back the old days of the canal-boat and stage-coach if you wish. The steamboat and the railroad are here. The new forces have produced both good and evil. We cannot get rid of them even if it were not undesirable to get rid of them; and our instant duty is to try to accommodate our social, economic, and legislative life to them, and to frame a system of law and conduct under which we shall get out of them the utmost possible benefit and the least possible amount of harm. It is foolish to pride ourselves upon our progress and prosperity, upon our commanding position in the international industrial world, and at the same time have nothing but denunciation for the men to whose commanding position we in part owe this very progress and prosperity, this commanding position.

Whenever great social or industrial changes take place, no matter how much good there may be to them, there is sure to be some evil, and it usually takes mankind a number of years and a good deal of experimenting before they find the right ways in which, so far as possible, to control the new evil, without at the same time nullifying the new good. I am stating facts so obvious that if each one of you will think them over, you will think them trite, but if you read or listen to some of the arguments advanced, you will come to the conclusion that there is need of learning these trite truths. In these the effort to bring the new tendencies to a standstill is always futile and generally mischievous; but it is possible somewhat to develop them aright. Law can to a degree guide, protect, and control industrial development, but it can never cause it, or play more than a subordinate part in its healthy development unfortunately it is easy enough by bad laws to bring it to an almost complete stop.

In dealing with the big corporations which we call trusts, we must resolutely purpose to proceed by evolution and not revolution. We wish to face the facts, declining to have our vision blinded either by the folly of those who say there are no evils, or by the more dangerous folly of those who either see, or make believe that they see, nothing but evil in all the existing system, and who if given their way would destroy the evil by the simple process of bringing ruin and disaster to the entire country. The evils attendant upon over-capitalization alone are, in my judgment, sufficient to warrant a far closer supervision and control than now exist over the great corporations. Wherever a substantial monopoly can be shown to exist, we should certainly try our utmost to devise an expedient by which it can be controlled. Doubtless some of the evils existing in or because of the great corporations, cannot be cured by any legislation which has yet been proposed, and doubtless others, which have really been incident to the sudden development in the formation of corporations of all kinds, will in the end cure themselves. But there will remain a certain number which can be cured if we decide that by the power of the Government they are to be cured. The surest way to prevent the possibility of curing any of them is to approach the subject in a spirit of violent rancor, complicated with total ignorance of business interests, and fundamental incapacity or unwillingness to understand the limitations upon all law-making bodies. No problem, and least of all so difficult a problem as this, can be solved if the qualities brought to its solution are panic, fear, envy, hatred, and ignorance. There can exist in a free republic no man more wicked, no man more dangerous to the people, than he who would arouse these feelings in the hope that they would redound to his own political advantage. Corporations that are handled honestly and fairly, so far from being an evil, are a natural business evolution and make for the general prosperity of our land. We do not wish to destroy corporations, but we do wish to make them subserve the public good. All individuals, rich or poor, private or corporate, must be subject to the law of the land; and the Government will hold them to a rigid obedience thereof. The biggest corporation, like the humblest private citizen, must be held to strict compliance with the will of the people as expressed in the fundamental law. The rich man who does not see that this is in his interest is, indeed, short-sighted. When we make him obey the law we insure for him the absolute protection of the law.

The savings banks show what can be done in the way of genuinely beneficent work by large corporations when intelligently administered and supervised. They now hold over twenty-six hundred millions of the people's money and pay annually about one hundred millions of interest or profit to their depositors. There is no talk of danger from these corporations; yet they possess great power, holding over three times the amount of our present national debt; more than all the currency, gold, silver, greenbacks, etc., in circulation in the United States. The chief reason for there being no talk of danger from them is that they are, on the whole, faithfully administered for the benefit of all, under wise laws which require frequent and full publication of their condition, and which prescribe certain needful regulations with which they have to comply, while at the same time giving full scope for the business enterprise of their managers within these limits.

Now, of course, savings banks are as highly specialized

a class of corporations as railroads, and we cannot force too far the analogy with other corporations; but there are certain conditions which I think we can lay down as indispensable to the proper treatment of all corporations which from their size have become important factors in the social development of the community.

Before speaking, however, of what can be done by way of remedy, let me say a word or two as to certain proposed remedies which, in my judgment, would be ineffective or mischievous. The first thing to remember is that if we are to accomplish any good at all it must be by resolutely keeping in mind the intention to do away with any evils in the conduct of big corporations, while steadfastly re fusing to assent to indiscriminate assault upon all forms of corporate capital as such. The line of demarcation we draw must always be on conduct, not upon wealth; our objection to any given corporation must be, not that it is big, but that it behaves badly. Perfectly simple again, my friends, but not always heeded by some of those who would strive to teach us how to act toward big corporations. Treat the head of the corporation as you would treat all other men. If he does well stand by him. You will occasionally find the head of a big corporation who objects to that treatment; very good, apply it all the more carefully. Remember, after all, that he who objects because he is the head of a big corporation to being treated like anyone else is only guilty of the same sin as the man who wishes him treated worse than anyone else because he is the head of a big corporation. Demagogic denunciation of wealth is never wholesome and generally dangerous; and not a few of the proposed methods of curbing the trusts are dangerous chiefly because all in sincere advocacy of the impossible is dangerous. It is an unhealthy thing for a community when the appeal is made to follow a course which those who make the appeal either do know or ought to know cannot be followed; and which if followed would result in disaster to everybody. Loose talk about destroying monopoly out of hand, without a hint as to how the monopoly should even be defined, offers a case in point.

Nor can we afford to tolerate any proposal which will strike at the so-called trusts only by striking at the general well-being. We are now enjoying a period of great prosperity. The prosperity is generally diffused through all sections and through all classes. Doubtless there are some individuals who do not get enough of it, and there are others who get too much. That is simply another way of saying that the wisdom of mankind is finite; and that even the best human system does not work perfectly. You don t have to take my word for that. Look back just nine years. In 1893 nobody was concerned in downing the trusts. Everybody was concerned in trying to get up himself. The men who propose to get rid of the evils of the trusts by measures which would do away with the general well- being, advocate a policy which would not only be a dam age to the community as a whole, but which would defeat its own professed object. If we are forced to the alternative of choosing either a system under which most of us prosper somewhat, though a few of us prosper too much, or else a system under which no one prospers enough, of course we will choose the former. If the policy advocated is so revolutionary and destructive as to involve the whole community in the crash of common disaster, it is as certain as anything can be that when the disaster has occurred all efforts to regulate the trusts will cease, and that the one aim will be to restore prosperity. A remedy much advocated at the moment is to take off the tariff from all articles which are made by trusts. To do this it will be necessary first to define trusts. The language commonly used by the advocates of the method implies that they mean all articles made by large corporations, and that the changes in tariff are to be made with punitive intent towards these large corporations. Of course, if the tariff is to be changed in order to punish them, it should be changed so as to punish those that do ill, not merely those that are prosperous. It would be neither just nor expedient to punish the big corporations as big corporations; what we wish to do is to protect the people from any evil that may grow out of their existence or mal-administration. Some of those corporations do well and others do ill. If in any case the tariff is found to foster a monopoly which does ill, of course no protectionist would object to a modification of the tariff sufficient to remedy the evil. But in very few cases does the so-called trust really monopolize the market. Take any very big corporation I could mention them by the score which controls say something in the neighborhood of half of the products of a given industry. It is the kind of corporation that is always spoken of as a trust. Surely, in rearranging the schedules affecting such a corporation it would be necessary to consider the interests of its smaller competitors which control the remaining part, and which, being weaker, would suffer most from any tariff designed to punish all the producers; for, of course, the tariff must be made light or heavy for big and little producers alike. Moreover, such a corporation necessarily employs very many thousands, often very many tens of thousands of workmen, and the minute we proceeded from denunciation to action it would be necessary to consider the interests of these workmen. Furthermore, the products of many trusts are unprotected, and would be entirely unaffected by any change in the tariff, or at most very slightly so. The Standard Oil Company offers a case in point; and the corporations which control the anthracite coal output offer another for there is no duty whatever on anthracite coal.

I am not now discussing the question of the tariff as such; whether from the standpoint of the fundamental difference between those who believe in a protective tariff and those who believe in free trade; or from the standpoint of those who, while they believe in a protective tariff, feel that there could be a rearrangement of our schedules, either by direct legislation or by reciprocity treaties, which would result in enlarging our markets; nor yet from the standpoint of those who feel that stability of economic policy is at the moment our prime economic need, and that the benefits to be derived from any change in schedules would not compensate for the damage to business caused by the wide-spread agitation which would follow any attempted general revision of the tariff at this moment. Without regard to the wisdom of any one of those three positions, it remains true that the real evils connected with the trusts cannot be remedied by any change in the tariff laws. The trusts can be damaged by depriving them of the benefits of a protective tariff, only on condition of damaging all their smaller competitors, and all the wage workers employed in the industry. This point is very important, and it is desirable to avoid any misunderstanding concerning it. I am not now considering whether or not, on grounds totally unconnected with the trusts, it would be well to lower the duties on various schedules, either by direct legislation, or by legislation or treaties designed to secure as an offset reciprocal advantages from the nations with which we trade. My point is that changes in the tariff would have little appreciable effect on the trusts save as they shared in the general harm or good proceeding from such changes. No tariff change would help one of our smaller corporations, or one of our private individuals in business, still less one of our wage workers, as against a large corporation in the same business; on the contrary, if it bore heavily on the large corporation, it would inevitably be felt still more by that corporation's weaker rivals, while any injurious result would of necessity be shared by both the employer and the employed in the business concerned. The immediate introduction of substantial free trade in all articles manufactured by trusts, that is, by the largest and most successful corporations, would not affect some of the most powerful of our business combinations in the least, save by the damage done to the general business welfare of the country; others would undoubtedly be seriously affected, but much less so than their weaker rivals, while the loss would be divided between the capitalists and the laborers; and after the years of panic and distress had been lived through, and some return to prosperity had occurred, even though all were on a lower plane of prosperity than before, the relative difference between the trusts and their rivals would remain as marked as ever. In other words, the trust, or big corporation, would have suffered relatively to, and in the interest of, its foreign competitor; but its relative position towards its American competitors would probably be improved; little would have been done towards cutting out or minimizing the evils in the trusts; nothing towards securing adequate control and regulation of the large modern corporations. In other words, the question of regulating the trusts with a view to minimizing or abolishing the evils existent in them, is separate and apart from the question of tariff revision.

You must face the fact that only harm will come from a proposition to attack the so-called trusts in a vindictive spirit by measures conceived solely with a desire of hurting them, without regard as to whether or not discrimination should be made between the good and evil in them, and without even any regard as to whether a necessary sequence of the action would be the hurting of other interests. The adoption of such a policy would mean temporary damage to the trusts, because it would mean temporary damage to all of our business interests; but the effect would be only temporary, for exactly as the damage affected all alike, good and bad, so the reaction would affect all alike, good and bad. The necessary supervision and control in which I firmly believe as the only method of eliminating the real evils of the trusts must come through wisely and cautiously framed legislation which shall aim, in the first place, to give definite control to some sovereign over the great corporations, and which shall be followed, when once this power has been conferred, by a system giving to the Government the full knowledge which is the essential for satisfactory action. Then when this knowledge one of the essential features of which is proper publicity has been gained, what further steps of any kind are necessary can be taken with the confidence born of the possession of power to deal with the subject, and of a thorough knowledge of what should and can be done in the matter.

We need additional power; and we need knowledge. Our Constitution was framed when the economic conditions were so different that each State could wisely be left to handle the corporations within its limits as it saw fit. Nowadays all the corporations which I am considering do what is really an interstate business, and as the States have proceeded on very different lines in regulating them, at present a corporation will be organized in one State, not because it intends to do business in that State, but because it does not, and therefore that State can give it better privileges, and then it will do business in some other States, and will claim not to be under the control of the States in which it does business; and of course it is not the object of the State creating it to exercise any control over it, as it does not do any business in that State. Such a system cannot obtain. There must be some sovereign. It might be better if all the States could agree along the same lines in dealing with these corporations, but I see not the slightest prospect of such an agreement. Therefore I personally feel that ultimately the nation will have to assume the responsibility of regulating these very large corporations which do an interstate business. The States must combine to meet the way in which capital has combined; and the way in which the States can combine is through the National Government. But I firmly believe that all these obstacles can be met if only we face them, both with the determination to overcome them, and with the further determination to overcome them in ways which shall not do damage to the country as a whole; which, on the contrary, shall further our industrial development, and shall help instead of hindering all corporations which work out their success by means that are just and fair towards all men.

Without the adoption of a constitutional amendment my belief is that a good deal can be done by law. It is difficult to say exactly how much, because experience has taught us that in dealing with these subjects where the lines dividing the rights and duties of the States and of the nation are in doubt it has sometimes been difficult for Congress to forecast the action of the courts upon its legislation. Such legislation (whether obtainable now, or obtainable only after a constitutional amendment) should provide for a reasonable supervision, the most prominent feature of which at first should be publicity; that is, the making public both to the governmental authorities and to the people at large the essential facts in which the public is concerned. This would give us exact knowledge of many points which are now not only in doubt but the subject of fierce controversy. Moreover, the mere fact of the publication would cure some very grave evils, for the light of day is a deterrent to wrong-doing. It would doubtless disclose other evils with which for the time being we could devise no way to grapple. Finally, it would disclose others which could be grappled with and cured by further legislative action.

Remember, I advocate the action which the President can only advise, and which he has no power himself to take. Under our present legislative and constitutional limitations, the national executive can work only between narrow lines in the field of action concerning great corporations. Between those lines, I assure you that exact and even-handed justice will be dealt, and is being dealt, to all men, without regard to persons.

I wish to repeat with all emphasis that, desirable though it is that the nation should have the power I suggest, it is equally desirable that it should be used with wisdom and self-restraint. The mechanism of modern business is tremendous in its size and complexity, and ignorant intermeddling with it would be disastrous. We should not be made timid or daunted by the size of the problem; we should not fear to undertake it; but we should undertake it with ever present in our minds dread of the sinister spirits of rancor, ignorance, and vanity. We need to keep steadily in mind the fact that besides the tangible property in each corporation there lies behind the spirit which brings it success, and in the case of each very successful corporation this is usually the spirit of some one man or set of men. Under exactly similar conditions one corporation will make a stupendous success where another makes a stupendous failure, simply because one is well managed and the other is not. While making it clear that we do not intend to allow wrongdoing by one of the captains of industry any more than by the humblest private in the industrial ranks, we must also in the interests of all of us avoid cramping a strength which, if beneficently used, will be for the good of all of us. The marvellous prosperity we have been enjoying for the past few years has been due primarily to the high average of honesty, thrift, and business capacity among our people as a whole; but some of it has also been due to the ability of the men who are the industrial leaders of the nation. In securing just and fair dealing by these men let us to do them justice in return, and this not only because it is our duty, but because it is our interest; not only for their sakes, but for ours. We are neither the friend of the rich man as such nor the friend of the poor man as such; we are the friend of the honest man, rich or poor; and we intend that all men, rich and poor alike, shall obey the law alike and receive its protection alike.

Document Analysis

As Theodore Roosevelt moved into the second year of his presidency, he was aware of the public's concerns about the unregulated growth and power of business trusts. Roosevelt noted that many people used the word trust "very loosely and almost always with technical inaccuracy." What the average person called a "trust," Roosevelt contended, was simply a large corporation. He further noted that this common conception of the trusts included large corporations that operated in several states "and often have a tendency to monopoly."

Roosevelt argues that large corporations had developed because of the new technologies in the transportation and communication fields. These changes have happened, and cannot be undone. The challenge, as Roosevelt sees it, is to adopt laws which shall allow society to develop from these changes "the utmost possible benefit and the least possible amount of harm." While Roosevelt believed there had to be regulation of the trusts, he contended that the behavior of a company, not simply its size, is the real issue. Attacking all big businesses could endanger the general prosperity the nation was experiencing at that time.

Roosevelt also addresses one reform that had been suggested—removing the tariff from products that were made by the trusts. Since the Civil War, the Republican Party had supported a high protective tariff—an import tax that made imported goods more expensive, and was therefore thought to protect American manufacturers from competition from cheaper foreign imports. Roosevelt notes that the trusts rarely achieved true monopoly, and removing tariff protections would harm the small businesses that were not part of any illegitimate trust; indeed, it might even harm the small companies more than the trusts.

Throughout his speech, Roosevelt called for sensible reforms, and rejected proposals that sprang from "rancor" or a "vindictive spirit." The government needed the power to regulate big businesses that behaved badly, but that power had to be exercised "with wisdom and self-restraint." While he gave few details of the kinds of reforms he envisioned, he did note that some might be accomplished by simple legislation, while others might require a constitutional amendment. He also suggested that some means was needed to force businesses to make accurate reports to the government about their activities and earnings, and that this information should be made public also, so that the people could know what wrongs were being committed and what needed to be done to correct them.

Essential Themes

President Roosevelt stressed a few key themes throughout this speech. One is the persistence of change. Changes in technology and in the structuring of business had led to the development of large corporations in America, and these changes could not be undone. The nation needed to address the problem of trusts being used in attempts to create monopolies, but the fact that big business exists, and that the technology that allowed such growth has been developed, must be accepted. The clock could not be turned back, even if the nation wished to do so.

THE WASHINGTON SCHOOLMASTER
From the *Chronicle* (Chicago)

"The Washington Schoolmaster," an editorial cartoon about the coal strike of 1902, by Charles Lederer.

While Roosevelt believed some means of regulating big business was needed, he stressed the themes of care and restraint in creating these regulations. He believed that some reforms that had been suggested were simply impossible; others would require amending the Constitution before the government could exercise the powers envisioned. Roosevelt argued these changes should be evolutionary, not revolutionary. This is in keeping with the general approach of the Progressive movement of the early 1900s—Progressivism was pragmatic, liberal reform, not radical utopianism. It aimed at practical reforms that would benefit consumers and workers. Roosevelt feared that attacking all big businesses, and not just those involved in monopolistic practices, might endanger the overall health of the economy, which benefitted all Americans to some extent.

A third theme Roosevelt emphasizes in this speech was a regular part of his speeches and writings on the trust issue. He argued that the mere size of a corporation was not the issue. The behavior of the company is the issue that must be addressed. Doing business on a large scale brought certain benefits to businesses, which were not necessarily illegitimate. But business combinations like the trusts, or cartels, or pools, which sought to limit competition and tended toward monopoly, had to be prohibited.

—Mark S. Joy

Bibliography and Additional Reading

Blum, John Morton. *The Republican Roosevelt*. New York: Atheneum, 1974.

Chessman, G. Wallace. *Theodore Roosevelt and the Politics of Power*. Boston: Little, Brown and Company, 1969.

Goodwin, Doris Kearns. *The Bully Pulpit: Theodore Roosevelt, William Howard Taft, and the Golden Ae of Journalism*. New York: Simon and Schuster, 2013.

McGerr, Michael. *A Fierce Discontent: The Rise and Fall of the Progressive Movement in America*. New York: Oxford University Press, 2003.

WHAT DIDN'T HAPPEN IN THE COAL CONTROVERSY—*Cleveland Plain Dealer.*

The two sides were supposed to listen to expert testimony and come to a friendly agreement; cartoon from the Cleveland Dealer.

■ "Echoes from the Recent Pennsylvania Coal Strike"

Date: February 12, 1903
Author: George F. Baer
Genre: Testimony; speech

Summary Overview

In a series of hearings on the conditions of American coal mines that lasted from October 1902 to February 1903, Philadelphia and Reading Railroad president George F. Baer testified that the 163-day anthracite coal strike conducted by the United Mine Workers (UMW) union was illegal and that the "lawlessness" and reckless conditions in the mines were created not by mine owners but by the workers and the unions themselves. Baer also argued that any reduction in "exertion" by workers would result in lower production and, therefore, less pay for the workers. His testimony was later published in the April 1903 issue of *Cassier's Magazine*, a monthly engineering journal.

Defining Moment

By the turn of the twentieth century, the United States was heavily dependent on coal for virtually every aspect of life, including transportation, home heating, factory operation, and many other elements of industrialized society. Demand for coal was high, and miners worked arduously, in dangerous conditions and for little pay. In 1900, John Mitchell, president of the UMW, successfully led a strike against bituminous coal field owners. Although he succeeded in securing improved wages—aided by the fact that President William McKinley, in an election year, intervened to end the strike—Mitchell and the UMW union could not gain recognition as the mines' representative in labor negotiations.

In May of 1902, anthracite coal miners, seeking higher pay, eight-hour workdays, and recognition of the UMW as their union, walked out of the mines in Pennsylvania. Anthracite coal was a cleaner and more efficient form of coal and was, therefore, in very high demand on the heavily populated Eastern Seaboard. As a result, this strike would have major implications for the American economy. Coal operators refused to negotiate with the UMW, and the strike continued well into the fall. The operators brought in thousands of security officers to keep striking workers away from the mines, but more workers walked off their jobs. There were a number of incidents of violence and vandalism, and eventually the Pennsylvania National Guard was deployed to maintain order in the region.

As winter approached, President Theodore Roosevelt pushed for a resolution, convening meetings in Washington between the UMW and the operators. Unfortunately, the meetings proved fruitless, and workers continued their strike. Roosevelt and the government understood the implications of failure to resolve this strike and moved toward a more heavy-handed approach. Roosevelt's next step was to threaten military intervention, an action that would benefit neither side. The two parties agreed to end the strike while a government-appointed commission was established to review the issues. The commission was taken on tours of the mines and given a firsthand view of the industry. After completing the tours, the commission returned to Washington and began three months of hearings.

The hearings would become a major spectacle, with a high-profile set of closing arguments between George F. Baer, a prominent attorney and president of the Philadelphia and Reading Railroad, and outspoken trial lawyer Clarence Darrow. After hours of Baer's and Darrow's arguments, the commission began its review of thousands of pages of findings and rendered its decision. The workers were granted a 10-percent wage increase and an eight-hour workday, but the UMW did not receive recognition as the official negotiator for the workers.

Author Biography

George Frederick Baer was born on September 26, 1842, in Somerset County in southwestern Pennsylvania. At the age of thirteen, he left school and began working in the printing office of a local newspaper, the *Somerset Democrat*, which he would later purchase in partnership with his brother. Baer entered Franklin and Marshall

College in 1860 but left a year later, after the Civil War broke out, to serve as a captain in the 133rd Pennsylvania Volunteers. Following the war, Baer was admitted to the bar in Berks County, Pennsylvania, and became local counsel to the Philadelphia and Reading Railroad. In 1896, after thirty-three years of service, he was elevated to the post of president of the railway. Baer would later become president of Franklin and Marshall College. A Social Darwinist, he continued his legal career until his death in Philadelphia in April 1914.

HISTORICAL DOCUMENT

I think there is, from lack of thought, much confusion in the minds of many people as to the rights, powers and duties which properly belong to industrial organisations, including both capital and labor organisations. In general, no one denies the right of men to organise for any lawful purpose; but the right to organise, and the power of the organisation when organized, must still be governed and controlled by the general law of the land under which individual and property rights are protected.

We constantly hear the phrase: "Capital organises. Why may not labor organise?" As if this settled the problem. But capital cannot organise for an illegal purpose. Organised capital is subjected to sharper scrutiny than any other kind of organisation. A possible violation of individual rights is at once seized upon by the public as requiring some new and drastic law, if existing laws are not sufficient to meet public expectations. For example, may capital organise in such a way that one manufacturer may employ pickets to surround the establishment of another competing manufacturer to prevent ingress or egress to the works, or interfere with the sale of its commodities by intercepting its customers, or interfere with the transportation of its products and the orderly conduct of the rival business? We concede to organised labor the same rights that we claim for organised capital. Each must keep, within the law. There cannot be one law for citizens and corporations and another law for labor organizations.

The lawlessness in the coal regions was the direct result of mistaken theories of the rights of the Mine Workers. It will not do to say that the leaders have not encouraged violence and crime. It is true, no doubt, that they did not directly advise it. They at times counseled against it and issued paper proclamations calling for peace, and at other times they have expressed regrets for it. Nevertheless, they are legally and morally responsible for the situation they created, and from which this violence and crime resulted.

They complain bitterly of the decisions of the legally constituted courts whereby riotous conduct, unlawful destruction of property and interference with legal rights of citizens are simply restrained. They even demand of their political supporters the passage of laws which will place trades unions above and beyond the customary and the ordinary jurisdiction of the courts. They blindly refuse to see that the peace and prosperity of the community and the rights of the citizen can be maintained only through the supremacy of the law and its just and equal administration. The overthrow of the civil power, whereby whole communities are at the mercy of the mob, so delights them that they cry out lustily against the soldiers who are sent to protect life and property. Why this denunciation of courts, of police, and of soldiers, if the measures to support a strike are to be only peaceful and persuasive? The law is a terror only to evil doers. In the exercise of lawful acts we need fear neither courts, police, nor soldiers.

We have been told time and again how boys to the number of over twenty or thirty thousand in the coal regions have been admitted to membership in the Mine Workers' organization; how foreigners, without reference to the fact as to whether they are or are not American citizens—foreigners of many nationalities and speaking diverse tongues—with the boys, compose a majority of this organization. These boys, like most boys, have not been disciplined to reverence law and order, and we do not expect boys to behave very well unless they are under strong restraint. The foreigners, many of them, have been governed in their old homes by stringent police regulations. The law, in the person of a policeman or a gendarme, confronted them everywhere. They have come to this country with confused ideas of what free government means. The distinction between liberty regulated by law, and license, is practically unknown to them. Therefore, when a powerful organization of which they are members, led by men who are upheld and encouraged in a respectable community, tells them that. Force may be used to compel men to join their union, that scabs should be ostracised, that they are given power to suspend operations at a colliery where the employees do not join the union, is it not a direct invitation,—nay, more,—a command to commit the violence and crime that characterised the reign of terror in the mining regions?

Men who teach these false doctrines, pose as they may, are inciting to riot. Every day they saw the results of their work in outrages against persons and property. They made no reasonable effort to restrain the violence. They even ease their conscience with the fallacy that until a man is convicted in the courts he is guilty of no crime, and, therefore, they can shut their eyes to what is going on around them.

The legal responsibility they incur gives them little concern. They assume that juries selected from among their own members or sympathizers will not find them guilty. They will not become incorporated for fear of civil suits resulting in heavy damages. Still, the moral and legal responsibility exists, even though there is at times no adequate remedy for its enforcement.

We do not object to our employees joining labor organizations. This is their privilege. But we will not agree to turn over the management of our business to a labor organization because some of our employees belong to it. Our employees, union and non union, must respect our discipline. It is essential to the successful conduct of our business, and is peculiarly necessary in mining operations to prevent accidents. We must be left free to employ and discharge men as we please. If any of our officers abuse this privilege, then it is our duty to hear the case and review the action so that substantial justice may be reached. But we do not admit the right of an organization, the moment we exercise the power of discipline, to coerce us, before inquiry, by strike, or interference with our management.

The employer ought, I think, to meet his employees personally or a representative of such employees, provided such representative acts only for the particular employees and does not act in the interests of persons who are not employees of the particular colliery. To illustrate—in a controversy as to conditions existing at one colliery, the employees of that colliery must limit their demands to the particular conditions affecting that colliery, and if they see fit to be represented by someone acting as their attorney—we do not care what name they give him, he may be president, or a vice president, or anything else—he must be limited in the same way, he must not inject a theory as to what would be fair towards employees of another company a hundred or a thousand miles away.

It is on this account that we have objected to the interference of the president of the United Mine Workers in our business. If he simply represented our own employees and was acting exclusively for them, there could be no objection to dealing with him. But he represents an organization having for its object some Utopian scheme of uniformity of wages and conditions in the mining of coal all over the United States. And instead, therefore, of considering only the questions at issue between our employees and ourselves he is considering a general proposition which relates to all the coal miners dwelling under the sun. The fact that the miners' organization does restrict the quantity of coal a man may mine is clearly proven. It is not only proven, but it is defended as a right. Restriction on production, limiting the quantity a man may produce, seems to be based on the theory that this is essential to give employment to the many. The illustration given by one of the miners' attorneys was this: that if there is only a loaf to divide, you must divide it equally and give no one man more than his just proportion. The illustration is fallacious in this, that it is not germane to the subject. Labor is not a division of an existing thing. It is a power which produces things. Labor is not the loaf, but that by which in various forms the loaf is produced. Any restriction, therefore, on labor must necessarily reduce the number of loaves which are essential to feed the hungry.

To limit the right of exertion, of work, is to limit production. It is not only a wrong done to the individual, but it is a violation of sound economic principles, and, therefore, an injury to society. The ultimate effect of restricting production so as to divide employment and increase wages, must be to keep on dividing the wage fund as often as new men seek employment. There must be a limit to an increase of wages, but there can be no limit to the increase of workmen. The process must inevitably lead to the destruction of the industry or the reduction of the wages of every man to a sum barely sufficient to sustain life. Wages can increase only when each individual is left free to exert himself to his fullest capacity, thereby creating which, in turn, gives new employment—creates demand for commodities and demand for workmen to produce them. Only in this way can the wage fund be increased.

The country is agitated over the possible dangers to the common welfare by combinations of capital. These combinations, or rather consolidations of many interests into one common company, are all based on the theory that they will result in greater economy, that the cost of production will be decreased, and that the public will be benefited in many ways, especially by regularity in production, stability of employment, and reduction in cost to the consumer.

The criticisms as to over valuation and capitalization are financial questions, and only indirectly affect the public economic questions. If men see fit to invest their money in watered securities, that is their business, and the public is not responsible for ultimate losses. Economic laws will in the final windup work out the financial problem. But the public are rightly anxious as to the effect on the consumer.

All free men oppose monopoly. It is instinctive, and the possibilities of it alarm us. The mere fear of it suggests all manner of devices to prevent it. It is unquestionably true that if the recent combinations of capital, instead of proving a benefit to the public, as their organisers honestly believe, shall prove detrimental and result in creating monopolies guilty of extortion and oppression, legal and peaceful remedies will surely be found to curb their rapacity and oppression. But these large industrial combinations produce only things which are desirable, not absolutely necessary to sustain life. If the price of steel or any other like commodity is too high, or its production is stopped by striking workmen, for the time being, because of low wages, or by owners because of low profits, the public will be put to temporary inconvenience, but it can cause no general suffering.

But if we are over anxious as to the probable effect of these mere possibilities of monopoly (I say possibilities, because it is not probable that in a rich, energetic country like ours any such industrial monopolies can be either created or maintained) what must be the measure of anxiety: as to placing the control of the fuel of the country in one organization, and that, too, an organization without capital or responsibility?

Fuel is the life's blood of our age. It is as essential as food. Food production can never be monopolized. However low the wages and small the reward of the tillers of the soil, the labor reformer has not succeeded in controlling farming. The farmers know no restriction in hours of labor.

But what of fuel? Without a dollar invested in property, the fuel of the country has been absolutely monopolized. Not a ton of coal could be mined in the United States without the consent of the United Mine Workers of America unless it was mined protected by guns and at the risk of destruction of life and property. Is this a serious situation? The dangers from combinations of capital are mere possibilities, but the results of the fuel monopoly are actual.

We are not left to conjecture. The facts are before us. The United Mine Workers have created a monster monopoly. They did shut up the anthracite mines for more than five months. They taxed the bituminous laborers and all laborers over whom organised labor had control to support the strike. The owners of bituminous mines, some in self defense, others in the hope of gain, contributed freely to the strike fund. The public contributed freely. More than three million dollars were raised to carry on what they called the industrial war. With what result? The price of both anthracite and bituminous coal more than doubled. The supply was inadequate. The public was suffering not only from the high price, but from the scarcity of coal. Industrial operations closed down and men were thrown out of employment. All over the land, except in the districts that could be supplied by the great anthracite coal companies, the poor, the honest workman and the well to do suffered for want of fuel. In the middle of winter, in a land of plenty, this gigantic monopoly had the power to create a scarcity of fuel and bring distress upon a whole nation.

It is seldom that the violation of sound economic business rules so quickly brings with it such a series of disasters. How far the public will take to heart the lesson that has been taught is, of course, as it always is, an unknown problem. But this Commission represents the dignity which ever must uphold law and order, the justice that is inherent in righteous judgment, and the wisdom that can respect the progress and mighty achievements of our social and business conditions which have produced such marvelous prosperity. And, holding fast to that which is good, it will be slow to recommend a new order of things that may lead to the dire results which a six months' trial has already produced.

But someone will say, "Oh, all these direful results might have been averted by you operators." How? By a surrender to unjust demands. Yes; the evil day could have been postponed.

Let us not deceive ourselves. Men charged with the management of property, conscious of no wrong doing, believing they are dealing justly with their employees, ought not to surrender at the dictation of labor leaders whose reputation and subsistence depend upon their success in formulating impractical demands, and thereby stirring up strife. The record shows that an honest effort was made to convince the United Mine Workers that their demands were unjust.

The anthracite coal trade has for fifty years been a most perplexing problem. It has, perhaps, aroused greater expectations and caused more disappointments than any large business enterprise in the country. To the untutored mind it seems so easy to dig coal and to sell it at a profit. But to the men who have given their best thoughts and years to the problem it becomes one of the most complex of all industrial problems. Indeed, when I look back over more than thirty years of my own connection with the Reading system and recall the struggles of the system and the able men who have gone before me, it seems that their labors were like those of Sisyphus.

You know that coal cannot be well stored. Bituminous coal cannot be stored in very large quantities because it is apt to ignite. Anthracite coal can be stored, but the cost of storing it is very great. We have made some experiments as to storing coal and picking it up again. The cost, with the breakage and the lowering of the grade of the coal, amounts, as near as we can get at it, to twenty six cents a ton. We have found that we cannot store coal and must not overlook the fact that if wages go up, then materials and supplies necessarily participate in the increase, and the general cost of mining coal is increased. The proportion of wages on a ton of coal is about $1.45 to $1.50 This represents the average cost under the present conditions of producing a ton of coal—that is, the wage labor of producing a ton of coal—and from 40 to 45 cents represent the supplies that go into the cost of the coal. Our coal roundly costs us about $2 to put on the car, and $1.45 to $1.50 represent wages.

The production of coal is one of the few industries in which there are three parties to be considered: first, the operator, because he controls the business—for the present at least; second, the workmen; and third, the consumer. In most industrial operations the consumer is only indirectly interested. He need not purchase the things if their cost is too great; but coal he must purchase. If he is a manufacturer, he requires it for power, and everyone needs it to cook his breakfast and warm his home. The price cannot be arbitrarily fixed. It is undoubtedly true that the mine workers must receive an adequate compensation, measured by like wages under similar conditions in other industries, and, I take it—with some hesitation—that the operator may be permitted, under a normal condition of society, to have a little profit on the capital and work he bestows in the business. If the anthracite mine operator fixes the price on anthracite coal so high that the manufacturer cannot use it, the manufacturer will do one of two things—purchase bituminous coal, or, if in the locality of his manufactory that cannot be had to advantage, he will abandon the site of his manufactory and go to a more favored locality where fuel is cheap and plentiful. In this problem of manufacturing, fuel is the foundation of everything. It, therefore, becomes a business duty and a business necessity to see that manufacturers are given coal at a reasonable price. If they cannot get it, they will be driven out of business. And if they are driven out of business, then the sources of trade for the railroads fail.

These are problems that captains of industry in these days must consider, and must daily consider—how to increase the wealth of the community they are serving by increasing its prosperity—because only in that way can they add to their revenues; how to return to their stockholders a just payment for the money they have invested, and how to give honest wages, fair and full wages, to the men they employ. These are burdens. You may think they are light; but to a man who is charged with responsibility they become terrible realities.

What, then, can be done practically? If you increase wages, what will you accomplish? If they are too low, increase them; it will pass on to the consumer, and that consumer will be the rich and the poor. If they are just, then let them alone.

What evidence have you that they are unjust? We were led to believe, when an attack was made upon the horrible conditions in the anthracite fields, that a condition existed whereby men were being oppressed. Attention, however, has been called to the fact that on the basis of wages supposedly being paid in the anthracite regions, the advance claimed makes less than the wages that have actually been paid.

Now, that the wages are fair we demonstrated by a number of things to which I want to call your attention. You will remember that it has been said that one of the evils in the coal region is that there is too much labor there. What does that indicate? Why, that labor there is attractive. There is plenty of work in the United States, and those men could get employment elsewhere. Are you going to increase the rate of wages, and attract still more people there to sit down and wait in the hope of getting enough money in a day to support them for a week? Will you improve the congested labor condition in the anthracite fields by raising the price of wages so as to attract all unemployed labor into that field and bring on a worse condition of things?

Remember how easily the trade of anthracite mining is acquired. There is no apprenticeship, such as in ordinary trades; no such conditions as many of us went through when, as boys, we served as apprentices, working night and day to acquire a trade, with little or no remuneration.

Under the mining laws of Pennsylvania a man, of course, must be a certified miner. But each year hordes of strong men come from over the sea. They come as laborers and obtain work in the mines. They are paid larger wages than they ever dreamed of in their own countries—from $1.50 up to $1.75 or $2 a day. They work as laborers for two years in the mines receiving this pay, and at the end of two years they can become certified miners. This is the only apprenticeship they serve. After that they can go into the mine early in the morning and drill their hole and blast their coal, and at eleven o'clock walk out to smoke their pipe and enjoy leisure.

It is no skilled trade. There is no apprenticeship such as prevails in the arts—with the carpenter and the mason and the bricklayer and all artisans, and, above all, the machinist, who has to devote years to acquiring great skill. Are these men who work five and six hours a day, and earn the sums of money we have shown you that they do earn, to become public pensioners at the expense of every honest workingman in this city and in all the cities of the seaboard? Shall he be made to buy coal to keep himself warm and to cook his meals at an unfair price?

If there is any sociological question involved here it requires you to consider most carefully whether, in trying to do some favor to the coal miners in the anthracite regions you are not only going to work injustice to the operators, but you are going to do a wrong to every consumer of coal.

I have heretofore called attention to the sliding scale. I intended to discuss the question of eight hours a day; but I will let that go. Enough has been said upon that subject. I do not believe in the theory. There are some trades where eight hours are enough, but there ought to be no limitation on work in the collieries. If the breaker time is reduced to eight hours per day, the output of coal would be so restricted that the cost of coal would be increased enormously. Of course, the answer would be, "Build new breakers and sink new shafts." That is easily said. Expend another half million dollars at each colliery, and then the public would have to pay the cost. It is one of the things that you cannot help. If you are oppressed in one direction, and the price has to go up, the public is the forgotten man; but there is where it falls all the time. The consumer pays for it. And those of us who stand up to protect the consumer, who represents the average man in the community, are always to be treated as merciless, tyrannical men.

That brings me to say one word in defense of our own companies. I submit that the companies I represent, the Philadelphia & Reading Coal and Iron Company and Lehigh & Wilkes-Barre Coal Company, have suffered the most at the hands of these people, in that a number of our collieries are destroyed. Where is the evidence of our wrong doing? What have we done? Have we ill treated our men? Have we wronged them in any way? Is there any testimony here to cast a shadow of doubt on the integrity and the honesty and the fairness of these companies in dealing with their men? Who is there that will dare to say, or has said, that the humblest man in our employment has been refused redress or consideration of any complaint?

Superintendents tell you that they hear every complaint and treat it justly. Such is their instruction. This company is too big to be dishonest. It means to deal fairly with all men. It means it because its management is honest and its policy is honest. And I protest that nothing has been more unfair than to drag us here into a controversy of this kind, without showing that there was any wrong done, or that anything in our system needed to be corrected.

Now, then, what is the practical suggestion that I have to make? I would gladly see a return to the sliding scale. For some reason or other the sliding scale meets with little favor among, labor leaders. You are asked to fix the price of coal practically for three years. I am not a prophet. I do not know what the business conditions of the next three years will be.

I can hope that the general prosperity of the country will continue so that wages can be even increased. But I know, as a business man, that I am not willing to commit myself to the payment of wages for three years based upon the existing condition of things. I do not know the day nor the hour when a break may come, and, as a cautious man of the world, charged with grave responsibilities, I want some system adopted that will work like the governor on an engine and regulate the speed at which we go.

I want to say that, while it is entirely true that some of the men have not been as prompt as we wished them in working on holidays, and some of them have shut down the breakers at one colliery and another to go to a funeral, and sometimes in times of great distress they would not work when we thought they ought to work, I will say that, taking the whole situation through, the behaviour of men in our companies since the strike is over has been admirable. They have rendered efficient work, and produced all the coal which, under the circumstances, could be produced, unless they had worked on these exceptional holidays, and while that would have been desirable, you cannot ignore the conditions and the traditions of people. These foreigners come here with many holidays. They have been accustomed to observe all their holidays. I am not going to find fault with a man who keeps his native holiday, even though it does deprive us of a little coal. There are some things that must be allowed to individual freedom, and this is one of them.

Now, what is my proposition? That the rate of wages now paid shall be the minimum basis for the next three years.

That from the first of November to the first of April, 1903, all employees, other than contract miners, shall be paid an additional five per cent.

That on and after April, 1903, for each five cents in excess of $4.50 per ton on the average price realized for white ash coal in the harbour of New York, on all sizes above pea, wages shall be advanced one per cent.; the wages to rise or fall one per cent. for each five cents increase or decrease in prices; but they shall never fall during the next three years below the present basis.

Now, before I give the result, let me just explain what that means. We will take the risk of guaranteeing for three years the present basis of wages. I say risk. We take a great risk in doing that. It means that the price of coal must be kept in New York harbour $4.50, or otherwise we are carrying on operations at a loss. We are willing to take that risk, and to pay, in addition, one per cent. increase in wages for each five cents increase on coal, taking the prices at New York harbour, which eliminates all calculations, as a basis.

The average price for each region to be ascertained by a competent accountant, to be appointed by judge Gray, chairman of the Commission, or by one of the United States Circuit judges holding courts in the City of Philadelphia, the compensation of the accountant to be fixed by the judge making the appointment, and to be paid by the operators in proportion to the tonnage of each mine; each operator to submit a full statement each month to said accountant of all the sales of white ash coal, and the prices realized therefrom, f. o. b. New York, with the right of the accountant to have access to the books to verify the statement.

Document Analysis

Baer's testimony makes an effort to undermine the UMW's position as well as assert the perceived rights of the owners and operators. He claims that there are limits to the mineworkers' perceived "right to organise," taking into consideration what he deems the "lawlessness" of the workers and the unions that attempted to organize them. Baer also argues that employers should retain the right to directly engage their employees with regard to grievances and business operations instead of working through union negotiators. He further calls into question the legitimacy of the United Mine Workers, accusing the union of taking monopolistic steps while undercutting one of the economy's most vital natural resource industries. The result of acceding to the workers' demands, he argues, would be lower wages for workers, higher prices for coal, and a negative overall trend in American industrial development.

Baer's first point is that he and his fellow operators do not object to the right of workers to join a union; rather, the problem at hand is one specific union, the UMW. Mitchell's group, Baer argues, organized under dubious and illegal means, including, he alleges, forcing foreigners and others to join their cause. The purpose of the UMW is not to protect the workers, he says, but to "incit[e them] to riot." He claims that the union made no effort to address the violence that occurred during the strike, preferring instead to teach members to simply push on with lawlessness. Baer insists that UMW's record speaks for itself: in 1900, they shut down countless bituminous mines "for more than five months," and now they encouraged similar closures in anthracite mines.

Baer also argues that the owners and operators should have the right to address employee issues directly with those workers rather than rely on an intermediary such as the UMW. An external party such as UMW operates without knowledge of the issues specific to each mine and instead attempts to address each issue using "some Utopian scheme of uniformity of wages and conditions." As an example, he criticizes the idea of limiting the amount of coal produced by each miner as an attempt to create work for additional workers, arguing that such ideals in fact only reduce production.

Baer uses economics to argue against the notion of raising wages for workers. Such a raise, he says, would directly impact the price of coal production, a cost that would then be passed along to the consumer. Rather, he suggests, wages for noncontract employees should be raised by five percent and maintained at that level until April 1903, after which pay would be tied to market prices for three years; though wages might decrease as well as increase under this scheme, he stipulates that they would never fall below the present level.

The anthracite coal strike had already had an impact, driving up the price of bituminous coal. Despite the best efforts of the operators to negotiate, Baer claims, the union refused to halt the strike. He alleges that the UMW is a monopolistic organization that seeks to perpetuate the strike despite the risks to the marketplace, the workers, and the American economy.

Essential Themes

George Baer's closing argument at the hearing in February 1903, delivered to a hostile audience that included labor activists, workers, and the famous civil libertarian Clarence Darrow, was greeted with considerable animosity. His expectation that employers should have the right to deal with their respective employees' issues in the manner of their choosing was perceived by many as reminiscent of the presumed "divine right" of monarchs to rule over their subjects. Nevertheless, Baer's comments represented the perspective of many mine owners and operators on the issue.

Baer did address the plight of the workers, touching on the issues of wages and working conditions, but he did so within the context of a broader argument: that workers performed their respective tasks as a result of the forces dictated by the marketplace. The exertion that workers experienced was necessary, he said, because Americans needed coal production, and any changes in hours or wages would impact coal prices and ultimately adversely impact workers. In order to avoid such conditions, Baer proposed a wage increase tied to market prices rather than one that he deemed arbitrary and imposed by external political entities.

As he argued for the right of owners to address wage and labor issues, Baer discounted the UMW as an illegal organization. Labor had the right to organize, he said, but the UMW, which he deemed a "monopoly" because of its singularity as a mineworkers union, could never serve as a legitimate advocate in negotiations simply because it was not knowledgeable of the specific interests and operations of each mine. Furthermore, according to Baer, UMW had a reputation for forcing workers to join and engage in illegal activity in strike situations. Given UMW's uneducated and illegal activity, Baer argued, it could not represent the workers at the negotiating table. On this point, the government agreed; while it allowed for a wage increase and permitted a fact-finding tour of the mines, the special commission still refused to identify UMW as the workers' representative.

—Michael P. Auerbach

Bibliography and Additional Reading

Bechtel, Ali. "Building Is Tribute to Prominent Berks Attorney Who Once Battled Clarence Darrow." *Berks Barrister* (Spring, 2013): 10–13.

Blatz, Perry K. *Democratic Miners: Work and Labor Relations in the Anthracite Coal Industry, 1875–1925.* Albany: State University of New York Press, 1994.

Connelly, Scott. "The Greatest Strike Ever." *Pennsylvania Center for the Book*. Pennsylvania State University, Spring 2010.

Lindermuth, John R. *Digging Dusky Diamonds: A History of the Pennsylvania Coal Region.* Mechanicsburg, PA: Sunbury, 2013.

McDonough, Jack. *The Fire Down Below: The Great Anthracite Strike of 1902 and the People Who Made the Decisions.* Scranton, PA: Avocado, 2002.

Painter, Nell Irvin. *Standing at Armageddon: A Grassroots History of the Progressive Era.* New York: Norton, 1987.

U.S. Anthracite Coal Strike Commission. *Report to the President on the Anthracite Coal Strike of May–October, 1902.* Washington, DC: Government Publishing Office, 1903.

A child labor standards poster from the 1940s. (U.S. National Archives and Records Administration)

Jane Addams: "Child Labor and Other Dangers of Childhood"

Date: December 1906
Author: Jane Addams
Genre: Speech; address

Summary Overview
In 1906, social activist and feminist Jane Addams addressed a convention of the American Humane Association on the issue of child labor. She argued that putting children to work in the growing American industrial complex denied them the ability to develop in a healthy manner. Child labor, she said, contributed to crime and societal ills. She called for new laws that kept children of a certain age from working. She also urged Americans to take notice of this issue and to take action to halt child-labor practices.

Defining Moment
During the latter half of the nineteenth century, the Industrial Revolution took hold in the United States. Across the spectrum of industries, the country saw unparalleled growth and prosperity. However, while this success strengthened the upper and middle classes, the American Industrial Revolution hinged upon the hard work of the country's poorest citizens. The manufacturing industry, for example, offered jobs, but those jobs commonly required extremely long hours, dangerous and unhealthy working conditions, and low wages.

As a result of these employment options, families who moved to U.S. cities (including a high volume of immigrants) in search of opportunities had little choice—parents and children alike needed to work in order to support themselves. While the parents were physically able to endure the harsh conditions prevalent at manufacturing "sweatshops," children were far less physically and mentally fit for this type of work, according to child-labor opposition groups. Even if children could handle the work, there remained a question about the effects of labor on children's long-term development and health.

In light of these concerns, the call for reform of the nation's child endangerment and labor laws increased steadily among child advocates and social reformers.

One such reformer was Addams, who, with her friend Ellen Starr, founded the social settlement known as Hull House in Chicago in 1889. Hull House was dedicated to combating society's ills through better understanding and volunteerism. In light of her work with Chicago's neediest children, Addams was particularly well-suited to see and appreciate the gravity of the child-labor issue.

Addams was not alone in her observations of the impacts of child labor. In 1904, the National Child Labor Committee (NCLC) was formed at a conference of Americans concerned about this issue. In 1911, Addams joined the NCLC's board of directors. In 1906, Lewis Hine, working for the NCLC, started taking photographs of children at work. He captured haunting images of children working arduously for little pay in cotton mills, mines, and other industrial complexes. These images further fueled public pressure for the reform of child-labor laws. To be sure, most states had passed laws regarding child labor, but, with lax enforcement, those laws were only effective if businesses chose to adhere to them. Activists, such as Addams, and members of the NCLC therefore advocated for stricter laws, passed at the federal level and enforced uniformly in each state.

Author Biography
One of nine children, Laura Jane Addams was born on September 6, 1860, in Cedarville, Illinois. Her father, John, was a prominent Illinois state legislator and friend to President Abraham Lincoln. Her mother, Sarah, died while giving birth to a stillborn child. Addams attended Rockford Female Seminary (later Rockford College, and as of 2013, Rockford University). She started medical school in Philadelphia in 1881, but health problems forced her to stop; she instead traveled throughout Europe. She became a prominent Chicago city leader and an internationally renowned feminist, labor leader, and activist. A founder of the American Civil Liberties Union

(ACLU) and a member of the executive board of the NCLC, Addams was awarded the Nobel Peace Prize in 1931, but was admitted to a Baltimore hospital with heart problems on the day she was to receive it. She died on May 21, 1935, from cancer.

HISTORICAL DOCUMENT

The whole problem of life is involved in that subject. It may be said that if a child is starving or neglected, society takes care of it and under the law it is the duty of the inspectors to investigate every case of that kind and relieve it, and in addition to that it is their duty to search around and find out such cases, and when such cases are discovered, it only needs to be brought to public notice to be remedied. But that is not the only or chief evil which threatens childhood in our city, and indeed in every city throughout this country. To my mind, much of the evil which threatens and surrounds childhood is due to the vast enterprises which are now being pushed forward with such vigor and are connected intimately with the industrial situation. I refer to the employment of children in industrial centers, in short, to child labor which we know exists to an alarming extent, and which it is the duty of every thinking man and woman to limit as far as possible, if it cannot be abolished. I think we all agree that the child is entitled to the advantages which result from an opportunity to play and develop, and the doctors put more stress on the child's advantages to play, as being the very basis of a healthy development of the mind and body; and if we assume, as we must, that the child is entitled to those advantages, then we must admit that putting him or her to work prematurely deprives the child of those advantages which by right it is entitled to.

There is no need to discuss that proposition, for it is too self-evident to need discussion. If we want to go into child labor as England goes into it, then it is easy to say that children should be put to work at 12 years of age, at which age child labor is legal in England; that is, the child may work half a day and attend school half a day, if the parents consent to it, but with such a law it has been proven that the child has been deprived of the advantages to which it is entitled, and that its development, both mentally and physically, is impaired and undermined thereby. It has been found by repeated examinations and tests, that if a child who has been put to work thus early is measured and weighed and the result compared with that of children who go to school all day and are afforded the opportunities for play and development which is natural, the first child was an inch and a half shorter, weighed considerably less, and was stunted in other directions. Those are facts, and cannot be controverted.

I quite agree with what was said by a probation officer in this room that an examination of the children brought in by their officers in every instance disclosed that they were abnormal, due solely to their being deprived of the advantages which as children they are entitled to. In cases where they have had children who were brought in there, most of them were found to be abnormal from a medical standpoint, and it has been stated that sixty-three per cent of the boys brought there are poorly nourished, and suffering from malnutrition and want of sleep. That is my experience, and the experience of everyone who is engaged in this work. That applied to children who are compelled to go to work. They do not have their meals properly and do not have sufficient food to stand the physical strain, and the result is their minds and nerves become overstrained, and the next result is, many of them become at an early age mental and physical wrecks.

We know one thing, too, that the requirements of the working man are that he shall be at his post early in the morning, and apply all his energies to his work during the day, and walk home soberly at night. All his working hours are required for his maintenance and that of his family, and his physical development enables him to do that. But that does not apply to a boy. There is one thing he will not do unless compelled to, and that is, work for his maintenance; but the very thing that is not demanded of him he will do the next moment, if opportunity is afforded him, and that is play, because that is his prerogative. Now, if we insist that the boy shall throw over all the natural tendencies of play, and the needs of his moral nature and his opportunity to go to school and receive mental and moral training, and yet expect him to walk along in moral paths, we are demanding of him that which he will not perform, and if he does it will be at the expense of his mental and physical development.

I remember in early years one of the mistakes we made in Hull House was in not having sufficient rooms at command to meet the wants of roomers, and particularly of those who were the victims of that pernicious system of child labor. I remember we had one little fellow there who had tried to support his mother and grandmother, and he got along very well and brought home to his mother his wages regularly and was the man of the house at twelve; and that continued for some years; but when he got to be eighteen he fell in with other boys, and exhibited a strange moral perversion, and finally became a tramp and threw the whole burden which he had carried for years on society. Why? Because we had put on him a man's burden when he was but twelve years of age. He was not old enough, had not the development physically, mentally and morally to assume the burden of life at that age and became a wreck at nineteen, whereas, if he had been kept at school and had had the advantages of natural development until the time he would naturally have quit school he would have taken to a man's duties the same as anyone else.

Over and over again we take children and put them into a position where they have no opportunity for development, compel them to work and leave them to acquire an education as best they may, and the inevitable result is, we break them down mentally and physically; they lose the mental vigor they would have acquired by play and education, and it is easy to understand that their mental standard is lowered at the same time.

Now it seems to me that this body, this society, deeply interested as it is in all humane measures, should take every possible step to remedy this evil and to remove the cause of it, and to look at it from every standpoint and see that humane laws are enacted where they are so much needed, for to my mind it is the most important question of the day.

I have told a story of a little child I once saw in a cotton mill who worked all night, although only five years old, and I spoke to the foreman of the mill about her. He said it was perfectly wonderful the way that child worked night after night, and spent her nights with other children in the same factory. This little child would walk around and join the threads on the cotton mill with little knots and entered into the work fully with others who were there. When she was tired she would lie down in a corner on some rags and rest a little while, and her place would be temporarily filled by one of the other children. The foreman did not enter into the situation at first, but when we called his attention to it, he became very much alarmed when the matter was shown to him in its proper light; but we did not dare to express ourselves very empathetically, because we were there only by courtesy. He did not see what he had to do with it, but permitted her to lie down at night in a corner when she became tired. Of course he said he would not make a rule of doing that with the others, but it was what we said to him went home.

Now that same thing is occurring all about us, and people do not see it, and if they can only be made to do so, their human instincts will at once be brought into play to put a stop to those things. Philanthropists do not stop to consider that this child labor causes the child to grow into an old young man, and there is no excuse for it, and it is up to this society to make clear that the demands for child labor in those large commercial industries, and in this commercial generation shall cease, and it should apply itself to securing the enactment of laws which will abolish this child suffering.

Take the sister states in the United States, and we have here the worst possible child legislation, a very great deal worse than it is in England, because there the child cannot commence work until it is twelve years old; and, as a whole, the laws relating to child labor in the United States are worse than can be found anywhere in Europe. Why is it we are willing to shirk our duty to the children? It is largely because we have directed our philanthropy in another direction, but I repeat it is the duty of this humane society to actively work along the line of saving children from brutal treatment, notwithstanding it means a long and bitter fight; and in this connection I urge upon you the necessity of having careful examinations made of children who are put out of work, and note the results. I know there are many who think it is all right to put boys to work, because they have made themselves obnoxious to society by getting into mischief; but I unhesitatingly assert that if an examination were made into the cases of the worn-out men we see so often around us, it would be found that in the large number of instances their condition was the result of being put to work too young. We once made an examination of men who came to us in Chicago, who were completely worn out and prematurely old, most of whom were Americans, and it was surprising to find how many of them were under thirty-five years of age, and their condition was brought about by their having been put to work too young. They have become disgusted with the whole business, and we know that in our own cases if we liked certain dishes of food but were compelled to eat them all the time we would revolt at them, so these young-old men have revolted at those burdens which were prematurely placed upon them, and finally developed into tramps.

I would subject to this society the proposition that it will be doing the most valuable work it can engage in by addressing itself to this question of the premature labor of children which prevails in every large city, and it is one of the things which sooner or later must be taken up with vigor. At times, when I see things around me, I am so ashamed that I sometimes wonder if we are civilized. It is one of those things that will be laid upon against us, and a hundred years hence people will ask if we could possibly have been civilized, and yet have permitted these things to continue. I do not favor idleness for children, but every child ought to have the advantage of industrial training, and it ought to have a chance for mental training, and to adjust its strength and development to the burdens it will have to bear.

Document Analysis

Addams reminds the conference participants of her primary concern: child welfare. In a society, Addams says, people are driven to action whenever a child is hungry, neglected, or otherwise mistreated. However, she identifies a particular danger to children looming at the turn of the century: that of industrial enterprises consistently using—and endangering—children in their pursuit of productivity.

For a child to work in a sweatshop instead of attending school or playing with other children, Addams argues, is to jeopardize that child's physical and mental development. She cites studies performed in England (which resulted in legal limitations on work hours and conditions for children there) showing that children who worked on assembly lines instead of attending school were shorter and otherwise physically stunted in comparison with their schoolyard counterparts. Americans need to take heed of such studies, the results of which she argues are undeniable fact, and implement similar child-labor laws.

Addams further comments on the social implications of child labor. Here, she cites her own personal experience at Hull House as well as her encounters with fellow child-protection advocates. Hull House has had a large number of clients who were working children, she says. These boys and girls were subjected to high levels of stress when they worked to support their families. In addition to the physical impacts of such stress—weight loss and chronic illness among them—many of the working children she encountered also suffered socially, demonstrating antisocial and criminal behavior. Addams adds that law-enforcement officers with whom she has interacted (including a probation officer she met at the conference where she spoke) revealed that children who worked at sweatshops and other industrial sites were more likely to commit crime.

Addams continues by underscoring the fact that adults who worked in such conditions could barely handle the stress of their work. In comparison, children are especially ill-equipped to take on such roles when they should instead be in the classroom, Addams argues. If they continue to be forced into the workforce at a young age, Addams says, child laborers will be so stunted and "worn out" that even when they reach an adult age, they would likely know and be able to handle menial tasks only.

Americans have long been blind to the issue of child labor and its impacts on young workers (as well as society as whole), Addams says. Congress and the rest of the federal government should enact the strictest child-labor laws, she argues, adding that government was acting far too slowly on the issue, allowing for working children to grow into maladjusted adult laborers with behavioral issues. Addams emphasizes that this trend was not based on speculation: she saw the effects of child labor on the adults with whom she worked daily at Hull House. It is time, she argues, for the federal government to act quickly and pass laws strictly regulating child labor in the

"Addie Card, 12 years. Spinner in North Pormal [i.e., Pownal] Cotton Mill. Vt." by Lewis Hine, 1912-1913)

United States. If no such laws are enacted, she states, American society can hardly consider itself "civilized" in the future.

Essential Themes
When Addams addressed the American Humane Association in 1906, she offered two perspectives to support her claims with regard to the nation's child-labor issue. First, she cited statistics and other trend information that revealed the short- and long-term ill effects of child labor on the Americans. Second, she offered her own experience with both child workers and adult former child laborers. The information revealed from both sources, she said, made enacting strict child-labor laws at the federal level not just a necessary legal step but a moral imperative that had implications on future American society.

Children were working long hours in sweatshops and other industrial complexes, Addams said, instead of going to school and learning a wide range of social skills. This trend meant that American laborers were increasingly maladjusted and unable to perform work beyond the menial tasks to which they were exposed as children. The education children received at school far exceeded the lessons learned on an assembly line. After all, she said, normal child development was the product of school and childhood social interaction: children who were denied these experiences were highly likely to have psychological problems (and even criminal tendencies) that would keep them from contributing meaningfully to society.

Addams also relied on her own experiences at Hull House to support her position. Far too many children, she said, were coming to Hull House with social and behavioral issues resulting from having to work. Some came back to Hull House as adults, suffering from a "moral perversion" that would ultimately cause harm to society.

Addams concluded that it was time for Congress to enact strict regulations on child labor. When children were old enough to handle the stress of the workplace, she said, they should be allowed to do so. However, she argued, in the meantime, children should be sent to school to prepare them for the adult world.

—*Michael P. Auerbach*

Bibliography and Additional Reading
Addams, Jane. *Twenty Years at Hull House*. London: Penguin, 1910.
"Childhood Lost: Child Labor during the Industrial Revolution." *Eastern Illinois University*. Eastern Illinois University, n.d.
Hindman, Hugh D. *Child Labor: An American History*. Armonk, NY: Sharpe, 2002.
Linn, James Weber. *Jane Addams: A Biography*. Champaign: University of Illinois Press, 1935.
Rosenberg, Chaim M. *Child Labor in America: A History*. Jefferson, NC: McFarland, 2013.

From *The Jungle*

Date: 1906
Author: Upton Sinclair
Genre: Novel (excerpt)

Summary Overview
In the 1906 novel *The Jungle*, novelist and journalist Upton Sinclair describes the success of Chicago's meatpacking industry in hiding unsanitary factory conditions, as well as the dangers of working in such facilities. Sinclair also comments on the political forces at play, telling the story of a Chicago meatpacker's union that helps decrease the political influence of the factory owners by voting sympathetic candidates into power. The novel was based on Sinclair's own experiences investigating Chicago's meatpacking industry, and his findings would inspire the passage of new food safety laws in the United States.

Defining Moment
Throughout the nineteenth century, the meatpacking industry was one of the largest employers in the Midwest. In the years leading up to the Civil War, this industry employed thousands of Americans, most of whom were located in Cincinnati, Ohio, and other parts of the Ohio River Valley. During and after the Civil War, the meatpacking industry shifted to Chicago, Illinois, a hub of the nation's growing railway system.

In 1865, the establishment of the Union Stock Yards, a meatpacking district just south of Chicago, bolstered Chicago's position as the nation's leader in meatpacking. The stockyards were tremendous, using fifteen miles of railway track to deliver livestock to the slaughterhouses and transport the final products throughout the nation. They also relied on the Chicago River for water, using 500,000 gallons per day, and sent contaminated wastewater back into a river fork. By the beginning of the twentieth century, the Union Stock Yards covered 475 acres, with fifty miles of roads and 130 miles of railway track servicing them.

The industry was highly lucrative, with a growing service area. During the Civil War era, the Cincinnati- and Chicago-based industries were focused on servicing the Midwest. However, the advent of the refrigerated boxcar made it possible to send fresh meat throughout the country, and even around the world. By 1900, the Union Stock Yards employed more than 25,000 people. The meatpacking companies wielded tremendous political and financial influence over the areas in which they operated, and government oversight was limited.

In light of the high degree of economic prosperity the Union Stock Yards brought to the Chicago area, as well as the insular manner in which the meatpacking industry managed itself, few people outside of the industry knew the realities of working at that massive complex. The thousands of workers there, mainly Eastern European immigrants, worked exceptionally long hours in unsanitary and highly dangerous conditions. It was not until the beginning of the twentieth century, when novelist and social activist Upton Sinclair published his novel *The Jungle*, that the nation as a whole began to pay attention to the harsh and unsanitary environment that was the meatpacking industry. The novel inspired the passage of the Federal Food and Drugs Act of 1906, which regulated the manufacture and sale of various foods and medicinal products.

Author Biography
Upton Beall Sinclair was born on September 20, 1878, in Baltimore, Maryland. He and his parents moved to New York City when he was ten. At the age of eighteen, he graduated from what is now the City University of New York and continued his education at Columbia University. Having developed an interest in writing as a teenager, Sinclair published short stories and dime novels throughout his time in college and continued to publish fiction after completing his education. He also became a socialist, and in 1904, embarked on an investigation of the meatpacking industry for the socialist newspaper Appeal to Reason. Sinclair traveled to Chicago and remained there for several weeks, observing the life of meatpacking workers and the conditions that surrounded them. These observations became the basis for The Jungle, serialized

in Appeal to Reason in 1905 and published in book form in 1906. Sinclair wrote numerous novels after *The Jungle*, some of which, including the 1927 novel *Oil!*, also proved influential. In 1934, Sinclair unsuccessfully ran for governor of California. Afterward he returned to the private sector, writing a number of historical novels. He died on November 25, 1968, at the age of ninety.

HISTORICAL DOCUMENT

...And then there was the condemned meat industry, with its endless horrors. The people of Chicago saw the government inspectors in Packingtown, and they all took that to mean that they were protected from diseased meat; they did not understand that these hundred and sixty-three inspectors had been appointed at the request of the packers, and that they were paid by the United States government to certify that all the diseased meat was kept in the state. They had no authority beyond that; for the inspection of meat to be sold in the city and state the whole force in Packingtown consisted of three henchmen of the local political machine!...

And then there was "potted game" and "potted grouse," "potted ham," and "deviled ham"—devyled, as the men called it. "De-vyled" ham was made out of the waste ends of smoked beef that were too small to be sliced by the machines; and also tripe, dyed with chemicals so that it would not show white, and trimmings of hams and corned beef, and potatoes, skins and all, and finally the hard cartilaginous gullets of beef, after the tongues had been cut out. All this ingenious mixture was ground up and flavored with spices to make it taste like something. Anybody who could invent a new imitation had been sure of a fortune from old Durham, said Jurgis's informant, but it was hard to think of anything new in a place where so many sharp wits had been at work for so long; where men welcomed tuberculosis in the cattle they were feeding, because it made them fatten more quickly; and where they bought up all the old rancid butter left over in the grocery stores of a continent, and "oxidized" it by a forced-air process, to take away the odor, rechurned it with skim milk, and sold it in bricks in the cities!...

There were the men in the pickle rooms, for instance, where old Antanas had gotten his death; scarce a one of these that had not some spot of horror on his person. Let a man so much as scrape his finger pushing a truck in the pickle rooms, and he might have a sore that would put him out of the world; all the joints of his fingers might be eaten by the acid, one by one. Of the butchers and floorsmen, the beef boners and trimmers, and all those who used knives, you could scarcely find a person who had the use of his thumb; time and time again the base of it had been slashed, till it was a mere lump of flesh against which the man pressed the knife to hold it. The hands of these men would be criss-crossed with cuts, until you could no longer pretend to count them or to trace them. They would have no nails,—they had worn them off pulling hides; their knuckles were swollen so that their fingers spread out like a fan. There were men who worked in the cooking rooms, in the midst of steam and sickening odors, by artificial light; in these rooms the germs of tuberculosis might live for two years, but the supply was renewed every hour. There were the beef luggers, who carried two-hundred-pound quarters into the refrigerator cars, a fearful kind of work, that began at four o'clock in the morning, and that wore out the most powerful men in a few years. There were those who worked in the chilling rooms, and whose special disease was rheumatism; the time limit that a man could work in the chilling rooms was said to be five years. There were the wool pluckers, whose hands went to pieces even sooner than the hands of the pickle men; for the pelts of the sheep had to be painted with acid to loosen the wool, and then the pluckers had to pull out this wool with their bare hands, till the acid had eaten their fingers off. There were those who made the tins for the canned meat, and their hands, too, were a maze of cuts, and each cut represented a chance for blood poisoning. Some worked at the stamping machines, and it was very seldom that one could work long there at the pace that was set, and not give out and forget himself, and have a part of his hand chopped off. There were the "hoisters," as they were called, whose task it was to press the lever which lifted the dead cattle off the floor. They ran along upon a rafter, peering down through the damp and the steam, and as old Durham's architects had not built the killing room for the convenience of the hoisters, at every few feet they would have to stoop under a beam, say four feet above the one they ran on, which got them into the habit of stooping, so that in a few years they would be walking like chimpanzees. Worst of any, however, were the fertilizer men, and those who served in the cooking rooms. These people could not be shown to the visitor—for the odor of a fertilizer man would scare away any ordinary visitor at a hundred yards, and as for the other men, who worked in tank rooms full of steam, and in some of which there were open vats near the level of the floor, their peculiar trouble was that they fell into the vats; and when they were fished out, there was never enough of them left to be worth exhibiting—sometimes they would be overlooked for days, till all but the bones of them had gone out to the world as Durham's Pure Leaf Lard!...

There was never the least attention paid to what was cut up for sausage; there would come all the way back from Europe old sausage that had been rejected, and that was mouldy and white—it would be dosed with borax and glycerine, and dumped into the hoppers, and made over again for home consumption. There would be meat that had tumbled out on the floor, in the dirt and sawdust, where the workers had tramped and spit uncounted billions of consumption germs. There would be meat stored in great piles in rooms; and the water from leaky roofs would drip over it, and thousands of rats would race about on it. It was too dark in these storage places to see well, but a man could run his hand over these piles of meat and sweep off handfuls of the dried dung of rats. These rats were nuisances, and the packers would put poisoned bread out for them, they would die, and then rats, bread, and meat would go into the hoppers together. This is no fairy story and no joke; the meat would be shovelled into carts, and the man who did the shoveling would not trouble to lift out a rat even when he saw one—there were things that went into the sausage in comparison with which a poisoned rat was a tidbit. There was no place for the men to wash their hands before they ate their dinner, and so they made a practice of washing them in the water that was to be ladled into the sausage. There were the butt-ends of smoked meat, and the scraps of corned beef, and all the odds and ends of the waste of the plants, that would be dumped into old barrels in the cellar and left there. Under the system of rigid economy which the packers enforced, there were some jobs that it only paid to do once in a long time, and among these was the cleaning out of the waste barrels. Every spring they did it; and in the barrels would be dirt and rust and old nails and stale water—and cart load after cart load of it would be taken up and dumped into the hoppers with fresh meat, and sent out to the public's breakfast. Some of it they would make into "smoked" sausage—but as the smoking took time, and was therefore expensive, they would call upon their chemistry department, and preserve it with borax and color it with gelatine to make it brown. All of their sausage came out of the same bowl, but when they came to wrap it they would stamp some of it "special," and for this they would charge two cents more a pound....

And then the editor wanted to know upon what ground Dr. Schliemann asserted that it might be possible for a society to exist upon an hour's toil by each of its members. "Just what," answered the other, "would be the productive capacity of society if the present resources of science were utilized, we have no means of ascertaining; but we may be sure it would exceed anything that would sound reasonable to minds inured to the ferocious barbarities of Capitalism. After the triumph of the international proletariat, war would of course be inconceivable; and who can figure the cost of war to humanity—not merely the value of the lives and the material that it destroys, not merely the cost of keeping millions of men in idleness, of arming and equipping them for battle and parade, but the drain upon the vital energies of society by the war-attitude and the war-terror, the brutality and ignorance, the drunkenness, prostitution, and crime it entails, the industrial impotence and the moral deadness? Do you think that it would be too much to say that two hours of the working time of every efficient member of a community goes to feed the red fiend of war?"

And then Schliemann went on to outline some of the wastes of competition: the losses of industrial warfare; the ceaseless worry and friction; the vices—such as drink, for instance, the use of which had nearly doubled in twenty years, as a consequence of the intensification of the economic struggle; the idle and unproductive members of the community, the frivolous rich and the pauperized poor; the law and the whole machinery of repression; the wastes of social ostentation, the milliners and tailors, the hairdressers, dancing masters, chefs and lackeys. "You understand," he said, "that in a society dominated by the fact of commercial competition, money is necessarily the test of prowess, and wastefulness the sole criterion of power. So we have, at the present moment, a society with, say, thirty per cent of the population occupied in producing useless articles, and one per cent occupied in destroying them..."

And then there were official returns from the various precincts and wards of the city itself! Whether it was a factory district or one of the "silk-stocking" wards seemed to make no particular difference in the increase; but one of the things which surprised the [Socialist] party leaders most was the tremendous vote that came rolling in from the stockyards. Packingtown comprised three wards of the city, and the vote in the spring of 1903 had been five hundred, and in the fall of the same year, sixteen hundred. Now, only a year later, it was over sixty-three hundred—and the Democratic vote only eighty-eight hundred! There were other wards in which the Democratic vote had been actually surpassed, and in two districts, members of the state legislature had been elected. Thus Chicago now led the country; it had set a new standard for the party, it had shown the workingmen the way!

—So spoke an orator upon the platform; and two thousand pairs of eyes were fixed upon him, and two thousand voices were cheering his every sentence. The orator had been the head of the city's relief bureau in the stockyards, until the sight of misery and corruption had made him sick. He was young, hungry-looking, full of fire; and as he swung his long arms and beat up the crowd, to Jurgis he seemed the very spirit of the revolution. "Organize! Organize! Organize!"—that was his cry. He was afraid of this tremendous vote, which his party had not expected, and which it had not earned. "These men are not Socialists!" he cried. "This election will pass, and the excitement will die, and people will forget about it; and if you forget about it, too, if you sink back and rest upon your oars, we shall lose this vote that we have polled today, and our enemies will laugh us to scorn! It rests with you to take your resolution—now, in the flush of victory, to find these men who have voted for us, and bring them to our meetings, and organize them and bind them to us! We shall not find all our campaigns as easy as this one. Everywhere in the country tonight the old party politicians are studying this vote, and setting their sails by it; and nowhere will they be quicker or more cunning than here in our own city. Fifty thousand Socialist votes in Chicago means a municipal-ownership Democracy in the spring! And then they will fool the voters once more, and all the powers of plunder and corruption will be swept into office again! But whatever they may do when they get in, there is one thing they will not do, and that will be the thing for which they were elected! They will not give the people of our city municipal ownership—they will not mean to do it, they will not try to do it; all that they will do is give our party in Chicago the greatest opportunity that has ever come to Socialism in America! We shall have the sham reformers self-stultified and self-convicted; we shall have the radical Democracy left without a lie with which to cover its nakedness! And then will begin the rush that will never be checked, the tide that will never turn till it has reached its flood—that will be irresistible, overwhelming—the rallying of the outraged workingmen of Chicago to our standard! And we shall organize them, we shall drill them, we shall marshal them for the victory! We shall bear down the opposition, we shall sweep it before us—and Chicago will be ours! Chicago will be ours! CHICAGO WILL BE OURS!"

GLOSSARY

orax: a white, crystalline powder (hydrated sodium borate) used as a cleaning agent

tripe: the stomach lining of a cow or ox, used as food

Workers in the union stockyards. (Suhling & Koehn Co., Chicago, Illinois)

Document Analysis

The Jungle tells the story of a Lithuanian immigrant, Jurgis Rudkus, who arrives in Chicago in search of work. He and his family settle in an area known as Packingtown, where they experience a wide range of hardships. Jurgis finds work in the meatpacking industry but continues to struggle with poverty and crime in addition to the physical dangers of his work environment. He eventually becomes interested in socialism and labor unions, seeing them as a possible solution to the rampant corruption of the meatpacking industry. Though *The Jungle* is a work of fiction, the novel is a thinly veiled commentary on life at the Union Stock Yards and expresses Sinclair's positive views of unionization and socialist ideals.

Throughout *The Jungle*, Jurgis witnesses firsthand many of the unsanitary conditions and unhealthy products being assembled in Packingtown. Some departments within the facility in which he works use dye and other chemicals, parts of older and unused meat segments, and even diseased animal corpses in the creation of household food products. The production of sausage continues even after rat droppings as well as cleaning chemicals, dirt, and sawdust have fallen into the openly stored piles of meat. Sinclair's descriptions of these unhygienic conditions are graphic and clearly demonstrate that meat products produced in such conditions are unfit for human consumption.

Sinclair likewise uses the novel to draw attention to the corruption of the meatpacking industry as well as its human cost. Government inspectors visit Packingtown but accomplish little, as the companies pay or otherwise influence the inspectors to sign off on their unsanitary practices. Workers, such as Jurgis, are unable to improve the sanitary conditions of their work environment; in fact, the plants of Packingtown are even said to lack handwashing facilities. Workers returning home carry germs and harmful substances on their hands and clothes, exposing their families to those environmental conditions as well. Furthermore, Sinclair, through Jurgis, emphasizes the extreme dangers associated with working in Packingtown. Picklers, boners, butchers, and other workers are said to be at constant risk of injury, and thanks to the unsanitary working conditions and numerous hazardous substances around them, even the smallest cut has the potential to develop a terrible infection. Other workers, such as those responsible for operating hoisting machinery, spend so much time bent over that they walk around "like chimpanzees."

After experiencing the hardships of meatpacking work, Jurgis eventually meets Dr. Nicholas Schliemann, a Swiss native whose socialist views appear to provide a solution. Schliemann convinces Jurgis of the value of unions, which could allow the meatpackers to unite and speak with one voice. Jurgis realizes that unionization could empower the people of Packingtown and give them the ability to take control of Chicago politics and put an end to the harmful and exploitative practices of the meatpacking industry.

Essential Themes

In *The Jungle*, Jurgis Rudkus arrives in the United States in search of opportunity, but he instead encounters hardship, crime, corruption, and danger in a large system of slaughterhouses known as Packingtown. The story is fictional, but Sinclair's novel is heavily based on his experiences and observations at the very real Union Stock Yards outside of Chicago. Sinclair believed that the secrets of the meatpacking industry—then hidden from the prying eyes of critics, activists, and the public at large—needed to be revealed to all Americans, and the novel form allowed him to do so in an accessible manner, presenting a depiction of the meatpacking industry that resonated with readers on several levels.

In the novel, it is common for workers to be injured, maimed, or even killed while working in Packingtown. Death can be immediate, Jurgis learns, or it can be long and painful due to infection. Sinclair calls attention to the terrible human cost of the meatpacking industry, presenting in unflinching detail the amputations, mutilations, and deaths that commonly occur in a work environment that favors production over worker safety. In addition, the meatpacking industry is shown to use extremely unsanitary and unhealthy practices in the production of its products. Chemicals, animal waste, and other foreign substances are commonly dumped into the meat, and expired and even rancid byproducts are packaged and sold to customers. The government is shown to monitor these practices, but, as Jurgis learns, government inspectors are on site as a service to the companies themselves rather than the public. By describing the unsanitary production of food products in detail, Sinclair made it clear to his readers that poor working conditions in meatpacking facilities affected not only the people who worked there, but also the unsuspecting consumers who ate the contaminated products—perhaps including the readers themselves.

—Michael P. Auerbach

Bibliography and Additional Reading

Barrett, James R. *Work and Community in the Jungle: Chicago's Packinghouse Workers, 1894–1922*. Champaign: University of Illinois Press, 1990.

Halpern, Rick. *Down on the Killing Floor: Black and White Workers in Chicago's Packinghouses, 1904–1954*. Urbana: University of Illinois Press, 1997.

Stromquist, Shelton, and Marvin Bergman. *Unionizing the Jungles: Labor and Community in the Twentieth-Century Meatpacking Industry*. Iowa City: University of Iowa Press, 1997.

Warren, Wilson J. *Tied to the Great Packing Machine: The Midwest and Meatpacking*. Iowa City: University of Iowa Press, 2007.

Fire Hazards in New York City Factories

Date: 1912
Author: New York Factory Investigating Commission
Genre: Report

Summary Overview

In 1911, a fire destroyed a garment factory in New York City, killing 145 workers. Community activists and political leaders called upon the New York General Assembly and the governor to investigate the conditions that started the fire, in the hope that other workplace disasters could be avoided. The Commission's findings and recommendations resulted in major revisions to the state's (and later the country's) occupational safety laws and regulations.

Defining Moment

On March 25, 1911, a fire broke out in a crowded workroom at the Triangle Waist Company, an apparel factory occupying the top three floors of a ten-story building in Manhattan. (A "waist" was an article of women's clothing in the nineteenth and early twentieth centuries, sometimes also called a "shirtwaist," and this disaster has become known to history as the Triangle Shirtwaist Factory fire.) The fire spread quickly throughout the factory, aided by the overabundance of flammable waste in the factory. Employees of the factory (and the rest of the building) were unable to escape the smoke and flame, as emergency exits were blocked by piles of fabric or otherwise locked, and the sole fire escape collapsed. When the fire department arrived, it could not elevate its ladders above the sixth floor and even their innovative high-pressure hoses were unequal to the task, leaving the upper floors vulnerable to the fire. Workers, unable to descend via fire escapes or stairs, dove from windows to their deaths on the street below. One hundred forty-five people, most of whom were women and teenagers, perished in the fire.

In the minds of those who worked for Triangle, the fire and massive loss of life were both foreseeable and avoidable. Two years earlier, the International Ladies Garment Workers' Union (ILGWU), representing many of Triangle's 900 employees, launched a strike to protest working conditions—including the illegal locking of exit doors and the lack of sufficient fire escapes. However, Triangle locked out its striking employees and hired replacements to continue working at the Washington Place factory. Ultimately, the strikers gained some concessions on wages and hours, and though management agreed to safety improvements, those were never undertaken, and conditions deteriorated.

The Triangle disaster sent shockwaves through New York City. Community, religious, and political leaders as well as citizens packed into the Metropolitan Opera House to discuss fire safety at the city's workplaces, and more than one hundred thousand mourners marched up Fifth Avenue to honor the dead. Shortly after the mass meeting, the march, and the funerals, the call went up to the state capitol in Albany: the government needed to intervene and examine the conditions that led to the deaths of 145 New Yorkers.

Author Biography

From the Metropolitan Opera House meeting, a special committee was established to lead the charge on the seat of state government. The New York Committee on Safety arrived to find a captive audience, as legislators only days before had seen a fire take place in the State House. Led by Senate majority leader Robert F. Wagner and Senator Alfred E. Smith, the New York General Assembly quickly established the Factory Investigating Commission. The commission was the first of its kind in the United States: it was granted the power to investigate all manner of working conditions at manufacturing facilities in every city in the state. It could assess inspection practices, review construction plans, compel testimony under oath, and enter any manufacturing facility for inspection.

The assembly had initially given the commission a one-year mandate but quickly extended that framework to three years. The commission's investigative work, however, was complete within two years, and was comprehensive and voluminous. Between 1911 and 1912, the commission had visited fifty plants across the state and investigated more than 3,300 others, interviewed nearly 500 witnesses, and conducted fifty-nine public hearings, generating more than 7,000 pages of testimony. Upon completion of its investigation of every major manufacturing industry in New York, the commission issued its findings and recommendations to the assembly, on which the burden to issue new workplace safety and health laws and regulations would next fall.

HISTORICAL DOCUMENT

CREATION OF COMMISSION.

On Saturday afternoon, March 25, 1911, a fire took place in the business establishment of the Triangle Waist Company, at No. 23–29 Washington Place, in the Borough of Manhattan, City of New York, in which 145 employees, mainly women and girls lost their lives.

This shocking loss of life aroused the community to a full sense of its responsibility. A superficial examination revealed conditions in factories and manufacturing establishments that constituted a daily menace to the lives of the thousands of working men, women and children. Lack of precautions to prevent fire, inadequate fire-escape facilities, insanitary conditions that were insidiously undermining the health of the workers were found existing everywhere. The need of a thorough and extensive investigation into the general conditions of factory life was clearly recognized.

THE EXISTING FIRE PROBLEM IN NEW YORK CITY.

Five kinds of buildings are used for factory purposes in the City of New York.

THE CONVERTED DWELLING OR TENEMENT.

Owing to the increase in land values and change in the residence localities, a number of buildings formerly used for living purposes have been made over into factories. The buildings are from four to six stories in height, usually 25 feet wide by about 60 to 85 feet deep. The exterior walls are brick or stone, the floors, interior trim, stairways, beams and doors are of wood. The stairways are usually from two to three feet in width, the doors often open inward; there are no automatic sprinkler systems, no fire prevention or extinguishing appliances except fire pails, which are not always preserved for fire purposes; the workrooms are divided by wooden partitions and crowded with employees, while the machines are placed as close together as space will permit, without regard to means of exit. There are exterior fire-escapes with balconies on each floor, connected by vertical ladders (those of late construction by inclined stairways), which usually lead to a yard in the rear of the premises, or to some blind alley from which there is no means of escape. There is ordinarily a ladder from the lowest balcony to the ground, but it is generally not in place, or very difficult to use in case of fire because of its weight. There is usually but one door leading from the street.

Here we have a type of building constructed for dwelling purposes only, in which the number of occupants is multiplied any number of times without any change in the exit facilities provided.

THE LOFT BUILDING

The loft building marks an evolution in the construction of factory buildings in the City of New York.

The first lofts were built about twenty-five years ago, for the storing and sale of merchandise, but the manufacturer soon found it desirable to have his goods manufactured in workrooms adjacent to his salesroom and directly under his supervision.

Increase in land values, moreover, forced the manufacturers to extend upwards instead of spreading out horizontally. The availability of the loft for manufacturing purposes was soon appreciated, and to-day this type of building is generally used for factory purposes.

THE NON-FIREPROOF LOFT BUILDING

The non-fireproof loft building is usually six or seven stories in height, 25 feet wide by 80 feet in depth, with brick, stone or iron fronts and rears, brick side walls, wooden floors and wooden trim. There is usually one unenclosed wooden stairway, varying in width from two to three and one-half feet, and often winding around the elevator shaft. Wooden doors lead to the stairways; very often the doors open inwardly.

Fire Hazards in New York City Factories • 199

Mourners from the Ladies Waist and Dressmakers Union Local 25 and the United Hebrew Trades of New York march in the streets after the Triangle fire. Date: 1911.

These buildings, as a rule, possess exterior fire-escapes similar to those found on the converted tenement described above. Usually every floor in these buildings is occupied by a different tenant, in some cases there being two or more tenants on each floor. The tenant uses the floor, or his portion of it, as salesroom, office and factory, dividing one from the other by wooden partitions. In the manufacturing part there are usually a number of machines placed as close together as possible with little aisle space between. These buildings are to be found in numbers on the lower east and west side. The number of people permitted to work on a floor is restricted only by a provision of the Labor Law which provides a minimum of 250 cubic feet of air space per person and entirely disregards the floor area. As the distance between floor and ceiling is at least ten feet, and often more, this cubic air space is easily obtained without any appreciable prevention of overcrowding and congestion. The present law does not require the posting of the number of people allowed even by this standard, and so prosecutions for violations of this law are practically unknown. These buildings usually do not contain any automatic sprinklers. They have fire pails, which are rarely kept for the proper purpose. A few of them have standpipes, with hose which is often useless.

THE FIREPROOF LOFT BUILDING LESS THAN 150 FEET HIGH

The fireproof loft building less than 150 feet in height, that is about 12 stories or under, has brick, stone or metal exterior walls, wooden floors and trim, stairways of metal or stone and elevators. Stairways are generally about three feet wide, enclosed by fireproof walls. These buildings are either 25, 50, 75 or 100 feet wide by 80 to 200 feet in depth, the usual size being 50 by 80 or 90 feet. The conditions of occupancy as to tenants are similar to those in the non-fireproof loft buildings just described. The Triangle Waist Company occupied a building of this type at 23–29 Washington Place. That building, in its construction and interior is typical of the so-called fireproof loft buildings, and indeed much better than hundreds of buildings used for similar purposes in New York city (sic) to-day. Some of these buildings have automatic sprinkler systems. They are usually provided with stand pipes, connected with the city water supply, and have on each floor a hose of required length, and some are provided with exterior fire-escapes. It is to be noted that in these buildings the elevators are used to go from the street to the upper floors not only by the employers but by the employees. In most cases the latter are absolutely unaware of the location of the stairways. Auxiliary fire appliances are present in most cases, but their existence is unknown to the workers and no care is given to their preservation. The interior arrangements are similar to those existing in the non-fireproof loft building, the same wooden partitions, the same congestion and doors opening inwardly.

Testimony shows that the danger in these so-called fireproof buildings results from the use of wood for floors, doors and trim. The buildings are usually of such a height that the Fire Department ladders and extensions, and even the water towers, do not reach the upper stories. Fire occurring in these places under conditions of manufacture which are hereafter described usually results in the destruction of the entire contents of the building while walls and floors remain substantially intact.

THE FIREPROOF LOFT BUILDING MORE THAN 150 FEET HIGH

This building is more than twelve stories in height. The walls are of brick, stone or metal, the floors are of cement or stone, the trim and doors are of metal or fire-resisting material, the stairways are of stone or metal, and enclosed by fireproof walls. There are usually several stairways and elevators. The buildings are sometimes supplied with automatic sprinkler systems and have standpipes to which hose is connected on each floor, and other appliances for extinguishing fires. In addition, these buildings sometimes have exterior stairways leading either to the street or to the ground in the rear. The buildings are usually 50, 75 or 100 feet or more in width and are from 75 to 200 feet deep. They are occupied for manufacturing and other purposes, and sometimes one tenant is found to occupy more than one floor. In these buildings, if a fire occurs, it is usually confined to the floor on which it starts since it cannot burn up or down except through the windows.

Above the sixth floor these buildings are open to the same objections as are fireproof buildings less than 150 feet high, namely the upper floors cannot be reached by the firemen. The exit facilities are usually well constructed, but the number of people who occupy these buildings is not determined by either exits, width of stairways, or floor space. The only restriction is, as in all other buildings, the 250 cubic feet of air space provision. The distance between the floors is usually 10 to 15 feet, so the cubic air space may fulfill the legal requirement while the floor presents a congested condition.

DANGER TO LIFE IN FIREPROOF BUILDINGS

Particular reference is made to the fireproof building which is believed on account of its construction to be safer for the occupants than the non-fireproof building and to require few if any precautions, either to prevent fire or to preserve the safety of the occupants in case of fire. The testimony discloses the weakness of these suppositions. While fireproof building itself will not burn, the merchandise, wooden partitions and other inflammable material burn as readily in a fireproof building as in any other. It is assumed by all fire insurance experts that when a fire occurs on any one floor, the contents of that entire floor will be destroyed. It is like placing paper in a fireproof box—it confines the fire to that locality, but the fire is just as hot and just as destructive within its bounds. Therefore, unless means are provided for automatically extinguishing fires and for the rapid escape of the occupants, loss of life may occur even in fireproof buildings.

The Triangle Waist Company fire is illustrative of this fact. There the building was practically left intact, yet the fire was severe enough to cause the death of a large number of the occupants. In the fireproof building the fire is confined to a limited area and is therefore more easily controlled. The occupants of floors over eighty feet from the ground cannot, however, be reached by the Fire Department's ladders, and must trust for escape to the stairways or exterior fire-escapes.

In many of these buildings the occupants manufacture garments and other inflammable articles. The floors are littered with a quantity of cuttings, waste material and rubbish, and are often soaked with oil or grease. No regular effort is made to clear the floors. No fireproof receptacles are provided for the accumulated waste, which in some cases is not removed from the floors for many days. Many of the workmen, foremen and employers smoke during business hours and at meal times.

Lighted gas jets are unprotected by globes or wire netting, and are placed near to the inflammable material. Very often quantities of made-up garments and inflammable raw material are stored in those lofts. Fire drills are not held, save in rare instances, exits are unmarked and the location of the stairways and exterior fire-escapes is often unknown. Access to the stairway and outside fire-escapes is obstructed by machinery, wooden partitions and piled-up merchandise, while in some cases the fire-escape balcony is at such a distance from the floor as to make it almost impossible for women employees to reach it without assistance. Wired glass is not used in the windows facing the balconies of the fire-escapes except in fireproof buildings over 150 feet high. In some cases the window leading to fire-escapes are not large enough to permit the passage of grown persons readily. Automatic or manual fire-alarms are hardly ever provided, except in the larger fireproof buildings.

RECOMMENDATIONS OF THE COMMISSION

1. PREVENTION OF FIRE

Testimony was given that at least 50 per cent of the fires occurring to-day could be prevented by taking certain simple and inexpensive precautions. Some experts placed the percentage of preventable fires as high as 75 per cent. Fire extinguishment has received careful attention in the past, and to-day the means supplied for extinguishing fires are many. But little attention until recently, has been given to the subject of fire prevention. An ounce of prevention in the case of fires, as in any other case, is worth a pound of cure.

The principal causes of fires in the city of New York during the past few years have been rubbish heaps, lighted matches, cigars and cigarettes, and exposed gas jets. It is believed by the Commission that the prohibition of smoking in manufacturing establishments, and the cleaning up or removal of rubbish, cutting and waste from the floors, and providing fireproof receptacles therefor, will be most effective in the prevention of fires.

The fire in the Triangle Waist Company building was caused by a lighted cigarette thrown upon a pile of cuttings. Smoking should be strictly prohibited to both employees and employers. The Commission in its investigation visited among other establishments, a cigar factory in a converted tenement house when there were several hundred employees at work. The foreman was asked whether smoking was allowed. He stated that smoking was prohibited—although at that moment he was busily engaged in smoking his own cigar.

A number of witnesses testified that while smoking ought to be prohibited, its prevention was a hopeless task. Such an attitude surprises the Commission, as it believes from its investigation that a little education upon the subject will convince both employee and employer of the wisdom and necessity of this law. Smoking in a factory is a constant menace to all employed therein.

2. NOTICE TO AUTHORITIES IN CASE OF FIRE

No matter what care and what precautions may be taken, fire will occur, and attempts are frequently made by employees to extinguish them before calling upon the public authorities. In almost every case this is a serious mistake. In the Triangle Waist Company and Equitable Building fires, lives would have been saved and the fire would not have been nearly so severe, the Fire Department had been promptly notified. In this regard the Commission can do no more than lay before the public the facts disclosed. It had been the intention of the Commission after examining into the matter, to recommend the installation of automatic or manual fire alarms in certain factories.

3. NOTICE TO OCCUPANTS IN CASE OF FIRE

The Commission gave much thought and attention to means of notifying the occupants of a building in case of fire. After consideration of the facts before it, the Commission is of the opinion that the dangers from panic and excitement caused by any alarm, such as the ringing of a bell indicating on which floor the fire had occurred, when the alarm might be false or the fire slight and readily controlled, outweighed the advantage to be gained. Therefore the Commission does not at this time recommend any automatic fire-alarm system, save as may become necessary in connection with the operation of a fire drill hereinafter provided for.

4. FIRE DRILLS

The Commission personally witnessed fire drills in factory buildings, and some testimony was taken upon this subject. The Commission believes that in factory buildings where more than twenty-five persons are regularly employed above the second story, a fire drill should be conducted. One of the purposes of the fire drill should be to indicate to the occupants where the stairways are, and the means of reaching them. It has been found in many of the larger buildings where the occupants use the elevators to go to and from their work, that the location of the stairs or exterior fire-escapes is unknown. The Commission is of the opinion that the drill should be supervised by the local Fire Departments. A fire drill is also extremely useful in preventing panic. While of course not so effective in the case of occupants of a loft or factory building as in the case of school children, it undoubtedly would go far in preventing a mad rush towards the exits. If the fire drill accomplishes nothing more than to acquaint the occupants of a building with the different exits, to compel them to use those exits at stated intervals, and to keep them clear and unobstructed, it will have served its purpose. The periodical fire drill will constantly bring to the minds of employee and employer alike the possibility of fire and the necessity for using every proper means to prevent the same.

5. PREVENTION OF SPREAD OF FIRE

The installation of the automatic sprinkler system has been recommended by Fire Chiefs throughout the State, and by nearly all of the experts on the fire problem. The Commission does not desire to make any drastic recommendation on this subject, but it is convinced that in buildings over seven stories or 90 feet in height, in which wooden floors or wooden trim are used, and more than 200 people are employed above the seventh floor, the only safe means to prevent the spread of fire and the loss of life incidental thereto would be the installation of an automatic sprinkler system.

Chief Kenlon of the New York Fire Department testified that had an automatic sprinkler system been installed in the Triangle Waist Company building, he believed that not a single life would have been lost. If manufacturing is carried on above the seventh story of a building, or 90 feet above the ground, the manufacturer should be required to furnish every possible device to safeguard the lives of his employees in case of fire.

6. ESCAPE FROM WORKROOMS

The Commission ascertained by investigation and testimony, that exits to outside fire-escapes and to interior stairways, especially when they lead through other portions of the loft, were often unknown to many of the operatives. It certainly is necessary to indicate clearly the location of these exits.

A contributing cause to the loss of life in the Triangle Waist Company fire was the lack of clear passageways leading to the fire-escapes and stairways. The employees were so crowded together, seated at tables containing machines, with chairs back to back, that when a great number of them attempted to leave at the same time there was panic and confusion. The following is a diagram showing the arrangement of the sewing machines, and the congestion prevailing on the ninth floor of this building, where most of the deaths occurred.

In the report made by the Superintendent of the New York Board of Fire Underwriters, it was stated that 20 dead bodies were found near the machines "apparently overcome before they could extricate themselves from the crowded aisles." The condition which prevailed in this building obtains in many similar buildings. The necessity for clear and unobstructed passageways to exits should be absolutely insisted upon, otherwise with the slightest panic, even without a fire, severe injuries, if not loss of life, would occur.

The Commission has already commented on the width of doors and windows leading to outside fire-escapes. It has also found that the doors leading to stairways are too narrow. This is especially so in the old converted tenements where these narrow doors are a source of danger in case of panic or fire. The first rush is always for the doors. The attempt upon the part of a number of persons to pass through at one time leads to a jam, and if the doors are dangerously narrow, many would lose their lives. When there are only a few persons employed upon a floor a narrow door is not a serious objection, but where a number of persons are employed, regard for their safety requires that such dangerous conditions be remedied.

7. HUMAN FACTORS

Results of the Data Obtained by the Investigation

NEGLECT OF THE HUMAN FACTOR

Brief as was the period devoted to the investigation, limited as was the number of industries and establishments inspected, and incomplete as was necessarily all our data, the conclusion that forcibly impressed itself, after the completion of the preliminary investigation, was that the human factor is practically neglected in our industrial system.

Many of our industries were found housed in palatial loft buildings, and employing the most improved machinery and mechanical processes, but at the same time greatly neglecting the care, health and safety of their employees.

Our system of industrial production has taken gigantic strides in the progressive utilization of natural resources and the exploitation of the inventive genius of the human mind, but has at the same time shown a terrible waste of human resources, of human health and life.

It is because of this neglect of the human factor that we have found so many preventable defects in industrial establishments, such a large number of workshops with inadequate light and illumination, with no provision for ventilation, without proper care for cleanliness, and without ordinary indispensable comforts such as washing facilities, water supply, toilet accommodations, dressing-rooms, etc. It is because of utter neglect on the part of many employers that so many dangerous elements are found in certain trades. These elements are not always necessary for the successful pursuit of the trade, and their elimination would mean a great improvement in the health of the workers, and would stop much of the misery caused by the occupational diseases incident to certain industries.

The construction of tenement houses in New York City is under the strict supervision of the Tenement House Department. There is no reason why the interests of the greater number of persons inhabiting factory buildings should not be conserved as much as the interests of the tenement house dwellers.

8. IGNORANCE OF THE NUMBER AND OF THE LOCATION OF INDUSTRIAL ESTABLISHMENTS

In the course the investigation, much difficulty was found in locating all the establishments in an industry or a district. At present there is no method by which every manufacturing establishment may be located, and its existence brought to the attention of the authorities. At present, any person who has the necessary capital or credit may build, lease, or hire any ramshackle building, engage as many workers as he can crowd into his premises, and work them under any conditions. The very existence of this establishment may not be known to the Labor Department, until it is discovered by accident.

In the investigation of the Cloak and Suit Industry, made during the last year, by the Joint Board of Sanitary Control, about 30 per cent of the shops were found unrecorded, and in our own investigation, our inspectors found the utmost difficulty in tracing many establishments which were never recorded by the Labor Department in the list sent by them to us.

9. LACK OF STANDARDS

The worker spends the greater part of his waking hours in the workshop and factory. The proper sanitation of the workplace is therefore of paramount importance to the worker, both to his health and to the security of his life.

It is only lately that intelligent employers have awakened to the fact that factory sanitation is very closely related to industrial efficiency, and that neglect of this subject by factory owners is detrimental to their own interests as well as extremely injurious to their workers.

It is also but lately that the workers themselves have realized the value of proper sanitation of factories, and have added this to the economic demands of their labor organizations.

Unfortunately, there is hardly a field of science where there is such a complete lack of standards as in industrial hygiene.

It is on account of this deplorable lack of standardization that many provisions of the labor laws are so vague and indefinite, and that large employers, willing to introduce modern safety devices and sanitary conveniences in their factories, are unable to do so with complete success. It is also this lack of standards that makes the enforcement of the sanitary clauses of the labor laws so unsatisfactory, for it is a most difficult matter for the inspector to exactly determine what is meant by "sufficient" fire protection, "proper light," "adequate" ventilation, "fit" toilet accommodations, etc.

The standardization of factory sanitation is one of the most important matters which the Commission has considered during its brief preliminary investigation, and we intend to devote much attention to it if our activities are continued.

The front page of the New York Evening Journal *announces "Fire Trap Victims Buried: Draft New Law to Save Shop Workers"; article, "Woman Tells of Fight for Life at Barred Doors," gives details of the Triangle fire. Editorial cartoon asks, "Who Is Responsible?"*

Document Analysis

The Factory Investigating Commission was established to review existing manufacturing facilities in New York and to ascertain areas in which fire prevention and occupational health might be improved. The central point of reference, understandably, was the Triangle Waist Company fire. However, the commission's recommendations spoke to a wide range of other potential disasters that loomed in New York's manufacturing facilities.

Among the commission's observations were that certain buildings that were believed to be "fireproof" were just as likely to experience a deadly fire as the former tenements and other, older buildings that contained flammable building products (such as wood) in their walls and floors. Factories, the commission reports, were found in a number of structures, including former residential buildings. Builders were increasingly building high-rise lofts to accommodate expanded manufacturing needs, and although these structures were made with cement and other flame-retardant materials (as opposed to wood), they still posed a danger. This risk was not associated with the building materials; instead, it was the prevalence of flammable materials such as cloth, paper, and lubricating oils. The fact that so many workstations were close to each other in such facilities meant that fire could start and spread rapidly even in a flame-resistant structure. The commission cites the fact that the Triangle fire left the building largely intact even when the interior was completely devastated by fire.

Another important finding in the report is the fact that many fires may be prevented by simply demonstrating sensible workplace behavior and practices. For example, the commission believed that the Triangle fire was caused by a lit cigarette. The commission, in its countless interviews, learned that although smoking in manufacturing facilities was considered dangerous, far too many workers continued to smoke on the job.

The commission cites the existence of guidelines for installing automatic sprinklers in certain buildings, but stops short of reiterating those rules. Rather, it focuses on other practices that could prevent another Triangle tragedy. For example, the commission cites the chaos in the Triangle facility when fire spread. Such conditions, the members recommend, could be mitigated by informing the workers of emergency escape protocols and even conducting fire drills. Such practices, the commission argues, could reduce panic and save lives.

Employers and building owners, the commission adds, had a role to play in ensuring the safety of the employees working in New York's factories. Unblocked exits, adequate fire escapes, and wider stairwells, for example, could have saved the lives of many Triangle employees during that fire. Better lighting and ventilation were also necessary for a healthy workplace, the commission recommends. Furthermore, the commission argues, there was a need for improved industrial hygiene and sanitary standards.

The commission acknowledges that economic development in New York (and the rest of the country) at times moved faster than employee safety regulations. In fact, the commission estimates the number of industrial and manufacturing facilities in the state to be upward of 44,000—its investigation was therefore limited—which meant that it was likely that far more facilities demonstrated subpar worker safety and hygiene issues. Still, the commission recommends that the assembly enact comprehensive standards and rules that would apply to all of the state's factories, with the goal of protecting the health and safety of employees.

Essential Themes

The Factory Investigating Commission was created in the wake of one of the worst industrial accidents in U.S. history. The commission's task was not just to ascertain the causes of the Triangle Waist Company fire but also to investigate the entire state's manufacturing sector to assess the risks of future, similar disasters. The city of Pittsburgh, Pennsylvania, had conducted a similar review of its manufacturing facilities. However, the Factory Investigating Commission was distinguished by both its extensive scope and its goal of reviewing every facility in every manufacturing industry New York contained within its borders. What it found and recommended could be reviewed in two general categories.

The first category is that of a disregard for rules and regulations already in place. The Asch Building, in which the Triangle Waist Company was housed, was what the commission deems a "fireproof" building, but a lit cigarette, overcrowded workspaces, and unkempt flammable waste helped the fire spread quickly. A lack of emergency exits and automatic sprinklers, and employee ignorance of fire-escape procedures, contributed to the massive casualty rate. Each of these practices and issues were not new concepts but had apparently been disregarded at Triangle.

The second category is the need for changes in the workplace. The Triangle plant's employees, like countless other facilities' workers, did not know what to do in

Photograph shows police or fire officials placing Triangle Shirtwaist Company fire victims in coffins.

the event of a fire because fire drills were not practiced consistently. Additionally, too many facilities in New York state had inadequate lighting and ventilation, insufficient waste management practices, and other issues that negatively affected worker health and safety. The commission's recommendations were extensive, moving far beyond fire prevention issues to include adequate dressing rooms, water supplies, toilets, and other necessary workplace resources. Attention to these matters would greatly improve workplace environments across the state, the commission's members concluded.

It was critical, the commission argued, that the state enact new laws that would impose new rules and protections for workers. The assembly did take this recommendation seriously, passing more than a dozen workplace safety laws in the two years that followed the commission's conclusion. The federal government, taking this commission's findings to heart, later followed suit when Frances Perkins, who had assisted with its investigation, became labor secretary in the administration of President Franklin D. Roosevelt.

—*Michael P. Auerbach*

Bibliography and Additional Reading

Gentzinger, Donna. *The Triangle Shirtwaist Factory Fire*. Greensboro, NC: Reynolds, 2008.

"The New York Factory Investigating Commission." U.S. Department of Labor, 2014.

New York (State) Factory Investigating Commission. *Preliminary Report of the Factory Investigating Commission*. 3 vols. Albany, NY: Argus, 1912.

Stein, Leon. *The Triangle Fire*. Centennial ed. Ithaca: Cornell University Press, 2011.

Von Drehle, David. *Triangle: The Fire That Changed America*. New York: Grove, 2004.

"The Bosses of the Senate" (1889). Reformers like the cartoonist Joseph Keppler depicted the Senate as controlled by the giant moneybags, who represented the nation's financial trusts and monopolies.

■ Clayton Act

Date: 1914
Author: Representative Henry De Lamar Clayton
Genre: Legislation

Summary Overview
The Clayton Antitrust Act both clarified and strengthened the Sherman Antitrust Act of 1890. While the wording of that previous legislation was purposefully vague, the Clayton Act listed practices that were definitely antitrust violations such as interlocking directorates and price discrimination for purchasers. While the legislation was originally intended to protect labor unions from legal injunctions, the final compromise provision that appeared in the final legislation proved essentially unenforceable.

Defining Moment
Woodrow Wilson had run on an antitrust platform during his 1912 election campaign. While some important trusts had been and continued to be broken up using the Sherman Antitrust Act of 1890, a new Congress easily passed new legislation designed to limit the discretion of courts in enforcing antitrust law so that more trusts could be busted. The Clayton Act was passed in late 1914, part of a spate of progressive legislation that Woodrow Wilson inspired at the beginning of his first term. This included the creation of the Federal Trade Commission, which is charged with enforcing the Clayton Act and other antitrust laws.

The prime motivation for the act was disappointment in the way that antitrust laws had been enforced over the previous twenty-five years. In particular, small businesses and farmers had expressed disappointment, frustration, and anger because so many trusts benefited from the government's laissez-faire attitude toward anticompetitive practices at their expense. The primary reason that the previous antitrust law was seldom enforced was that the Supreme Court had created a "rule of reason" to guide its decisions. This, in effect, gave the justices total discretion over how the law would be enforced and their interpretation depended more upon their political philosophy than the public good. By explicitly spelling out what practices were illegal, judicial discretion was supposed to disappear.

Another prime mover behind the passage of the Clayton Act was the labor movement, which wanted relief from having antitrust laws enforced against them. What they got in the bill was an unsatisfying compromise that did little to stop this kind of persecution. In the next fifteen years, courts would hand down more labor injunctions than in the twenty-four years before the bill's passage. Other demands by labor unions and other progressive groups were watered down in the first draft of the bill and later watered down further in the Senate. The initial bill passed the House 275–54, with every Democrat but one voting in favor. The final bill passed the House 244–54 and the Senate by a margin of 35–24.

Author Biography
Henry De Lamar Clayton (1857–1929) was a Democratic Representative from Alabama from 1897 to 1914 when he accepted a federal judgeship in his home state. His father, also named Henry Clayton, was a general in the Confederate army during the Civil War. He is primarily remembered for being the primary sponsor of the Clayton Antitrust Act.

HISTORICAL DOCUMENT

An Act to supplement existing laws against unlawful restraints and monopolies, and for other purposes.

Be it enacted by the Senate and House of Representatives of the United States of America in Congress assembled, That "antitrust laws," as used herein, includes the Act entitled "An Act to protect trade and commerce against unlawful restraints and monopolies," approved July second, eighteen hundred and ninety; sections seventy-three to seventy-seven, inclusive, of an Act entitled "An Act to reduce taxation, to provide revenue for the Government, and for other purposes," of August twenty-seventh, eighteen hundred and ninety-four; an Act entitled "An Act to amend sections seventy-three and seventy-six of the Act of August twenty-seventh, eighteen hundred and ninety-four, entitled 'An Act to reduce taxation, to provide revenue for the Government, and for other purposes,' " approved February twelfth, nineteen hundred and thirteen; and also this Act.

"Commerce," as used herein, means trade or commerce among the several States and with foreign nations, or between the District of Columbia or any Territory of the United States and any State, Territory, or foreign nation, or between any insular possessions or other places under the jurisdiction of the United States, or between any such possession or place and any State or Territory of the United States or the District of Columbia or any foreign nation, or within the District of Columbia or any Territory or any insular possession or other place under the jurisdiction of the United States: Provided, That nothing in this Act contained shall apply to the Philippine Islands.

The word "person" or "persons" wherever used in this Act shall be deemed to include corporations and associations existing under or authorized by the laws of either the United States, the laws of any of the Territories, the laws of any State, or the laws of any foreign country.

Section 2. That it shall be unlawful for any person engaged in commerce, in the course of such commerce, either directly or indirectly to discriminate in price between different purchasers of commodities, which commodities are sold for use, consumption, or resale within the United States or any Territory thereof or the District of Columbia or any insular possession or other place under the jurisdiction of the United States, where the effect of such discrimination may be to substantially lessen competition or tend to create a monopoly in any line of commerce: Provided, That nothing herein contained shall prevent discrimination in price between purchasers of commodities on account of differences in the grade, quality, or quantity of the commodity sold, or that makes only due allowance for difference in the cost of selling or transportation, or discrimination in price in the same or different communities made in good faith to meet competition: And provided further, That nothing herein contained shall prevent persons engaged in selling goods, wares, or merchandise in commerce from selecting their own customers in bona fide transactions and not in restraint of trade.

Section 3. That it shall be unlawful for any person engaged in commerce, in the course of such commerce, to lease or make a sale or contract for sale of goods, wares, merchandise, machinery, supplies or other commodities, whether patented or unpatented, for use, consumption or resale within the United States or any Territory thereof or the District of Columbia or any insular possession or other place under the jurisdiction of the United States, or fix a price charged therefor, or discount from, or rebate upon, such price, on the condition, agreement or understanding that the lessee or purchaser thereof shall not use or deal in the goods, wares, merchandise, machinery, supplies or other commodities of a competitor or competitors of the lessor or seller, where the effect of such lease, sale, or contract for sale or such condition, agreement or understanding may be to substantially lessen competition or tend to create a monopoly in any line of commerce.

Section 4. That any person who shall be injured in his business or property by reason of anything forbidden in the antitrust laws may sue therefor in any district court of the United States in the district in which the defendant resides or is found or has an agent, without respect to the amount in controversy, and shall recover threefold the damages by him sustained, and the cost of suit, including a reasonable attorney's fee.

Section 5. That a final judgment or decree hereafter rendered in any criminal prosecution or in any suit or proceeding in equity brought by or on behalf of the United States under the antitrust laws to the effect that a defendant has violated said laws shall be prima facie evidence against such defendant in any suit or proceeding brought by any other party against such defendant under said laws as to all matters respecting which said judgment or decree would be an estoppel as between the parties thereto: Provided, This section shall not apply to consent judgments or decrees entered before any testimony has been taken: Provided further, This section shall not apply to consent judgments or decrees rendered in criminal proceedings or suits in equity, now pending, in which the taking of testimony has been commenced but has not been concluded, provided such judgments or decrees are rendered before any further testimony is taken.

Whenever any suit or proceeding in equity or criminal prosecution is instituted by the United States to prevent, restrain or punish violations of any of the antitrust laws, the running of the statute of limitations in respect of each and every private right of action arising under said laws and based in whole or in part on any matter complained of in said suit or proceeding shall be suspended during the pendency thereof.

Section 6. That the labor of a human being is not a commodity or article of commerce. Nothing contained in the antitrust laws shall be construed to forbid the existence and operation of labor, agricultural, or horticultural organizations, instituted for the purposes of mutual help, and not having capital stock or conducted for profit, or to forbid or restrain individual members of such organizations from lawfully carrying out the legitimate objects thereof; nor shall such organizations, or the members thereof, be held or construed to be illegal combinations or conspiracies in restraint of trade, under the antitrust laws.

Section 7. That no corporation engaged in commerce shall acquire, directly or indirectly, the whole or any part of the stock or other share capital of another corporation engaged also in commerce, where the effect of such acquisition may be to substantially lessen competition between the corporation whose stock is so acquired and the corporation making the acquisition, or to restrain such commerce in any section or community, or tend to create a monopoly of any line of commerce.

No corporation shall acquire, directly or indirectly, the whole or any part of the stock or other share capital of two or more corporations engaged in commerce where the effect of such acquisition; or the use of such stock by the voting or granting of proxies or otherwise, may be to substantially lessen competition between such corporations, or any of them, whose stock or other share capital is so acquired, or to restrain such commerce in any section or community, or tend to create a monopoly of any line of commerce.

This section shall not apply to corporations purchasing such stock solely for investment and not using the same by voting or otherwise to bring about, or in attempting to bring about, the substantial lessening of competition. Nor shall anything contained in this section prevent a corporation engaged in commerce from causing the formation of subsidiary corporations for the actual carrying on of their immediate lawful business, or the natural and legitimate branches or extensions thereof, or from owning and holding all or a part of the stock of such subsidiary corporations, when the effect of such formation is not to substantially lessen competition.

Nor shall anything herein contained be construed to prohibit any common carrier subject to the laws to regulate commerce from aiding in the construction of branches or short lines so located as to become feeders to the main line of the company so aiding in such construction or from acquiring or owning all or any part of the stock of such branch lines, nor to prevent any such common carrier from acquiring and owning all or any part of the stock of a branch or short line constructed by an independent company where there is no substantial competition between the company owning the branch line so constructed and the company owning the main line acquiring the property or an interest therein, nor to prevent such common carrier from extending any of its lines through the medium of the acquisition of stock or otherwise of any other such common carrier where there is no substantial competition between the company extending its lines and the company whose stock, property, or an interest therein is so acquired.

Nothing contained in this section shall be held to affect or impair any right heretofore legally acquired: Provided, That nothing in this section shall be held or construed to authorize or make lawful anything heretofore prohibited or made illegal by the antitrust laws, nor to exempt any person from the penal provisions thereof or the civil remedies therein provided.

Section 8. That from and after two years from the date of the approval of this Act no person shall at the same time be a director or other officer or employee of more than one bank, banking association or trust company, organized or operating under the laws of the United States, either of which has deposits, capital, surplus, and undivided profits aggregating more than $5,000,000; and no private banker or person who is a director in any bank or trust company, organized and operating under the laws of a State, having deposits, capital, surplus, and undivided profits aggregating more than $5,000,000 shall be eligible to be a director in any bank or banking association organized or operating under the laws of the United States. The eligibility of a director, officer, or employee under the foregoing provisions shall be determined by the average amount of deposits, capital, surplus, and undivided profits as shown in the official statements of such bank, banking association, or trust company filed as provided by law during the fiscal year next preceding the date set for the annual election of directors, and when a director, officer, or employee has been elected or selected in accordance with the provisions of this Act it shall be lawful for him to continue as such for one year thereafter under said election or employment.

No bank, banking association or trust company, organized or operating under the laws of the United States, in any city or incorporated town or village of more than two hundred thousand inhabitants, as shown by the last preceding decennial census of the United States, shall have as a director or other officer or employee any private banker or any director or other officer or employee of any other bank, banking association, or trust company located in the same place: Provided, That nothing in this section shall apply to mutual savings banks not having a capital stock represented by shares: Provided further, That a director or other officer or employee of such bank, banking association, or trust company may be a director or other officer or employee of not more than one other bank or trust company organized under the laws of the United States or any State where the entire capital stock of one is owned by stockholders in the other: And provided further, That nothing contained in this section shall forbid a director of class A of a Federal reserve bank, as defined in the Federal Reserve Act, from being an officer or director or both an officer and director in one member bank.

That from and after two years from the date of the approval of this Act no person at the same time shall be a director in any two or more corporations, any one of which has capital, surplus, and undivided profits aggregating more than $1,000,000, engaged in whole or in part in commerce, other than banks, banking associations, trust companies and common carriers subject to the Act to regulate commerce, approved February fourth, eighteen hundred and eighty seven, if such corporations are or shall have been theretofore, by virtue of their business and location of operation, competitors, so that the elimination of competition by agreement between them would constitute a violation of any of the provisions of any of the antitrust laws. The eligibility of a director under the foregoing provision shall be determined by the aggregate amount of the capital, surplus, and undivided profits, exclusive of dividends declared but not paid to stockholders, at the end of the fiscal year of said corporation next preceding the election of directors, and when a director has been elected in accordance with the provisions of this Act it shall be lawful for him to continue as such for one year thereafter.

When any person elected or chosen as a director or officer or selected as an employee of any bank or other corporation subject to the provisions of this Act is eligible at the time of his election or selection to act for such bank or other corporation in such capacity his eligibility to act in such capacity shall not be affected and he shall not become or be deemed amenable to any of the provisions hereof by reason of any change in the affairs of such bank or other corporation from whatsoever cause, whether specifically excepted by any of the provisions hereof or not, until the expiration of one year from the date of his election or employment.

Section 9. Every president, director, officer or manager of any firm, association or corporation engaged in commerce as a common carrier, who embezzles, steals, abstracts or willfully misapplies, or willfully permits to be misapplied, any of the moneys, funds, credits, securities, property or assets of such firm, association or corporation, arising or accruing from, or used in, such commerce, in whole or in part, or willfully or knowingly converts the same to his own use or to the use of another, shall be deemed guilty of a felony and upon conviction shall be fined not less than $500 or confined in the penitentiary not less than one year nor more than ten years, or both, in the discretion of the court.

Prosecutions hereunder may be in the district court of the United States for the district wherein the offense may have been committed.

That nothing in this section shall be held to take away or impair the jurisdiction of the courts of the several States under the laws thereof; and a judgment of conviction or acquittal on the merits under the laws of any State shall be a bar to any prosecution hereunder for the same act or acts.

Section 10. That after two years from the approval of this Act no common carrier engaged in commerce shall have any dealings in securities, supplies or other articles of commerce, or shall make or have any contracts for construction or maintenance of any kind, to the amount of more than $50,000, in the aggregate, in any one year, with another corporation, firm, partnership or association when the said common carrier shall have upon its board of directors or as its president, manager or as its purchasing or selling officer, or agent in the particular transaction, any person who is at the same time a director, manager, or purchasing or selling officer of, or who has any substantial interest in, such other corporation, firm, partnership or association, unless and except such purchases shall be made from, or such dealings shall be with, the bidder whose bid is the most favorable to such common carrier, to be ascertained by competitive bidding under regulations to be proscribed by rule or otherwise by the Interstate Commerce Commission. No bid shall be received unless the name and address of the bidder or the names and addresses of the officers, directors and general managers thereof, if the bidder be a corporation, or of the members, if it be a partnership or firm, be given with the bid.

Any person who shall, directly or indirectly, do or attempt to do anything to prevent anyone from bidding or shall do any act to prevent free and fair competition among the bidders or those desiring to bid shall be punished as prescribed in this section in the case of an officer or director.

Every such common carrier having any such transactions or making any such purchases shall within thirty days after making the same file with the Interstate Commerce Commission a full and detailed statement of the transaction showing the manner of the competitive bidding, who were the bidders, and the names and addresses of the directors and officers of the corporations and the members of the firm or partnership bidding; and whenever the said commission shall, after investigation or hearing, have reason to believe that the law has been violated in and about the said purchases or transactions it shall transmit all papers and documents and its own views or findings regarding the transaction to the Attorney General.

If any common carrier shall violate this section it shall be fined not exceeding $25,000; and every such director, agent, manager or officer thereof who shall have knowingly voted for or directed the act constituting such violation or who shall have aided or abetted in such violation shall be deemed guilty of a misdemeanor and shall be fined not exceeding $5,000, or confined in jail not exceeding one year, or both, in the discretion of the court.

Section 11. That authority to enforce compliance with sections two, three, seven and eight of this Act by the persons respectively subject thereto is hereby vested: in the Interstate Commerce Commission where applicable to common carriers, in the Federal Reserve Board where applicable to banks, banking associations and trust companies, and in the Federal Trade Commission where applicable to all other character of commerce, to be exercised as follows:

Whenever the commission or board vested with jurisdiction thereof shall have reason to believe that any person is violating or has violated any of the provisions of sections two, three, seven and eight of this Act, it shall issue and serve upon such person a complaint stating its charges in that respect, and containing a notice of a hearing upon a day and at a place therein fixed at least thirty days after the service of said complaint. The person so complained of shall have the right to appear at the place and time so fixed and show cause why an order should not be entered by the commission or board requiring such person to cease and desist from the violation of the law so charged in said complaint. Any person may make application, and upon good cause shown may be allowed by the commission or board, to intervene and appear in said proceeding by counsel or in person. The testimony in any such proceeding shall be reduced to writing and filed in the office of the commission or board. If upon such hearing the commission or board, as the case may be, shall be of the opinion that any of the provisions of said sections have been or are being violated, it shall make a report in writing in which it shall state its findings as to the facts, and shall issue and cause to be served on such person an order requiring such person to cease and desist from such violations, and divest itself of the stock held or rid itself of the directors chosen contrary to the provisions of sections seven and eight of this Act, if any there be, in the manner and within the time fixed by said order. Until a transcript of the record in such hearing shall have been filed in a circuit court of appeals of the United States, as hereinafter provided, the commission or board may at any time, upon such notice and in such manner as it shall deem proper, modify or set aside, in whole or in part, any report or any order made or issued by it under this section.

If such person fails or neglects to obey such order of the commission or board while the same is in effect, the commission or board may apply to the circuit court of appeals of the United States, within any circuit where the violation complained of was or is being committed or where such person resides or carries on business, for the enforcement of its order, and shall certify and file with its application a transcript of the entire record in the proceeding, including all the testimony taken and the report and order of the commission or board. Upon such filing of the application and transcript the court shall cause notice thereof to be served upon such person and thereupon shall have jurisdiction of the proceeding and of the question determined therein, and shall have power to make and enter upon the pleadings, testimony, and proceedings set forth in such transcript a decree affirming, modifying, or setting aside the order of the commission or board. The findings of the commission or board as to the facts, if supported by testimony, shall be conclusive. If either party shall apply to the court for leave to adduce additional evidence, and shall show to the satisfaction of the court that such additional evidence is material and that there were reasonable grounds for the failure to adduce such evidence in the proceeding before the commission or board, the court may order such additional evidence to be taken before the commission or board and to be adduced upon the hearing in such manner and upon such terms and conditions as to the court may seem proper. The commission or board may modify its findings as to the facts, or make new findings, by reason of the additional evidence so taken, and it shall file such modified or new findings, which, if supported by testimony, shall be conclusive, and its recommendation, if any, for the modification or setting aside of its original order, with the return of such additional evidence. The judgment and decree of the court shall be final, except that the same shall be subject to review by the Supreme Court upon certiorari as provided in section two hundred and forty of the Judicial Code.

Any party required by such order of the commission or board to cease and desist from a violation charged may obtain a review of such order in said circuit court of appeals by filing in the court a written petition praying that the order of the commission or board be set aside. A copy of such petition shall be forthwith served upon the commission or board, and thereupon the commission or board forthwith shall certify and file in the court a transcript of the record as hereinbefore provided. Upon the filing of the transcript the court shall have the same jurisdiction to affirm, set aside, or modify the order of the commission or board as in the case of an application by the commission or board for the enforcement of its order, and the findings of the commission or board as to the facts, if supported by testimony, shall in like manner be conclusive.

The jurisdiction of the circuit court of appeals of the United States to enforce, set aside, or modify orders of the commission or board shall be exclusive.

Such proceedings in the circuit court of appeals shall be given precedence over other cases pending therein, and shall be in every way expedited. No order of the commission or board or the judgment of the court to enforce the same shall in any wise relieve or absolve any person from any liability under the antitrust Acts.

Complaints, orders, and other processes of the commission or board under this section may be served by anyone duly authorized by the commission or board, either (a) by delivering a copy thereof to the person to be served, or to a member of the partnership to be served, or to the president, secretary, or other executive officer or a director of the corporation to be served; or (b) by leaving a copy thereof at the principal office or place of business of such person; or (c) by registering and mailing a Copy thereof addressed to such person at his principal office or place of business. The verified return by the person so serving said complaint, order, or other process setting forth the manner of said service shall be proof of the same, and the return post-office receipt for said complaint, order, or other process registered and mailed as aforesaid shall be proof of the service of the same.

Section 12. That any suit, action, or proceeding under the antitrust laws against a corporation may be brought not only in the judicial district whereof it is an inhabitant, but also in any district wherein it may be found or transacts business; and all process in such cases may be served in the district of which it is an inhabitant, or wherever it may be found.

Section 13. That in any suit, action, or proceeding brought by or on behalf of the United States subpoenas for witnesses who are required to attend a court of the United States in any judicial district in any case, civil or criminal, arising under the antitrust laws may run into any other district: Provided, That in civil cases no writ of subpoena shall issue for witnesses living out of the district in which the court is held at a greater distance than one hundred miles from the place of holding the same without the permission of the trial court being first had upon proper application and cause shown.

Section 14. That whenever a corporation shall violate any of the penal provisions of the antitrust laws, such violation shall be deemed to be also that of the individual directors, officers, or agents of such corporation who shall have authorized, ordered, or done any of the acts constituting in whole or in part such violation, and such violation shall be deemed a misdemeanor and upon conviction therefor of any such director, officer, or agent he shall be punished by a fine of not exceeding $5,000 or by imprisonment for not exceeding one year, or by both, in the discretion of the court.

Section 15. That the several district courts of the United States are hereby invested with jurisdiction to prevent and restrain violations of this Act, and it shall be the duty of the several district attorneys of the United States, in their respective districts, under the direction of the Attorney General, to institute proceedings in equity to prevent. and restrain such violations. Such proceedings may be by way of petition setting forth the case and praying that such violation shall be enjoined or otherwise prohibited. When the parties complained of shall have been duly notified of such petition, the court shall proceed, as soon as may be, to the hearing and determination of the case; and pending such petition, and before final decree, the court may at any time make such temporary restraining order or prohibition as shall be deemed just in the premises. Whenever it shall appear to the court before which any such proceeding may be pending that the ends of justice require that other parties should be brought before the court, the court may cause them to be summoned, whether they reside in the district in which the court is held or not, and subpoenas to that end may be served in any district by the marshal thereof.

Section 16. That any person, firm, corporation, or association shall be entitled to sue for and have injunctive relief, in any court of the United States having jurisdiction over the parties, against threatened loss or damage by a violation of the antitrust laws, including sections two, three, seven and eight of this Act, when and under the same conditions and principles as injunctive relief against threatened conduct that will cause loss or damage is granted by courts of equity, under the rules governing such proceeding's, and upon the execution of proper bond against damages for an injunction improvidently granted and a showing that the danger of irreparable loss or damage is immediate, a preliminary injunction may issue: Provided, That nothing herein contained shall be construed to entitle any person, firm, corporation, or association, except the United States, to bring suit in equity for injunctive relief against any common carrier subject to the provisions of the Act to regulate commerce, approved February fourth, eighteen hundred and eighty-seven, in respect of any matter subject to the regulation, supervision. or other jurisdiction of the Interstate Commerce Commission.

Section 17. That no preliminary injunction shall be issued without notice to the opposite party.

No temporary restraining order shall be granted without notice to the opposite party unless it shall clearly appear from specific facts shown by affidavit or by the verified bill that immediate and irreparable injury, loss, or damage will result to the applicant before notice can be served and a hearing had thereon. Every such temporary restraining order shall be indorsed with the date and hour of issuance, shall be forthwith filed in the clerk's office and entered of record, shall define the injury and state why it is irreparable and why the order was granted without notice, and shall by its terms expire within such time after entry, not to exceed ten days, as the court or judge may fix, unless within the time so fixed the order is extended for a like period for good cause shown, and the reasons for such extension shall be entered of record. In case a temporary restraining order shall be granted without notice in the contingency specified, the matter of the issuance of a preliminary injunction shall be set down for a hearing at the earliest possible time and shall take precedence of all matters except older matters of the same character; and when the same comes up for hearing the party obtaining the temporary restraining order shall proceed with the application for a preliminary injunction, and if he does not do so the court shall dissolve the temporary restraining order. Upon two days' notice to the party obtaining such temporary restraining order the opposite party may appear and move the dissolution or modification of the order, and in that event the court or judge shall proceed to hear and determine the motion as expeditiously as the ends of justice may require.

Section two hundred and sixty-three of an Act entitled "An Act to codify, revise, and amend the laws relating to the judiciary," approved March third, nineteen hundred and eleven, is hereby repealed.

Nothing in this section contained shall be deemed to alter, repeal, or amend section two hundred and sixty-six of an Act entitled "An Act to codify, revise, and amend the laws relating to the judiciary," approved March third, nineteen hundred and eleven.

Section 18. That, except as otherwise provided in section 16 of this Act, no restraining order or interlocutory order of injunction shall issue, except upon the giving of security by the applicant in such sum as the court or judge may deem proper, conditioned upon the payment of such costs and damages as may be incurred or suffered by any party who may be found to have been wrongfully enjoined or restrained thereby.

Section 19. That every order of injunction or restraining order shall set forth the reasons for the issuance of the same, shall be specific in terms, and shall describe in reasonable detail, and not by reference to the bill of complaint or other document, the act or acts sought to be restrained, and shall be binding only upon the parties to the suit, their officers, agents, servants, employees, and attorneys, or those in active concert or participating with them, and who shall, by personal service or otherwise, have received actual notice of the same.

Section 20. That no restraining order or injunction shall be granted by any court of the United States, or a judge or the judges thereof, in any case between an employer and employees, or between employers and employees, or between employees, or between persons employed and persons seeking employment, involving, or growing out of, a dispute concerning terms or conditions of employment, unless necessary to prevent irreparable injury to property, or to a property right, of the party making the application, for which injury there is no adequate remedy at law, and such property or property right must be described with particularity in the application, which must be in writing and sworn to by the applicant or by his agent or attorney.

And no such restraining order or injunction shall prohibit any person or persons, whether singly or in concert, from terminating any relation of employment, or from ceasing to perform any work or labor, or from recommending, advising, or persuading others by peaceful means so to do; or from attending at any place where any such person or persons may lawfully be, for the purpose of peacefully obtaining or communicating information, or from peacefully persuading any person to work or to abstain from working; or from ceasing to patronize or to employ any party to such dispute, or from recommending, advising, or persuading others by peaceful and lawful means so to do; or from paying or giving to, or withholding from, any person engaged in such dispute, any strike benefits or other moneys or things of value; or from peaceably assembling in a lawful manner, and for lawful purposes; or from doing any act or thing which might lawfully be done in the absence of such dispute by any party thereto; nor shall any of the acts specified in this paragraph be considered or held to be violations of any law of the United States.

Section 21. That any person who shall willfully disobey any lawful writ, process, order, rule, decree, or command of any district court of the United States or any court of the District of Columbia by doing any act or thing therein, or thereby forbidden to be done by him, if the act or thing so done by him be of such character as to constitute also a criminal offense under any statute of the United States, or under the laws of any State in which the act was committed, shall be proceeded against for his said contempt as hereinafter provided.

Section 22. That whenever it shall be made to appear to any district court or judge thereof, or to any judge therein sitting, by the return of a proper officer on lawful process, or upon the affidavit of some credible person, or by information filed by any district attorney, that there is reasonable ground to believe that any person has been guilty of such contempt, the court or judge thereof, or any judge therein sitting, may issue a rule requiring the said person so charged to show cause upon a day certain why he should not be punished therefor, which rule, together with a copy of the affidavit or information, shall be served upon the person charged, with sufficient promptness to enable him to prepare for and make return to the order at the time fixed therein. If upon or by such return, in the judgment of the court, the alleged contempt be not sufficiently purged, a trial shall be directed at a time and place fixed by the court: Provided, however, That if the accused, being a natural person, fail or refuse to make return to the rule to show cause, an attachment may issue against his person to compel an answer, and in case of his continued failure or refusal, or if for any reason it be impracticable to dispose of the matter on the return day, he may be required to give reasonable bail for his attendance at the trial and his submission to the final judgment of the court. Where the accused is a body corporate, an attachment for the sequestration of its property may be issued upon like refusal or failure to answer.

In all cases within the purview of this Act such trial may be by the court, or, upon demand of the accused, by a jury; in which latter event the court may impanel a jury from the jurors then in attendance, or the court or the judge thereof in chambers may cause a sufficient number of jurors to be selected and summoned, as provided by law, to attend at the time and place of trial, at which time a jury shall be selected and impaneled as upon a trial for misdemeanor; and such trial shall conform, as near as may be, to the practice in criminal cases prosecuted by indictment or upon information.

If the accused be found guilty, judgment shall be entered accordingly, prescribing the punishment, either by fine or imprisonment, or both, in the discretion of the court. Such fine shall be paid to the United States or to the complainant or other party injured by the act constituting the contempt, or may, where more than one is so damaged, be divided or apportioned among them as the court may direct, but in no case shall the fine to be paid to the United States exceed, in case the accused is a natural person, the sum of $1,000, nor shall such imprisonment exceed the term of six months: Provided, That in any case the court or a judge thereof may, for good cause shown, by affidavit or proof taken in open court or before such judge and filed with the papers in the case, dispense with the rule to show cause, and may issue an attachment for the arrest of the person charged with contempt; in which event such person, when arrested, shall be brought before such court or a judge thereof without unnecessary delay and shall be admitted to bail in a reasonable penalty for his appearance to answer to the charge or for trial for the contempt; and thereafter the proceedings shall be the same as provided herein in case the rule had issued in the first instance.

Section 23. That the evidence taken upon the trial of any persons so accused may be preserved by bill of exceptions, and any judgment of conviction may be reviewed upon writ of error in all respects as now provided by law in criminal cases, and may be affirmed, reversed, or modified as justice may require. Upon the granting of such writ of error, execution of judgment shall be stayed, and the accused, if thereby sentenced to imprisonment, shall be admitted to bail in such reasonable sum as may be required by the court, or by any justice, or any judge of any district court of the United States or any court of the District of Columbia.

Section 24. That nothing herein contained shall be construed to relate to contempts committed in the presence of the court, or so near thereto as to obstruct the administration of justice, nor to contempts committed in disobedience of any lawful writ, process, order, rule, decree or command entered in any suit or action brought or prosecuted in the name of, or on behalf of, the United States, but the same, and all other cases of contempt not specifically embraced within section twenty-one of this Act, may be punished in conformity to the usages at law and in equity now prevailing.

Section 25. That no proceeding for contempt shall be instituted against any person unless begun within one year from the date of the act complained of; nor shall any such proceeding be a bar to any criminal prosecution for the same act or acts; but nothing herein contained shall affect any proceedings in contempt pending at the time of the passage of this Act.

Section 26. If any clause, sentence, paragraph, or part of this Act shall, for any reason, be adjudged by any court of competent jurisdiction to be invalid, such judgment shall not affect, impair, or invalidate the remainder thereof, but shall be confined in its operation to the clause, sentence, paragraph, or part thereof directly involved in the controversy in which such judgment shall have been rendered.

GLOSSARY

common carrier: a term for any company that transports goods across state lines; in the context of this law at this time, the term applied primarily to railroads

estoppel: a way for court to prevent a party to a case from going back on assertions made during the case

injunction: an order from a judge designed to get parties to obey a court ruling or final decision; injunctions were a major concern to trade unions that had experienced judicial harassment during strikes and labor actions of all kinds for decades by the time this law was passed

Document Analysis
Sections 2 and 3 of the Clayton Act deal with price discrimination and anticompetitive no-purchase agreements. These are among the most important sections of the Clayton Act because they deal with two very common practices that had helped make large monopolies possible. Most notably, Section 3 prevents companies from have two different pricing strategies in different communities depending on the amount of competition they face in each. If they undersold a competitor in one community, they have to keep the same price in a different community where the competition is less. While difficult to enforce, this provision suggests the important role that government can play in limiting the potential excesses of capitalism.

Another important section of this law is Section 7, which bans corporations from acquiring "the whole or any part of the stock or other share capital of another corporation engaged also in commerce," if that acquisition leads to "substantially lessen competition." This provision applies specifically to mergers, which actually increased after the passage of the Sherman Act. It also applies to holding companies, which aligned the interests of apparently competing companies through mutual stock ownership. These had been a significant cause of monopolistic behavior and were made substantially worse by the fact, as was the case with Standard Oil, that these incestuous relationships were unknown to the public. Here is an important provision of the law that was enforced at the time and strengthened by subsequent legislation in later years.

Another key change in the Clayton Act from previous antitrust law is in Section 4, which states, "That any person who shall be injured in his business or property by reason of anything forbidden in the antitrust laws may sue" and can "recover threefold the damages by him sustained, and the cost of suit, including a reasonable attorney's fee." Only the government could enforce the Sherman Act, but now anyone who could afford an attorney could make an argument that might bankrupt the aggrieved party. Unfortunately for labor unions, their employers were often keen to use the Clayton Act in this way.

For all the controversy over its labor provisions, the Clayton Act is surprisingly weak on trade union concerns. While the language about human labor not being a commodity was supposed to indemnify labor unions from antitrust prosecution, it was really just a restatement of common law principles. Nevertheless, Samuel Gompers of the American Federation of Labor (AFL) proclaimed that the passage of this law was "Labor's Magna Carta," referring to the famous English document that gave English lords rights in opposition to King John in 1215.

What it did do was declare strikes, boycotts, and the existence of labor unions legal, even if they were still subject to judicial harassment under this legislation. This was a theoretical improvement even though these organizations and practices had a long history by this point in time. The key phrase here is "lawfully carrying out the legitimate objects." The existence of unions became institutionalized, but their actions remained subject to review from a largely hostile judiciary.

Essential Themes
While the Clayton Act persists as a crucial part of American antitrust law, its initial impact proved limited. For example, it contained a provision against interlocking directorates. An interlocking directorate was the practice of businessmen serving on the boards of directors of each other's companies, which made coordinating activities and prices much easier since seemingly competitive companies then contained the same leadership. Congress postponed the enforcement of this provision in the text of the law and eventually dropped it entirely. Since the passage of the Clayton Act, its provisions have been amended many times, making its impact much stronger.

Despite its limitations, the Clayton Act still marked a number of other important symbolic changes in American history. Most notably, the use of the Constitution's Commerce Clause to justify the power to enact this legislation marked an important precedent for the legislation of the late New Deal years. Similarly, it is also marked a major milestone in the courtship of labor unions by the Democratic Party. While other antitrust legislation followed this law, its provisions continue to regulate American commerce today.

—*Jonathan Rees*

Bibliography and Additional Reading
Cooper, Jr., John Milton. *Woodrow Wilson: A Biography*. New York: Alfred A. Knopf, 2009.
Dawley, Alan. *Struggles for Justice: Social Responsibility and the Liberal State*. Cambridge, MA: Harvard University Press, 1991.
Link, Arthur S. *Woodrow Wilson and the Progressive Era, 1910–1917*. New York: Harper and Row, 1954.
Painter, Nell Irvin. *Standing at Armageddon: A Grassroots History of the Progressive Era*. New York: W.W. Norton, 2008.

Albert B. Fall was the first U.S. cabinet official sentenced to prison. (Bain News Service, publisher. - Library of Congress Prints and Photographs Division. George Grantham Bain Collection.)

■ On the Teapot Dome Scandal

Date: May 1922; February 1924
Authors: Robert La Follette; U.S. Congress; Calvin Coolidge
Genre: Speech; law

Summary Overview

The Teapot Dome scandal was a case of political corruption within the administration of President Warren G. Harding. It erupted in 1922, when Harding's secretary of the interior, Albert B. Fall, was accused of setting up drilling leases on public lands for two top oil industry executives and receiving a payback in return. As a result, congressional hearings were initiated, an independent prosecutor assigned, and witnesses called beginning in late 1923, after Harding's death from heart failure. Although the scandal never directly implicated Harding, it occurred at a time when other, lesser administrative scandals were unfolding and ended up blackening Harding's reputation and his standing as a president. There is no one key document associated with the scandal, but only a series of statements and legal testimonies given over a period of several years. The selection of materials included here is made up of: (1) a short argument delivered in the Senate by the Progressive Wisconsin Senator Robert La Follette in favor of prosecuting the case; (2) a congressional resolution canceling the oil leases at the center of the scandal, after it had been determined that they were questionable; and (3) two brief statements by President Calvin Coolidge regarding the removal of an administrative official implicated in the case.

Defining Moment

The Teapot Dome scandal took its name from an oil reserve in Wyoming that featured a rock outcropping resembling a teapot. The reserve was leased by Secretary of the Interior Albert B. Fall to the industrialist Harry F. Sinclair—head of Mammoth Oil Co. (later Sinclair Oil Co.)—in early 1922. It and another reserve in Elk Hills, California, which was leased to Edward L. Doheny, head of Pan-American Petroleum Co., were part of an effort by Fall to demonstrate the utility of allowing private oil companies to make use of oil reserves on public lands—to the benefit of both the government and private industry. Fall had recently won President Warren G. Harding to his cause, although some in the administration felt that these oil fields, which were dedicated to maintaining a supply of fuel for the U.S. Navy, were best left untapped and overseen by the government. Fall and his business associates noted that private companies were already drilling in areas adjacent to the reserves, and it would be prudent to act before the oil at the site was depleted. They sweetened the deal by agreeing to erect fuel storage facilities at Navy shipyards in California and Hawaii. However, as an April 1922 article in the *Wall Street Journal* noted, the entire arrangement had been made without any open, competitive bidding. It thus appeared to be an instance of crony capitalism.

The practice of conservation of natural resources—of holding public goods in reserve—was relatively new at the time. Under the presidencies of Theodore Roosevelt, William H. Taft, and Woodrow Wilson inroads were made into this arena. (Taft, in fact, had designated Elk Hills a naval reserve in 1912, and Wilson did the same for Teapot Dome in 1915.) In the case of oil, it was thought wise to leave some of that resource in natural reservoirs, or domes, for future use. Both Democrats and Republicans generally supported the policy and in 1920 passed a law mandating the maintenance of adequate reserves for such purposes. On the other hand, private oil interests, along with many politicians, opposed the policy, holding that the oil supply was plentiful enough to make reserves unnecessary, and that, in any case, private oil companies were capable of supplying the needs of the U.S. government. Albert Fall, a former senator from New Mexico, represented the latter school of thought.

Adding to suspicions regarding the Teapot Dome deal was an air of secrecy surrounding Fall and his associates. A perception of favoritism and bribery seemed to be confirmed when Fall started making improvements to his private ranch in New Mexico. Fall claimed that the secrecy was necessary to protect the storage facilities from attack during war. Despite the fact that the Harding administration enjoyed the benefit of having Congress politically aligned with it (under Republican control), the Senate voted to launch an investigation. The senator most responsible for pushing for the review was the Progressive Wisconsin politician Robert M. La Follette. The senator put in charge of the investigation, under the Committee on Public Lands, was Montana Democrat Thomas J. Walsh, respected for his legal skills and personal integrity. Thus, following months of information gathering and analysis, the hearings got underway—in late 1923, after President Harding's death and Secretary Fall's departure from the cabinet.

Author Biographies
Robert M. La Follette was born in Primrose, Wisconsin, in 1855. He served as a county district attorney and in the U.S. House of Representatives before returning to Wisconsin to run for governor, which led to his serving in that office as a Progressive from 1901 to 1906. From there he moved to the U.S. Senate (1906–24), sponsoring bills, among other legislation, to limit the power of the railroads. His *La Follete's Weekly* expanded his reach and helped build a wider reform movement, partly aligned with the Populist movement. As the Progressive Party's presidential candidate in 1924, he won 5 million votes, about one-sixth of the total. La Follette died in Washington, D.C., the following year.

Calvin Coolidge was born in 1872 in Plymouth, Vermont. His mother and sister died early in his life; his father was a prominent public official. Coolidge graduated from Amherst College and pursued a career in law and government. While living in Northampton, Massachusetts, he won a seat on the city council in 1900, chairmanship of the Northampton Republican Committee in 1904, a position on the Massachusetts General Court in 1907, and, eventually, the office of governor in 1919. He left office to serve as vice president to Warren G. Harding. In August 1923, Harding died, leaving Coolidge as president. In 1924, Coolidge won reelection, holding office until 1929. He retired to Northampton and died in 1933.

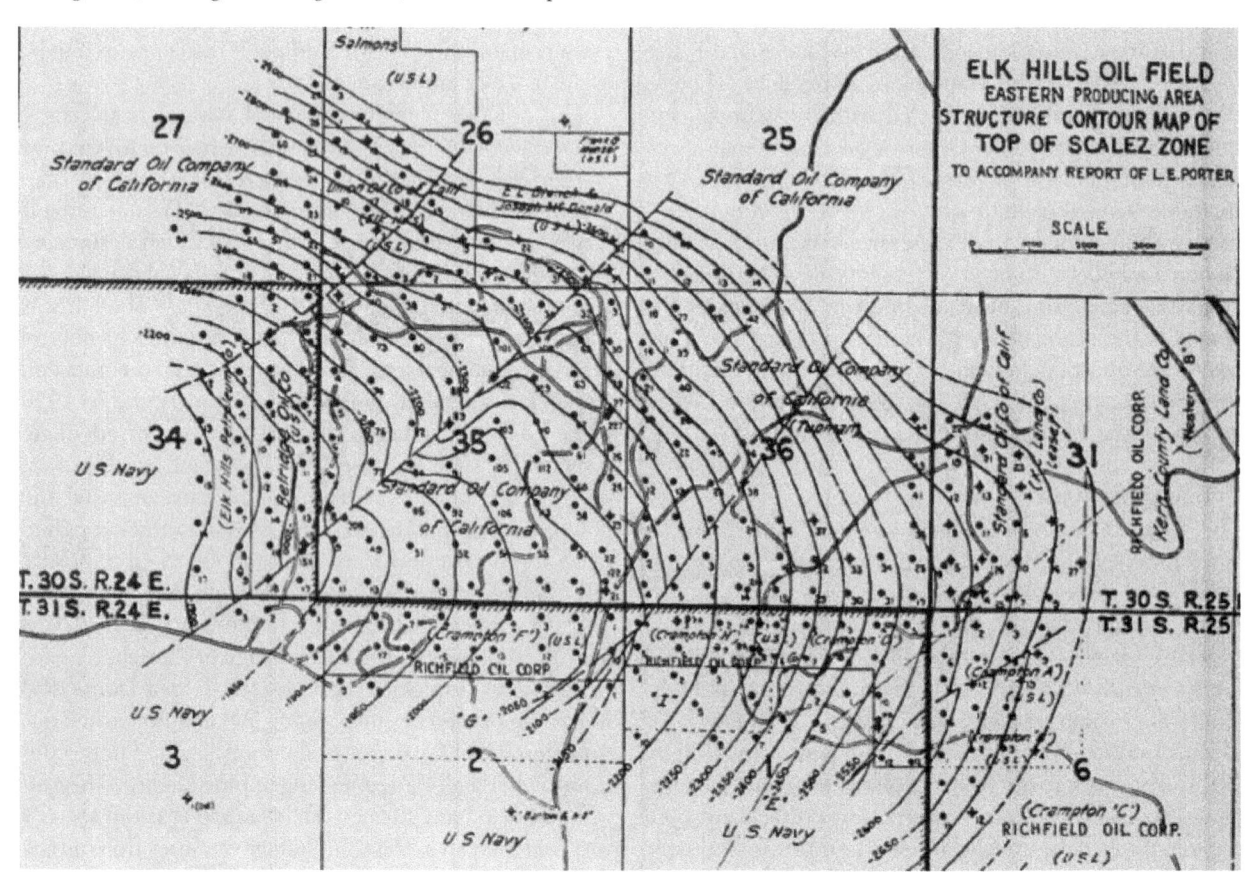

Elk Hills Oil field structure map. (State of California Dept. of Natural Resources Division of Mines Bulletin 118 - Geologic Formations and Economic Development of the Oil and Gas Fields of California)

HISTORICAL DOCUMENT

[Senator Robert La Follette, on the Senate floor, May 13, 1922, noting what he is opposed to in the leasing deal between Albert Fall and Harry Sinclair]

First. Against the policy of the Secretary of the Interior and the Secretary of the Navy in opening the naval reserves at this time for exploitation.

Second. Against the method of leasing public lands without competitive bidding, as exemplified in the recent contract entered into between Secretary Fall of the Interior and Secretary Denby of the Navy and the Standard Oil-Sinclair-Doheny interest.

Third. Against the policy of any department of the Government of the United States entering into a contract of any character whatsoever, whether competitive or not, which would tend to continue or perpetuate a monopolistic control of the oil industry of the United States or create a monopoly on the sale of fuel oil or refined oil to the Navy or any other department of the Government.

For the following reasons:

There exists no emergency or necessity which would warrant the opening of the naval reserves at this time for exploitation in order that the Navy might be supplied with the various grades of oil required by it, there being already above ground and in storage in the United States the greatest amount of oil that has been in storage in the history of all times.

The prices of fuel oil at the seaboard are lower than they have been in years, and there is an abundant supply.

The oil industry of the United States is just now convalescing from the greatest depression it has ever suffered, the daily production now being the largest in its history, and therefore, the turning over of Government lands to the large pipe-line interests for exploitation will have the direct result of depressing the price of crude oil without in any way relieving the people of the onerous and burdensome high prices of refined products.

* * *

[Joint Resolution of Congress Canceling Oil Leases, February 8, 1924]

Joint Resolution Directing the President to institute and prosecute suits to cancel certain leases of oil lands and incidental contracts, and for other purposes.

WHEREAS it appears from evidence taken by the Committee on Public Lands and Surveys of the United States Senate that certain lease of Naval Reserve Numbered 3, in the State of Wyoming, bearing date April 7, 1922, made in form by the Government of the United States, through Albert B. Fall, Secretary of the Interior, and Edwin Denby, Secretary of the Navy, as lessor, to the Mammoth Oil Company, as lessee, and that certain contract between the Government of the United States and the Pan American Petroleum and Transport Company, dated April 25, 1922, signed by Edward C. Finney, Acting Secretary of the Interior, and Edwin Denby, Secretary of the Navy, relating among other things to the construction of oil tanks at Pearl Harbor, Territory of Hawaii, and that certain lease of Naval Reserve Numbered 1, in the State of California, bearing date December 11, 1922, made in form by the Government of the United States through Albert B. Fall, Secretary of the Interior, and Edwin Denby, Secretary of the Navy, as lessor, to the Pan American Petroleum Company, as lessee, were executed under circumstances indicating fraud and corruption; and

WHEREAS the said leases and contract were entered into without authority on the part of the officers purporting to act in the execution of the same for the United States and in violation of the laws of Congress; and

WHEREAS such leases and contract were made in defiance of the settled policy of the Government, adhered to through three successive administrations, to maintain in the ground a great reserve supply of oil adequate to the needs of the Navy in any emergency threatening the national security: Therefore be it

Resolved by the Senate and House of Representatives of the United States of America in Congress assembled, That the said leases and contract are against the public interest and that the lands embraced therein should be recovered and held for the purpose to which they were dedicated; and

Resolved further, That the President of the United States be, and he hereby is, authorized and directed immediately to cause suit to be instituted and prosecuted for the annulment and cancellation of the said leases and contract and all contracts incidental or supplemental thereto, to enjoin the further extraction of oil from the said reserves under said leases or from the territory covered by the same, to secure any further appropriate incidental relief, and to prosecute such other actions of proceedings, civil and criminal, as may be warranted by the facts in relation to the making of the said leases and contract.

And the President is further authorized and directed to appoint, by and with the advice and consent of the Senate, special counsel who shall have charge and control of the prosecution of such litigation, anything in the statutes touching the powers of the Attorney General of the Department of Justice to the contrary notwithstanding.

* * *

[President Calvin Coolidge addressing the public]

The dismissal of an officer of the government [i.e., Secretary of the Navy Edwin Denby], such as is involved in this case, other than by impeachment, is exclusively an executive function. The President is responsible to the people for his conduct relative to the retention or dismissal of public officials. I assume that responsibility, and the people may be assured that as soon as I can be advised so that I may act with entire justice to all parties concerned and fully protect the public interests, I shall act. I do not propose to sacrifice any innocent man for my own welfare, nor do I propose to retain in office any unfit man for my own welfare. I shall try to maintain the functions of the government unimpaired, to act upon the evidence and the law as I find it, and to deal thoroughly and summarily with every kind of wrongdoing. [February 11, 1924]

It is my duty to extend to every individual the constitutional right of a presumption of innocence until proven guilty. But I have another duty equally constitutional, and even more important, of assuring the enforcement of the law. In that duty I do not intend to fail.

Character is the only secure foundation of the State. We know well that all plans of improving the machinery of government and all measures for social betterment fail, and the hopes of progress wither, when corruption touches administration. At the revelation of greed making its subtle approaches to public officers, of the prostitution of high place to private profit, we are filled with scorn and indignation. We have a deep sense of humiliation at such gross betrayal of trust, and we lament the undermining of public confidence in official integrity.

But we can not rest with righteous wrath; still less can we permit ourselves to give way to cynicism. The heart of the American people is sound. Their officials with rare exception are faithful and high minded. For us, we propose to follow the clear, open path of justice. There will be immediate, adequate, unshrinking prosecution, criminal and civil, to punish the guilty and to protect every national interest. In this effort there will be no politics and no partisanship. It will be speedy, it will be just.

I am a Republican but I can not on that account shield anyone because he is a Republican. I am a Republican, but I can not on that account prosecute anyone because he is a Democrat. I want no hue and cry, no mingling of innocent and guilty in unthinking condemnation, no confusion of mere questions of law with questions of fraud and corruption…I ask the support of our people, as chief magistrate, intent on the enforcement of our laws without fear or favor, no matter who is hurt or what the consequences.

[February 12, 1924]

GLOSSARY

competitive bidding: a process by which work or products needed by the government are presented to private businesses, who then make their best offers regarding costs, time, etc.

convalesce: to return to health and strength; recuperate

joint resolution: a formal statement passed by both the Senate and the House of Representatives

lessor and lessee: the parties that lease property to another and make use of property owned by another, respectively

naval reserves: in this context, oil deposits designated for use by the U.S. Navy

Document Analysis

The Teapot Dome scandal was one of the most captivating and damaging cases of political corruption in American history. Although not the sole force responsible for launching congressional hearings, Senator Robert La Follette was one of the main driving forces. In the course of investigating the matter, Congress discovered that Fall had worked to convince the secretary of the Navy, Edwin Denby, to shift authority for the oil reserves from the military to the Interior Department, under Fall's leadership. Then came the leasing of Teapot Dome to Sinclair and of Elk Hills to Doheny. The investigation revealed, moreover, that Fall had received over $400,000 (or $5 million in today's currency) in interest-free loans and government bonds from the two businessmen in return for arranging the leases. Although in the early part of the proceedings Fall had his protectors in the administration and elsewhere in government, they began to withdraw their support as more disclosures came forth. One such supporter, Attorney General Harry M. Daugherty, faced his own problems in connection with his running of the Department of Justice; he was forced to resign his office in 1924. The Navy Department's Denby, under pressure to resign as well, eventually did so. It is pressure to fire Denby that Coolidge is responding to in the statements given above. Congress also asked President Calvin Coolidge to appoint a special prosecutor in order to uncover any criminal wrongdoing in the case. Ultimately, Coolidge appointed two: one Republican and one Democrat. Ongoing press coverage of the scandal drew in a large public audience.

Various criminal and civil suits unfolded as time went by. In a ruling by the Supreme Court in 1927, well after the cancellation of the oil leases by Congress (in 1924), the leases were found to improper and return of the reserves to the government was deemed right and just. Fall, his reputation in tatters, was found guilty of bribery in 1929 and sentenced to one year in prison and a $100,000 fine. Sinclair and Doheny were acquitted of all charges—a somewhat surprising outcome. (Most observers expected to see convictions on conspiracy charges.) Sinclair, however, was subsequently charged in a second investigation with contempt because he refused to cooperate and was found to have tampered with the jury. He received a short sentence as a result.

The Teapot Dome scandal was used by political opponents of the Harding administration to paint a picture of graft and corruption, a picture that has colored popular opinion about the Harding presidency ever since. The Republican Party, too, was blasted at the time for its close ties to the business community and its alleged interest in fostering deals between politicians and business owners. While Harding's reputation has long suffered as a result of the scandal, his party benefitted from the efforts of his vice president and successor, Calvin Coolidge, toward restoring public trust in Republican leadership and confidence in government. Coolidge made a point of having zero tolerance for corruption in his administration and of appointing only men of the "highest character" to his cabinet. And character, as Coolidge notes in the second of his two statements above, "is the only secure foundation of the State." Republicans may also have been helped by the fact that Edward Doheny was found to have had links to leading Democrats as well as Republicans; some of them were even on his payroll. Thus, when Democrats tried in 1924 and 1928 to win the presidency through claims of honest government, they failed to win over voters and were defeated—by Coolidge and Herbert Hoover, in turn.

Essential Themes

Besides the political dimension, Teapot Dome is remembered for having been one of the first successes of the budding conservation movement. The public came to realize that, although natural resource issues are complex and planning for the needs of future generations is difficult, such planning must take place, and having a government conservation policy makes good sense. After Teapot Dome, petroleum development came to be overseen by the Federal Oil Conservation Board (FOCB), which focused on the "wise use" of the resource and maintaining stability in the oil market. The program was short-lived, however. Business groups such as the American Petroleum Institute pressured the government to limit the FOCB's authority and allow big oil companies, together with the many smaller, independent refiners, to develop drilling sites and bring their product to market under less restrictive conditions.

Teapot Dome is also noted for having inspired the writer Upton Sinclair's 1927 novel *Oil!*, which features a self-made oil millionaire (modeled on Edward Doheny) and his more skeptically-minded son. That novel, in turn, inspired the filmmaker Paul Thomas Anderson's award-winning 2007 movie *There Will Be Blood*, which highlights some of the ruthless business practices in the early oil industry and features a cast of odd and colorful characters. (The actor Daniel Day-Lewis, who plays the main character, won an Academy Award for best actor.)

—*Michael Shally-Jensen*

Bibliography and Additional Reading

Bennett, Leslie E. *One Lesson from History: Appointment of Special Counsel and the Investigation of the Teapot Dome Scandal*. Washington, DC: Brookings Institution, 1999.

Davis, Margaret Leslie. *Dark Side of Fortune: Triumph and Scandal in the Life of Oil Tycoon Edward L. Doheny*. Berkeley: University of California Press, 1998.

McCartney, Laton. *The Teapot Dome Scandal: How Big Oil Bought the Harding White House and Tried to Steal the Country*. New York: Random House, 2008.

Stratton, David H. *Tempest over Teapot Dome: The Story of Albert B. Fall*. Norman: University of Oklahoma Press, 1998.

From *My Life and Work*, by Henry Ford

Date: 1922
Authors: Henry Ford, with collaboration by Samuel Crowther
Genre: Autobiography; memoir

Summary Overview

Twenty years after the founding of the Ford Motor Company, Henry Ford had recently acquired total ownership and control. Although rumors had circulated that he was going bankrupt and was out of touch, Ford had demonstrated that he had the financial and personal resources to meet the challenges of the early 1920s. As the most respected business leader of that time, Ford wanted to influence others who sought to become entrepreneurs. In this book, he set forth his philosophy of business and of life. The economy of the United States had been in a short, but significant, recession in 1920–21, and many looked to the future with uncertainty. Ford believed that the principles that had guided him in prior years would serve him well in the years to come. Thus, he and Crowther wrote a book that outlined a foundation to assist in strengthening the American economy and improving all levels of American society.

Defining Moment

Although Ford had been a peace activist prior to 1917, when the United States finally entered the First World War he shifted the company's production lines to help support the war effort. Up to that time, the company had been very successful, with its focus on the production of the Model T. In the first months after the end of the war, Ford and the company prospered, owing to the pent-up demand for automobiles. However, in 1920, when the first general economic recession since the development of the auto industry started, Ford was not well positioned to face it. There were pressures from his creditors, who were uneasy due to rumors that the company was insolvent. Adding to the credit problem was the fact that Ford had borrowed twenty million dollars in 1919 to buy out all the other company owners. With decreasing sales of its Model T, the Ford Motor Company and its owner were thought, by some, to be facing their end.

However, Ford, aided by key executives, transformed the company. They refocused their efforts, doing away with many of the products they had added to help the war effort. The number of administrative positions was greatly decreased. In line with Ford's personal philosophy of caring for his workers, most laid-off office employees were offered jobs in the factory. Resources not necessary for the newly focused company were sold. But the most important change was the development of the first just-in-time production system. Ford could pressure his suppliers to insure on-time delivery. This allowed him to reduce his inventory by more than enough to allow him to pay off all the loans. He also pressured his dealers, resulting in an increased cash flow for the company. Thus, while Ford and the Ford Motor Company had been expected to be eventual failures, instead they were once again seen as the leaders of American industry. As a privately held company, rather than one with shares traded on a major stock exchange, Ford Motor Company differed from other major corporations. Partly because of this, Ford was even more admired by many Americans. It was at this point that Ford, with the assistance of Crowther, decided to publish what was publicized as an autobiography, but which was in reality more of a philosophical statement. Read not only in America but translated into numerous languages, *My Life and Work* impacted political and economic thought around the world.

Author Biographies

Henry Ford (1863–1947) was an American industrial leader of the early twentieth century. Growing up on a farm, he demonstrated an early mechanical aptitude. After being a machinist's apprentice in Detroit, he left to work on portable steam engines, eventually ending up as an engineer for Thomas Edison. In the 1890s, he began developing a quadricycle (automobile). After two failed attempts, in 1902, he, with several partners, formed what became the Ford Motor Company. His most successful car, the Model T, began production in 1908. An excellent engineer and shrewd businessman, he established the moving assembly line, set the forty-hour workweek as the norm, and supported a living wage for workers, although he was sternly antiunion. Although Ford was inclusive in his business dealings and treatment of his workforce, he supported an anti-Semitic publication in the 1920s. However, when asked in 1924, he refused to support Germany's Nazi Party.

Samuel Crowther (1880–1947) was a journalist and author. In addition to articles in numerous publications, Crowther wrote, or cowrote, fifteen books, mainly on business. He collaborated with Henry Ford on four books, this being the first.

HISTORICAL DOCUMENT

When we talk about improvements usually we have in mind some change in a product. An "improved" product is one that has been changed. That is not my idea. I do not believe in starting to make until I have discovered the best possible thing. This, of course, does not mean that a product should never be changed, but I think that it will be found more economical in the end not even to try to produce an article until you have fully satisfied yourself that utility, design, and material are the best. If your researches do not give you that confidence, then keep right on searching until you find confidence. The place to start manufacturing is with the article. The factory, the organization, the selling, and the financial plans will shape themselves to the article. You will have a cutting edge on your business chisel and in the end you will save time. Rushing into manufacturing without being certain of the product is the unrecognized cause of many business failures. People seem to think that the big thing is the factory or the store or the financial backing or the management. The big thing is the product, and any hurry in getting into fabrication before designs are completed is just so much waste time. I spent twelve years before I had a Model T—which is what is known to-day as the Ford car—that suited me. We did not attempt to go into real production until we had a real product. That product has not been essentially changed.

We are constantly experimenting with new ideas. If you travel the roads in the neighbourhood of Dearborn you can find all sorts of models of Ford cars. They are experimental cars—they are not new models. I do not believe in letting any good idea get by me, but I will not quickly decide whether an idea is good or bad. If an idea seems good or seems even to have possibilities, I believe in doing whatever is necessary to test out the idea from every angle. But testing out the idea is something very different from making a change in the car. Where most manufacturers find themselves quicker to make a change in the product than in the method of manufacturing—we follow exactly the opposite course.

Our big changes have been in methods of manufacturing. They never stand still. I believe that there is hardly a single operation in the making of our car that is the same as when we made our first car of the present model. That is why we make them so cheaply. The few changes that have been made in the car have been in the direction of convenience in use or where we found that a change in design might give added strength. The materials in the car change as we learn more and more about materials. Also we do not want to be held up in production or have the expense of production increased by any possible shortage in a particular material, so we have for most parts worked out substitute materials. Vanadium steel, for instance, is our principal steel. With it we can get the greatest strength with the least weight, but it would not be good business to let our whole future depend upon being able to get vanadium steel. We have worked out a substitute. All our steels are special, but for every one of them we have at least one, and sometimes several, fully proved and tested substitutes. And so on through all of our materials and likewise with our parts. In the beginning we made very few of our parts and none of our motors. Now we make all our motors and most of our parts because we find it cheaper to do so. But also we aim to make some of every part so that we cannot be caught in any market emergency or be crippled by some outside manufacturer being unable to fill his orders. The prices on glass were run up outrageously high during the war; we are among the largest users of glass in the country. Now we are putting up our own glass factory. If we had devoted all of this energy to making changes in the

From *My Life and Work*, by Henry Ford

Ford assembly line, 1913.

product we should be nowhere; but by not changing the product we are able to give our energy to the improvement of the making.

The principal part of a chisel is the cutting edge. If there is a single principle on which our business rests it is that. It makes no difference how finely made a chisel is or what splendid steel it has in it or how well it is forged—if it has no cutting edge it is not a chisel. It is just a piece of metal. All of which being translated means that it is what a thing does—not what it is supposed to do—that matters. What is the use of putting a tremendous force behind a blunt chisel if a light blow on a sharp chisel will do the work? The chisel is there to cut, not to be hammered. The hammering is only incidental to the job. So if we want to work why not concentrate on the work and do it in the quickest possible fashion? The cutting edge of merchandising is the point where the product touches the consumer. An unsatisfactory product is one that has a dull cutting edge. A lot of waste effort is needed to put it through. The cutting edge of a factory is the man and the machine on the job. If the man is not right the machine cannot be; if the machine is not right the man cannot be. For any one to be required to use more force than is absolutely necessary for the job in hand is waste.

The essence of my idea then is that waste and greed block the delivery of true service. Both waste and greed are unnecessary. Waste is due largely to not understanding what one does, or being careless in doing of it. Greed is merely a species of nearsightedness. I have striven toward manufacturing with a minimum of waste, both of materials and of human effort, and then toward distribution at a minimum of profit, depending for the total profit upon the volume of distribution. In the process of manufacturing I want to distribute the maximum of wage—that is, the maximum of buying power. Since also this makes for a minimum cost and we sell at a minimum profit, we can distribute a product in consonance with buying power. Thus everyone who is connected with us—either as a manager, worker, or purchaser—is the better for our existence. The institution that we have erected is performing a service. That is the only reason I have for talking about it. The principles of that service are these:

1. An absence of fear of the future and of veneration for the past. One who fears the future, who fears failure, limits his activities. Failure is only the opportunity more intelligently to begin again. There is no disgrace in honest failure; there is disgrace in fearing to fail. What is past is useful only as it suggests ways and means for progress.

2. A disregard of competition. Whoever does a thing best ought to be the one to do it. It is criminal to try to get business away from another man—criminal because one is then trying to lower for personal gain the condition of one's fellow man—to rule by force instead of by intelligence.

3. The putting of service before profit. Without a profit, business cannot extend. There is nothing inherently wrong about making a profit. Well-conducted business enterprise cannot fail to return a profit, but profit must and inevitably will come as a reward for good service. It cannot be the basis—it must be the result of service.

4. Manufacturing is not buying low and selling high. It is the process of buying materials fairly and, with the smallest possible addition of cost, transforming those materials into a consumable product and giving it to the consumer. Gambling, speculating, and sharp dealing, tend only to clog this progression.

GLOSSARY

Dearborn: a city in Michigan, near Detroit, that was Henry Ford's home and his company's headquarters

vanadium steel: steel with the element vanadium added, providing greatly increased strength

Mr. and Mrs. Henry Ford in his first car, the Ford Quadricycle.

Document Analysis

Henry Ford understood that his approach to business was different from that of most other people. Early in the introduction to this book, he stated that his theory of business was really, "a theory that looks toward making this world a better place in which to live." Although Ford did not object to all the money his approach made for him, he claimed that this should not be the sole focus of business. He used the word "service" to encapsulate the essence of what should be one's life's goal. The section of the introduction to *My Life and Work*, which is reprinted above, is the last four pages. After outlining his principles in the introduction, nineteen chapters followed, with each focusing on a different aspect of Ford's business and personal philosophy. Because Ford was not an accomplished writer, Crowther was the one who put the words on paper. While the philosophy of the text was clearly Ford's, much of the phrasing represented Crowther's contribution to the text.

Although an engineer by inclination, Ford was a manufacturer by profession. Thus, he began this passage by focusing on the central aspect of what he did. This was to provide a service to the public, by manufacturing a reliable automobile at a reasonable price. This was the Model T, in production for twenty years, which he had developed twelve years after his first car, the quadricycle. From 1903 to 1908, Ford Motor Company produced eight models prior to the Model T's debut; during most of that period, Ford was not the major shareholder in the company. While these were successful products, none of them met his goal of a car that would be affordable to everyone. Although in the late 1920s, Ford was forced to follow the pattern of slightly changing car designs every model year, he was convinced that this was a wasteful exercise. In his mind, making the manufacturing process more efficient was a better change than slight changes in the product. When this book was written, the Ford Motor Company produced about forty percent of the cars sold in the United States. This allowed it to develop the multiple suppliers necessary to reliably provide essential components to its manufacturing plants.

Given his focus on the manufacturing process, rather than on continually redesigning cars, it is understandable why Ford considered waste a major problem. His adaptation of the assembly line, learned from meatpacking plants, was an example of reducing waste in the human effort required, resulting in a lower manufacturing cost. While such efficiency added to his profits, he saw it as a byproduct of good service to the customer. He truly believed that his efforts to streamline the manufacturing process made all people "the better for our existence." While not everyone saw the steps he took to control the manufacturing process as positive for the nation, Ford believed that it allowed him to reduce waste and control costs. Similarly, some thought it was easy for Ford to say that greed was a bad thing, while at the same time, making more money than most people in the country (or any country). While ignoring that aspect of his success, Ford asserts elsewhere in the introduction that it takes strong individual leadership to direct a company; he uses the failing Soviet experiment in running factories by committee as a counterexample.

Four principles, which essentially close the introduction, illustrate some of what set Ford apart from most other businessmen. He advocates pushing for progress, being the best, serving the public, and seeking only a fair return for one's efforts—not extraordinary profits. This is a different mind-set from that of most of his contemporaries in industry. While his views distinguished Ford from his competitors, it also allowed him to become a dominant force in the American economic system.

Essential Themes

As with many great men, Henry Ford was a contradiction: a man of his times as well as one far ahead of his times. This book, and related material, was a widely studied treatise on how to conduct business. While Ford could use his economic muscle to force suppliers to do things his way, he could also pay factory workers more than some of his competitors, while selling quality cars at a lower price. Two of the ideas he advocated, and which have had a big impact, were: (1) achieving efficiency by eliminating waste, and (2) what is now known as a "just-in-time" system of manufacturing, or making the next part in the line only when it is needed (as opposed to building up an inventory). By the end of the twentieth century, many did not associate key portions of these innovations with Henry Ford; rather, they were associated with Japanese business practices, especially with Toyota. After World War II, Japanese business leaders were searching for a model that would help them rebound from the war. Toyota executives studied Ford's approach to business and developed their model based partly on his, albeit without as much pressure on their suppliers. Thus, through a circuitous route, what was Ford's unique approach to business in the United States during the early twentieth century has continued to influence American business leaders into the twenty-first.

Ford's focus on an efficient manufacturing system, whether by using the assembly line or by not having a large inventory of components sitting idle in a warehouse, was his major contribution. When *My Life and Work* was written, not only was the United States coming out of an economic recession, but there was great turmoil in the larger world. Both extreme right-wing (i.e., Nazi) and left-wing (i.e., Communist) groups were not only challenging the political structure, they were advocating different economic systems. Ford's response was to promote an economic system he believed served the needs of society as well as his fellow industrialists. For him, this was possible only if wasteful and greedy practices were abandoned. Thus, "service," to use his term, was the key not only to producing a quality product, but to creating a stable foundation for society.

—Donald A. Watt

Bibliography and Additional Reading

Brinkley, Douglas. *Wheels for the World: Henry Ford, His Company, and a Century of Progress.* New York: Viking Adult, 2003.

Ford, Henry, with Samuel Crowther. *My Life and Work.* New York: Garden City Pub. Co., 1922.

"Henry Ford." *American Experience.* Narr. Oliver Platt. PBS. WGBH, Boston, July 15, 2014.

"The Life of Henry Ford." *The Henry Ford Museum.* Dearborn, MI: The Henry Ford, 2013.

Watts, Stephen. *The People's Tycoon: Henry Ford and the American Century.* New York: Vintage Books, 2009.